MW01144638

ft

Architecting Microsoft Azure Solutions

Exam Ref 70-534

Haishi Bai
Steve Maier
Dan Stolts

PHI Learning Private Limited
Delhi-110092
2017

This Indian Reprint—₹ 595.00
(Original U.S. Edition—₹ 2744.00)

EXAM REF 70-534: ARCHITECTING MICROSOFT AZURE SOLUTIONS
by Haishi Bai, Steve Maier and Dan Stolts

ISBN-978-81-203-5191-2

Published by Asoke K. Ghosh, PHI Learning Private Limited, Rimjhim House, 111, Patparganj Industrial Estate, Delhi-110092 and Printed by Rajkamal Electric Press, Plot No. 2, Phase IV, HSIDC, Kundli-131028, Sonepat, Haryana.

Contents at a glance

Contents

What do you think of this book? We want to hear from you!

Microsoft is interested in hearing your feedback so we can continually improve our books and learning resources for you. To participate in a brief online survey, please visit:

www.microsoft.com/learning/booksurvey/

**Chapter 6   Design a management, monitoring, and business
continuity strategy   305**

What do you think of this book? We want to hear from you!

Microsoft is interested in hearing your feedback so we can continually improve our
books and learning resources for you. To participate in a brief online survey, please visit:

www.microsoft.com/learning/booksurvey/

Introduction

Most books take a very low-level approach, teaching you how to use individual classes and accomplish fine-grained tasks. This book takes a high-level architectural view, building on your knowledge of lower-level Microsoft Azure systems management experience and content. Both the exam and the book are so high-level, in fact, that there are very few step-by-step instructions involved. There is some coding (Windows PowerShell and Azure PowerShell) but it is minimized to getting started with managing Azure with PowerShell and an introduction to how you can use Windows and Azure PowerShell to design, build, and deploy systems in the Azure cloud. The Exam Ref has a huge advantage over other study mechanisms: It demonstrates what is on the exam while also helping you to understand what it takes to design systems in real-world scenarios.

This book covers every exam objective, but it does not cover every exam question. Only the Microsoft exam team has access to the exam questions themselves and Microsoft regularly adds new questions to the exam, making it impossible to cover specific questions. You should consider this book a supplement to your relevant real-world experience and other study materials. If you encounter a topic in this book that you do not feel completely comfortable with, use the links you'll find in the text to gain access to more information and take the time to research and study the topic. Great information is available on MSDN, TechNet, and in blogs and forums.

Microsoft certifications

Microsoft certifications distinguish you by proving your command of a broad set of skills and experience with current Microsoft products and technologies. The exams and corresponding certifications are developed to validate your mastery of critical competencies as you design and develop, or implement and support, solutions with Microsoft products and technologies, both on-premises and in the cloud. Certification brings a variety of benefits to the individual and to employers and organizations.

> **MORE INFO**   **ALL MICROSOFT CERTIFICATIONS**
>
> For information about Microsoft certifications, including a full list of available certifications, go to *http://www.microsoft.com/learning.*

Acknowledgments

It takes many people to make a book, and even more to make a technical exam reference. Thanks to the content authors:

- Haishi Bai (*http://haishibai.blogspot.com*)
- Steve Maier (*http://42base13.net*)
- Dan Stolts (*http://ITProGuru.com*)

You can visit them and follow them on their blogs. Thanks to content providers and editors: Karen Szall, Devon Musgrave, Roberto Freato, and Bob Russell. Thanks to all those at Microsoft Press and Microsoft Learning for driving this certification, content, and resulting book. Most of all, thank you, for taking the time to learn about Azure cloud architecture through this exam reference guide.

Free ebooks from Microsoft Press

From technical overviews to in-depth information on special topics, the free ebooks from Microsoft Press cover a wide range of topics. These ebooks are available in PDF, EPUB, and Mobi for Kindle formats, ready for you to download at:

http://aka.ms/mspressfree

Check back often to see what is new!

Microsoft Virtual Academy

Build your knowledge of Microsoft technologies with free expert-led online training from Microsoft Virtual Academy (MVA). MVA offers a comprehensive library of videos, live events, and more to help you learn the latest technologies and prepare for certification exams. You'll find what you need here:

http://www.microsoftvirtualacademy.com

Errata, updates, & book support

We've made every effort to ensure the accuracy of this book and its companion content. You can access updates to this book—in the form of a list of submitted errata and their related corrections—at:

http://aka.ms/ER534/errata

If you discover an error that is not already listed, please submit it to us at the same page.

If you need additional support, email Microsoft Press Book Support at *mspinput@ microsoft.com*.

Please note that product support for Microsoft software and hardware is not offered through the previous addresses. For help with Microsoft software or hardware, go to *http:// support.microsoft.com*.

We want to hear from you

At Microsoft Press, your satisfaction is our top priority, and your feedback our most valuable asset. Please tell us what you think of this book at:

http://aka.ms/tellpress

The survey is short, and we read every one of your comments and ideas. Thanks in advance for your input!

Stay in touch

Let's keep the conversation going! We're on Twitter: *http://twitter.com/MicrosoftPress*.

Preparing for the exam

Microsoft certification exams are a great way to build your resume and let the world know about your level of expertise. Certification exams validate your on-the-job experience and product knowledge. Although there is no substitute for on-the-job experience, preparation through study and hands-on practice can help you prepare for the exam. We recommend that you augment your exam preparation plan by using a combination of available study materials and courses. For example, you might use the Exam ref and another study guide for your "at home" preparation, and take a Microsoft Official Curriculum course for the classroom experience. Choose the combination that you think works best for you.

Note that this Exam Ref is based on publicly available information about the exam and the authors' experience. To safeguard the integrity of the exam, authors do not have access to the live exam questions.

## CHAPTER 1

Design Microsoft Azure infrastructure and networking

What is the cloud? Among all the possible definitions, one captures the essence of the cloud in the simplest way: "The cloud is a huge pool of resources that supports a variety of services."

The foundation of the cloud is a large pool of storage, compute, and networking resources. A key value proposition of the cloud is that you can acquire any amount of these resources at any time, from anywhere, without needing to worry about managing any underlying infrastructures. And when you are done with these resources, you can return them to the cloud just as easily to avoid the unnecessary cost to keep them around.

> **IMPORTANT**
> **Have you read page page xviii?**
> It contains valuable information regarding the skills you need to pass the exam.

You can run services on top of these resources. Some of the services give you access to the infrastructure, such as virtual machines (VMs) and virtual networks—these services are called Infrastructure as a Service (IaaS). Some of the services provide support for building your own services in the cloud—these services are called Platform as a Service (PaaS). On top of IaaS and PaaS run Software as a Service (SaaS), which handle all kinds of workloads in the cloud.

After presenting a brief introduction of Microsoft Azure datacenters, this chapter focuses mostly on IaaS. It introduces tools and services for managing compute and network resources. In addition, it discusses design considerations and patterns to orchestrate these resources into complete solutions.

Objectives in this chapter:

- Objective 1.1: Describe how Azure uses Global Foundation Services (GFS) datacenters
- Objective 1.2: Design Azure virtual networks, networking services, DNS, DHCP, and IP addressing configuration
- Objective 1.3: Design Azure Compute
- Objective 1.4: Describe Azure virtual private network (VPN) and ExpressRoute architecture and design
- Objective 1.5: Describe Azure services

Objective 1.1: Describe how Azure uses Global Foundation Services (GFS) datacenters

To serve more than 1 billion customers across more than 140 countries and regions, Microsoft has built huge datacenters that have a combined total of more than 1 million servers. These datacenters are strategically placed at different geographic locations and are connected by high-performance fiber-optic networks. They provide continuous supports to more than 200 cloud services, such as Microsoft Bing, Office 365, OneDrive, Xbox Live, and Azure platform.

Managing enormous resource pools is not an easy task. Microsoft has invested tremendous resources to build reliable, secure, and sustainable datacenters. The team that manages and runs Azure infrastructure is called Microsoft Cloud Infrastructure and Operations (MCIO), formerly known as Global Foundation Service (GFS). This objective goes behind the scenes and reveals how these datacenters are designed, built, and maintained.

This section covers the following topics:

- Learning about Azure's global footprints
- Understanding the design of cloud-scale data centers
- Designing for the cloud

EXAM TIP

You might find both MCIO and GFS are used in documentation, online materials, and white papers to refer to the team that operates Azure datacenters. As far as the exam is concerned, the two names are interchangeable. Also, sometimes Azure datacenters are referred to as Microsoft datacenters. The exam doesn't distinguish between the two, either.

Azure's global footprints

Azure is available in 140 countries and supports 10 languages and 19 currencies. Massive datacenters at 17 geographic regions provide scalable services to all Azure customers around the globe. For example, Azure Storage stores more than 30 trillion objects and serves on average in excess of 3 million requests per second.

Regions and datacenters

Azure operates in 17 regions. Each region contains one or more datacenters. Table 1-1 lists current Azure regions and their corresponding geographic locations.

TABLE 1-1 Azure regions and locations

Azure region	Location
Central US	Iowa
East US	Virginia
East US 2	Virginia
US Gov Iowa	Iowa
US Gov Virginia	Virginia
North Central US	Illinois
South Central US	Texas
West US	California
North Europe	Ireland
West Europe	Netherlands
East Asia	Hong Kong SAR
Southeast Asia	Singapore
Japan East	Saitama Prefecture
Japan West	Osaka Prefecture
Brazil South	Sao Paulo State
Australia East	New South Wales
Australia Southeast	Victoria

Be aware that in some texts the terms "regions" and "locations" are often used inter-changeably. A datacenter is also sometimes referred as a *facility*. Azure doesn't have a formal concept of "zones," although a zone roughly maps to a datacenter or a facility in some con-texts. For example, Azure Storage provides Zone-Redundant Storage (ZRS), which maintains three copies of your data across two to three facilities within a single region or across two regions.

Another concept regarding compute resource placements is the *Affinity Group*. Affinity Group is a way to group your cloud services by proximity to each other in an Azure data-center to minimize communication latency. When you put your services in the same Affinity Group, Azure knows that they should be deployed on hardware that is close to one another to reduce network latency.

> **MORE INFO   STAMPS**
>
> In some online literatures, you might also see references to *stamps*. A stamp loosely refers to a group of server racks. It's not an official concept and is never stipulated as a manage-ment or deployment boundary.

Regional differences

Not all Azure regions provide the same set of services. As a new service is being rolled out, it might at first become available only at a small set of regions and then become avail-able across all regions. Some regions have additional constraints. For example, the Australia regions are available only to customers with billing addresses in Australia and New Zealand. For a complete region/service cross-reference table, go to *http://azure.microsoft.com/en-us/regions/#services*.

Azure is available in China. However, you might have noticed that China is not listed as one of the regions in Table 1-1. This is because Azure in China is independently operated by 21Vianet, one of the largest Internet Service Providers (ISPs) in China. Your Azure subscrip-tions provisioned for the China region cannot be used for other regions. The reverse is also true: your subscriptions outside the China region cannot be used for the China region.

Azure's multilanguage support is not tied to specific regions. You can choose your Azure Management Portal language as a user preference. For example, it's perfectly fine to use a user interface (UI) localized in Japanese to manage resources around the globe. However, many Azure objects don't allow non-English characters in their names or identifiers.

Designing cloud-scale datacenters

A single Azure datacenter can be as big as three large cruise ships placed end to end and host tens of thousands of servers. This level of unprecedented scale brings additional challenges in datacenter design and management. A radically different strategy is needed to design and operate cloud-scale datacenters.

Embracing errors

Cloud-scale datacenters use commodity servers to reduce cost. The availability of these servers is often not as high as the more expensive ones you see in traditional datacenters. And when you pack hundreds of thousands of servers and switches into the same facility, hardware failures become the norm of day-to-day operation. It's unimaginable to remedy these failures individually. A different approach is needed.

Traditionally, datacenter designs focus on increasing Mean Time between Failures (MTBF). With a few servers available to host certain workloads, each of the servers is required to be highly reliable so that a healthy server can remain online for an extended period of time when a failing server is being repaired or replaced. With commodity servers, such long MTBF can't be guaranteed. However, cloud-scale datacenters do have an advantage: they have lots of servers. When one server is failing, its workloads can be directed to another healthy server for recovery. This workload migration mechanism makes it possible for customer services to recover from hardware failures quickly. In other words, cloud-scale datacenters focus more on Mean Time to Recover (MTTR) instead of MTBF, because, in the end, what customers care about is the availability of their services, not the availability of underlying hardware.

Due to the sheer number of servers, such workload migrations can't happen manually in cloud-scale datacenters. To bring MTTR to its minimum requirement, automation is the key. Errors must be detected and handled automatically so that they can be fixed with minimum delays.

Human factors

When it comes to following rules and avoiding mistakes, humans are much less reliable than machines. Unfortunately, humans have the ultimate controlling power over all machines (or so it seems in the present day). Looking back a bit, some of the massive outages in cloud-scale datacenters were caused by humans. As the saying goes, to err is human, and such mistakes will happen, regardless of what countermeasures have been put in place. However, there are some key strategies that can help cloud-scale datacenters to reduce such risks.

Abundant training, rigorous policy reinforcement, continuous monitoring, and auditing form the foundation of an error-resilient team. However, using privileged accounts still has its inherent risks. Azure adopts polices such as just-in-time administrator accesses and just-enough administrator accesses. Microsoft staff doesn't have access to customer data by default. When Microsoft personnel need access to Azure resources for diagnosing specific customer problems, they are granted access to the related resources for no more than a predetermined window. All activities are carefully monitored and logged. At the same time, Azure also encourages customers managing their accesses to resources to follow best practices by providing tools, services, and guidance such as Azure Active Directory (Azure AD) multifactor authentication, built-in Role-Based Access Control (RBAC) with Azure Resource Groups, and Azure Rights Management.

Automation is undoubtedly one of the most effective means to reduce human errors. Azure provides several automation options, including Azure Management API, Azure Power-Shell, and Azure Cross-Platform Command-Line Interface (xplat-cli). In addition, Azure also provides managed automation services such as Azure Automation, which is covered in Chapter 6. In terms of automating resource state management at scale, you can use first-party solutions such as Custom Script Extension and Windows PowerShell Desired State Configuration (DSC), or use integrated third-party solutions such as Puppet and Chef.

Trust-worthy computing

Although the adoption of the cloud has been accelerating, many organizations still have doubts when it comes to handing their valuable business data and mission-critical workloads to a third party. Cloud platforms such as Azure need to work with the highest standards and greatest transparency to build their credibility as trust-worthy business partners. This is a challenge not unique to Azure, but to the entire cloud industry.

It is the policy of Microsoft that security, privacy, and compliance are a shared responsibility between Azure and Azure's customers. Azure takes over some of the burden for implementing operational processes and technical safeguards, including (but not limited to) the following:

- Physical security and continuous surveillance.

  Azure datacenters are protected by physical barriers and fencing, with integrated alarms, cameras and access controls. The facilities are constantly monitored from the operations center.

- Protection against virus, malware, and DDoS attacks.

  Azure scans all software components for malware and viruses during internal builds and deployments. Azure also enables real-time protection, on-demand scanning and monitoring for Cloud Services and VMs. To prevent attacks such as DDoS, Azure performs big data analysis of logs to detect and respond to intrusion risks and possible attacks.

- Activity monitoring, tracing and analysis, and abnormality detection.

  Security events are continuously monitored and analyzed. Timely alerts are generated so that hardware and software problems can be discovered and mitigated early.

- System patching, such as applying security patches.

  When patch releases are required, they are analyzed and applied to the Azure environment based on the severity. Patches are also automatically applied to customer guest VMs unless the customer has chosen manual upgrades, in which case the customer is responsible for patching.

- Customer data isolation and protection.

  Azure customers are logically isolated from one another. An Azure customer has no means to access another customer's data, either intentionally or unintentionally. We cover data protection in more detail in Chapter 2.

On the other hand, Azure provides tools and services to help customers to realize their own security and compliance goals. A good example is data encryption for Azure Storage. Azure offers a wide range of encryption options to protect data at rest. Azure also provides a Key Vault service to manage security keys. However, it's up to the customers to make appropriate choices based on their security and performance requirements. The customers must decide which technologies to use and how to balance between security and performance overheads. Furthermore, customers need to utilize security communication channels such as SSL and TLS to protect their data during transition.

To help customers to achieve compliance goals, Microsoft has developed an extensible compliance framework by which Azure can adapt to regulatory changes. Azure has been independently verified by a diverse range of compliance programs, such as ISO 27001/27002, FISMA, FedRAMP, HIPPA, and EU Model Clauses.

> **MORE INFO** **MICROSOFT AZURE TRUST CENTER**
>
> Microsoft Azure Trust Center (*http://azure.microsoft.com/en-us/support/trust-center/*) is a central point of reference for materials related to security and compliance. For an up-to-date compliance program list, go to *http://azure.microsoft.com/en-us/support/trust-center/compliance/*.

Sustainable reliability

Each of the Azure datacenters hosts a large number of services. Many of these are mission-critical services that customers rely on to keep their businesses running. There's a lot at stake for both Microsoft and its customers. So, the very first mission of Azure datacenter design is to ensure infrastructure availability. For critical infrastructural components such as power supplies, Azure builds multiple levels of redundancies. Azure datacenters are equipped with Uninterruptible Power Supply (UPS) devices, massive battery arrays, and generators with on-site fuel reserves to ensure uninterrupted power supply even during disastrous events.

These extreme measures incur significant cost. Azure datacenters must be carefully designed so that such additional layers of protections can be provided while the total cost of ownership is still well controlled. Microsoft takes a holistic approach to optimize its datacenters. Instead of focusing on optimizing a single component, the entire ecosystem is considered as a whole so that the Total Cost of Ownership (TCO) remains low without compromising efficiency.

As a matter of fact, Microsoft runs some of the most efficient cloud-scale datacenters in the world with Power Usage Effectiveness (PUE) measures as low as 1.125. PUE is the ratio between total facility power usage and IT equipment's power usage. A lower PUE means less power is consumed to support day-to-day facility operations such as providing office lighting and running elevators. Because such additional power consumption is unavoidable, A PUE of 1.125 is very hard to achieve. For comparison, the industry norm is about 1.8.

Last but not least, Azure datacenters are environment-friendly. Microsoft is committed to reducing the environmental footprint of its datacenters. To make these datacenters sustainable, Microsoft has implemented a comprehensive strategy that involves every aspect of datacenter design and operation, such as constructing datacenters using recycled materials, utilizing renewable power sources, and pioneering in efficient open-air cooling.

Since its first datacenter was constructed in 1989, Microsoft has never stopped innovating how datacenters are designed and operated. Four generations later, Azure datacenters are looking forward to the next new generation of datacenters—and they're just on the horizon—which will be even more efficient and sustainable. The benefits of these innovations are passed to Azure's customers and eventually billions of end users around the world.

Designing for the cloud

The unique characteristics of cloud-scale datacenters bring both challenges and opportunities to designing your applications. On one hand, you need to ensure that your application architecture is adapted for these characteristics so that your application can function correctly. On the other hand, you want to take advantage of Quality of Service (QoS) opportunities that the cloud offers, allowing your applications to thrive.

This section focuses on the first aspect, which is to ensure that your applications function correctly in cloud-scale datacenters. Chapter 4 discusses how to improve QoS in the cloud.

Datacenter maintenance

Azure performs two types of maintenances: planned and unplanned. Planned maintenance occurs periodically on a scheduled basis; unplanned maintenance is carried out in response to unexpected events such as hardware failures.

PLANNED MAINTENANCE

Azure periodically performs maintenance on the hosting infrastructure. Many of these maintenances occur at the hosting operation system level and the platform software level without any impact to hosted VMs or cloud services. However, some of these updates will require your VMs to be shut down or rebooted.

You can configure VMs on Azure in two ways: multi-instance and single-instance. Multi-instance VMs are joined to a same logical group called an *Availability Set*. When Azure updates VMs, it guarantees that not all machines in the same Availability Set will be shut down at the same time. To ensure your application availability, you should deploy your application on an Availability Set with at least two VMs. Only multi-instance VMs qualify for the Service Level Agreement (SLA) provided by Azure.

> *MORE INFO* **UPDATE DOMAIN AND FAULT DOMAIN**
>
> Two concepts related to Availability Set are *Update Domain* and *Fault Domain*. Chapter 4 introduces these two concepts in more detail within the context of service availability and reliability.

Single-instance VMs are stand-alone VMs. During datacenter updates, these VMs are brought down in parallel, upgraded, and brought back online in no particular order. If your application is deployed on a single-instance VM, the application will become unavailable during this maintenance window. To help preclude any problems, Microsoft sends email notices to single-instance customers, indicating the exact date and time on which the maintenance is scheduled, as shown in Figure 1-1. Thus, if your Availability Set contains only a single VM, the availability of your application will be affected because there will be no running instances when the only machine is shut down.

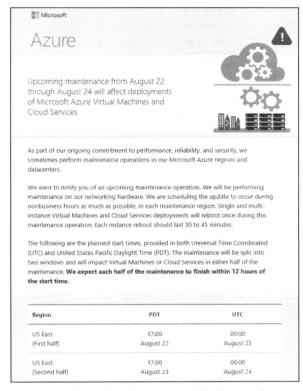

FIGURE 1-1   A sample maintenance notification email

UNPLANNED MAINTENANCE

Unplanned maintenances are triggered by unexpected physical infrastructure problems such as network failures, rack-level failures and other hardware failures. When such a failure is detected, Azure automatically moves your VMs to a healthy host. When multiple VMs are deployed in the same Availability Set, they are allocated to two Fault Domains (you can read more on this in Chapter 4). At the hardware level, Fault Domains don't share a common power source or network switch, so the probability of two Fault Domains failing at the same time is low.

Azure's autorecovery mechanism significantly reduces MTTR. In traditional datacenters, recovering or replacing a server often needs a complex workflow that can easily take days or even weeks. By comparison, Azure can recover a VM in minutes. Regardless of how short the window is, the VM is still restarted. Your application needs to be able to restart itself when this happens. Otherwise, although the VM is recovered, your application is still unavailable.

Azure Cloud Service has a built-in mechanism to monitor and recover your application process. For applications deployed on VMs, you can define endpoints with load-balanced sets. A load-balanced set supports custom health probes, which you can use to detect if your application is in running state. Load-balanced sets are discussed further in Objective 1.3.

Datacenter outages

No cloud platform is immune to some large-scale outages caused by natural disasters and occasionally human errors. Microsoft has adopted a very transparent policy that shares very thorough Root Cause Analysis (RCA) reports with customers when such outages happen. These reports disclose the exact cause of the outage, no matter if it is because of code defects, architecture flaws, or process violations. Microsoft works very hard to ensure that the mistake is not repeated in the future.

Cross-region redundancy is an effective way to deal with region-wide outages. Later in this book, you'll learn technologies such as Azure Traffic Manager and Service Bus paired namespaces that help you to deploy cross-region solutions.

Service throttling

The cloud is a multitenant environment occupied by many customers. To ensure fair resource consumption, Azure throttles service calls according to subscription limits. When throttling occurs, you experience degraded services and failures in service calls.

Different Azure services throttle service calls based on different criteria, such as the amount of stored data, the number of transactions, and system throughputs. When you subscribe to an Azure service, you should understand how the service throttles your calls and ensure that your application won't exceed those limits.

Most Azure services offer you the option to gain additional capacities by creating multiple service entities. If you've decided that a single service entity won't satisfy your application's needs, you should plan ahead to build multi-entity support into your architecture so that your application can be scaled out as needed.

Another effective way to offset some of the throttling limits is to use caches such as application-level caching and Content Delivery Networks (CDNs). Caches help you not only to reduce the amount of service calls, but also to improve your application performance by serving data directly from cache.

Service security

With the exception of a few read-only operations, Azure requires proper authentication information to be present before it grants a service request. Azure services supports three different authentication strategies: using a secret key, using a Shared Access Signature (SAS), and using federated authentication via Azure AD.

When a secret key is used, you need to ensure that the key itself is securely stored. You can roll out a protection strategy yourself, such as using encryptions. Later in this chapter, you'll see how Azure Key Vault provides an efficient, reliable solution to this common problem.

SAS is a proven way to provide detailed level of access control over entities. With SAS, you can grant access to specific data with explicit rights during given time windows. The access is automatically revoked as soon as the window is closed.

Azure AD is discussed in depth in Chapter 2.

Thought experiment
Explaining the benefits of cloud

In this thought experiment, apply what you've learned about this objective. You can find answers to these questions in the "Answers" section at the end of this chapter.

Although cloud adoption has been accelerating over the past few years, many enterprise decision makers remain very cautious when deciding on cloud strategies. In particular, they are concerned about data security and service reliability. They have doubts when it comes to handling valuable business data to a third-party. And their doubts are reinforced by occasional news outbursts on cloud datacenter outages and breaches. As a technical lead, you need to come up with a strategy to convince these decision makers to adopt a cloud strategy.

With this in mind, answer the following questions:

1. How would you explain the benefits of the cloud in terms of data security?
2. How would you explain the benefits of the cloud in terms of reliability?

Objective summary

- Azure serves more than 1 billion customers out of 17 global locations. Azure runs more than 200 online services in more than 140 countries.

- A key strategy to improve service availability in the cloud is to reduce MTTR. Workload is reallocated to healthy servers so that the service can be recovered quickly.
- Automation, just-in-time access, and just-enough access are all effective ways to reduce possible human errors.
- Azure datacenters take over some of the responsibilities of infrastructure management by providing trust-worthy and sustainable infrastructures.
- Your application needs to be designed to cope with service interruptions and throttling. In addition, your application needs to adopt appropriate security policies to ensure that your service is only accessed by authenticated and authorized users.

Objective review

Answer the following questions to test your knowledge of the information in this objective. You can find the answers to these questions and explanations of why each answer choice is correct or incorrect in the "Answers" section at the end of this chapter.

1. Which are the effective ways to reduce human errors?

   A. Sufficient training

   B. Automation

   C. Just-in-time access

   D. Reinforced operation policy

2. Azure has been independently verified by which of the following compliance programs?

   A. ISO 27001/27002

   B. FedRAMP

   C. HIPPA

   D. EU Model Clauses

3. Which of the following VM configurations qualifies for availability SLA?

   A. Single-instance VM

   B. Multi-instance VMs on an Availability Set

   C. Single-instance VM on an Availability Set

   D. Two single-instance VMs

Objective 1.2: Design Azure virtual networks, networking services, DNS, DHCP, and IP addressing configuration

Today, just about any computer you see is connected to some network. Computers on Azure are no exception. When you provision a new VM on Azure, you never gain physical access to the hosting machine. Instead, you need to operate the machine through remote connections such as remote desktop or Secure Shell (SSH). This is made possible by the networking infrastructure provided by Azure.

This objective introduces Azure Virtual Networks, with which you can create virtualized private networks on Azure. VMs deployed on a virtual network can communicate with one another just as if they were on an on-premises local area network (LAN).

Furthermore, you can connect your virtual networks with your on-premises networks, or with other virtual networks, through cross-network connections. You'll learn about hybrid networks in objective 1.4.

> **This section covers the following topics:**
> - Creating a cloud-only virtual network
> - Understanding ACLs and Network Security Groups

Creating a cloud-only virtual network

It's fairly easy to create a new virtual network on Azure. This section walks you through the steps to set up a new virtual network with two subnets on Azure. Then, you will review some of the differences between a virtual network and an on-premises network that you should be aware of when you design your network infrastructures in the cloud.

> **NOTE   REVIEW OF BASIC NETWORKING CONCEPTS**
>
> This objective doesn't require readers to have deep networking knowledge. Instead, it assumes most readers don't routinely maintain networks and might need refreshers of basic networking concepts. These concepts are explained as side notes throughout this chapter. Feel free to skip these notes if you are already familiar with the concepts.

Creating a virtual network by using the Azure management portal

There are several different ways you can create a new virtual network on Azure, including using the Azure management portal, Azure PowerShell, and xplat-cli. This section walks you through how to use the management portal to create a new virtual network. Scripting options are discussed later in this chapter.

1. Sign in to the management portal (*https://manage.windowsazure.com*).

2. Select New, Network Services, Virtual Network, and then Custom Create, as shown in Figure 1-2.

FIGURE 1-2 Creating a new virtual network

The Create A Virtual Network Wizard opens.

3. On the Virtual Network Details page, in the Name box, type a name for the virtual network. In the Location box, select a location where you want the network to reside. If you have multiple Azure subscriptions, you also need to pick which Azure subscription to use. Then, click the right-arrow button to continue, as illustrated in Figure 1-3.

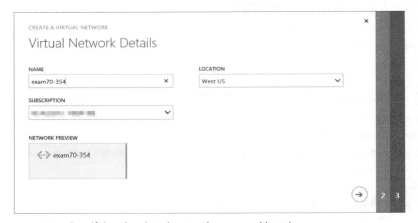

FIGURE 1-3 Specifying the virtual network name and location

> **NOTE** **ABOUT AFFINITY GROUPS FOR VIRTUAL NETWORKS**
>
> Previously, when you created a virtual network, you needed to associate the network with an Affinity Group. This is no longer a requirement. Now, virtual networks are associated directly with a region (location). Such virtual networks are called *regional virtual network* in some texts. The previous requirement of having Affinity Groups was because Azure networks were designed in layers. Communication among hardware within the same "branch" was much faster than communication across branches. A new

flat network design makes it possible for VMs across the entire region to communicate effectively, eliminating the need to put a virtual network in an Affinity Group.

4. On the DNS Servers And VPN Connectivity page, click Next to continue. (You'll come back to these options later in this chapter.)

The Virtual Network Address Spaces page opens, as shown in Figure 1-4.

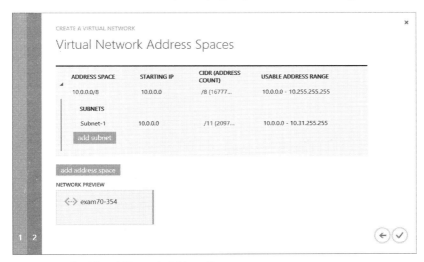

FIGURE 1-4 The Virtual Network Address Spaces page

When you manage a larger virtual network, you might want to create multiple subnets to improve performance. To describe this briefly, a network is like a web of roads. When you have more computers sending and receiving packets on the same network, packets can collide and must be resent again. Using subnets, you can control and limit traffic in different areas. It's similar to using local roads for a short commute, and using shared highways to travel longer distances.

In many cases, subnets are created not only for performance, but also for manageability. You can create subnets in alignment with business groups. For example, you can create one subnet for the sales department, and another subnet for engineering. You can also create subnets based on server roles. For example, you can have a subnet for web servers and another subnet for file servers.

> **NOTE** **ABOUT CIDR NOTATION**
> Classless Inter-Domain Routing (CIDR) notation is a shorthand representation of a subnet mask. It uses the number of bits to represent a subnet mask. For example, a subnet mask of 255.0.0.0 uses 8 bits, hence it's written as /8. And a subnet mask of 255.255.0.0 uses 16 bits, which is written as /16 in CIDR notation. With CIDR, 10.0.0.0/8 in Figure 1-4

represents a network ID of 10.0.0.0 and a subnet mask of 255.0.0.0, which corresponds to the address range 10.0.0.0 to 10.255.255.255.

5. Click the Add Subnet button to create a new subnet. The updated address space is illustrated in Figure 1-5. In the lower-right corner, click the check button to complete the set up.

ADDRESS SPACE	STARTING IP	CIDR (ADDRESS COUNT)	USABLE ADDRESS RANGE
10.0.0.0/8	10.0.0.0	/8 (16777...	10.0.0.0 - 10.255.255.255
SUBNETS			
Subnet-1	10.0.0.0	/11 (2097...	10.0.0.0 - 10.31.255.255
Subnet-2	10.32.0.0	/11 (2097...	10.32.0.0 - 10.63.255.255
add subnet			

FIGURE 1-5 A virtual network with two subnets

Now, your network has two subnets, each has 2,097,152 (2^{21}) addresses.

> **NOTE ABOUT SUBNET BITS AND THE NUMBER OF SUBNETS**
>
> When you create a subnet, you are borrowing a number of bits from the host ID and adding them to the network ID. In previous example, we are borrowing 3 bits, which means you can create up to 8 (2^3) subnets. Because the bits borrowed are high bits, they correspond to 0, 32, 64, 96, 128, 160, 192, and 224. This is why the first IP address on the second subnet is 10.32.0.0.

IP Addresses

Each VM has at least two associated IP addresses: a public-facing virtual IP (VIP) address, and an internal dynamic IP (DIP) address.

A VIP comes from a pool of IP addresses managed by Microsoft. It is not assigned directly to the VM. Instead, it's assigned to the Cloud Service that contains the VM. You can reserve VIPs so that you can assign static public IPs to your VMs. At this point, each Azure subscription is allowed to reserve up to 20 VIPs.

> **NOTE ABOUT VMS AND CLOUD SERVICES**
>
> Each VM you create belongs to a cloud service. Cloud Services is introduced in Chapter 4. For now, you can understand a cloud service as a management and security boundary for VMs. VMs residing in the same cloud service have a logical private scope, within which they can communicate with one another directly using host names.

To reserve a VIP, use the following Azure PowerShell command:

```
New-AzureReservedIP -ReservedIPName "MyReservedIP" -Label "MyLabel" -Location "West US"
```

After you have the static VIP allocated, you can use it as part of the VM configuration when you create a new VM. VMs are discussed in the next objective.

The DIP address is a dynamic IP address associated with your VM. A DIP is assigned by DHCP with a near-infinite lease. So, it remains stable as long as you don't stop or deallocate the machine. However, it's not a static IP address. If your VM resides in a virtual network, you can assign a static IP address to it. For example, when you set up a domain controller or a Domain Name System (DNS) server on your virtual network, you'll need to assign static IPs to these machines because both services require static IP addresses.

With Azure, you can create multiple virtual network interfaces (NICs) on your VM residing on a virtual network. In this case, your VM has multiple associated DIPs, one for each NIC.

In addition to VIP and DIP, there's another type of IP address, which is called Instance-Level Public IP (PIP) Address. As stated previously, a VIP is not assigned to a VM, but to the Cloud Service containing the VM. A PIP, on the other hand, is directly assigned to a VM. PIP is appropriate for workloads that need a large number of ports to be opened, such as passive FTP.

Name resolution and DNS servers

VMs on the same network can address one another by DIP addresses. If you want to refer to VMs by hostnames or fully qualified domain name (FQDN) directly, you need name resolutions. Azure provides a built-in hostname resolution for VMs and role instances within the same cloud service. However, for VMs across multiple cloud services, you'll need to set up your own DNS server.

HOST NAMES AND FQDNS

As is discussed in Objective 1.3, when you create a new VM, the host name is specified by you. And when you define a cloud service role (you can read more about Cloud Services in Chapter 4), you can define the VM host name by using the *vmName* property in the service configuration file. In this case, Azure will append an instance number to the name to distinguish different role instances. For example, if *vmName* is *MyRole*, the actual host names of role instances will be *MyRole01*, *MyRole02,* and so on.

When you create a VM (or a cloud service), a DNS name is assigned to the machine with the format *[machine name].cloudapp.net*, where *[machine name]* is the name you specify. You can use this FQDN to address your machine directly over Internet. When the VM is provisioned, a public-facing VIP is associated with the machine, and then the DNS name is associated with this VIP.

You can also use CNAME or A records to associate a custom domain name with your VM. When you use A records, however, you need to note that the VIP of your VM might change. When you deallocate a VM, the associated VIP is released. And when the VM is restarted later, a new VIP will be picked and assigned. If you want to ensure that your VM has a static public IP address, you'll need to configure a static IP address for it as described earlier.

Last but not least, for simple name resolutions, you can also use hosts files (%System32%\Drivers\etc\hosts for Windows; /etc/hosts for Linux) and cross-enter IP-to-host mappings to all the VMs in the same virtual network.

DNS SERVERS

You can set up DNS servers on your virtual network to provide a name resolution service to the machines on the same network. Objective 1.3 presents a couple of examples.

Understanding Access Control Lists and Network Security Groups

You can use both network Access Control Lists (ACLs) and Network Security Groups (NSGs) to control traffic to your VMs. In either case, the traffic is filtered before it reaches your VM so that your machine doesn't need to spend extra cycles on packet filtering.

Before you continue learning about ACLs and NSGs, you need to first understand how VM endpoints work.

VM endpoints

When you provision a VM on Azure by using the management portal, by default the device is accessible through Remote Desktop and Windows PowerShell Remoting for Windows-based VMs, and through SSH for Linux-based VMs. This is because Azure automatically defines the corresponding endpoints.

Each endpoint maps a public port to a private port. The private port is used by the VM to listen for incoming traffic. For Example, your device might have an Internet Information Services (IIS) server running on it, listening to the private port 80. The public port is not used by the VM itself, but by another entity called Azure Load Balancer.

As mentioned earlier, a VM has a VIP address as well as a DIP address. However, the VIP address is actually not directly associated with the VM. Instead, the VIP address is associated with Load Balancer. It's Load Balancer that listens to the traffic to the VIP address and the public port, and then forwards the traffic to the VM listening to the DIP address and the private port. Figure 1-6 shows how this traffic forwarding works. At the top, the traffic reaches the endpoint at *VIP:[public port]*. Then, Load Balancer forwards the traffic to *DIP:[private port]*. In this example, an endpoint is defined to map a public port 8080 to a private port 80. The IIS server on a VM named *myvm* is listening to local address 10.0.0.1:80. An end user accesses the website by the public address myvm.cloudapp.net:8080. Note that the "myvm" in the FQDN "myvm.cloudap.net" is the name of the Cloud Service in which the VM resides. It's not necessarily the same as the VM name (you can have multiple VMs in the same Cloud Service).

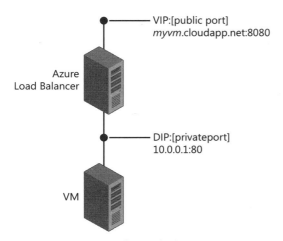

FIGURE 1-6 Construct of an endpoint

Endpoints can be stand-alone or load-balanced. When a load-balanced endpoint is defined, Load Balancer distributes traffic evenly among the VMs within the same load-balanced set. Figure 1-7 shows how it works.

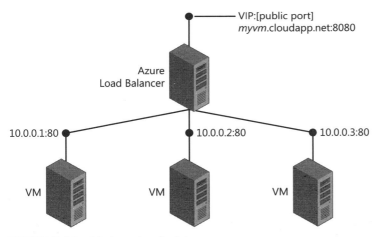

FIGURE 1-7 A load-balanced endpoint

Endpoints are for public accesses. When you provision a VM on a virtual network, it can communicate with other VMs on the same network just as if they were on a physical local network. There are no endpoints needed for private communications.

Network ACLs

ACL provides the ability to selectively permit or deny traffic to a VM endpoint. An ACL comprises an ordered list of rules that either permit or deny traffic to the endpoint. Packets are filtered on the hosting server before they can reach your VM. When a new endpoint is created, by default all traffic from all IP addresses are allowed. Then, you can define ACLs to constrain accesses to certain ranges of IP addresses by defining blocked lists and safe lists, each of which is defined here:

- **Blocked list**   You can block ranges of IP addresses by creating *deny rules*. Table 1-2 shows an example of ACL that blocks accesses from a specific subnet:

TABLE 1-2   A sample blocked list

Rule #	Remote subnet	Endpoint	Permit/deny
100	10.32.0.0/11	80	Deny

- **Safe list**   You can also create a safe list that allows only specific IP addresses to access an endpoint. First, you'll define a rule that denies all traffic to the endpoint. Then, you add additional rules to allow accesses from specific IP addresses (ACL uses *lowest takes precedence* rule order). Table 1-3 shows a sample safe list:

TABLE 1-3   A sample safe list

Rule #	Remote subnet	Endpoint	Permit/deny
100	0.0.0.0/0	80	Deny
200	10.0.0.0/11	80	Permit

You can apply ACLs to load-balanced endpoints, as well. When you apply an ACL to a load-balanced endpoint, it's applied to all VMs in the same load-balanced set. You can specify up to 50 ACL rules per VM endpoint.

NSGs

For VMs deployed on a virtual network, NSGs provide more detailed access controls. An NSG is a top-level object of your Azure subscription that you can apply to a VM or a subnet to control traffic to the VM or the subnet. You can also associate different NSGs to a subnet and the VMs contained in the virtual network to establish two layers of protections.

Similar to an ACL, an NSG is made up by a number of prioritized rules. Each NSG comes with a number of default rules that you can't remove. However, as these rules have lower priorities, you can override them by additional rules. There are two types of rules: inbound rules and outbound rules. Each rule defines whether the traffic should be denied or allowed to flow from a source IP range and port to a destination IP range and port. You can also specify protocols in NSG rules. The supported protocols are TCP and UDP, or * for both.

In NSG rules, IP ranges are represented by named tags. There are three default tags:

- **VIRTUAL_NETWORK** This tag specifies all network address space on your virtual network. It also includes connected on-premises address spaces and vNet-to-vNet address spaces (you'll learn about on-premises connections and vNet-to-vNet connections in Objective 1.4).

- **AZURE_LOADBALANCER** This tag denotes Azure Load Balancer. Load Balancer sends health probe signals to VMs in a load-balanced set. This tag is used to identify the IP address from which the health probes originate.

- **INTERNET** This tag specifies all IP address that are outside the virtual network.

With an NSG, inbound traffic is denied by the default rules, with the exception of allowing health probes from Load Balancer. Table 1-4 lists the default inbound rules of an NSG. The first rule allows all internal traffic within the same virtual network; the second rule allows health probes from Load Balancer; and the third rule denies all other accesses.

TABLE 1-4 Default inbound rules of an NSG

Priority	Source IP	Source port	Destination IP	Destination port	Protocol	Access
65000	VIRTUAL_NETWORK	*	VIRTUAL_NETWORK	*	*	Allow
65001	AZURE_LOADBALANCER	*	*	*	*	Allow
65000	*	*	*	*	*	Deny

Table 1-5 lists the default outbound rules of a NSG. The first rule allow outbound traffic to the virtual network. The second rule allows outbound traffic to Internet. And the third rule denies all other outbound traffic.

TABLE 1-5 Default outbound rules of a NSG

Priority	Source IP	Source Port	Destination IP	Destination Port	Protocol	Access
65000	VIRTUAL_NETWORK	*	VIRTUAL_NETWORK	*	*	Allow
65001	*	*	INTERNET	*	*	Allow
65000	*	*	*	*	*	Deny

NSGs are different from ACLs in a couple of aspects:

- ACLs are applied to traffic to a specific VM endpoint, whereas NSGs are applied to all traffic that is inbound and outbound on the VM.

- ACLs are associated to a VM endpoint, whereas NSGs are associated to a VM, or a subnet within a virtual network.

> **NOTE   INCOMPATIBILITY BETWEEN ACL AND NSG**
>
> You cannot use both ACL and NSG on the same VM instance. You must first remove all endpoint ACLs before you can associate an NSG.

Thought experiment

Implementing perimeter networks in Azure Virtual Network

In this thought experiment, apply what you've learned about this objective. You can find answers to these questions in the "Answers" section at the end of this chapter.

Using isolated security zones is an effective way for enterprises to reduce many types of risks on their networks. For example, many enterprises use a perimeter network to isolate their Internet-facing resources from other parts of their internal network. You can implement the same level of protection in Azure Virtual Network, as well. In this case, you have a number of VMs that will be exposed to the Internet. And you have a number of application servers and database servers on the same virtual network.

With this in mind, answer the following questions:

1. What technologies would you use to implement a perimeter network in Virtual Network?

2. How would you design your network topology?

Objective summary

- You can create private virtual networks in Azure. VMs deployed on the same virtual network can communicate with one another as if they were on the same local network.

- Each machine has a public VIP address and one or multiple PIP addresses, one per NIC.

- You can associate both static virtual IP addresses and static private IP addresses to VMs on a virtual network.

- ACLs are associated to VM endpoints to control traffic to VMs.

- NSGs are associated to VMs or subnets to provide greater traffic control to VMs or virtual networks.

- Both ACLs and NSGs define prioritized rules to control network traffic, but they cannot be used in conjuction.

Objective review

Answer the following questions to test your knowledge of the information in this objective. You can find the answers to these questions and explanations of why each answer choice is correct or incorrect in the "Answers" section at the end of this chapter.

1. A VM can have multiple associated IP addresses. Which of the following are possible IP addresses associated with a VM?

   A. Public virtual IP

   B. Dynamic private IP

   C. Static public IP

   D. Static private IP

2. NSGs define a number of default tags. Which of the following tags are default tags?

   A. VIRTUAL_NETWORK

   B. AZURE_LOADBALANCER

   C. INTERNET

   D. VIRTUAL_MACHINE

3. Which of the following are NSG rule fields?

   A. Source IP and source port

   B. Target IP and target port

   C. Protocol

   D. Priority

4. Which of the following are ACL rule fields?

   A. Rule number

   B. Remote subnet

   C. Endpoint

   D. Permit/deny

Objective 1.3: Design Azure Compute

You can run both Windows and Linux VMs on Azure to host your workloads. You can provision a new VM easily on Azure at any time so that you can get your workload up and running without spending the time and money to purchase and maintain any hardware. After the VM is created, you are responsible for maintenance tasks such as configuring and applying software patches.

To provide the maximum flexibility in workload hosting, Azure provides a rich image gallery with both Windows-based and Linux-based images. It also provides several different series of VMs with different amounts of memory and processor power to best fit your workloads. Furthermore, Azure supports virtual extensions with which you can customize the standard images for your project needs.

Selecting VM sizes

The easiest way to create a VM is to use the management portal. You can use either the current portal (*https://manage.windowsazure.com*) or the new Azure Preview Management Portal (*https://portal.azure.com*). The following steps use the new portal.

1. Sign in to the Preview Management Portal (*http://portal.azure.com*).

2. In the lower-left corner of the screen that opens, click the New icon, and then, in the center pane, select Compute, as shown in Figure 1-8. (As of this writing, the portal is still in preview, so the exact layout and naming may change.)

FIGURE 1-8 Creating a new VM

In the lower-left corner of Figure 1-8, at the bottom of the list, is the option for the Azure Marketplace. This Marketplace provides thousands of first-party and third-party templates for you to deploy necessary Azure resources to support various typical workloads.

3. In this exercise, you'll create a new Windows Server 2012 R2 VM, which happens to be the first item in the list. If the VM image is not listed, click Azure Marketplace, then click Everything, and then type in a search keyword to locate the image.

4. On the Create VM blade (the UI panes on the new Azure Portal are called *blades*). Type a Host Name, a User Name, and a Password, as demonstrated in Figure 1-9.

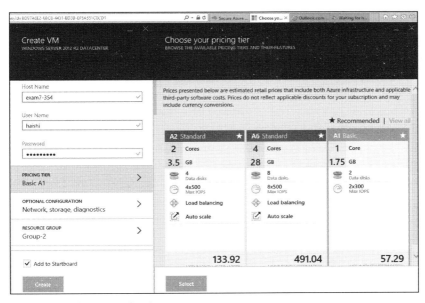

FIGURE 1-9 Choosing price tier

The Host Name will become the host name of your VM. Recall from Objective 1.2 that a Cloud Service with the same name will be automatically created as a container of the VM. The VM is also placed into a logical group called a Resource Group. Resource Groups are discussed when Azure Template is introduced later in this objective. The user name and the password becomes the credential of your local administrator.

5. Click Pricing Tier, which opens a new blade where you can choose from a variety of configurations (to see the complete list, click the View All link). Click a VM size that you want to use, and then click the Select button to return to the previous blade.

6. Optionally, click Optional Configuration to examine default settings and to make changes as needed. For example, you can choose to join the VM to a virtual network or create public endpoints using this blade.

7. Back on the Create VM blade, scroll down to examine other options, such as which Azure subscription to use and the region to which the VM is to be deployed. Make changes as needed.

8. Leave the Add To Starboard option selected, and then click the Create button to create the VM. After the machine is created, you'll see a new icon on your start board (the customizable home page of the new Preview Management Portal), which provides direct access to the VM.

9. Click the icon to open the VM blade. Click the Connect icon to establish a remote desktop connection to the VM. You'll be asked to sign in. Sign in using the credentials you entered at step 4. You'll also see a certificate warning. Click Yes to continue.

10. After the connection is established, you can manage the VM just as if you were managing any servers through remote desktop.

Choosing pricing tiers and machine series

Azure provides two pricing tiers: Basic and Standard. Basic tier is most suitable for development, tests, and simple production workloads. It doesn't have features such as load balancing and autoscaling. And, there are fewer VM sizes from which to choose. On the other hand, the Standard tier provides a wide range of VM sizes with features such as load balancing and autoscaling to support production workloads.

Azure organizes VM sizes into machine series—A-series, D-series, DS-series, and G-series. Only a part of A-series is available to the Basic tier. All series are available for the Standard tier. Following is a description of each series:

■ **A-series** A-series VMs are designed for generic.workloads. Table 1-6 lists all available sizes in the A-series. A0 to A4 sizes are available to both the Basic tier and the Standard tier. Each VM has an operating system (OS) drive and a temporary drive. The OS drives are persistent, but the temporary drives are transient. You can attach 1-TB data drives to your VMs, as well. Each has a maximum Input/Output Operations Per Second (IOPS) of 300 for the Basic tier, and 500 for the Standard tier. With more drives, you gain more overall IOPS with parallel IO operations. Among A-series sizes, A8 through A11 are designed for high-performance computing, which is discussed in Chapter 4.

TABLE 1-6 A-series VM sizes

Size	CPU cores	Memory	OS drive size (GB)/ temporary drive size (GB)	Maximum number of data drives	Maximum IOPS
A0	1	768 MB	1,023/20	1	1X300/1X500
A1	1	1.75 GB	1,023/40	2	2X300/2X500
A2	2	3.5 GB	1,023/60	4	4X300/4X500
A3	4	7 GB	1,023/120	8	8X300/8X500
A4	8	14 GB	1,023/240	16	16X300/16X500
A5	2	14 GB	1,023/135	4	4X500
A6	4	28 GB	1,023/285	8	8X500
A7	8	56 GB	1,023/605	16	16X500
A8	8	56 GB	1,023/382	16	16X500
A9	16	112 GB	1,023/382	16	16X500
A10	8	56 GB	1,023/382	16	16X500
A11	16	112 GB	1,023/382	16	16X500

> *NOTE* **ABOUT TEMPORARY DISKS**
>
> Both OS drives and data drives are virtual hard drives (VHDs) stored in Azure Blob Storage. Their data is automatically duplicated three times for reliability. However, the temporary drives reside on the hosting servers. If the host fails, your VM will be moved to a healthy host, but not the temporary drive. In this case, you'll lose all temporary data. By default, the temporary drive is mounted as drive D on a Windows system, and /dev/sdb1 on a Linux system.

- **D-series** This series of VMs is designed for workloads with high processing power and high-performance temporary drives. D-series VMs use solid-state drives (SSDs) for temporary storage, providing much faster IO operations compared to what traditional hard drives provide. Table 1-7 lists all available sizes in the D-series.

TABLE 1-7 D-series VM sizes

Size	CPU cores	Memory (GB)	OS drive size (GB)/ temporary drive size (GB)	Maximum number of data drives	Maximum IOPS
Standard_D1	1	3.5	1,023/50 (SSD)	2	2X500
Standard_D2	2	7	1,023/100 (SSD)	4	4X500
Standard_D3	4	14	1,023/200 (SSD)	8	8X500
Standard_D4	8	28	1,023/400 (SSD)	16	16X500
Standard_D11	2	14	1,023/100 (SSD)	4	4X500
Standard_D12	4	28	1,023/200 (SSD)	8	8X500
Standard_D13	8	56	1,023/400 (SSD)	16	16X500
Standard_D14	16	112	1,023/800 (SSD)	32	32X500

EXAM TIP

A0 to A4 are called by different names in the Basic tier and the Standard tier. In the Basic tier, they are referred as Basic_A0 to Basic_A4, whereas in the Standard series, each of the sizes has its own corresponding names, which are used in scripts and API calls. You should know how these names mapped to VM sizes:

- A0: extra small
- A1: small
- A2: medium
- A3: large
- A4: extra large

- **DS-series** DS-Series VMs are designed for high I/O workloads. They use SSDs for both VM drives and a local drive cache. Table 1-8 lists all DS-series sizes.

TABLE 1-8 DS-series VM sizes

Size	CPU cores	Memory (GB)	OS drive size (GB)/ local drive size (GB)	Maximum number of data drives	Cache Size (GB)	Maximum IOPS/band-width (Mbps)
Standard_DS1	1	3.5	1,023/7 (SSD)	2	43	3,200/32
Standard_DS2	2	7	1,023/14 (SSD)	4	86	6,400/64
Standard_DS3	4	14	1023/28 (SSD)	8	172	12,800/128
Standard_DS4	8	28	1,023/56 (SSD)	16	344	25,600/256
Standard_DS11	2	14	1,023/28 (SSD)	4	72	6,400/64
Standard_DS12	4	28	1,023/56 (SSD)	8	144	12,800/128
Standard_DS13	8	56	1,023/112 (SSD)	16	288	25,600/256
Standard_DS14	16	112	1,023/224 (SSD)	32	576	50,000/512

- **G-series**   This series of VMs is one of the biggest on cloud with Xeon E5 V3 family processors. Table 1-9 lists all available sizes in the G-series.

TABLE 1-9 G-series VM sizes

Size	CPU cores	Memory (GB)	OS drive size (GB)/local drive size (GB)	Maximum number of data drives	MAX IOPS
Standard_G1	2	28	1,023/384 (SSD)	4	4X500
Standard_G2	4	56	1,023/768 (SSD)	8	8X500
Standard_G3	8	112	1,023/1,536 (SSD)	16	16X500
Standard_G4	16	224	1,023/3,072 (SSD)	32	32X500
Standard_G5	32	448	1,023/6,144 (SSD)	64	64X500

Using data disks

As previously mentioned, temporary drives are transient and you should not use them to maintain permanent data. If your application needs local storage to keep permanent data, you should use data drives. The Tables 1-6 through 1-9 show that for each VM size you can attach a number of data drives. You can attach both empty data drives and data drives with data to a VM. To attach a data drive, go to the Settings blade of your VM, click Disks, and then select either Attach New to create a new data drive, or Attach Existing to attach an existing data drive. Figure 1-10 shows demonstrates attaching a new data drive to a VM using the Preview Management Portal.

FIGURE 1-10 Attaching a data drive

After a new data drive is attached to a VM, you need to initialize it before you can use it.
For Windows-based VMs, you can use the Disk Manager tool in Server Manager to initialize
the drive, and then create a simple volume on it, or a striped volume across multiple drives.
For Linux-based VMs, you need to use a series of commands such as *fdisk*, *mkfs*, *mount*, and
blkid to initialize and mount the drive.

You can choose a host caching preference—None, Read Only, or Read/Write—for each
data drive. The default settings usually work fine, unless you are hosting database workloads
or other workloads that are sensitive to small I/O performance differences. For a particular
workload, the best way to determine which preference to use is to perform some I/O bench-
mark tests.

Generally speaking, using striped drives usually yields better performance for I/O-heavy
applications. However, you should avoid using geo-replicated storage accounts for your
striped volumes because data loss can occur when recovering from a storage outage (for
more information, go to *https://msdn.microsoft.com/en-us/library/azure/dn790303.aspx*).

Managing images

There are three sources for Azure VM: the Azure VM gallery, VM Depot, and custom images. You can use these images as foundations to create, deploy, and replicate your application run-time environments consistently for different purposes such as testing, staging, and production.

- **VM gallery**   The Azure VM gallery offers hundreds of VM images from Microsoft, partners, and the community at large. You can find recent Windows and Linux OS images as well as images with specific applications, such as SQL Server, Oracle Database, and SAP HANA. MSDN subscribers also have exclusive access to some images such Windows 7 and Windows 8.1. For a complete list of the images, go to *http://azure. microsoft.com/en-us/marketplace/virtual-machines/.*

- **VM Depot**   The VM Depot (*https://vmdepot.msopentech.com/List/Index*) is an open-source community for Linux and FreeBSD images. You can find an increasing number of images with various popular open-source solutions such as Docker, Tomcat, and Juju.

- **Custom images**   You can capture images of your VMs and then reuse these images as templates to deploy more VMs.

Capturing custom images

You can capture two types of images: generalized or specialized.

A generalized image doesn't contain computer or user-specific settings. These images are ideal for use as standard templates to rollout preconfigured VMs to different customers or users. Before you can capture a generalized image, you need to run the System Preparation (Sysprep) tool in Windows, or use the **waagent –deprovision** command in Linux. All the OS images you see in the VM gallery are generalized. Before you can capture a generalized image, you need to shut down the VM. After the VM is captured as an image, the original VM is automatically deleted.

Specialized images, conversely, retain all user settings. You can think of specialized images as snapshots of your VMs. These images are ideal for creating checkpoints of an environment so that it can be restored to a previously known good state. You don't need to shut down a VM before you capture specialized images. Also, the original VM is unaffected after the images are captured. If a VM is running when an image is captured, the image is in crash-consistent state. If application consistency or cross-drive capture is needed, it's recommended to shut down the VM before capturing the image.

To capture an image, on the Virtual Machine blade, click the Capture button, as shown in Figure 1-11.

FIGURE 1-11 Command icons on the Virtual Machine blade

Using custom images

You can use your custom images to create new VMs just as you would use standard images. If you use a specialized image, you skip the user provisioning step because the image is already provisioned. When a new VM is created, the original VHD files are copied so that the original VHD files are not affected.

As of this writing, there's no easy way to use custom images on the new Preview Management Portal. However, with the full management portal, you can use custom images by clicking the My Images link on the Choose An Image page of the Create A Virtual Machine Wizard, as illustrated in Figure 1-12.

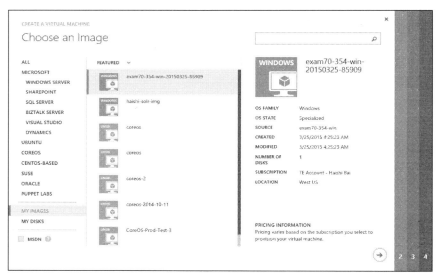

FIGURE 1-12 Choosing image in the Create A Virtual Machine Wizard

Alternatively, you can use Azure PowerShell to create a new VM by using a custom image. For example, to create a new VM from the custom image *myVMImage*, use the following command:

```
New-AzureQuickVM –Windows –Location "West US" –ServiceName "examService" –Name "examVM"
–InstanceSize "Medium" –ImageName "myVMImage" –AdminUsername "admin"–Password "sh@ang3!"
–WaitForBoot
```

Managing VM states

Custom images provide basic supports for deploying workloads consistently across different environments. However, custom images have some undesirable characteristics. First, it's difficult to revise a custom image. To make any changes, you need to provision the image as a new VM, customize it, and then recapture it. Second, it's also difficult to track what has been changed on an image because of the manual customizations. Third, rolling out a new version is difficult, as well. To deploy a new image version, the VM needs to be re-created, making upgrade a lengthy and complex process. What you need are more light-weight, traceable, agile, and scalable state management solutions. This section discusses a number of technologies that enable efficient VM state managements.

VM extension

When you provision a new VM, a light-weight Azure Virtual Machine Agent (VM Agent) is installed on the VM by default. VM Agent is responsible for installing, configuring, and managing Azure VM Extensions (VM Extensions). VM Extensions are first-party or third-party components that you can dynamically apply to VMs. These extensions make it possible for you to dynamically customize VMs to satisfy your application, configuration, and compliance needs. For example, you can deploy the McAfee Endpoint Security extension to your VMs by enabling the *McAfeeEndpointSecurity* extension.

You can use Azure PowerShell cmdlet *Get-AzureVMAvailableExtension* to list currently available extensions. Listing 1-1 shows a sample of the cmdlet.

LISTING 1-1 Listing available VM extensions

```
PS C:\> Get-AzureVMAvailableExtension | Format-Table -Wrap -AutoSize -Property
ExtensionName, Description
ExtensionName                 Description
-------------                 -----------
VS14CTPDebugger               Remote Debugger for Visual Studio 2015
ChefClient                    Chef Extension that sets up chef-client on VM
LinuxChefClient               Chef Extension that sets up chef-client on VM
DockerExtension               Docker Extension
DSC                           PowerShell DSC (Desired State Configuration) Extension
CustomScriptForLinux          Microsoft Azure Custom Script Extension for Linux IaaS
BGInfo                        Windows Azure BGInfo Extension for IaaS
CustomScriptExtension         Windows Azure Script Handler Extension for IaaS
VMAccessAgent                 Windows Azure Json VMAccess Extension for IaaS
….
```

> **NOTE   VM AGENT OPT-OUT**
>
> When creating a VM, you can choose not to install VM agent. You can install VM Agent to an existing VM; however, when a VM agent is installed, removing it is not a supported scenario. You can, of course, physically remove the agent, but the exact behavior after removal is unsupported.

Custom Script Extension and DSC

Custom Script Extension downloads and runs scripts you've prepared on an Azure Blob storage container. You can upload Azure PowerShell scripts or Linux Shell scripts, along with any required files, to a storage container, and then instruct Custom Script Extension to download and run the scripts. The following code snippet shows a sample Azure CLI command to use the Custom Script Extension for Linux (*CustomScriptForLinux*) to download and run a mongodb.sh shell script:

```
azure vm extension set -t '{"storageAccountName":"[storage account]","storageAccount
Key":"…"}' -i '{"fileUris":["http://[storage account].blob.core.windows.net/scripts/
mongodb.sh"],"commandToExecute":"sh mongodb.sh"}' [vm name] CustomScriptForLinux
Microsoft.OSTCExtensions 1.*
```

Using scripts to manage VM states overcomes the shortcomings of managing them with images. Scripts are easier to change and you can apply them faster. And an added benefit is that you can trace all changes easily by using source repositories.

However, writing a script to build up a VM toward a target state is not easy. For each of the requirement components, you'll need to check if the component already exists and if it is configured in the desired way. You'll also need to deal with the details of acquiring, installing, and configuring various components to support your workloads. Windows PowerShell Desired State Configuration (DSC) takes a different approach. Instead of describing steps of how the VM state should be built up, you simply describe what the desired final state is with DSC. Then, DSC ensures that the final state is reached. The following is a sample DSC script that verifies the target VM has IIS with ASP.NET 4.5 installed:

```
Configuration DemoWebsite
{
  param ($MachineName)
  Node $MachineName
  {
    #Install the IIS Role
    WindowsFeature IIS
    {
      Ensure = "Present"
      Name = "Web-Server"
    }
    #Install ASP.NET 4.5
    WindowsFeature ASP
    {
      Ensure = "Present"
      Name = "Web-Asp-Net45"
    }
  }
}
```

State management at scale

For larger deployments, you often need to ensure consistent states across a large number of VMs. You also need to periodically check VM states so they don't drift from the desired parameters. An automated state management solution such as Chef and Puppet can save you from having to carry out such repetitive and error-prone tasks.

For both Chef and Puppet, you write cookbooks that you can then apply to a large number of VMs. Each cookbook contains a number of "recipes" or "modules" for various tasks, such as installing software packages, making configuration changes, and copying files. They both facilitate community contributions (Puppet Forge and Chef Supermarket) so that you can accomplish common configuration tasks easily. For example, to get a Puppet module that installs and configures Redis, you can use Puppet tool to pull down the corresponding module from Puppet Forge:

```
puppet module install evenup-redis
```

Both Chef and Puppet install agents on your VMs. These agents monitor your VM states and periodically check with a central server to download and apply updated cookbooks. Azure provides VM extensions that bootstrap Chef or Puppet agents on your VMs. Furthermore, Azure also provides VM images that assist you in provisioning Chef and Puppet servers. Chef also supports a hosted server at *https://manage.chef.io*.

Managing VM states is only part of the problem of managing application run-time environments in the cloud. Your applications often depend on external services. How do you ensure that these external services remain in desired states? The solution is Azure Automation. With Automation, you can monitor events in VMs as well as external services such as Azure App Service Web Apps, Azure Storage, and Azure SQL Server. Then, workflows can be triggered in response to these events.

Automation's cookbooks, called *runbooks*, are implemented as Azure PowerShell Workflows. To help you to author these runbooks, Azure has created an Azure Automation Runbook Gallery where you can download and share reusable runbooks. Figure 1-13 shows how you can create a new runbook based on existing runbooks in the gallery.

FIGURE 1-13 Choosing a runbook from the Runbook Gallery

Capturing infrastructure as code

Traditionally, development and operations are two distinct departments in an Independent Software Vendor (ISV). Developers concern themselves with writing applications, and the folks in operations are concerned with keeping the applications running. However, for an application to function correctly, there are always explicit or implicit requirements regarding how the supporting infrastructure is configured. Unfortunately, such requirements are often lost during communication, which leads to many problems such as service outages because of misconfigurations, frictions between development and operations, and difficulties in re-creating and diagnosing issues. All these problems are unacceptable in an Agile environment.

In an Agile ISV, the boundary between development and operations is shifting. The developers are required to provide consistently deployable applications instead of just application code; thus, the deployment process can be automated to rollout fixes and upgrades quickly. This shift changed the definition of application. An application is no longer just code. Instead, an application is made up of both application code and explicit, executable description of its infrastructural requirements. For the lack of better terminology, such descriptions can be called *infrastructure code*. The name has two meanings. First, "infrastructure" indicates that it's not business logics but instructions to configure the application runtime. Second "code" indicates that it's not subject to human interpretation but can be consistently applied by an automation system.

Infrastructure code is explicit and traceable, and it makes an application consistently deployable. Consistently deployable applications are one of the key enabling technologies in the DevOps movement. The essence of DevOps is to reduce friction so that software lifecycles can run smoother and faster, allowing continuous improvements and innovations. Consistently deployable applications can be automatically deployed and upgraded regularly across multiple environments. This means faster and more frequent deployments, reduced confusion across different teams, and increased agility in the overall engineering process.

Azure Resource Template

Azure Resource Templates are JSON files that capture infrastructure as code. You can capture all the Azure resources your application needs in a single JSON document that you can consistently deploy to different environments. All resources defined in an Azure Resource Template are provisioned within a Resource Group, which is a logical group for managing related Azure resources.

> **NOTE SUPPORTING ALL AZURE RESOURCE TYPES**
>
> Supports of all Azure resource types are added gradually over time. Each Azure resource type is implemented as a Resource Provider that can be plugged into Azure Resource Manager, the service that governs resource creation. At this point, there are only a number of Azure resource types that are supported. Eventually, though, all Azure resource types are expected to be supported.

You can write an Azure Resource Template from scratch using any text editor. You can also download a template from an Azure template gallery by using Azure PowerShell:

1. In Azure PowerShell, switch to Azure Resource Manager mode:

    ```
    Switch-AzureMode AzureResourceManager
    ```

2. Use the *Get-AzureResourceGroupGalleryTemplate* cmdlet to list gallery templates. The command returns a large list. You can use the *Publisher* parameter to constrain the results to a specific publisher:

    ```
    Get-AzureResourceGroupGalleryTemplate -Publisher Microsoft
    ```

3. Save and edit the template of interest:

    ```
    Save-AzureResourceGroupGalleryTemplate -Identity Microsoft.JavaCoffeeShop.0.1.3-
    preview -Path C:\Templates\JavaCoffeeShop.json
    ```

4. At the top of the file, an Azure Resource Template contains a schema declaration (Figure 1-14). This consists of a content version number and a "resources" group, which contains resource definitions.

```
{
    "$schema": "http://schema.management.azure.com/schemas/2014-04-01-preview/deploymentTemplate.json#",
    "contentVersion": "1.0.0.0",
    "parameters": {...},
    "resources": {...}
}
```

FIGURE 1-14 Sample Azure Template

Optionally, you can also define parameters, variables, tags, and outputs. A complete introduction of the template language is beyond the scope of this book. You can use the *Test-AzureResourceGroupTemplate* cmdlet to validate your template at any time. You need an actual Resource Group in order to use the cmdlet. However, creating a Resource Group is easy:

```
New-AzureResourceGroup –Name [resource group name]
```

5. Supply the resource group name to the command along with other required parameters, and then validate if your template is ready to be deployed.

   To deploy a template, use the *New-AzureResourceGroupDeployment* cmdlet:

```
New-AzureResourceGroupDeployment -Name [deployment name] -ResourceGroupName
[resource gorup] -TemplateFile [template file] -TemplateParameterFile [parameter
file]
```

An Azure Resource Template captures the entire topology of all Azure resources required by your application. And, you can deploy it with a single Azure PowerShell command. This capacity greatly simplifies resource management of complex applications, especially service-oriented architecture (SOA) applications that often have many dependencies on hosted services.

Containerization

In the past few years, container technologies such as Docker have gained great popularity in the industry. Container technologies make it possible for you to consistently deploy applications by packaging them and all their required resources together as a self-contained unit. You can build a container manually, or it can be fully described by metadata and scripts. This way, you can manage containers just as source code. You can check them in to a repository, manage their versions, and reconcile their differences just as how you would manage source code. In addition, containers have some other characteristics that make them a favorable choice for hosting workloads on cloud, which are described in the sections that follow.

AGILITY

Compared to VMs, containers are much more light weight because containers use process isolation and file system virtualization to provide process-level isolations among containers. Containers running on the same VM share the same system core so that the system core is not packaged as part of the container. Because starting a new container instance is essentially the same as starting a new process, you can start containers quickly—usually in time frames less than a second. The fast-start time makes containers ideal for the cases such as dynamic scaling and fast failover.

COMPUTE DENSITY

Because container instances are just processes, you can run a large number of container instances on a single physical server or VM. This means that by using containers, you can achieve much higher compute density in comparison to using VMs. A higher compute density means that you can provide cheaper and more agile compute services to your customers. For example, you can use a small number of VMs to host a large number of occasionally accessed websites, thus keeping prices competitive. And you can schedule a larger number of time-insensitive batch jobs.

DECOUPLE COMPUTE AND RESOURCE

Another major benefit of using containers is that the workloads running in them are not bound to specific physical servers or VMs. Traditionally, after a workload is deployed, it's pretty much tied to the server where it's deployed. If the workload is to be moved to another server, the new one needs to be repurposed for the new workload, which usually means the entire server needs to be rebuilt to play its new role in the datacenter. With containers, servers are no longer assigned with specific roles. Instead, they form a cluster of CPUs, memory, and disks within which workloads can roam almost freely. This is a fundamental transformation in how the datacenter is viewed and managed.

Container orchestration

There are many container orchestration solutions on the market that provide container clustering, such as Docker Swarm, CoreOS Fleet, Deis, and Mesosphere. Orchestrated containers form the foundation of container-based PaaS offerings by providing services such as coordinated deployments, load balancing, and automated failover.

> **EXAM TIP**
>
> Container technology has gained considerable momentum in the past few years. New capabilities, new services, and new companies are emerging rapidly and the landscape is changing continually. For example, there are many variations in capabilities of different orchestration offerings. At this point, the container should not be a focus of the test, so you shouldn't spend a lot of energy to chase new developments in the field. However it's very important to understand the benefits of containers because they will become increasingly important in future tests.

Orchestrated containers provide an ideal hosting environment for applications that use Microservices architecture. You can package each service instance in its own corresponding container. You can join multiple containers together to form a replica set for the service. You can automate container cluster provisioning by using a combination of Azure Resource Template, VM Extensions, Custom Script Extension, and scripts. The template describes the cluster topology, and VM extensions perform on-machine configurations. Finally, automated scripts in containers themselves can perform container-based configurations.

Scaling applications on VMs

In Azure, you can configure applications to *scale-up* or *scale-out*.

Scaling-up refers to increasing the compute power of the hosting nodes. In an on-premises datacenter, scaling up means to increase the capacity of the servers by increasing memory, processing power, or drive spaces. Scaling-up is constrained by the number of hardware upgrades you can fit into the physical machines. In the cloud, scaling-up means to choose a bigger VM size. In this case, scaling-up is constrained by what VM sizes are available.

Scaling-out takes a different approach. Instead of trying to increase the compute power of existing nodes, scaling-out brings in more hosting nodes to share the workload. There's no theoretical limit to how much you can scale-out—you can add as many nodes as needed. This makes it possible for an application to be scaled to very high capacity that is often hard to achieve with scaling-up. Scaling-out is a preferable scaling method for cloud applications.

The rest of this section will focus on scaling out.

Load balancing

When you scale-out an application, the workload needs to be distributed among the participating instances. This is done by load balancing. (Load-balanced endpoints were introduced earlier in this chapter.) The application workload is distributed among the participating instances by the Azure public-facing load-balancer in this case.

However, for multitiered applications, you often need to scale-out middle tiers that aren't directly accessible from the Internet. For instance, you might have a website as the presentation layer, and a number of VMs as the business layer. You usually don't want to expose the business layer, and thus you made it accessible only by the presentation layer. How would you scale the business layer without a public-facing load balancer? To solve this problem, Azure introduces Internal Load Balancers (ILB). ILBs provide load balancing among VMs residing in a Cloud Service or a regional virtual network.

The ILBs are not publically accessible. Instead, you can access them only by other roles in the same Cloud Services, or other VMs within the same virtual network. ILB provides an ideal solution for scaling a protected middle tier without exposing the layer to the public. Figure 1-15 shows a tiered application that uses both a public-facing load balancer and an internal load balancer. With this deployment, end users access the presentation layer through Secure Sockets Layer (SSL). The requests are distributed to the presentation layer VMs by Azure Load Balancer. Then, the presentation layer accesses the database servers through an internal load balancer.

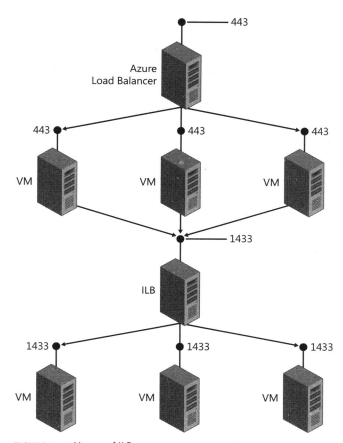

FIGURE 1-15 Usage of ILB

As mentioned earlier, you can define custom health probes when you define a load-balanced set. You can configure your VMs to respond to health probes from the load balancer via either TCP or HTTP. If a VM fails to respond to a given number of probes, it is considered unhealthy and taken out of the load balancer. The load balancer will keep probing all of the VMs (including the unhealthy ones) so that when the failed VM is recovered, it will automatically be rejoined to the balanced set. You can use this feature to temporarily take a VM off the load balancer for maintenance by forcing a false response to probe signals.

Autoscale

With Azure, you can scale your VMs manually in a Cloud Service. In addition, you can also set up autoscale rules to dynamically adjust the system capacity in response to average CPU usage or number of messages in a queue.

To use autoscaling, you need to add the VMs to an Availability Set. Availably Sets are discussed in Chapter 4. At the moment, you can consider an Availability Set as a group of VMs for which Azure attempts to keep at least one VM running at any given time. Figure 1-16 shows a sample autoscaling policy on the management portal.

FIGURE 1-16 Sample autoscaling policy

Let's go through the above policy item by item.

- **Edit Scale Settings For Schedule**   You can specify different scaling policies for different times of the day, different days of the week, and specific date ranges. For example, if you are running an ecommerce site that expects spikes in traffic during weekends, you can set up a more aggressive scaling policy to ensure that the performance of the system under heavier loads during those periods.

- **Scale By Metric**   You can choose None, CPU, or Queue. An autoscaling policy without a scale metric is for scheduled scaling scenarios. For the latter two options, Azure monitors the performance of your VMs and adjusts the number of instances accordingly to ensure that the metric falls into the specified range.

- **Instance Range**   The Instance Range specifies the lower and upper boundaries of scaling. The lower boundary makes certain that the system maintains a minimum capacity, even if the system is idle. The upper boundary controls the cost limit of your deployment. Each VM instance has its associated cost. You want to set up an appropriate upper limit so that you don't exceed your budget.

- **Target CPU** The Target CPU specifies the desired range of the specific metric. If the value exceeds the upper limit, scaling up (in this case, a more precise term would be "scaling out") will be triggered. If the value falls below the lower limit, scaling down (again, in this case a more precise term would be "scaling in") will be triggered. Please note that the autoscaling system doesn't respond to every metric value changes. Instead, it makes decisions based on the average value in the past hour.

> **NOTE AUTOSCALING AFTER THE FIRST HOUR**
>
> Because autoscaling uses the average value of the past hour, it's not triggered as frequently as you might have expected. This is a very common point of confusion for many users who set up the autoscaling policy for the first time.

- **Scale Up By** You can specify how fast the system is to be scaled-out by specifying scaling steps and delays between scaling actions.
- **Scale Down By** You can control how the system is scaled down. Depending on how your workload pattern changes, you might want to set an aggressive scale-down policy to de-provision the resources quickly after busy hours to reduce your costs.

Thought experiment
Lift and ship

In this thought experiment, apply what you've learned about this objective. You can find answers to these questions in the "Answers" section at the end of this chapter.

When it comes to adopting the cloud, many enterprises would consider lifting and shipping existing applications to Azure VMs as the starting point. After all, if an application runs well on a local server, the chances are good that it will run well on a VM in Azure, won't it? However, there are often more things to consider than just deploying the applications to a VM, such as reliability, availability, security, and performance.

With this in mind, answer the following questions:

1. What challenges do you think you need to prepare for?

2. What are the next steps after an application has been moved to Azure?

Objective summary

- Azure supports various VM sizes and a gallery of both Linux images and Windows images.
- You can automate VM state management with Azure Automation and third-party solutions such as Chef and Puppet.
- VM Extension and Azure PowerShell DSC automates on-machine configuration tasks.
- DevOps requires infrastructure to be captured as code. With DevOps, an application consists of both application code and infrastructure code so that the application can be deployed consistently and rapidly across different environments.
- Azure Resource Template captures the entire topology of your application as code, which you can manage just as you do application source code. Resource Templates are JSON files that you can edit using any text editors.
- Containerization facilitates agility, high compute density, and decoupling of workloads and VMs. It transforms the datacenter from VMs with roles to resource pools with mobilized workloads.
- You can use autoscale to adjust your compute capacity to achieve balance between cost and customer satisfaction.

Objective review

Answer the following questions to test your knowledge of the information in this objective. You can find the answers to these questions and explanations of why each answer choice is correct or incorrect in the "Answers" section at the end of this chapter.

1. What VM series should you consider if you want host applications that require high-performance IO for persisted data?

   A. A-series

   B. D-series

   C. DS-series

   D. G-series

2. How many data drives can you attach to a Standard_G5 VM (the biggest size in the series)?

   A. 8

   B. 16

   C. 32

   D. 64

3. What's the format of an Azure Resource Template?

   A. JSON

   B. XML

   C. YAML

   D. PowerShell

4. Which of the following technologies can help you to manage consistent states of VMs at scale?

   A. Custom Script Extension

   B. Chef or Puppet

   C. Azure Automation

   D. Containerization

Objective 1.4: Describe Azure virtual private network (VPN) and ExpressRoute architecture and design

Microsoft realizes that for many of its existing enterprise customers, migration to cloud will be a long process that might take years or event decades. In fact, for some of these customers, a complete migration might never be feasible. To ensure smooth cloud transitions, Azure provides a pathway for enterprises to adopt cloud at their own pace. This means that for the foreseeable future, many enterprises will be operating *hybrid* solutions that have components running both on-premises and in the cloud. Thus, reliable, secure, and efficient connectivity between on-premises datacenters and cloud becomes a necessity. This objective discusses two of the connectivity options: Azure Virtual Network and Azure ExpressRoute. Then, we briefly introduce some of the other hybrid solution options.

> **This section covers the following topics:**
> - Designing hybrid solutions with Virtual Network and ExpressRoute
> - Understanding other hybrid solution options

Designing hybrid solutions with Virtual Network and ExpressRoute

Virtual Network offers several types of hybrid connections that bridge resources located at different facilities. You can choose one or several connection options that best suit your requirements. Note that this objective does not focus on detailed steps of setting up the connections. Instead, it describes the steps in general and then focuses on how each connection type suits different scenarios.

Point-to-Site VPN

Point-to-Site VPN is the simplest hybrid connection by which you can securely connect your local computer to an Azure virtual network. No specific VPN devices are needed in this case. Instead, you install a Windows VPN client through which you can connect to any VMs and Cloud Services within the virtual network. Figure 1-17 shows the topology of a Point-to-Site VPN.

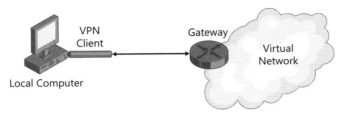

FIGURE 1-17 Point-to-site connectivity

Establishing a point-to-site connection involves several steps:

1. Specify an IP address range. When your VPN clients connect, they will receive IP addresses from this range. You need to ensure that this range doesn't overlap with IP ranges within your on-premises network.

2. Add a gateway subnet.

3. Create a dynamic routing gateway.

   You can choose between a standard gateway, which gives you about 80 Mbps and 10 S2S tunnels, and a high-performance gateway, which gives you about 200 Mbps and 30 S2S tunnels.

4. Create a client certification to be used for client authentication. The client machine that makes the VPN connection needs to have the certificate installed.

5. Download the VPN client configuration package from your virtual network's Dashboard page. When the client is installed, you'll see a new VPN connection with the same name as your virtual network.

With Point-to-Site connection, you can connect to your VMs on Azure from anywhere. It uses Secured Socket Tunneling Protocol (SSTP), which means that you can establish the connection through firewalls and Network Address Translation (NAT). It works well to support a small mobile workforce. However, because each client PC in this case establishes a separate connection to the gateway, you are limited to the number of S2S tunnels that the gateway can support.

Point-to-Site enables scenarios such as remote administration of cloud resources, troubleshooting, monitoring, and testing. It can be applied to use cases such as remote education, mobile office, and occasional command and control. However, for bridging on-premises networks and Azure Virtual Networks, you'll probably want to use Site-to-Site VPN.

Site-to-Site VPN

Site-to-Site VPN is designed for establishing secured connections between site offices and the cloud, or bridging on-premises networks with virtual networks on Azure. To establish a Site-to-Site VPN connection, you need a public-facing IPv4 address and a compatible VPN device, or Routing and Remote Access Service (RRAS) running on Windows Server 2012. (For a list of known compatible devices, go to *https://msdn.microsoft.com/en-us/library/azure/jj156075. aspx#bkmk_KnownCompatibleVPN*.) You can use either static or dynamic gateways for Site-to-Site VPN. However, if you want to use both Site-to-Site VPN and Point-to-Site VPN at the same time, you'll need a dynamic gateway. Figure 1-18 shows the topology of a Site-to-Site VPN.

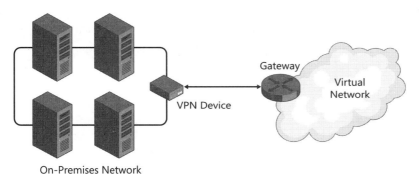

FIGURE 1-18 Site-to-site connectivity

Site-to-Site VPN extends your local network to the cloud. As you move your workloads gradually to the cloud, you often need the servers in the cloud and the local servers to still work together before the migration is complete. Using Site-to-Site VPN, these servers can communicate with each other as if they were on the same local network. This becomes handy when you move some domain-joined servers to the cloud but you still want to keep them on your local Active Directory.

Site-to-Site works in the other direction, as well: it brings your VMs in the cloud into your local network. You can join these servers into your local domain and apply your security policies on them. In many migration cases, moving the application servers is easier compared to moving a large amount of data. And some enterprises prefer to keep their data local for various reasons. With Site-to-Site VPN, your cloud VMs can reach back to your on-premises data. They also can be joined to Azure Load Balancer to provide high-availability services.

Although Site-to-Site connections provide reasonable reliability and throughput, some larger enterprises require much more bandwidth between their datacenters and the cloud. Moreover, because VPNs go through the public Internet, there's no SLA to guarantee the connectivity. For these enterprises, ExpressRoute is the way to go.

ExpressRoute

ExpressRoute provides private connections between your on-premises datacenters and Azure datacenters. You can achieve up to 10 Gbps bandwidth with the dedicated, secure, and reliable connections. These connections don't go through the public Internet, and you can get connectivity SLAs from your selected service providers. If you have frequent large-volume data transfers between your on-premises datacenters and Azure, ExpressRoute provides a faster solution that in some cases is even more economical.

There are two ways to use ExpressRoute to connect to Azure. One way is to connect to Azure through an exchange provider location. The other way is to connect Azure through a network service provider. The exchange provider option provides up to 10 Gbps bandwidth. The network service provider option provides up to 1 Gbps bandwidth. In either case, Azure configures a pair of cross-connections between Azure and the provider's infrastructure in an active-active configuration to ensure availability and resilience against failures. Figure 1-19 shows the topology of an ExpressRoute connection.

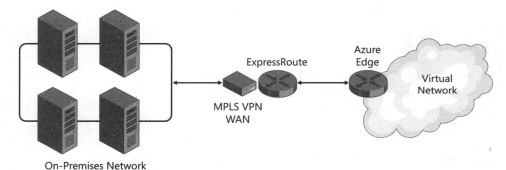

FIGURE 1-19 ExpressRoute connectivity

ExpressRoute's fast and reliable connection is ideal for scenarios such as data storage access, backups, and disaster recovery. For example, you can transfer and store a large amount of data to Azure Storage service while keeping your applications running on your own datacenter. For backup and disaster recovery, ExpressRoute makes data replication faster and more reliable, improving the performance as well as the reliability of your disaster recovery strategies. Moreover, you can access other Azure-hosted services such as Office 365 by using the same private connection for fast, secure access.

> **NOTE** **AVAILABILITY OF EXPRESSROUTE TO OFFICE 365**
>
> ExpressRoute to Office 365 connectivity is expected to be available to Office 365 customers beginning in the latter part of 2015.

When working together, many servers need frequent exchanges of data. When some of the servers are moved to the cloud, the additional latency introduced by Internet connections can have a serious impact on the performance of the overall system and sometimes render the entire system unusable. ExpressRoute provides a fast connection between your on-premises datacenters and Azure so that you can extend your local infrastructure to the cloud without having to make significant architecture or code changes.

vNet-to-vNet VPN

Just as you can establish Site-to-Site connections between your on-premises datacenters and Azure, you also can connect two virtual networks on Azure by using a VPN connection. Figure 1-20 shows the topology of a vNet-to-vNet connection.

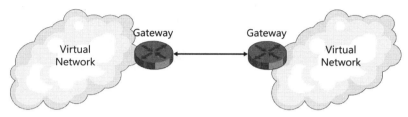

FIGURE 1-20   vNet-to-vNet connectivity

You can use vNet-to-vNet VPN to support georedundancy and geopresence. For example, you can use vNet-to-vNet VPN to set up SQL Always On across multiple Azure regions. Figure 1-21 shows another example, which is a cross-region three-node MongoDB replica set with a primary node and a secondary node in West US, and a secondary in West Europe. The West Europe node is for disaster recovery and is not allowed to be elected as a primary.

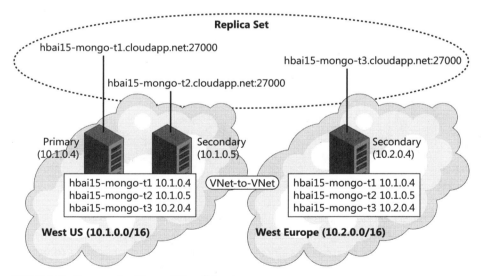

FIGURE 1-21   Cross-region MongoDB replica set

You also can use vNet-to-vNet VPN in business integration scenarios. With global corporations, business units sometimes remain independent from one another, but at the same time some workflows need to be integrated. Using vNet-to-vNet, resources owned by different business units can communicate with one another while maintaining isolations between the resources (refer to the earlier discussions on ACLs and NSGs). Some multitiered applications need such kind of isolations, as well. For instance, a new corporate website might need to consume services and data from multiple regional sites, which have their own virtual networks and security policies.

Multi-site VPN

You can use an Azure Virtual Network gateway to establish multiple Site-to-Site connections. This capability makes it possible to join multiple on-premises networks. Figure 1-22 shows the topology of a Multi-site VPN.

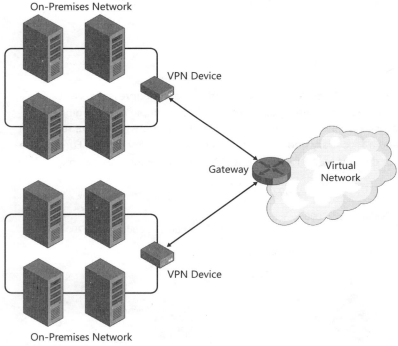

FIGURE 1-22 Multi-site VPN

Using Multi-site VPN, branch offices from different geographic locations can connect with one another to exchange data and share Azure-based resources such as a common hosted services. This topology is also referred to as a *hub-and-spoke* topology, which is quite common for scenarios in which a head office connects to multiple branch offices.

Understanding other hybrid solution options

In addition to various networking solutions, Azure also provides other services and tools that help you to implement hybrid scenarios. This section provides a brief review of these services and tools in the contexts of different scenarios.

Reaching out to the cloud

In this scenario, you have some locally hosted services that you want to expose to the cloud.

- **Service Bus Relay** With this service, you can expose your Windows Communication Foundation (WCF) services by registering a relay endpoint. Even if your service is behind a firewall and on a NAT, service consumers can still access the service via the public relay endpoint.

- **API Management** Using Azure API Management, you can modernize, manage, protect, and monitor your existing APIs hosted either on-premises or on cloud.

Reaching back to on-premises

In this scenario, your cloud-based services need to reach back to your on-premises resources such as databases in your local datacenter. You can use Azure App Service BizTalk API Apps Hybrid Connection to connect your web applications back to any on-premises resources that use a static TCP port, such as SQL database and Web APIs. This service is introduced briefly in Chapter 4.

Thought experiment

Dealing with network latency

In this thought experiment, apply what you've learned about this objective. You can find answers to these questions in the "Answers" section at the end of this chapter.

When you have servers running on both on-premises and the cloud, it's almost unavoidable that you will experience some performance degradation because of the extra network latency. When the degradation becomes unacceptable, some modifications to the code or to the architecture become necessary.

With this in mind, answer the following questions:

1. What code changes would you make to reduce latency?
2. What architecture changes would you make to reduce latency?

Objective summary

- You can use Point-to-Site connections to connect local compute to Azure Virtual Networks.

- You can use Site-to-Site connections to connect on-premises network to Azure Virtual Networks.

- You can use ExpressRoute to create a private, dedicated connection between your datacenters and Azure datacenters.

- To connect two Azure virtual networks, use vNet-to-vNet VPN.

- To connect multiple on-premises networks to the same Azure virtual network, use Multi-site VPN.

- You can use Service Bus Relay and API Management to expose local services to cloud.

- You can use BizTalk API Apps Hybrid Connection to connect back to on-premises resources from cloud.

Objective review

Answer the following questions to test your knowledge of the information in this objective. You can find the answers to these questions and explanations of why each answer choice is correct or incorrect in the "Answers" section at the end of this chapter.

1. What VPN types are supported by Azure?

   A. Point-to-Site

   B. Site-to-Site

   C. vNet-to-vNet

   D. Multi-set

2. What's the maximum bandwidth provided by ExpressRoute?

   A. 80 Mbps

   B. 200 Mbps

   C. 1 Gbps

   D. 10 Gbps

Objective 1.5: Describe Azure Services

Because your solution spans across multiple regions and facilities, you need to take additional care to ensure that the system performs at a global level. This objective introduces a couple of Azure services that can help you to optimize performance of a globally distributed system. Chapter 4 introduces more Azure services in the contexts of different scenarios.

Using Azure Traffic Manager

Traffic Manager routes incoming traffic to your application deployments at different geographic locations based on performance and availability.

To use Traffic Manager, you define a Traffic Manager profile that consists of a domain name, a list of endpoints, and a load-balancing policy. When a user tries to access a service, the following activities happen:

1. The user accesses the service by the domain name provided by Traffic Manager (*.trafficmanager.net). If a custom domain is used, another DNS resolution is performed to first resolve the custom domain name to the Traffic Manager domain name.

2. When Traffic Manager receives the DNS resolution request, it evaluates its policy and picks an endpoint address based on availability, performance, or a round-robin policy.

3. Traffic Manager returns a CNAME record that maps the Traffic Manager domain name to the selected endpoint.

4. The user's DNS server resolves the endpoint address to its IP address and sends it to the user.

5. The user calls the endpoint directly by the IP address.

A couple of points are worth discussing here. First, Traffic Manager functions during the DNS resolution phase. The actual traffic doesn't go through Traffic Manager. Second, because DNS records are often cached, Traffic Manager isn't involved in every service request. Third, the endpoints don't need to be on Azure. They can be on other cloud platforms, or even in on-premises datacenters.

Traffic Manager picks endpoints based on one of the following three methods:

- **Round-robin**   Traffic is distributed to all endpoints evenly or based on weights.

- **Performance**   Traffic Manager periodically updates a table that records the response time between various IP ranges to Azure datacenters. When a new request comes in, it picks the datacenter with the best response time in corresponding IP range.

- **Failover**   Traffic Manager returns the primary endpoint by default. However, if the primary endpoint becomes unavailable, it will return backup endpoints according to their assigned priorities.

These three methods are suitable for different scenarios. The round-robin method can be used for load-balancing in a same region or across multiple regions. The performance method can be used to optimize user traffic distribution. And the failover method can be used in failover scenarios.

You can also nest Traffic Manager profiles, which means a profile at a higher level uses other Traffic Manager endpoints as candidate endpoints. Using nested profiles, you can implement more complex policies. For example, you can have a top-level profile that uses the failover method to establish a primary site and a secondary site, and a second-level profile that distributes user traffics based on performance. You can have up to 10 levels of nested profiles.

Using CDN

Azure operates out of facilities located in 17 regions around the world, and that number is increasing every year. In addition, Azure also strategically places CDN point of presence (POP) locations to deliver content to end users. You can cache content from Azure Storage, Web Apps, and Azure Cloud Services.

When a user requests content by the CDN URL, the content is directly served from the CDN node, if the content exists. Otherwise, the content will be retrieved from the content origin and stored at the CDN node for future requests.

Using CDN has two major benefits. First, because content is served directly from the CDN node that is closest to the user, user experience can be greatly improved. Second, because a large portion of requests will be served from CDN nodes instead of from the original service nodes, the loads on the original service nodes are greatly reduced, making it possible for the service to scale-out to support a much greater number of users.

CDN is used mostly to cache static contents. However, you can cache dynamic outputs from your websites and cloud services as well because CDN content is identified by URLs, including the query parameters. For example, http://<*identifier*>.vo.msecnd.net/chart. aspx?item=1 and http://<*identifier*>.vo.msecnd.net/chart.aspx?item=2 represent two different cached objects. You need to be careful not to cache volatile data in CDN, because doing so can adversely affect your performance or even cause content problems, all at increased cost.

Thought experiment
Failover to the cloud

In this thought experiment, apply what you've learned about this objective. You can find answers to these questions in the "Answers" section at the end of this chapter.

When you have to perform maintenance on you on-premises system, how do you continue to provide service without having to acquire additional infrastructure to have a secondary deployment on-premises? By using Traffic Manager, you can failover to the cloud as you perform maintenance on your local system.

With this in mind, answer the following questions:

1. How would you set up the Traffic Manager policy in this case?

2. What would the customer experience be?

Objective summary

- Traffic Manager can distribute user traffic based on availability and performance.
- Traffic Manager uses the round-robin, performance, or failover method to decide to which endpoint to route traffic.
- CDNs serve cached content directly from CDN nodes that are closest to end users.
- CDNs can reduce traffic to original service nodes by serving static content directly.

Objective review

Answer the following questions to test your knowledge of the information in this objective. You can find the answers to these questions and explanations of why each answer choice is correct or incorrect in the "Answers" section at the end of this chapter.

1. Which of the following are methods Traffic Manager uses to pick endpoints?

   A. Round-robin

   B. Failover

   C. Performance

   D. Random

2. What are the benefits of using a CDN?

   A. Reduce response time

   B. Reduce traffic to the original service

   C. Improve data consistency

   D. Enable faster upgrades

Answers

This section contains the solutions to the thought experiments and answers to the objective review questions in this chapter.

Objective 1.1: Thought experiment

1. There's no single best way to explain how data is secured in the cloud. However, a simple analogy is quite effective: Ask if one would deposit money in a bank or keep cash under a couch cushion. Sure, the cash is closer to the owner when stored under the cushion, but the owner won't be able to provide the level of protection a bank can offer. When you save data to Azure, your data is replicated at least three times for high availability. And Azure makes sure your data is accessible only by you.

2. Again, there's no single correct answer. One possible approach is to talk about service recovery. Applications will fail, no matter where an application is deployed. The key to improving service availability is how quickly you can recover from errors. In traditional datacenters, MTTR is usually quite lengthy. Referring to previous service interruption cases if a good strategy to illustrate how reduced MTTR can help to dramatically increase service availability.

Objective 1.1: Review

1. **Correct answers:** A, B, C, and D
   - **A.** **Correct:** Sufficient training is the foundation of building up a high-quality team.
   - **B.** **Correct:** Automation is one of the most effective means to reduce human errors.
   - **C.** **Correct:** Just-in-time access ensures that there's no standing access to Azure resources, reducing the risk of accidental operations being carried out on customer data.
   - **D.** **Correct:** Operation policies must be reinforced to ensure established workflows and practices are precisely followed.

2. **Correct answers:** A, B, C, and D
   - **A.** **Correct:** Azure is committed to annual certification against ISO/IEC 27001/27002:2013.
   - **B.** **Correct:** Azure has been granted a Provisional Authority to Operate (P-ATO) from the Federate Risk and Authorization Management Program (FedRAMP).
   - **C.** **Correct:** Microsoft currently offers HIPPA Business Associate Agreement (BAA) to customers who have an Enterprise Agreement (EA).
   - **D.** **Correct:** Microsoft offers customers European Union Standard Contractual Clauses.

3. **Correct answers:** B

    A. **Incorrect:** Single-instance VMs don't qualify for SLA.

    B. **Correct:** Azure SLA requires at least two multi-instance VMs be deployed in the same Availability Set.

    C. **Incorrect:** If an Availability Set only contains a single VM, the VM doesn't qualify for SLA.

    D. **Incorrect:** Two VMs must be in the same Availability Set to qualify for SLA.

Objective 1.2: Thought experiment

1. Although you can use both ACL and NSG to control network traffic to VMs, NSG is a better choice in this case because, 1) you can define rules that apply to a subnet instead of a VM, and 2) you can gain greater control by defining inbound rules and outbound rules independently.

2. One possible way to design the topology is to put Internet-facing resources, application servers, and database servers into different subnets. The Internet-facing resources can communicate only to application servers through specific ports. And only application servers can access database servers governed by another set of rules.

Objective 1.2: Review

1. **Correct answers:** A, B, C, and D

    A. **Correct:** Each VM has an associated public virtual IP (VIP).

    B. **Correct:** Each VM has one or multiple private IP addresses, one per NIC.

    C. **Correct:** A static public IP can be associated with a VM.

    D. **Correct:** A private static IP address can be associated to a VM on a virtual network.

2. **Correct answers:** A, B, and C

    A. **Correct:** VIRTUAL_NETWORK denotes all IP ranges in the same virtual network, including connected networks.

    B. **Correct:** AZURE_LOADBALANCER denotes the IP address of the Azure load balancer.

    C. **Correct:** INTERNET denotes all IP addresses outside the virtual network.

    D. **Incorrect:** VIRTUAL_MACHINE is not a default tag.

3. **Correct answers:** A, B, C, and D

   A. **Correct:** An NSG rule defines traffic flow control from a source range to a destination range. The source range is defined by source IP and source port.

   B. **Correct:** An NSG rule defines traffic flow control from a source range to a destination range. The destination range is defined by target IP and source port.

   C. **Correct:** You can apply an NSG rule to TCP, UPD, or * for both protocols

   D. **Correct:** Each NSG rule has an associated priority. Rules with lower priority can be overridden by rules with higher priorities.

4. **Correct answers:** A, B, C, and D

   A. **Correct:** Each ACL rule has a rule number, which denotes the priority of the rule.

   B. **Correct:** The remote subnet defines the IP range that the rule will be applied to.

   C. **Correct:** An ACL rule is associated with a VM endpoint.

   D. **Correct:** An ACL rule can be either a permitting rule or denying rule.

Objective 1.3: Thought experiment

1. Reliability, availability, security, and performance are all valid concerns. Especially, because Azure provides SLAs only if there are at least two VMs in an Availability Set, to ensure availability, you'll need to deploy the application to at least two VMs and join them behind a load balancer. This might immediately cause some problems because not all applications are designed for such deployment. For instance, some of the legacy systems are designed to have a single central server that handles all user transactions. When the transactions are distributed to multiple instances, you might have two centers of truth that can't be reconciled. Data replication and customer partition are two effective approaches in some cases.

2. To take full advantage of the cloud, you should explore the possibility of moving the application to PaaS. With VMs, you are still responsible for managing the virtualized infrastructure. With PaaS, you can focus almost entirely on implementing your business logics and leave the rest to Azure.

Objective 1.3: Review

1. **Correct answer:** C

   A. **Incorrect:** A-series is designed for generic workload, with A8 through A11 designed for HPC.

   B. **Incorrect:** D-series is designed for applications with high CPU and high temporary data IO.

   C. **Correct:** DS-series is designed for applications with high persisted data IO.

   D. **Incorrect:** G-series is for application with high CPU and memory demands.

2. **Correct answer:** D

    A. **Incorrect:** 8 is below limitations of any series.

    B. **Incorrect:** 16 is the limit of A-series.

    C. **Incorrect:** 32 is the limit of D-series and DS-series.

    D. **Correct:** G-series supports up to 64 data drives.

3. **Correct answer:** A

    A. **Correct:** Azure Resource Template uses JSON format.

    B. **Incorrect:** Azure Resource Template doesn't support XML format.

    C. **Incorrect:** Azure Resource Template doesn't support YAML format.

    D. **Incorrect:** Azure PowerShell is a scripting language, it's not used to describe an Azure Resource Template.

4. **Correct answers:** A, B, C, and D

    A. **Correct:** Custom Script Extension downloads and runs configuration scripts such as DSC to designated VMs.

    B. **Correct:** Chef and Puppet are both integrated third-party solutions.

    C. **Correct:** Azure Automation can periodically check and fix your resource states so they don't drift away from standard settings.

    D. **Correct:** Containerization is an effective way to pack applications as consistently deployable unit.

Objective 1.4: Thought experiment

1. Common techniques include introducing cache to reduce accesses to databases, using asynchronous IO operations, compressing data, sending deltas and only required data instead of complete data sets, and paging.

2. You can use queues to decouple components to break hard dependencies among services so that they can run at different paces. You can also consider SOA and Microservices to decompose complex applications into smaller services that can evolve separately.

Objective 1.4: Review

1. **Correct answers:** A, B, C, and D

    A. **Correct:** Use Point-to-Site connections to connect local compute to Azure Virtual Networks.

    B. **Correct:** Use Site-to-Site connections to connect on-premises network to Azure Virtual Networks.

    C. **Correct:** Use vNet-to-vNet VPN to connect two Azure virtual networks.

    D. **Correct:** Use Multi-site VPN to connect multiple on-premises networks to the same Azure virtual network.

2. **Correct answers:** D

    A. **Incorrect:** 80 Mbps is roughly the bandwidth a standard Azure Virtual Network gateway provides.

    B. **Incorrect:** 200 Mbps is roughly the bandwidth a high-performance Azure Virtual Network gateway provides.

    C. **Incorrect:** 1 Gbps is the maximum ExpressRoute bandwidth when a network service provider is used.

    D. **Correct:** 10 Gbps is the maximum ExpressRoute bandwidth when an exchange provider is used.

Objective 1.5: Thought experiment

1. In this case, the Traffic Manger policy will use the failover method, with a primary endpoint pointing to on-premises deployment and a secondary endpoint pointing to cloud deployment.

2. As the maintenance begins, the on-premises site is brought down. Some customers will still be redirected to the on-premises endpoint, leading to service interruption. As DNS records expires, new customer requests will be redirected to the cloud endpoint. You should note that this is not a zero-downtime solution.

Objective 1.5: Review

1. **Correct answers:** A, B, and C

    A. **Correct:** Traffic Manager supports the round-robin method that distributes traffic evenly to endpoints.

    B. **Correct:** Traffic Manager supports the failover method that routes traffic to the primary endpoint and then to the secondary endpoint when the primary is unavailable.

    C. **Correct:** Traffic Manager supports performance-based routing that picks the endpoint with the least response time.

    D. **Incorrect:** Traffic Manager doesn't support random routing.

2. **Correct answers:** A and B

   A. **Correct:** CDN reduces response time by serving content directly from CDN locations.

   B. **Correct**: With static contents served from CDN locations, the traffic to the original service nodes can be greatly reduced.

   C. **Incorrect**: With CDNs serving cached contents, data could be out-of-sync with server versions and will eventually become consistent with server when local cache expires.

   D. **Incorrect:** CDN has nothing to do with your application server upgrades. On the other hand, because older static contents are served from CDNs, it will take time for the new static content to propagate to all CDN nodes.

## CHAPTER 2

Secure resources

This chapter covers topics on managed identity; specifically, using an external identity provider that manages identities as well as handles authentication requests for you. Then, the discussion moves on to how to make data secure in the cloud. You'll cover a number of techniques and services to ensure that data storages are reliable and available, and you'll be briefly introduced to Microsoft Azure backup and disaster recovery solutions, before they are fully covered in Chapter 6. Finally, you'll learn how Azure Directory assists system administrators to design, develop, and reinforce effective security policies across large enterprises.

Objectives in this chapter:

- Objective 2.1: Secure resources by using managed identities
- Objective 2.2: Secure resources by using hybrid identities
- Objective 2.3: Secure resources by using identity providers
- Objective 2.4: Identify an appropriate data security solution
- Objective 2.5: Design a role-based access control strategy

Objective 2.1: Secure resources by using managed identities

The core idea of using managed identities is to delegate complex identity management and user authentication tasks to a trusted party so that you can focus on developing business logics. Instead of managing identities yourself, you choose a trustworthy party that manages identities and handles user authentication requests for you. After a user is authenticated, this trusted party issues security tokens to you, which contain various claims about the user. Then, you can use these claims to make decisions such as whether to grant access and apply corresponding security rules.

The key to a successful implementation of a system using managed identities is to keep a clear picture of the relationships among the participants of the authentication/authorization workflow. Before going deeper, you first need to learn some terms. Then, you'll view them in a complete picture to examine how they interact with one another.

Understanding claims-based architecture

The system design that uses an external party to manage identities is sometimes called a *claims-based architecture*. The following are some of the key components of this architecture. (the sections that follow introduce each component separately, and then you'll see them put into a complete authentication workflow).

Securable entity and its attributes

A *securable entity* refers to a user, an application, or a service identity that makes service requests. An entity often has one or more associated attributes, such as user name, telephone number, and security roles.

Claim

A *claim* is an assertion made on an attribute of an entity. For example, the street address printed on a driver's license is an assertion made by an authority (such as a state office) with respect to an individual's home address (attribute). Any party can make assertions, but only claims from a trusted authority should be trusted.

Security token

A *security token* is a collection of claims. It is often digitally signed, encrypted, and transferred through secured channels to ensure its confidentiality, integrity, and authenticity. A consumer of a security token should trust the claims in the token only if the consumer can validate that the token is genuine and has not been altered.

Service provider/relying party

A *service provider* provides requested services. Within the context of a claims-based architecture, a service provider is also called a *relying party* because it relies on a third party to manage identities on its behalf.

Identity provider

An *identity provider* authenticates entities and issues security tokens to relying parties. The security token contains the claims that the identity provider made about the entity. Then, the relying party can use claims in the token for authorization. An identity provider offers one or multiple ways for an entity to authenticate, such as using a password or a security key, a digital certificate, a security token, or a biometric signature. Some identity providers also support authentications with a combination of multiple methods, which is called *multifactor authentication*.

Trust

A *trust relationship* is what ties an identity provider and a service provider together. A service provider assumes that the assertions in a security token are true because the token is issued by a trusted party. A service provider can choose to trust multiple identity providers, and an identity provider can provide authentication services to multiple service providers. These trusted parties form a circle of trust, in which an entity (such as a user) only needs to sign on once with any of the trusted identity providers to gain access to services provided by any of the service providers in the same trust circle. This is the so-called Single Sign-On (SSO) experience.

Authentication

The task of *authentication* is to verify if an entity is indeed what it claims to be. To authenticate, a user usually needs to provide certain proofs, such as a password, a digital certificate, or an issued security token. After the user is authenticated, an identity provider issues a security token to the requesting service provider.

Authorization

Authorization is the process of determining whether an authenticated user has access to certain functionalities provided by the service provider. An service provider uses claims in the security token to determine whether certain actions should be allowed. For example, certain actions are allowed only when there's a claim stating that the authenticated user has a role attribute with a value of "System Administrator."

To help you to remember the difference between authentication and authorization, simply remember that authentication contends with the question of who are you, whereas authorization establishes what are you allowed to do.

EXAM TIP

Quite a few components participate in an authentication and authorization workflow. Understanding how they interact with one another is the key to a successful implementation. Swim-lane diagrams such as that shown in Figure 2-1 are a proven, effective method to explain, or to memorize, how different parties work together. As an exercise in preparing for the exam, you should try to re-create these diagrams by yourself to ensure that you clearly understand how the process works.

Understanding basic authentication and authorization workflow

Figure 2-1 illustrates the basic authentication and authorization workflow within a claims-based architecture. This workflow applies to a typical scenario in which a user makes use of a browser to access a web application.

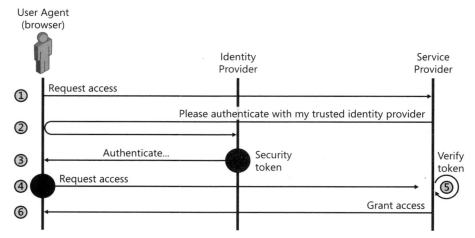

FIGURE 2-1 Basic authentication and authorization process

The following describes each numbered step in the workflow in Figure 2-1:

1. A user (agent) requests access to a service offered by a service provider.

2. The service provider is configured to use a trusted service provider for authentication. Instead of granting access to the service, it redirects the user agent to the designated service provider to first be authenticated.

3. The user completes the authentication process with the identity provider. When the authentication process is successfully completed, the identity provider issues a security token to the user agent.

4. The user agent requests access to the service again, but this time it attaches the security token to the request.

5. The service provider verifies the token. When the token is validated, it retrieves the claims contained in the token.

6. Based on the claims, the service provider decides whether the access request should be granted.

Working with native clients and multitiered applications

The workflow in Figure 2-1 is based on a browser as the user agent, which is also called a *passive client* in this context. The workflow relies on URL redirections to carry the process forward. In the case of a native application such as a Windows Desktop application or a mobile-phone application, a different workflow based on OAuth 2.0 specification is often used, as shown in Figure 2-2.

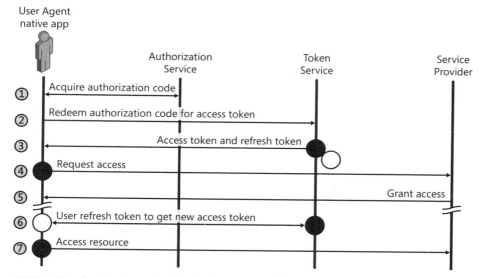

FIGURE 2-2 Authentication and authorization process with native client

The following describes each numbered step in the workflow in Figure 2-2:

1. A user (agent) requests an authorization code from an authorization service. In the request, the user agent identifies itself and specifies which application or service it is trying to access. The authorization service authenticates the user. If consent is required to use the service or the application, the authorization service also asks for the user's consent before continuing with the process. Otherwise, it issues an authorization code to the user agent.

2. The user redeems the authorization code for an access token from a token service.

3. After the authorization code, the client identification, and the service identification is verified, the token service issues an access token as well as a refresh token.

4. The user agent uses the access token to make service requests.

5. The service provider verifies the token and makes authorization decisions before providing the service.

6. When the access token expires, the user agent uses the refresh token it received earlier in step 3 to acquire a new access token. The purpose of the refresh token is to avoid reauthentication, which requires the user to sign in again.

7. The user agent makes additional service requests using the new access token, and the process continues.

Working with multitiered applications

When working with a multitiered application, a common workflow involves a user signing in to the front tier, and the front tier making service calls to the business tier within the context of the user's session. In this case, the service requests to the business tier need to be authenticated without explicit user actions. One way to achieve this is to use an application identity, which the front end uses for authentication as an independent entity. The business tier will simply trust that the front tier has authenticated the requesting user. This pattern is also called a *trusted subsystem*. When using application identity, the business tier can't distinguish which user has issued the original request. Thus, it's up to the tiers to communicate over application protocols when user contexts are needed.

A second way to implement the scenario is to use delegated user identity. In this case, a user requests an authorization code as well as an ID token from the authorization service. An ID token uniquely identifies the combination of a client program and a user. It is submitted to the front end along with authorization code. The front end can then use this token, along with the authorization code, to request an access token (and refresh token) to access the business tier. Figure 2-3 depicts a simplified diagram of the second approach.

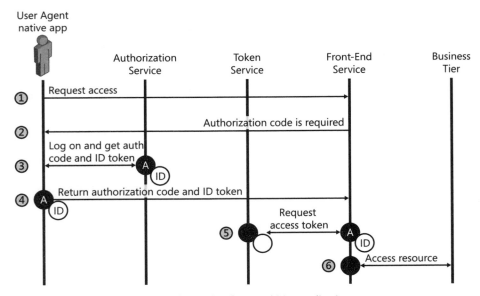

FIGURE 2-3 Authentication and authorization for a multitier application

The following describes each numbered step in the workflow in Figure 2-3:

1. A user agent requests access to business tier via the front end.

2. The front-end service replies that an authorization code is required to access the business tier.

3. The user signs in and receives an authentication code along with an ID token.

4. The authorization code and the ID token are returned to the front-end service.

5. The front-end service requests an access token from the token service.

6. The front-end service accesses the business tier with the access token.

Additional scenarios

When a server daemon needs to invoke another service, the daemon must carry out the authentication workflow without any user interactions. In this case, the daemon needs to have its own identity and credential (such as a digital certificate) so that it can directly request an access token by itself.

When a service needs to call another service, it needs to request an access token for the second service on behalf of the user. This can be done by following the OAuth 2.0 On-Behalf-Of (draft) specification (*http://tools.ietf.org/html/draft-jones-oauth-token-exchange-01*).

Azure Active Directory

Azure Active Directory (Azure AD) is a comprehensive managed-identity that provides identity management and authentication services to your applications using standard protocols such as SAML 2.0, ws-Federation, and OpenID Connect. In addition to acting as an identity provider under the claims-based architecture, Azure AD also provides other enterprise-focused services such as a multifactor authentication service, a centralized application access panel to manage access to Software as a Service (SaaS) applications, an application proxy by which you can set up remote access to your on-premises services, as well as a Graph API that you can use to directly interact with Azure AD objects for scenarios such as user managements and role-based access control (RBAC).

Azure AD is a highly scalable and reliable service with redundant deployments in data-centers around the globe. It handles billions of authentication requests every day. Some of the most popular SaaS applications such as Microsoft Office 365 and Microsoft Intune rely on Azure AD for authentication.

Azure AD supports all of the aforementioned authentication/authorization workflows that were introduced in the previous section. Understanding how the participating parties interact with one another in these workflows will definitely help you to ensure that all necessary configurations are in place. However, you don't need to cope with such details, because most of them are abstracted away by Azure AD Authentication Library (ADAL). This library facilitates authentication processes with both cloud and on-premises directories. And, it provides additional features, such as automatically refreshing expired access tokens, to further simplify the development process. In the sample scenario later in this chapter, you'll see how ADAL and Microsoft Visual Studio tooling work together to make implementing common authentication and authorization scenarios a breeze.

Azure AD is offered in three tiers: Free, Basic, and Premium. The Free tier covers the basic cloud-first application scenarios. The Basic and Premium tiers (currently only available through Microsoft Enterprise Volume Licensing Programs) are designed for enterprise usages at scale. Both tiers come with a Service Level Agreement (SLA) of 99.9 percent. In addition, the Premium tier also provides advanced features, such as machine learning–based security and usage reports, alerting, and multifactor authentication. For a detailed comparison of feature sets provided by these tiers, go to *http://azure.microsoft.com/en-us/pricing/details/active-directory/*.

Differences between Azure AD and on-premises Active Directory Domain Services

Azure AD and on-premises Active Directory Domain Services (AD DS) share many similarities. They both provide authentication and authorization services; they both facilitate managing directory objects such as users and groups; and they both provide SSO experience to enterprise users. Moreover, you can use tools such as Azure AD Synchronization (AAD Sync) to synchronize users and groups between your on-premises directories and your cloud-based directories. However, it's important to realize that these are two different technologies designed for different purposes and applied for different scopes. Some key differences exist between the two.

First, Azure AD and on-premises AD DS are designed for different scopes and they operate in different environments. On-premises AD DS is designed to secure on-premises resources. It usually works within local networks of a single enterprise. By contrast, Azure AD is designed to protect cloud-based resources. It is a multitenant system that works over the Internet.

The second difference is that Azure AD and on-premises AD DS use different protocols. On-premises AD DS uses protocols such as Kerberos and Lightweight Directory Access Protocol (LDAP), whereas Azure AD uses Internet-oriented protocols, such as SAML 2.0, ws-Federation, OpenID Connect, and RESTful Graph API.

Third, although their functionalities overlap in terms of authentication and authorization, they have mutually exclusive features. For instance, only on-premises AD DS supports constructs such as forests, domains, and organization units. Conversely, only Azure AD natively provides features such as Azure Access Panel and RESTful interfaces.

On-premises Active Directory and Azure AD working together

Obviously, Azure AD can operate on its own to provide a pure cloud-based identity-management solution, which is ideal for companies that have most of their resources in the cloud. On the other hand, you can also configure Azure AD as an extension to the existing enterprise on-premises Active Directory. In the second case, an enterprise can "project" part of its directory to the cloud so that users can utilize the same set of credentials to access both on-premises resources and cloud resources.

The way to connect Azure AD to Windows Server Active Directory is to use the AAD Sync service. The service provides a downloadable component that you can install on your on-premises Windows Server. Then, you can configure fine-grained object synchronization between your on-premises directories and your cloud-based directories.

Another way to use Windows Server Active Directory for cloud application authentication is to use Active Directory Federation Service (AD FS) and Azure Access Control Service (ACS), both of which you can learn more about in the next objective.

A sample scenario with ADAL and Visual Studio

This section walks you through a simple scenario that implements the basic authentication/ authorization workflow presented earlier in Figure 2-1 to help you to become familiar with common development processes with Azure AD. In this sample scenario, you'll create a simple ASP.NET application and then use Azure AD to provide authentication.

Prerequisites

- Visual Studio 2013 with Update 3 or above, with Azure SDK for .NET 2.4 or above.
- An active Azure subscription.

Part 1: Provision an Azure AD tenant and a user

In this part, you'll create a new Azure AD tenant and a new user that you'll use for the remainder of the exercise.

1. Sign in to the Azure management portal.
2. Click New, App Services, Active Directory, Directory, and then click Custom Create.
3. On the Add Directory page, type a name to identify your directory tenant, and a domain name. The final domain name of your tenant will be the name you enter, plus the *.onmicrosoft.com* postfix. In this example, you'll use *exam70354.onmicrosoft.com*, but, obviously, you'll need to use a different domain name. Next, select your country or region, and then click the check mark to continue.
4. When the directory tenant is provisioned, click the directory name to open its Quick Start page, and then click Add A User. You also can go to the user list page by clicking Users (located at the top of the page) and then, on the command bar, click Add User.
5. On the Add User page, type a user name, and then click the right arrow to continue. In this example, you'll use **sample1@exam70345.onmicrosoft.com**.
6. On the next page, type a first name, a last name, and a display name for the user. Change the role to Global Administrator, which is required to complete the second part of this sample. Provide an alternative email address, and then click the right arrow to continue.

7. On the last page, click Create to create a temporary password for the user. Then, on the password page, you can copy the password to the clipboard or send the password (as clear text) to the email addresses of your choice. Click the check mark to complete the process.

Part 2: Create and secure an ASP.NET application

In this part, you'll create a new ASP.NET application, and then turn on authentication by using the Azure AD tenant you just created in Part 1.

1. Start Visual Studio and create a new ASP.NET web application.

2. In the New ASP.NET Project dialog box, select the MVC template, and then click Change Authentication, as shown in Figure 2-4.

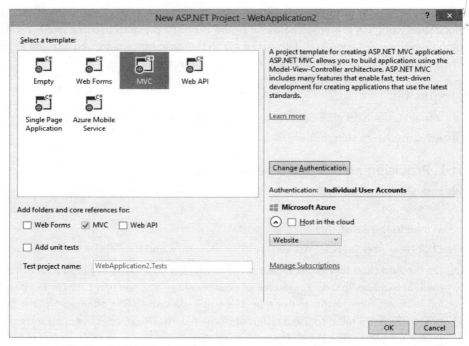

FIGURE 2-4 The New ASP.NET Project dialog box

3. In the Change Authentication dialog box, select the Organizational Accounts option. Then, in the Domain box, type your Azure AD tenant domain name. For Access Level, you can leave it at the default option, which, as illustrated in Figure 2-5, is Single Sign On, Read Directory Data, or choose options that allow you to read or write directory data, as well.

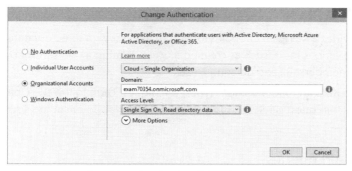

FIGURE 2-5 The Change Authentication dialog box

4. Click the OK button. A browser message displays, asking you to sign in to your Azure AD tenant. Sign in using the user credential you've just created. Because this is the first time you've signed in using this credential, you'll also be asked to change the temporary password. Follow the wizard to change your password, and then complete the sign-in process.

5. Back in the New ASP.NET Project dialog box, click the OK button to complete creating the project. When the project is being created, the Active Directory Authentication Library, which is a NuGet package, is automatically downloaded and installed to your project.

6. Press F5 to start the ASP.NET application.

   Take a look at the browser address bar; you'll see it begins with a *localhost* address, which is the service provider you try to access. Then, the browser is redirected to a sign-in page, which is provided by the trusted identity provider (Azure AD in this case).

7. Sign in via the user credential you've just created.

8. After you've signed in successfully, the browser is redirected back to your ASP.NET application. Note that the user name is displayed on the navigation bar, in the upper-right corner, as shown in Figure 2-6.

ASP.NET

ASP.NET is a free web framework for building great Web sites and Web applications using HTML, CSS and JavaScript.

FIGURE 2-6 The authenticated user name displayed on the navigation bar

Azure AD Graph API

Azure AD Graph API provides a REST API endpoint for you to interact with directory data and objects. You can perform various tasks, such as creating a user, updating a user's properties, checking a user's group membership, and deleting a user.

The API supports both XML and JSON content types; the request URLs follow the Open Data (OData) Protocol. Each request is required to present a JSON Web Token in the authorization header.

Structure of Graph API queries

Graph API URLs are structured using the following format:

```
https://graph.windows.net/{tenant identifier}/{resource path}?{query parameters}
```

The tenant identifier can be in one of the following three formats:

- **Tenant object ID**   Each Azure AD tenant is assigned a globally unique identifier (GUID). You can obtain this by using the *Get-AzureAccount* Windows PowerShell cmdlet.

- **A verified domain name**   Each registered Azure AD tenant has a default domain name of *{tenant name}*.onmicrosoft.com. However, you can add custom domain names to improve the user sign-in experience. When constructing Graph API URLs, you can use custom domain names instead of the default domain name to identify your Azure AD tenant.

- **"*MyOrganization*" or "*Me*" aliases**   Both aliases are only available for OAuth Authorization Code Grant types. When aliases are used, Graph API uses claims presented in the access token to derive the tenant.

For example, the following query returns a list of security groups under the *exam70354. onmicrosoft.com* tenant:

```
https://graph.windows.net/exam70354.onmicrosoft.com/groups?api-version=1.5
```

Each Graph API request needs to have three headers:

- **Host**   This is *graph.windows.net*.
- **Authorization**   This is your access token.
- **Content-Type**   This can be either *application/json* or *application/xml*.

When a request body is used, the payload is a JSON or an XML structure carrying the necessary parameters. For example, the request to create a new security group is a *POST* request with the following body:

```
{
    "displayName": "<display name>",
    "mailNickname": "<mail nick name>",
    "mailEnabled": <true or false>,
    "securityEnabled": <true of false>
}
```

MORE INFO **GRAPH EXPLORER**

You can use a sample graphic explorer at *https://graphexplorer.cloudapp.net/* to try out
graphic queries. The site generates necessary authentication headers for you.

Using the Azure AD Graph API Client Library

This client library helps developers to interact with Azure AD tenants in their .NET applications targeting the Windows Store, Windows Phone, and MVC web applications. You can also target the same code on Android and iOS by using Xamarin.

The library is a NuGet package (*Microsoft.Azure.ActiveDirectory.GraphClient*) that you can include in your projects. The library makes it possible for you to use Language Integrated Query (LINQ) queries to operate on your directory objects. For example, the following code queries for a user by name:

```
List<IUser> users = activeDirectoryClient.Users.Where(user =>
        user.UserPrincipalName.Equals("sample1@exam70354.onmicrosoft.com")).
        ExecuteAsync().Result.CurrentPage.ToList();
```

Thought experiment
Deciding whether you should use an external identity provider

In this thought experiment, apply what you've learned about this objective. You can find answers to these questions in the "Answers" section at the end of this chapter.

A user base is a very important asset to many companies. So, it's not uncommon to see people having doubts regarding whether to allow an external party to handle user management. As an architect, you need to convince your team why using an external identity provider is a better choice. Think about how you would answer these two questions:

1. Why do you want to use an external party such as Azure AD?

2. What challenges are you likely to face if you don't?

Objective summary

- Using managed identities makes it possible for developers to focus on improving business logics and be assured that their cloud resources are accessible only by authenticated and authorized users. Azure AD is such a managed identity solution, designed to secure cloud-based applications.

- Azure AD is different from on-premises AD DS. They are designed for different goals and they operate under different protocols. However, you can use Azure AAD Sync to link the two together so that your customers can still use their on-premises credentials to access cloud-based applications.

- Azure AD provides a RESTful Graph API with which you can interact with directory objects, such as performing Create, Read, Update and Delete (CRUD) operations and RBAC checks.

- Azure AD also provides client libraries such as ADAL and Azure AD Graph Client Library to facilitate application development.

Objective review

Answer the following questions to test your knowledge of the information in this objective. You can find the answers to these questions and explanations of why each answer choice is correct or incorrect in the "Answers" section at the end of this chapter.

1. Which of the following protocols are not supported by Azure AD?
    - **A.** ws-Federation
    - **B.** SAML 2.0
    - **C.** OpenID Connect
    - **D.** Kerberos

2. To ensure confidentiality, integrity, and authenticity of security tokens, you can use the following techniques. (Choose all that apply.)
    - **A.** Transmit over HTTPS
    - **B.** Digital signature
    - **C.** Encryption
    - **D.** Token expiration

3. To interact with Azure AD objects, what are the available options?
    - **A.** Graph API
    - **B.** ADAL and Azure AD Graph Client Library
    - **C.** LDAP
    - **D.** X.500

4. In a claims-based architecture, which of the following components issue security tokens?

   A. Identity provider

   B. Relying party

   C. User agent

   D. User

Objective 2.2: Secure resources by using hybrid identities

As large enterprises make the transition to the cloud era, they face the practical challenge of making their existing on-premises resources and their new cloud resources work together seamlessly. The key to achieving this goal is to provide an SSO experience across both on-premises resources and cloud resources.

As Objective 2.1 demonstrates, you can make Azure AD and your on-premises AD DS work together by using AAD Sync. In this objective, you'll dig deeper into the implementation details.

Before you begin looking at directory synchronization options, let's first review AD FS, which has been used to extend the reach of on-premises credentials.

> **This section covers the following topics:**
> - Setting up directory synchronization with AD FS
> - Configuring Azure AD Application Proxy

Setting up directory synchronization with AD FS

AD FS existed long before Azure AD, and it has been a proven way to extend the reach of on-premises AD DS to external networks. AD FS is the Microsoft implementation of the ws-Federation Passive Requestor Profile protocol. With it, cloud-based applications can use on-premises AD DS user credentials to authenticate by using standard protocols and SAML tokens.

You can continue to use AD FS as part of your hybrid identity solutions. But, if you'd like to have a centralized management plane and you want to take advantage of the new monitoring, analysis, and self-service capabilities provided by Azure AD, you should consider using directory synchronization to bring your directory objects into Azure AD.

Directory synchronization

Historically, there have been several synchronization solutions provided by Azure AD, including the aforementioned AAD Sync, DirSync, and FIM + Azure AD Connector. As of this writing, the three engines are being consolidated into a new, unified Sync Engine along with an Azure AD tool that greatly simplifies directory synchronization configuration tasks.

> **NOTE   THE EVOLUTION OF AZURE AD**
>
> Azure AD undergoes constant improvement. New features are being released quickly. As of this writing, DirSync is still the default synchronization mechanism when you follow the management portal links. At the same time, AAD Sync is also supported via a separate download link. Both are used in the sample scenarios that follow.

To conceptually understand directory synchronization, you need to understand three concepts: connector space, metaverse, and synchronization rules.

- **Connector space**   Each participating directory is connected to a connector space, which caches shadow copies of objects that contain a subset of actual directory objects. Directory object operations such as additions, deletions, and modifications are written to connector spaces before they are synchronized with the actual directories.

- **Metaverse**   A metaverse sits at the center of a directory synchronization. It holds a consolidated view of all the objects being synchronized.

- **Synchronization rules**   Synchronization rules define how attributes flow when certain criteria are met. You use synchronization rules to control how objects are synchronized and optionally transformed across multiple directories.

Figure 2-7 shows a simplified view of a directory synchronization with two participating directories.

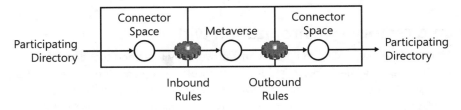

FIGURE 2-7 Directory synchronization

During synchronization, you can choose whether hashes of user passwords are synchronized, as well. If the password hashes are synchronized, the target directory can carry out authentications without the involvement of the original directory. Otherwise, the actual authentication operations are passed back to the original directory. For instance, when you synchronize an on-premises AD DS with Azure AD, if password hashes are synchronized, authentications are carried out by Azure AD. Otherwise, the authentication operations are passed back to the on-premises directory.

Sample scenario: setting up directory synchronization

This scenario walks you through the steps needed to set up basic directory synchronization between an on-premises AD DS forest and an Azure AD tenant.

1. Create a new user in your Azure AD tenant for directory synchronization. The user needs to be a Global Administrator. It's recommended that you set the account password expiration policy to never expire, which you can do by using the following Windows PowerShell cmdlet (for more information, go to *https://msdn.microsoft.com/ en-us/library/azure/dn757602.aspx*):

```
Set-msoluser -UserPrincipalName dirsync@exam70354.onmicrosoft.com
-PasswordNeverExpires $True
```

> **NOTE AZURE AD MODULE FOR WINDOWS POWERSHELL**
>
> To use the preceding cmdlet, you first need to download and install Azure AD Module for Windows PowerShell (*http://go.microsoft.com/fwlink/p/?linkid=236297*), and then use the *connect-msolservice* command to connect to the Azure AD tenant.

2. Change your Azure AD tenant configurations to turn on directory synchronization. You can do this on your tenant's Directory Integration page by selecting Activated, as shown in Figure 2-8. On the command bar, click Save to keep this change.

FIGURE 2-8 Turning on directory integration

3. After you have activated the feature, you can download the directory synchronization tool by using the download link on the same page.

4. Follow the wizard to complete the installation. Then, start the AAD Sync tool Configuration Wizard.

> **NOTE ERROR: A CONSTRAINT VIOLATION HAS OCCURRED**
>
> The user who runs the configuration wizard needs to be a member of the FIMSync-Admins group. Although the installation wizard adds the current user account to the group, you must log off and log on again for it to take effect. Otherwise, you might receive the error message "a constraint violation has occurred" during configuration.

5. Type the Azure AD credential you just created in step 1, and then click Next to continue.

6. Type the on-premises AD DS credential that you want to use for directory synchronization.

7. The account needs to have Administrator permissions on your organization's Active Directory directory service.

8. On the Hybrid Deployment page, if you want to allow data to be synchronized back to your on-premises Active Directory, select the Enable Hybrid Deployment check box.

    This is optional for this exercise; for now, you'll synchronize in only one direction, which is from on-premises to cloud.

9. On the Password Synchronization page, if you want passwords (hashes) to be synchronized, select the Enable Password Sync check box. For this exercise, select the check box. Click Next again to start the configuration.

10. When the configuration is done, confirm that the Synchronize Your Directories Now check box is selected, and then click Finish.

11. After a few minutes, you'll see your on-premises users and groups begin to appear in your Azure AD tenant. For example, a user named *joe@{your on-premises domain}.com* will be mapped *to joe@{your Azure AD tenant}.com* on your Azure AD tenant.

> **NOTE DIRSYNC AND AAD SYNC**
>
> As mentioned earlier in this objective, to use the AAD Sync agent, you need to follow a separate download URL instead of using the download link provided by the management portal. However, this might change by the time you read this text. Check the title of your application window to see which agent you are using.

12. Try out the newer AAD Sync services. First, download the service client from *http://www.microsoft.com/en-us/download/details.aspx?id=44225*. Note that this client cannot be installed on a Domain Controller.

13. On the Microsoft Azure Active Directory Sync Services page, click Install to begin installing the client.

When installation is complete, sign out and then sign in again. This is to ensure that your account's new ADSyncAdmins membership is activated.

14. Start the client by clicking the desktop shortcut (DirectorySyncTool).

15. On the Connect To Azure AD page, type the Azure AD credential that you want to use for directory synchronization. You should reuse the user you created in step 1.

16. On the Connect To AD FS page, type the domain, user name, and password of the on-premises account that you want to use for directory synchronization, and then click Add Forest. You can add multiple forests to join the synchronization on this page. When you're done, click Next to continue.

17. On the next page, specify User Matching rules.

18. With User Matching rules, you can define how user accounts from multiple forests are to be synchronized to Azure AD. For example, you might have two accounts representing the same user in two different forests. Using these rules, you can match these accounts by selected attributes. Because you are not synchronizing from multiple forests in this exercise, you can simply choose the Your Users Are Only Represented Once Across All Forests option, as shown in Figure 2-9. Table 2-1 summarizes the attributes that you can use to match user accounts, including custom attributes.

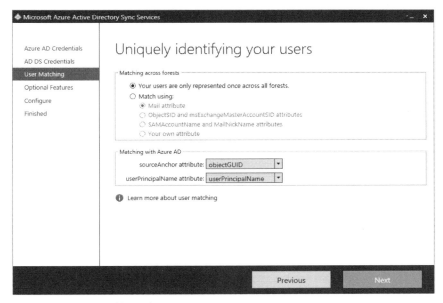

FIGURE 2-9 User Matching rules

TABLE 2-1 User Matching rules attributes*

Setting	Description
Your Users Are Only Represented Once Across All Forests	All users are created as individual objects in Azure AD. The objects are not joined in the metaverse.
Mail Attribute	This option joins users and contacts if the mail attribute has the same value in different forests. It is recommended to use this option when your contacts have been created by using GALSync.
ObjectSID And msExchange-MasterAccountSID Attributes	This option joins an enabled user in an account forest with a disabled user in an Exchange resource forest. This is also known as linked mailbox in Exchange.
SAMAccountName And MailNickName Attributes	This option joins on attributes where it is expected the logon ID for the user can be found.
My Own Attribute	With this option, you can select your own attribute. Limitation in CTP: ensure that you pick an attribute that will already exist in the Metaverse. If you pick a custom attribute, the wizard will not be able to complete.

*Source: http://msdn.microsoft.com/en-us/library/azure/dn757602.aspx

19. On the next page, you can select optional features. Select the Password Synchronization check box and then click Next to continue.

20. On the next page, click Configure to continue.

21. On the last page, confirm that the Synchronize Now check box is selected, and then click Finish.

Configuring Azure AD Application Proxy

Azure AD Application Proxy is a Premium-tier service with which you can expose on-premises applications to the cloud with the protection of Azure AD. This service provides a different approach to facilitate seamless resource access in a hybrid environment. Instead of focusing on bringing identities to the cloud, the service makes it possible for on-premises resources to be exposed to the cloud without complex network configuration changes. All you need to do is to install a connector that uses outbound connections only to connect to the proxy service.

Application management is another important part of Azure AD features. You'll see application management in more detail in Objective 2.5. The following sample scenario shows you how to use Azure AD Application Proxy to expose an on-premises application to the cloud. In this sample scenario, you'll expose a locally hosted ASP.NET web application to the cloud and turn on authentication with Azure AD.

Prerequisites

- Visual Studio 2013 with Update 3 or above, with Azure SDK for .NET 2.4 or above.
- Windows 8.1 or Windows Server 2012 R2.
- An active Azure subscription.

- An Azure AD tenant with Premium tier activated. If you haven't purchased Premium service, you can use the Licenses page of your Azure AD tenant on the management portal to try a free trail.

Creating a test application

As a starting point, you'll create a default ASP.NET application that you'll use for the remainder of the exercise.

1. Start Visual Studio, and then create a new ASP.NET web application using the MVC template.

2. You don't need to modify any code; simply press F5 to start the application. Make note of the local application address (*http://localhost:[port]*). You should keep this application running throughout the exercise because it simulates your on-premises application.

Publishing an application to the cloud

In this part, you'll expose the application to the Internet through Azure AD Application Proxy.

1. In the management portal, select the Azure AD tenant that you want to use, and then go to the Configure page.

2. Scroll down to the Application Proxy section, click the Enabled button, and then, on the command bar, click Save.

3. Go to the Applications page.

4. On the command bar, click the Add button.

5. On the configuration page, click the link Publish An Application That Will Be Accessible From Outside Your Network.

6. Type a display name for the application, and then click the right arrow to continue.

7. On the Application Properties page, note that in the External URL box, the proxy service provides a URL for your on-premises application. In the Internal URL box, paste the local address of your web application, and then click the check mark icon to complete the operation, as shown in Figure 2-10.

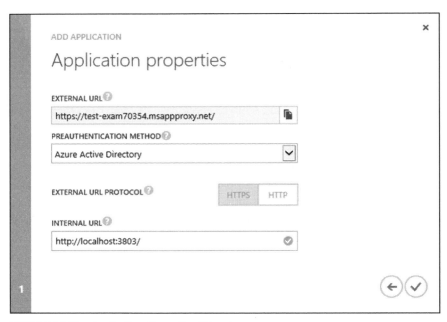

FIGURE 2-10 The Application Properties Wizard page

8. Back on the Applications page, click Download The Connector.

9. On the download page, review and accept the license terms and privacy statement, and then click the Download button.

10. Follow the installation wizard to install the connector. During the installation you'll need to sign in to your Azure AD tenant; the installer will complete all necessary configurations for you.

11. Back on the Applications page, click Assign Users.

12. Look for the users or groups that you want to assign to the application. By default, the filter sorts by groups, but you can change this to All Users. You'll need to click the check mark icon to refresh the screen. Select the user who you want to assign, and then, on the command bar, click the Assign icon.

13. Access the application by using the External Link shown earlier in Figure 2-10.

    Notice that the browser is redirected to your Azure AD tenant to sign in before you can access the application.

14. As an additional exercise, open another browser window and go to *https://myapps.microsoft.com*. This is the address of the Azure AD Access Panel, which provides enterprise users a centralized place to access all of the SaaS applications that the enterprise uses. You will examine the access panel more closely in Objective 2.5. Figure 2-11 shows how the test application you just exposed appears on the panel.

FIGURE 2-11 An application as viewed on the Azure AD Access Panel

Thought experiment

Identity solution for a hybrid environment

In this thought experiment, apply what you've learned about this objective. You can find answers to these questions in the "Answers" section at the end of this chapter.

As an architect who is designing a solution to provide an SSO experience for enterprise users to access both on-premises applications and cloud applications, you have two choices: using AD FS or AAD Sync. However, in a complex enterprise environment, you might need to employ a combination of several different techniques and services.

With this in mind, answer the following questions:

1. When would you pick Azure AD Application Proxy?

2. When would you pick AAD Sync?

Objective summary

- Modern enterprises face the challenge of implementing SSO for enterprise users to seamlessly access both on-premises and cloud-based resources.

- Azure AD supports synchronization between on-premises directories and cloud-based directories so that enterprise users can use their existing credentials to access both local and cloud resources.

- Using Azure AD Application Proxy, you can securely expose on-premises applications to the Internet.

Objective review

Answer the following questions to test your knowledge of the information in this objective. You can find the answers to these questions and explanations of why each answer choice is correct or incorrect in the "Answers" section at the end of this chapter.

1. You can use some of the following techniques for directory synchronization. (Choose all that apply.)

    A. DirSync

    B. AAD Sync

    C. Azure AD Connector

    D. Azure AD Graph API

2. To allow users to use their on-premises credentials from external networks, the following are viable options.

    A. AD FS

    B. AAD Sync

    C. ADAL

    D. FIM + Azure AD Connector

3. In a scenario of synchronizing multiple on-premises directories to a single Azure AD tenant, you have two user accounts representing a same user in two different forests, and both accounts have the same email address. What is the best way to handle this situation?

    A. Delete one of the accounts

    B. Employ User Matching rules to match the two accounts by email addresses

    C. Rename one of the accounts

    D. Synchronize the accounts as they are

Objective 2.3: Secure resources by using identity providers

A common barrier to adopting a new SaaS is often the process of registering a new user account. As a result, many SaaS vendors try to take advantage of the massive user bases of popular social networks such as Microsoft account, Facebook, and Yahoo by allowing these users to directly sign in to their services.

Before going into more details, it needs to be clarified that enterprise users accessing an increasing number of public and private SaaS services is a different challenge; this is discussed in greater depth in Objective 2.5. This objective focuses on the perspective of a SaaS vendor enabling users to authenticate by using their existing credentials.

Azure Access Control Service (ACS) is designed so that a service provider can work with multiple identity partners.

This section covers the following topics:

- Understanding Azure ACS
- Using Azure ACS with AD FS
- Using Azure ACS with social networks
- Using external identity providers with Azure Mobile Services

Understanding Azure ACS

Before going into specifics, you need to first understand what an authentication broker is and how Azure ACS fits into the overall picture.

Azure ACS as an authentication broker

The idea of an authentication broker is to provide an additional abstraction layer between service providers (or relying parties) and identity providers. An authentication broker provides the following benefits:

- It simplifies service provider development and maintenance. An authentication broker hides protocol details of working with different identity providers. It also makes it possible for an identity provider to be swapped out without impacting the service provider.

- A service provider can work with multiple identity providers at the same time. This is discussed in greater detail in Objective 2.4.

- It provides claim transformations so that a service provider can work with identity providers that don't provide the required claims out of the box.

Figure 2-12 shows how an authentication broker participates in the authentication workflow.

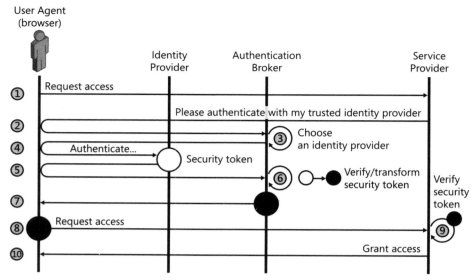

FIGURE 2-12 Authentication with an authentication broker

The following describes each numbered step in the workflow in Figure 2-12:

1. The user (agent) requests access to a resource provided by the service provider.

2. The service provider redirects the user agent to be authenticated with a trusted identity provider, which in this case is the authentication broker.

3. If the service provider supports multiple identity providers, the authentication broker can allow a user to pick which identity provider to use via a process called *home realm discovery*.

   One option to achieve this is for the authentication broker to present a web page with a list of identity providers from which the user can choose. Or, the authentication broker can attempt to automatically choose an appropriate identity provider based on user accounts (by examining email domains, for instance).

4. The user agent is redirected to the selected identity provider for authentication.

5. A security token is issued to the authentication broker.

   Note that during this part of the workflow, the authentication broker acts as a relying party to the selected identity provider.

6. The authentication broker verifies the token, and then, based on configuration, the authentication broker transforms the claims as needed.

7. The authentication broker issues a new token to the service provider.

8. The user agent sends a new request with the security token attached.

9. The service provider verifies the token and makes authorization decisions.

10. Access is granted.

Key Azure ACS concepts

Azure ACS introduces several additional components into the authentication workflow:

- **ACS namespaces**   An ACS namespace defines a trust circle to which multiple identity providers and relying parties can be added. Note that ACS namespaces and Azure AD tenants are separate concepts.

- **Rule groups**   A rule group is a set of claim rules that define how identity claims are transformed before they are passed to a relying party.

- **Claim rule**   A claim rule defines how a claim from an identity provider should be transformed. In the simplest form, a claim can be passed through to the relying party as it is. Or, a claim can be transformed into a different claim type that is supported by the relying party blindly or only when the claim contains certain values.

- **Service identities**   ACS also supports service identities, which you can use to authenticate directly with ACS instead of using an identity provider. Remember, from the perspective of the relying party, ACS is an identity provider. So, you can choose to allow users to use service identities to directly authenticate against this identity provider.

- **Identity providers**   This can be a ws-Federation Identity Provider (such as AD FS), a Facebook application, Microsoft account, or a Yahoo! ID.

- **Relying party applications**   These can be websites, applications, and services for which you want to use ACS for authentication.

Using Azure ACS with AD FS

You can directly configure your AD FS service as an identity provider to your cloud applications. You also can use Azure ACS as an authentication broker to connect your applications with your AD FS deployments.

Configuring Azure ACS and AD FS to work together requires several steps, which is beyond the scope of this book. The following is a high-level description:

1. Provision an Azure ACS namespace. To do so, in the management portal, select New, App Services, Active Directory, Access Control, and then Quick Create.

2. Configure the trust relationship between the AD FS deployment and the ACS namespace. The trust relationship is mutual, which means it needs to be configured on both the AD FS side and the ACS side. From the AD FS side, you'll need to configure ACS as a trusted relying party; from the ACS side, you'll need to configure AD FS as a trusted identity provider.

3. Configure ACS as a trusted identity provider to your cloud application. To do this, you need to register your application as a relying party with your ACS namespace, and then configure AD FS as a trusted relying party.

Figure 2-13 shows the relationship between AD FS, ACS, and the application. You can see how Azure ACS acts as two different roles in this workflow.

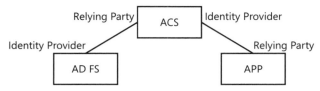

FIGURE 2-13 Azure ACS as an authentication broker

Using Azure ACS with social networks

In addition to AD FS, Azure ACS also supports popular social networks as identity providers, including Microsoft account, Facebook, and Yahoo!.

> **NOTE GOOGLE SUPPORT**
>
> As of May 19, 2014, new ACS namespaces cannot use Google as an identity provider, because Google is phasing out support for OpenID 2.0 and has closed registration for new applications. Existing ACS namespaces that use Google will continue to function until April 20, 2015.

The procedure to configure these identity providers is identical to that for configuring AD FS with Azure ACS.

Using identity providers with ASP.NET applications

As mentioned earlier in this objective, Azure ACS tooling is not being brought forward to new Visual Studio versions (you can still use the ACS ws-Federation metadata endpoint in any standard tools that support ws-Federation). However, there are still other tools with which your applications can use social network credentials. In this section, we'll focus on how to set up ASP.NET applications to use social network logons such as Microsoft account, Yahoo!, Facebook, Twitter, and Google.

Newer versions of ASP.NET have adopted Open Web Interface for .NET (OWIN). To understand how authentication works, you first need a high-level understanding of OWIN itself.

OWIN and authentication middleware

OWIN is an open specification that defines an abstraction layer between web applications and web servers. The primary goal of OWIN is to decouple web applications and web servers to stimulate growth of an open-source ecosystem for web modules and web hosts as well as web development tools.

Katana is an implementation of OWIN. It uses a layered architecture that consists of four layers: Host, Server, Middleware, and Application. Figure 2-14 shows the high-level architecture of a Katana implementation as well as how user requests flow through the pipeline.

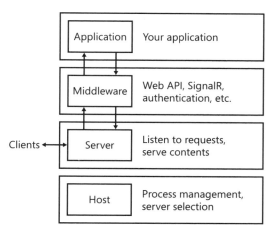

FIGURE 2-14 Katana architecture

- **Host**   This layer is responsible for management of the underlying process, selection of Server, and construction of the OWIN pipeline.

- **Server**   This layer manages application processes. It listens to requests and sends them through a user-defined OWIN pipeline.

- **Middleware**   This contains layers of components that are chained together into a pipeline. Requests flow through this pipeline before they reach the application. OWIN defines a very simple interface between layers called the *application delegate* or *AppFunc*, which takes an *IDictionary<string, object>* environment and returns a *Task*. Middleware is where you can introduce extensions and crosscutting components, including authentication middleware.

  ASP.NET uses a cookie authentication middleware for authentication. The middle tier issues cookies and validates cookies on subsequent requests. Katana ships a number of cookie authentication middleware for a number of external identity providers that support OAuth2 or OpenID protocol, including Microsoft account, Yahoo!, Facebook, and Google. In addition, ASP.NET templates provide the necessary UI and controller constructs for you to choose which external identity providers to use.

- **Application**   This is the layer on which the application logic is implemented. The application is mostly OWIN unaware, except for the startup code that sets up OWIN pipelines based on the application's requirements.

The best way to understand how OWIN cookie authentication works with ASP.NET is to walk through an actual sample scenario, which is what you're going to do next.

Sample scenario: using external authentication services with ASP.NET

In this sample scenario, you'll create a simple ASP.Net application and then turn on federated authentication using Google as an identity provider.

1. Start Visual Studio 2013 and then create a new ASP.NET web application using the Single Page Application template.

2. Open Startup.Auth.cs. By default, external identity providers are all disabled—you can see all related code is commented out in the *ConfigAuth* method:

```
// Uncomment the following lines to enable logging in with third party login
// providers
//app.UseMicrosoftAccountAuthentication(
//    clientId: "",
//    clientSecret: "");
//app.UseTwitterAuthentication(
//    consumerKey: "",
//    consumerSecret: "");
//app.UseFacebookAuthentication(
//    appId: "",
//    appSecret: "");
//app.UseGoogleAuthentication(new GoogleOAuth2AuthenticationOptions()
//{
//    ClientId = "",
//    ClientSecret = ""
//});
```

3. It's easy to include an external authentication service. To do so, uncomment the corresponding lines and supply the necessary configuration parameters. In this exercise, you'll turn on Google by uncommenting the Google-related lines (the last four lines in the preceding code). The process of turning on other identity providers is similar.

4. To turn on Google authentication, which uses OAuth2 protocol, you first need to obtain a Google Developer account. Then, you can manage your account and applications by using the Google Developers Console (*https://console.developers.google.com*).

5. Using the console, create a new project.

6. After the project is created, click APIs & Auth, and then click Credentials to open the Credentials page. Click Create New Client ID to create a new Client ID.

7. On the Create Client ID page, select the Web Application option, and then click the Configure Consent Screen button.

8. On the Consent Screen Configuration page, at a minimum you need to provide an email address and a product name. You can further customize the page by providing a logo file, product, privacy policy, and terms of service URLs. Then, click Save to keep the configuration.

9. On the Create Client ID page, click Create Client ID.

    After the Client ID is created, you can examine the generated Client ID and Client Secret on the console page, as shown in Figure 2-15.

Client ID for web application	
CLIENT ID	
EMAIL ADDRESS	
CLIENT SECRET	
REDIRECT URIS	http://localhost:3945/signin-google
JAVASCRIPT ORIGINS	https://www.example.com

Edit settings   Reset secret   Download JSON   Delete

FIGURE 2-15 The Client ID and Client Secret

10. For the authentication to work, you need to ensure that the Redirect URL matches the actual address of your web application. Press F5 to start your web application, and then note the address (*http://localhost:[port]*). Click the Edit Settings button, and then change the Redirect URL to *http://localhost:[port]/signin-google*.

11. Uncomment the last four lines of the code in the previous code snippet to turn on Google authentication:

```
app.UseGoogleAuthentication(new GoogleOAuth2AuthenticationOptions()
        {
ClientId = "…",
ClientSecret = "…"
});
```

Then, paste in the Client ID and the Client Secret shown in Figure 2-15.

12. Press F5 to start the application. Click Google to select authentication through Google, as shown in Figure 2-16.

Application name   Home   API   Register   Log in

Log in.

Use a local account to log in.

			Use another service to log in.
Email			Google
Password			

☐ Remember me?

Log in

FIGURE 2-16 The Google button on the Log In page

13. You can turn on authentication with other identity providers in a similar manner.

Using external identity providers with Azure Mobile Services

Azure Mobile Services provides mobile-application developers an easy way to create a cloud-based service layer for their applications. The service provides features such as data storage; push notifications; offline support; and integration with on-premises systems, Office 365, and Microsoft SharePoint. It also makes it possible to incorporate an SSO experience to mobile applications with Active Directory, Facebook, Twitter, Google, and Microsoft account.

To add a new identity provider, you follow a similar process as that used in the ASP.NET scenario. First, you create a new application with the identity provider. Next, you get an identifier and security key for your application (as was just demonstrated in the previous sample scenario). Finally, you provide the information to the Identity page of your mobile service.

 Thought experiment
Choosing a provider for a new SaaS application

In this thought experiment, apply what you've learned about this objective. You can find answers to these questions in the "Answers" section at the end of this chapter.

When you design a new SaaS application, authentication is something you must consider to ensure that only authenticated users can access the service. Now, you are facing the problem of choosing an identity provider.

With this in mind, answer the following questions:

1. When would you choose a specific identity provider?

2. When would you choose Azure ACS?

Objective summary

- SaaS vendors can use Azure ACS so that social network users can directly sign in using existing Microsoft account, AD FS, Facebook, and Yahoo! credentials.

- Azure ACS defines a trust circle in which multiple identity providers and relying parties can be added to deliver SSO experience to end users.

- ASP.NET uses OWIN cookie authentication middleware for authentication. It provides authentication middleware for identity providers such as Google, Microsoft account, Facebook, and Twitter.

- Azure Mobile Services provides built-in support for a number of identity providers, including Microsoft account, Facebook, Twitter, Google, and Azure AD.

Objective review

Answer the following questions to test your knowledge of the information in this objective. You can find the answers to these questions and explanations of why each answer choice is correct or incorrect in the "Answers" section at the end of this chapter.

1. Select all identity providers that are supported by Azure ACS.

    A. Microsoft account

    B. Facebook application

    C. Yahoo!

    D. AD FS

2. What can you do by defining claim rules?

    A. Change claim types

    B. Change claim values

    C. Combine two claims

    D. Pass through the claim

3. During an authentication workflow, what roles does Azure ACS play?

    A. Authentication broker

    B. Identity provider

    C. Relying party

    D. Application server

Objective 2.4: Identify an appropriate data security solution

Microsoft is committed to helping customers secure their data. Azure provides multiple layers of security and governance technologies, rigid compliance policies, and hardened operational practices to ensure data integrity and privacy while maintaining data availability for rightful users.

This objective discusses data security from three perspectives: data protection, access control, and disaster recovery.

This section covers the following topics:

- Understanding data protection technologies
- Implementing effective access control policies
- Using data reliability and disaster recovery services
- Understanding Azure Rights Management Services
- Managing security keys with Azure Key Vault

> **NOTE AZURE TRUST CENTER**
>
> Azure Trust Center provides valuable information regarding Azure's security, privacy, and compliance practices. For more information, go to *http://azure.microsoft.com/en-us/support/trust-center/*.

Understanding data protection technologies

Data protection involves protecting data at rest, in transit, and in use. At-rest data refers to data that is being stored on physical media. In-transit data refers to data that is being transmitted between two components, such as two networks, a service and a client, and two services. In-use data refers to the dynamic data used in computation, such as CPU cache and memory state.

As a leading cloud platform provider, Microsoft has made considerable investments in Azure datacenters to ensure that they provide the best protection of customer data. At the physical level, Azure datacenters deploy ISO-compliant safeguards such as 24x7 surveillance, Smartcard access, and key-locked racks. At the process level, rigorous operation processes are in place to ensure that the datacenters are fully audited and that only authorized personnel can access them. For example, a "just-in-time" policy ensures that Microsoft personnel don't have persistent access to customer data. They might be granted just-in-time accesses to resolve urgent issues, but those accesses are revoked as soon as the issue is closed.

Data encryption is one of the most important methods to protect data, especially at-rest data. Azure has three fundamental data repositories: Azure Storage, SQL Database, and Azure AD. Azure provides different encryption supports for these repositories. This section discusses Azure Storage encryption and SQL data encryption supports. Azure AD data encryption is left out because it's a service implementation detail that will likely not concern you.

Azure Storage

Azure Storage is a scalable, durable, and highly available data storage service provided by Azure. It offers Binary Large Object (Blob) storage for maintaining any type of text or binary data, Table storage as a NoSQL key-value data store, and Queue storage for reliable messaging between two components. In addition, it also provides File storage that can be shared by multiple applications and services using the SMB 2.1 protocol.

Azure Storage is one of the fundamental services of Azure. It provides data storage capability for many other Azure services. For instance, the operating system disks and data disks used by Azure Virtual Machines are based on Azure Blob storage.

Azure doesn't provide an out-of-the-box encryption feature on top of Azure Storage services. Instead, you can bring your own encryption solutions based on the performance, cost, and compliance requirements of your specific scenarios.

At the application level, you can use the .NET cryptography API or cryptography libraries provided by other programming languages. You can also encrypt data by using SDKs provided by on-premises Active Directory Rights Management Services (AD RMS) or Azure Rights Management Services (RMS).

At the platform level, you can use Azure StorSimple, which provides primary storage, archive, and disaster recovery. When configuring StorSimple, you can specify a data-at-rest encryption key for data encryption. StorSimple uses AES-256 with Cipher Block Chaining (CBC), which is the strongest commercially available encryption. You can manage encryption keys using your own key management system (KMS) or Azure Key Vault service, which you'll see later in this objective.

At the system level, you can use Windows features such as Encrypting File System (EFS), BitLocker drive encryption, or a third-party volume-level encryption to protect the data on your guest operating system drives and data drives (VHDs). System-level encryptions are often transparent to the operating system and the applications, so no application changes are needed to adopt such protections.

Azure provides an Import/Export service by which you can transmit large amounts of data to Azure by shipping physical data drives. BitLocker is mandatory when you use this service. For data import, you need to turn on BitLocker before you send the drives to Azure. The BitLocker key is communicated separately. For exports, you need to send empty drives to Azure, whereupon the service will load the data onto them and then encrypt the data before shipping the drives back to you.

SQL databases

You have two options to run SQL Server databases on Azure. First, you can use Azure SQL Database, which is a Platform as a Service (PaaS) offering provided by Azure that gives you hosted SQL database instances. Because the database instances are managed by Azure, you don't need to worry about database availability or low-level data protection; Azure takes care of that for you. On the other hand, you can set up your own SQL Server instances on top of Azure VMs. In this case, you own every aspect of the database instances, including ensuring high availability of database instances as well as implementing appropriate data-protection solutions.

SQL Server Transparent Data Encryption (TDE) provides protection for at-rest data by performing real-time I/O encryption and decryption of the data and log files. With TDE, developers can encrypt data by using AES and 3DES encryption algorithms without application changes. TDE provides protection over physical or logical breaches when underlying file systems are compromised and data files are exposed.

For a more granular encryption, you can use SQL Server Column-Level Encryption (CLE). CLE ensures that data remains encrypted until it is used. When a data page is loaded in memory, sensitive data is decrypted only when SQL Server is processing it. However, using CLE has a couple of downsides. First, applications need to be changed to invoke encryption/decryption. Second, there could be performance impacts not only because of the extra processing time, but also the negative effects on query optimizations.

By default, SQL Server keeps encryption keys in its master database. However, SQL Server also provides an extensible key management (EKM) provider architecture to delegate key management to an independent KMS.

Implementing effective access control policies

Access control ensures that only authorized users can access data. Azure employs multiple levels of access controls over customer data. These are discussed in the following sections.

Azure Storage

First, customer data is segmented by Azure subscriptions so that data from one customer can't be intentionally or accidentally accessed by another customer. Within a subscription, Azure Storage provides container-level and Blob-level access controls for Blob storage, and table-level and row-level access controls for Table storage. Each Azure Storage account has two associated keys: a primary key and a secondary key. Having two keys means that you can perform planned and unplanned (such as when the primary key is compromised) key rotations as needed.

In addition, Azure Storage also supports URL-based access with Shared Access Signatures (SAS). Using SAS, you can grant direct access to storage entities (containers, Blobs, queues, tables, or table rows) with a specified set of permissions during a specified time frame. For example, when you share a file, instead of sharing your storage account key, you can create an SAS signature with read privilege that allows users to read the specific file within a specified span of time. You don't need to revoke the access, because the SAS address automatically becomes invalid upon expiration of the predefined time frame.

Listing 2-1 shows how to generate a SAS signature by using Azure Storage Client Library for .NET. The code specifies the time window to be 4 hours (line 4 of the function) and grants read privilege (line 5). The code also specifies the time window to be open at –5 minutes (line 3) to ensure that the policy is active immediately, even if there were some time differences in server time due to clock drifts.

LISTING 2-1 Generating an SAS signature by using Azure Storage Client Library

```
string GenerateSASURL(CloudBlobContainer container, string blobName)
{
        CloudBlockBlob blob = container.GetBlockBlobReference(blobName);
        SharedAccessBlobPolicy policy = new SharedAccessBlobPolicy();
        policy.SharedAccessStartTime = DateTime.UtcNow.AddMinutes(-5);
        policy.SharedAccessExpiryTime = DateTime.UtcNow.AddHours(4);
        policy.Permissions = SharedAccessBlobPermissions.Read;
        string signature = blob.GetSharedAccessSignature(policy);
        return blob.Uri + signature;
}
```

This code generates a URL that looks like this:

```
https://storageaccount.blob.core.windows.net/sascontainer/myfile.txt?sv=2012-02-
12&st=2013-04-12T23%3A37%3A08Z&se=2013-04-13T00%3A12%3A08Z&sr=b&sp=rw&sig=dF2064yHtc8Rus
QLvkQFPItYdeOz3zR8zHsDMBi4S30%3D
```

In addition, you can use Stored Access Policy (SAP) to manage SASs in bulk. For example, you can change the access window, or deny access to a group of SASs, using an SAP. Listing 2-2 shows an example policy that allows SAS holders to perform *List* and *Read* operations on a container within a five-hour window.

LISTING 2-2 Creating a five-hour SAP granting list and read access to a container

```
CloudBlobContainer container;
string policyName = "samplepollicy";
...
BlobContainerPermissions permissions = new BlobContainerPermissions();
permissions.SharedAccessPolicies.Add(policyName, new SharedAccessBlobPolicy
{
    SharedAccessExpiryTime = DateTime.UtcNow.AddHours(8),
    Permissions = SharedAccessBlobPermissions.Read
                    | SharedAccessBlobPermissions.List
});
permissions.PublicAccess = BlobContainerPublicAccessType.Off;
container.SetPermissions(permissions);
var sas = container.GetSharedAccessSignature(permissions.SharedAccessPolicies
                                        [policyName]);
```

Azure SQL Database

Azure SQL Database uses an access security model that is very similar to on-premises SQL Server. Because Azure SQL Database instances are not domain-joined, only standard SQL authentication by user ID and password is supported. For SQL Server instances running on Azure Virtual Machines, they can also authenticate by using Kerberos tokens if the virtual machines (VMs) are domain-joined.

Azure AD

Azure AD provides a number of built-in roles with different administrative rights. For a simple deployment, a global administrator can take on all administrative responsibilities. For a more complex deployment, you can assign different administrators to manage specific areas of the tenant. Azure AD provides the following roles:

- **Global administrator** This role has access to all administrative features. Only global administrators can assign other administrative roles.
- **Billing administrator** This role can makes and manage subscriptions. A billing administrator also manages support tickets and monitors service consumption and health.
- **Service administrator** The service administrator manages requests and monitors the health of designated services.
- **User administrator** This role manages groups, user accounts, and service requests. However, a user administrator has limited capability in managing administrative accounts. For more details, see Table 2-2.
- **Password administrator** The password administrator can reset passwords for users and other password administrators.
- **User** This role can sign in and access directory objects when granted access. Azure AD Basic tier and Premium tier also support user self-service password reset. You can turn on this feature by going to the Configure page of your Azure AD tenant and changing the Users Enabled For Password Reset option to All.

Table 2-2 summarizes the administrator roles and their associated permissions.

TABLE 2-2 Administrator roles and associated permissions

Permission	Billing admin.	Global admin.	Password admin.	Service admin.	User admin.
View company and user information	Yes	Yes	Yes	Yes	Yes
Manage Microsoft Office support tickets	Yes	Yes	Yes	Yes	Yes
Reset user passwords	No	Yes	Yes	No	Yes[1]
Perform billing and purchasing operations for Office products	Yes	Yes	No	No	No
Create and manage user views	No	Yes	No	No	Yes
Create, edit, and delete users and groups, and manage user licenses	No	Yes	No	No	Yes[2]
Manage domains	No	Yes	No	No	No
Manage company information	No	Yes	No	No	No
Delegate administrative roles to others	No	Yes	No	No	No
Use directory synchronization	No	Yes	No	No	No

[1] Yes, with limitations. This role cannot reset passwords for billing, global, and service administrators.
[2] Yes, with limitations. This role cannot delete a global administrator or create other administrators.
Source: https://msdn.microsoft.com/en-us/library/azure/dn468213.aspx

Access control in other Azure services

In addition to providing access control mechanisms for data storages, Azure also provides ways to control accesses to other Azure resources. This section provides a couple of examples of several different access control mechanisms that exist in Azure.

AZURE VIRTUAL NETWORK

You can use network Access Control Lists (ACLs) to control traffic to your VM endpoints. Or, you can use Network Security Groups (NSGs) to implement more detailed control for VMs that are deployed in virtual networks (VNets).

An ACL is a group of rules that are applied to VM endpoints. By default, all inbound traffic is blocked. When a new endpoint is added, a new rule is added to the ACL to allow inbound traffic on that endpoint. The packet filtering is done by the host of your VM. Outbound traffic is allowed by default.

An ACL rule defines whether access should be allowed or denied from a certain network address range. You can define either "Allow" rules or "Deny" rules. Allow rules permit access from the given IP range, and they deny accesses from any other IPs. Conversely, Deny rules allow accesses from all IP ranges except for the one specified in the rule.

You can apply multiple rules to an endpoint; the rules will be evaluated according to their order. The lowest rule takes precedence. If an ACL is applied to a load-balanced set, it's applied to all VMs in that set.

You can manage ACLs by using either Azure PowerShell cmdlets or the management portal. Figure 2-17 shows how ACL settings look in the Azure Preview Management Portal.

FIGURE 2-17 ACL settings in the Azure Preview Management Portal

An NSG is a subscription-level object that you can associate to one or more VMs in regional virtual networks. Each Azure subscription can have 100 NSG rules, and each NSG rule can contain up to 200 rules, which can be either inbound rules or outbound rules. You can apply an NSG to either a VM, or a virtual network subnet. When applied to a VM, an NSG controls all traffic that goes in and out of the VM. When applied to a virtual network, an NSG applies to all traffic going through all VM on that subnet.

The difference between an ACL and an NSG is that an ACL is applied to traffic through an endpoint, whereas an NSG is applied to all traffic to and from a VM. You cannot apply NSG and ACL to the same VM.

AZURE SERVICE BUS

Service Bus provides a reliable messaging system for system integration and Internet of Things (IoT) scenarios. Service Bus supports SAS authentication on various Service Bus entities, such as queues, topics, and Event Hubs.

You can manage SAS keys in three ways: by using the management portal, programmatically by using Service Bus client SDK, or by using scripts. Figure 2-18 shows an example of configuring SAS for a Service Bus queue in the management portal. The figure shows that three SASs have been created: one for administrators with all access rights, one for receiving messages only, and the last one for sending messages only.

FIGURE 2-18 SAS on a Service Bus queue

Using data reliability and disaster recovery services

Cloud platforms are built on commodity hardware. With tens of thousands of servers running in a datacenter, hardware failures are unavoidable. A critical mission of a cloud platform is to ensure service availability regardless of these failures. A key strategy to achieving availability is redundancy.

In addition to built-in redundancy, Azure also provides a comprehensive set of services for backups and disaster recovery.

Data reliability

When you save your data on Azure, it automatically makes multiple copies of the data. When a single copy of the data is lost, you can restore your original data from these copies.

AZURE STORAGE

When a piece of data is saved to the Azure Storage service, the data is replicated multiple times for availability. Azure Storage provides the following data replication options to ensure reliable storage of data:

- **Locally Redundant Storage (LRS)**   Maintains three copies of your data within a single facility in a single region. LRS protects against common hardware failures, but not against facility-wide failures.

- **Zone-Redundant Storage (ZRS)**   Maintains three copies of your data across two or three facilities, either within a single region or across two regions.

- **Geo-Redundant Storage (GRS)**   Maintains six copies of your data, with three copies residing in the primary region, and another three copies residing in a backup region that is hundreds of miles away from the primary region.

- **Read-Access Geo-Redundant Storage (RA-GRS)**   Provides all of the benefits of GRS, plus permits read access to data at the secondary region when the primary region becomes unavailable.

AZURE SQL DATABASE

When you use SQL Database, you automatically take advantage of its many built-in fault-tolerance features.

Each SQL Database has three database replicas running at any given time. If the primary replica fails, SQL Database automatically fails-over to a secondary replica to ensure continuous data access. If a replica fails, a new one is automatically created to always maintain three replicas.

In addition, SQL Database provides an automatic "Point in Time Restore" feature, which automatically backs up your SQL database and retains the backups for 7 days for Basic tier, 14 days for Standard tier, and 35 days for Premium tier. This feature is active by default and it incurs no additional charges, except when you use the restore capability.

Another fault tolerance feature you get automatically is "geo-restore." When backing up your databases, Azure stores the most recent daily backup of your database in a different geographical location. In the event of a large-scale outage in a region, your data can be restored within 24 hours from another region.

If you have more aggressive recovery requirements, you can use "Standard geo-replication" or "Active geo-replication." Standard geo-replication (available to Standard and Premium-tier users) creates additional secondary replicas in a different region than the region in which your database is deployed (this region is called a *paired region*). These replicas are offline, but they can be brought online for an application to fail-over to them in the event of a datacenter disruption. Active geo-replication (available to Premium-tier users) provides the most rapid recovery time by keeping four geo-replicated live secondaries.

On top of the aforementioned features, you can also manually back up your databases. First, you can create transactional consistent copies of your databases to the same or different servers in the same or different regions. Second, you can use SQL Database Import and Export Service to export BACPACK files, which contain a logical copy of the schema as well as the data of a database. You can then import the file back to your database for disaster recovery.

AZURE AD

Azure AD is a highly available, geo-redundant service that handles billions of authenticate requests every day. It's deployed across a number of datacenters around the globe, and it securely stores hundreds of millions of objects. These objects are saved in different partitions for scaling. In addition, each partition has multiple replicas for high availability.

Azure Backup

Azure Backup is a simple yet powerful service with which you can back up your files to the reliable storage on Azure. Your data is saved in Azure Storage with geo-redundancy and at-rest encryption.

To back up your files, you first need to create a Backup Vault on Azure and then deploy a Backup Agent. Finally, you can configure which files or folders that you want backed up as well as backup schedules. The following sample scenario presents the basic steps to use Azure Backup:

1. In the management portal, click New, Data Services, Recovery Services, Backup Vault, and then Quick Create. Type a name for the backup vault and pick a region where the vault is to reside, and then click the Create Vault link.

2. After the vault is created, open its Quick Start page and click the Download Vault Credentials link to download a .VaultCredentials file, which you need to configure your Backup Agent.

3. There are two versions of Azure Backup Agent: one for Windows Server Essentials, and another for Windows Server, System Center Data Protection, or Windows Clients. Click the corresponding link to download and install the appropriate agent.

4. Follow the installation wizard pages to complete the installation process. At the last step, click Proceed To Registration to continue.

5. In the Register Server Wizard, pick your vault credential file, and then click Next to continue.

6. Type a passphrase or use the Generate Passphrase button to create one. Pick a folder where you want the passphrase to be saved, and then click Finish.

7. You can schedule, manage, and restore from your backups by using the installed agent. For instance, Figure 2-19 shows backups scheduled at 10 P.M. every Monday, Wednesday, and Friday, with the file retention policy set to 120 days. You can also use the Back Up Now feature to back up the selected files at any time. When you have file snapshots stored in your backup vault, you can restore to any archived versions at any time, whenever needed.

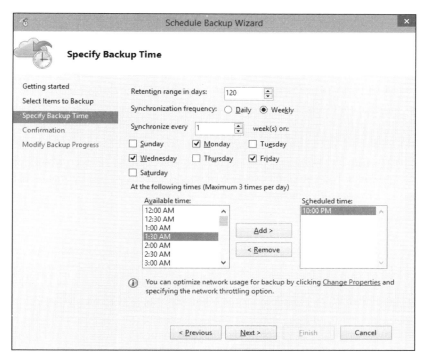

FIGURE 2-19 The Schedule Backup Wizard

StorSimple

StorSimple and Azure provide a unique hybrid storage and backup model. An enterprise can deploy a physical StorSimple appliance on local networks to provide efficient storage. In addition, a StorSimple appliance is paired with a virtual appliance on Azure for backup and disaster recovery.

StoreSimple and Azure provide a well-balanced solution between performance and scalability. On one hand, because data is stored on a local appliance, you achieve the responsiveness provided by the high-performance local hardware. On the other hand, you can create multiple snapshots in the cloud for backups, relieving you of local hardware capacity constraints.

Furthermore, because you can configure and monitor multiple local hardware appliances remotely through the management portal, you can effectively control backup and data restore of multiple on-premises sites at the same time.

Azure Site Recovery

Site Recovery helps you to protect important applications by coordinating the replication and recovery of physical or VMs. You can replicate these machines to a different on-premises datacenter, a hosting service provider, or Azure as the target site. Then, Site Recovery works with existing technologies such as SQL Server AlwaysOn, Microsoft Hyper-V Replica, and System Center to coordinate ongoing replications.

Using Site Recovery, you can create comprehensive recovery plans to ensure that resources are brought back online in an orderly fashion. For instance, you probably want to bring back the machines running the data tier before you attempt to bring back those running the application tier, which have dependency on the data tier. You can also include scripted and manual steps in your recovery plan to ensure that established processes are followed during the recovery process.

Last but not least, with Site Recovery, you can test out your disaster recovery solutions by running planned failovers. You can run these tests at your own convenience to ensure everything is in place for unexpected catastrophic events.

EXAM TIP

Azure Backup, StorSimple, and Azure Site Recovery provide tiered protection over your business data. Backup works at the file and folder level, StoreSimple works at the volume level, and Site Recovery works at the VM and topology level. They can work separately and they can work together. When preparing for the exam, you should keep their relationships in mind to help you identify appropriate technologies to use for different scenarios. Knowing their differences will also help you to easily eliminate some of the choices when asked specific questions.

Understanding Azure Rights Management Services

In modern workspaces, data is often shared across different services, applications, users, organizations, and devices. Using Azure Rights Management Services (RMS), encryption and access policies can travel with your data so that it has protection regardless of how it's accessed. With Azure RMS, you can do the following:

- Encrypt and decrypt data
- Manage and track encryption key distributions
- Manage key management and data access policies

Azure RMS comprises three components: an Azure RMS server, RMS-aware applications, and Azure RMS SDKs. Azure RMS provides SDKs for Windows, iOS, and Android environments, making it possible for you to write Azure RMS–aware applications for all popular mobile devices.

Microsoft provides three different Azure RMS server implementations: Microsoft Rights Management for Individuals, which is a free, hosted service; Microsoft Rights Management Service or Azure RMS, which is a hosted premium service; and Active Directory Rights Management Services, which is an on-premises implementation.

Managing security keys with Azure Key Vault

Key management is a very important aspect of cloud security solutions. If your security keys are not properly protected, data encryption is useless because data can easily be decrypted by using compromised keys. With Azure Key Vault, customers can help protect and control keys and secrets by using Hardware Security Module (HSM) in the cloud. Currently, Key Vault is available only through Management API and Windows PowerShell. The service is hosted, scalable, and available, so it provides an easier and more economical way to manage security keys. For example, in previous sections, you've seen that you can use SQL Server TDE to encrypt SQL data. Now, you can manage TDE secrets using Azure Key Vault by using a SQL Server Connector for Key Vault.

EXAM TIP

Encryption, replication, and appropriate access control are three key technologies for data security. All of the tools and services mentioned in this objective revolve around these three elements. If you learn best by hands-on practice, you can try to set up Backup using a client machine fairly easily following the example scenario in this section. To try out Site Recovery with minimum configuration, you can use a Hyper-V replica set as the primary site and back it up to Azure. With this configuration, you can walk through the major Site Recovery workflows with minimum hardware requirements. It's hard to set up StorSimple yourself because special hardware is needed.

Thought experiment
Prepare for region-wide outages

In this thought experiment, apply what you've learned about this objective. You can find answers to these questions in the "Answers" section at the end of this chapter.

For Line of Business (LoB) applications, it's important to maintain availability of the application because these applications are tightly connected with day-to-day business processes. Not being able to access the application can have a serious negative impact on the business. Although cloud platforms help you to improve your application availability, as an IT manager, you still need to prepare for region-wide disasters. With this in mind, answer the following questions:

1. How do you ensure business continuity when region-wide outages occur?

2. How do you recover from a region-wide outage?

Objective summary

- Azure provides comprehensive features that help to protect customer data.
- Azure provides built-in redundancies in all major data stores. Customer data is replicated multiple times to ensure data availability. Geo-redundancies are also supported for recovery from large-scale regional outages.
- Azure provides a rich set of disaster-recovery services, including Backup for backups at the file level, StorSimple for backups at volume level, and Site Recovery for backups at the machine and whole-topology level.
- With Microsoft RMS, encryption and access policies can travel along with data, regardless of where the data is accessed.
- Key Vault provides an easy-to-use, efficient, and secure solution to store and protect your security keys in the cloud.

Objective review

Answer the following questions to test your knowledge of the information in this objective. You can find the answers to these questions and explanations of why each answer choice is correct or incorrect in the "Answers" section at the end of this chapter.

1. Select all Azure services that provide solutions for data backup and disaster recovery.

    A. Backup

    B. StorSimple

    C. Site Recovery

    D. Azure RMS

2. Which of the following data stores doesn't provide built-in replication for reliable data storage?

    A. Azure Storage

    B. SQL Database

    C. SQL Server running on Azure VMs

    D. Azure AD

3. Which of the following replication models are supported by Azure Storage?

    A. Locally Redundant Storage (LRS)

    B. Zone Redundant Storage (ZRS)

    C. Geo-Redundant Storage (GRS)

    D. Read-Access Geo-Redundant Storage (RA-GRS)

Objective 2.5: Design a role-based access control strategy

Many enterprises need to manage large numbers of users with different access requirements, spanning many services, applications, locations, and devices. Add to that the dynamic nature of the modern workplace, which calls for an efficient solution that can quickly adapt to changes, and you can clearly see that this is no mean feat.

This objective discusses some of the proven strategies and Azure services that help large enterprise to manage identities and application accesses.

> **This section covers the following topics:**
> - Understanding access control challenges faced by large enterprises
> - Implementing RBAC
> - Using RBAC for Azure resources
> - Empowering users with self-service
> - Using Azure AD Access Panel
> - Managing devices with Azure AD Device Registration Service
> - Improving security policies over time

Understanding access control challenges faced by large enterprises

The rapid growth of SaaS applications and mobile devices has brought with it new challenges for IT professionals of modern enterprises. Among other tasks, instead of managing relatively static on-premises resources, they often need to quickly revise security policies to adapt to a much more dynamic and complex service ecosystem.

Access to SaaS applications

Today, more and more enterprise users rely on various public or private SaaS services to carry out day-to-day business functions. For example, many marketing teams use social networks such as Twitter and Facebook for customer engagements and marketing campaigns. And, many users take advantage of public storage services such as Box and OneDrive for file storage and sharing. Managing access to these SaaS applications is challenging because identities are scattered among different identity providers, managed by individual users in a self-service fashion. In fact, many enterprises don't even have a clear picture of what services are being used, much less the capability to manage them effectively.

Adapting to dynamic teams

In a dynamic enterprise environment, security policies must be constantly revised and refined to keep up with the rapid changes in working environments. A static privilege model strategy doesn't work. Administrators must find a balance between centralized control and appropriate distribution of management responsibilities so that groups of users can manage access to their working resources in a self-service model.

Bring your own devices

The traditional boundaries between work and personal life have been blurred by the explosion of consumer devices. More and more employees bring their personal devices to work environments in what is commonly referred to as "bring your own devices," or BYOD, and use those devices to access corporate data such as email and files. However, such usage has very little visibility to system administrators, because these devices often are not registered with the company.

It's very important for modern system administrators to gain insights into how all of these devices that are accessing their organization's information are used. It is equally important that they be able to place controls over that usage.

Implementing RBAC

RBAC is a proven method to manage access to resources at scale. RBAC has been widely adopted in the industry, and is natively supported by most modern operating systems and many programming languages.

A detailed introduction of RBAC is beyond the scope of this book; however, in this section, you'll go through some of its basic concepts and then you'll see how RBAC is implemented in Azure.

Groups

A group is an effective way to manage the access rights of collections of users. Instead of managing access rights of individual users, these users can be organized into logical groups so that they can inherit access rights assigned to these groups.

A typical use-case for groups is for a business unit or a team to create a team-wide group, in which everyone in the team shares the same access rights. For example, a test team can create a separate "Test team" group to control access to all test resources the team manages in the cloud.

Roles

A role defines a collection of permissions. Exactly what actions are allowed are explicitly defined in some systems (such as RBAC for Azure resources) but are implied in some other systems. For instance, the specific actions that an "operator" can do are subject to authorization decisions made by particular applications.

A role can be assigned to Groups, Users, or other identity subjects, as needed. Role assignments are often inherited along hierarchies. For example, a User belonging to a Group inherits role assignments of the Group.

RBAC and claims

RBAC and claims-based architecture work well together. With claims-based architecture, a relying party can request a trusted identity provider to provide a role claim, which reflects role assignments of the user. Then, the relying party can use the content of this claim to make authorization decisions.

For cases in which a user belongs to too many groups to be returned in a security token, the application needs to issue a separate directory query to verify whether the user belongs to a specific group, or groups.

Multifactor authentication

Multifactor authentication (MFA) requires a user to authenticate by using multiple authentication methods. The most common variation of MFA is 2-factor authentication (2FA). Common authentication methods use something you know (such as a passwords, SMS or call-based security codes), something you have (such as hardware or software tokens, smart cards, and mobile applications), or something that is unique to you (such as fingerprints and retinas).

Azure supports 2FA for securing Azure AD (included in Azure subscriptions), on-premises resources, and Active Directory, as well as custom applications. The Azure service that enables MFA is Azure Multi-Factor Authentication service.

Using RBAC for Azure resources

In addition to managing access to SaaS services, enterprise Azure users also require fine-grained access control for Azure resources. Azure provides built-in RBAC for Azure resources at different levels, and all access controls are integrated with Azure AD.

Roles and resource scopes

Azure has three levels of resource scopes: Subscription, Resource Group, and Resource. Azure provides the following three built-in roles that you can assign to users, groups, or services:

- **Owner**   Has complete control over all Azure resources in the scope.
- **Contributor**   Can perform all management operations except access management.
- **Reader**   Can only view resources. A Reader can't read any associated secrets (such as access keys) of resources. Moreover, Azure also provides roles for controlling accesses to specific services. For example, for SQL Database, there is a SQL DB Contributor role, a SQL Security Manager role, and a SQL Server Contributor role with corresponding access rights. For an updated list, go to *http://azure.microsoft.com/en-us/documentation/articles/role-based-access-control-configure/*.

Azure Subscriptions

An enterprise often maintains multiple Azure Subscriptions for different purposes. For instance, an enterprise might have a Subscription for development, and another Subscription for production. By using RBAC for Azure resources, administrators can assign different users or groups of users to corresponding Subscriptions with appropriate roles.

> **NOTE** **EXISTING SUBSCRIPTION ADMINISTRATORS AND CO-ADMINISTRATORS**
>
> Existing Azure subscription administrators and co-administrators are automatically assigned to the Owner role in this access control model.

Azure Resource Groups

The next level down is Resource Groups. With Resource Groups, you can gather related Azure resources into logical groups. You can have multiple Resource Groups under a Subscription, and each Resource Group can contain a number of Azure Resources, such as VMs, virtual networks, storage accounts, and websites. A Resource Group defines a management and security boundary. You can provision and de-provision a Resource Group as a complete unit, and you can assign security policies that apply to all resources in the group.

Resources

By default, all Resources within a Resource Group inherit all access rights assignments of the group, so you don't need to explicitly grant access to each individual Resource. However, if you choose to, you can override these access rights for each Resource, as needed.

Empowering users with self-service

Self-service is a great addition to RBAC because it brings flexibility into an enterprise's security policy. By allowing users to take on some of the common access management tasks themselves, system administrators are free to focus on more important tasks such as analyzing and improving security policies. Such common tasks include resetting passwords, changing passwords, managing groups and group memberships, and so on.

Inviting external users

Sometimes, an external user needs to have access to certain resources. When permitted by the tenant administrator, an Azure AD user can invite external users who have Microsoft accounts to access your Azure resources. These invited users don't need to be on your directory tenant, and they don't need to have an Azure subscription, either.

Furthermore, the tenant administrator can even allow invited users to invite more users. The administrator controls these settings through the User Access section of the tenant's Configure page.

Self-service password reset

With Azure AD Premium and Basic, users can reset their own passwords. Tenant owners configure the user password reset policy by using the Configure page of the tenant through the management portal. Figure 2-20 shows the page on which the policy is configured.

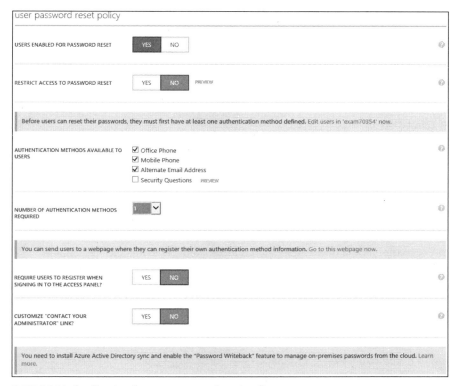

FIGURE 2-20 Configuring the user password reset policy

The Configure page presents the following options:

- **User Enabled For Password Reset**   Select this if users are allowed to reset their own password. When this feature is turned on, a user can go to *http://passwordreset. microsoftonline.com* to reset her password. She can also use the Can't Access Your Account link on sign-in pages to reset her password. On the other hand, if the feature is turned off, the user must contact her administrator to reset her password. Password issues are among the most frequent IT assistance requests. Allowing self-service password reset can greatly reduce this burden on system administrators.

- **Restrict Access To Password Reset**   Select this if only a specified group of users is allowed to reset their own passwords. When this feature is turned on, you can specify a group that can perform password reset.

- **Authentication Methods Available To Users**   Use this to select which challenges a user can employ to reset her password. When enabling user self-service password reset, at least one challenge option needs to be selected. Two options are recommended to provide users more flexibility in resetting passwords.

- **Number Of Authentication Methods Required**   This specifies a minimum number of authentication methods (one or two) a user needs to go through to reset her password.

> *NOTE* **SECURITY QUESTIONS**
>
> Security questions are less secure than phone or email-based password reset methods. You should avoid using security questions alone.

Self-service group management

Self-service group management is available to Azure AD Premium-tier users. Users can create security groups and manage group memberships by themselves. A user can also request to join groups, and the group owner can approve or reject these requests without involving administrators.

The following sample scenario shows how self-service group management works in an enterprise context.

In this sample scenario, Jack, a new employee has just joined the team, and he needs access to a number of Azure resources. The following steps show the process of Jack requesting access to these resources from Jane, the Azure subscription owner.

1. Jane has created a group named "Jane's team," which includes all members on her team. Jack already has his Azure AD credential, but he has not joined Jane's team. Jane's team is using Azure AD Premium.

2. Jack signs in to the Azure Preview Management Portal, *https://portal.azure.com*, and discovers that he doesn't have access to any resources.

3. Jack browses to the Azure AD Access Panel (*https://myapps.microsoft.com*).

4. He clicks the Groups link, searches for Jane's team, and then requests to join the group.

5. When Jane signs in to the Azure AD Access Panel, she sees Jack's request under Approvals, My Approvals.

6. Jane approves the request, and now Jack inherits all access rights assigned to the group.

7. Later, Jane can use the management portal to fine-tune Jack's access rights to specific resources.

Using Azure AD Access Panel

Azure AD Access Panel is a web portal where enterprise users can browse and start SaaS applications to which they have been granted access by AD tenant administrators or group owners. You can get to the Access Panel through its public URL at *http://myapps.microsoft.com*. This opens to the Applications tab, which displays your applications.

Or, you can use a tenant-specific URL by appending your organization's domain to the URL; for example, *http://myapps.microsoft.com/exam70354.onmicrosoft.com*.

The Access Panel supports a large number of SaaS applications out of the box. When you add an application to the portal, you can choose from one of the 2000-plus applications, as shown in Figure 2-21.

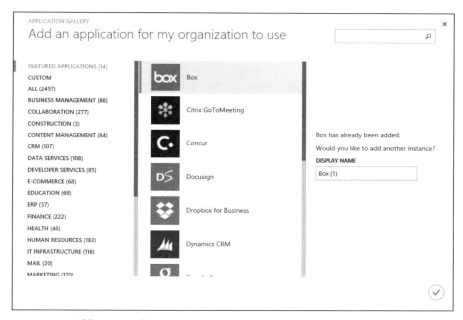

FIGURE 2-21 Adding an application to Azure AD Access Panel

Not all SaaS applications support federated authentications with Azure AD. To provide a smooth SSO experience, Azure AD Access Panel can securely save user credentials and automatically complete the sign-in process on the user's behalf. The following scenario shows how to enable an SSO experience to Twitter by using Azure AD Access Panel.

Sample scenario: enabling SSO access to Twitter

In this sample scenario, an enterprise uses a company-owned Twitter account to drive marketing campaigns and community awareness. The administrator wants to allow several enterprise users to monitor and contribute to the account. However, the administrator doesn't want to share the Twitter credential with these users. This way, when a user leaves the group the credential doesn't need to be reset. You can easily achieve this scenario by using the Azure AD Access Panel.

1. Sign in to the management portal and then go to to the Application page of your Azure AD tenant.

2. On the command bar, click Add to add a new application.

3. In the dialog box that opens, click the Add An Application From The Gallery link to continue.

4. On the next page, in the Search box, type **twitter** and press Enter to search for the Twitter application. Then, select the application and click the check mark to add it.

5. After the application is added, the applications Quick Start page opens. Click Configure Single Sign-On.

6. In the Configure Single Sign-On dialog box, select the Password Single Sign-On option, and then click the check mark.

7. Click Assign Users, select the users or groups that you want to grant access to the application, and then, on the command bar, click Assign.

8. In the Assign Users dialog box, select the I Want To Enter Twitter Credentials On Behalf Of The User check box.

9. Type the Twitter credential that represents your enterprise or your business unit, and then click the check mark.

10. Open Azure AD Access Panel and sign in as one of the users who have been assigned to the application.

11. Click the Twitter icon to access Twitter. You'll need to install and enable an Access Panel Extension the first time you do this, and you'll need to restart your browser after installation.

12. Go to to the Access Panel again. Now, the user can access Twitter by using the business Twitter account. The user's access to Twitter will be revoked when the user's access to the application is revoked from Azure AD.

Managing devices with Azure AD Device Registration Service

Azure AD Device Registration Service makes it possible for a system administrator to register personal devices that need access to on-premises resources. After a device is registered, the administrator can monitor and control how the device accesses on-premises data.

The process of registering a device is called Workplace Join, which is very similar to the Workplace Join process provided by Active Directory in Server 2012 R2. The detailed description of how to configure the service is beyond the scope of this book. The following are high-level steps:

1. Turn on Device Registration in you Azure AD tenant.

2. Configure your company DNS so that devices can discover your Azure AD Device Registration Service.

3. Apply Windows Server 2012 R2 schema extensions.

4. Deploy AD FS service with the Web Application Proxy.

5. Set up federation relationship with your on-premises Active Directory.

6. Configure directory synchronization between your Azure AD tenant and your on-premises Active Directory.

7. Join the device to your workplace by using the management portal.

8. Create an application access policy, which can use the value of an "Is Registered User" claim to make authorization decisions.

Improving security policies over time

As you learned earlier, a static security policy doesn't work in a modern, dynamic workplace. It's very important for system administrators to continually refine their security policies to ensure that these policies remain effective over time. However, to achieve this, system administrators need to be equipped with tools with which they can gain insights into user behaviors, to discover problems, and to design more effective policies.

Azure AD provides a rich set of tools and services for system administrators to continuously improve their security policies.

Discover

Azure AD helps administrators to discover what SaaS services are being used in the enterprise via the Cloud App Discovery (preview) service. By deploying agents on enterprise devices, Cloud App Discovery is capable of discovering what services are being used as well as their usage patterns. The results provide a great starting point for administrators to begin consolidating application access controls into the Azure AD Access Panel or to close down access to certain services.

After the agents have been deployed, a system administrator can go to the Cloud App Discovery dashboard (*https://appdiscovery.azure.com/*) to review applications, users, AD integrations, and application usages discovered by these agents. Figure 2-22 shows the Cloud App Discovery dashboard several minutes after I deployed a single agent. You can see already that a lot of useful information has been collected.

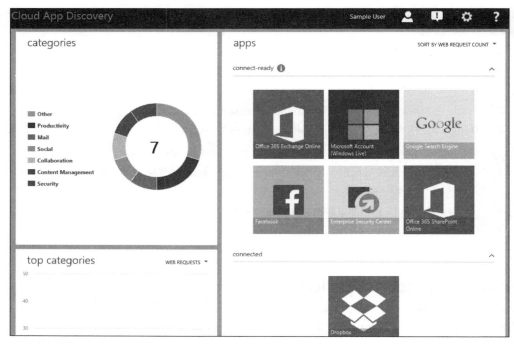

FIGURE 2-22 The Cloud App Discovery dashboard

Moreover, Azure AD runs analysis on your directory usages by using machine-learning modules. These modules help administrators to identify usage abnormalities, potential risks, and security policy violations that are usually hard to discover otherwise. For example, Azure AD can detect sign-in activities from multiple geographies. If a user signs in from two different locations within a timeframe that is shorter than usual traveling time, a flag can be raised because this event suggests that the account might have been compromised.

Monitor

Azure AD also provides enhanced auditing and reporting features to help administrators maintain continuous monitoring over security activities. In current preview, the following activity logs are provided:

- **Audit report** This log shows audited events in your directory. It reflects key changes in the directory over the past 30 days. An increasing number of events are tracked in this report, including adding, removing, or updating users; adding or removing applications; changing role memberships; and so on.
- **Password reset activity** This shows how passwords are being reset.
- **Password reset registration activity** This log specifies which users have registered their methods for password reset and which methods are being used.

- **Group activity** This reports activities of a group; that is, when users are added or removed.

Figure 2-23 shows a list of reports that are currently available on the management portal.

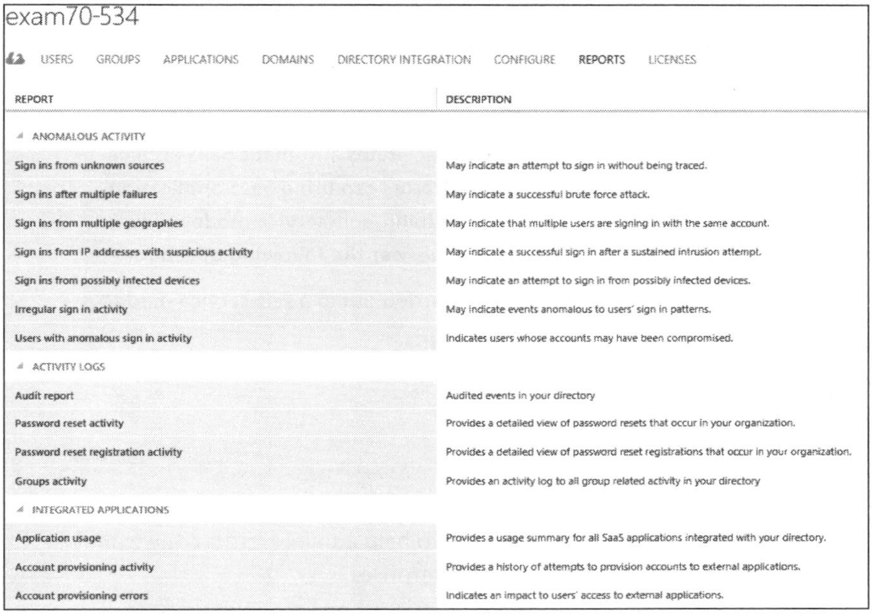
exam70-534

USERS GROUPS APPLICATIONS DOMAINS DIRECTORY INTEGRATION CONFIGURE REPORTS LICENSES

REPORT	DESCRIPTION
ANOMALOUS ACTIVITY	
Sign ins from unknown sources	May indicate an attempt to sign in without being traced.
Sign ins after multiple failures	May indicate a successful brute force attack.
Sign ins from multiple geographies	May indicate that multiple users are signing in with the same account.
Sign ins from IP addresses with suspicious activity	May indicate a successful sign in after a sustained intrusion attempt.
Sign ins from possibly infected devices	May indicate an attempt to sign in from possibly infected devices.
Irregular sign in activity	May indicate events anomalous to users' sign in patterns.
Users with anomalous sign in activity	Indicates users whose accounts may have been compromised.
ACTIVITY LOGS	
Audit report	Audited events in your directory
Password reset activity	Provides a detailed view of password resets that occur in your organization.
Password reset registration activity	Provides a detailed view of password reset registrations that occur in your organization.
Groups activity	Provides an activity log to all group related activity in your directory
INTEGRATED APPLICATIONS	
Application usage	Provides a usage summary for all SaaS applications integrated with your directory.
Account provisioning activity	Provides a history of attempts to provision accounts to external applications.
Account provisioning errors	Indicates an impact to users' access to external applications.

FIGURE 2-23 Azure AD reports

Azure AD also supports a number of notifications to which administrators can subscribe to be notified when certain events happen, such as when anomalous sign-ins are detected.

React

The management portal makes Azure AD configuration and management readily available to administrators from anywhere, on any device. Scripting options are available for administrators to automate configuration tasks through Azure Cross-Platform Command-Line Interface (xplat-cli), Windows PowerShell script, or direct invocations of the Azure Management API. Furthermore, you can manage such automated tasks by many of the existing tools and systems such as System Center. This way, administrators can continue to use their familiar tools to manage both on-premises and cloud resources. Last but not least, through integration with configuration systems such as Chef and Puppet, administrators can manage a large number of cloud and on-premises resources in a consistent manner.

In summary, Azure AD provides a continuous discover-monitor-react workflow that helps administrators to discover problems, adjust for changes, and ensure that security policies are followed all the time.

Thought experiment

Prepare for region-wide outages

In this thought experiment, apply what you've learned about this objective. You can find answers to these questions in the "Answers" section at the end of this chapter.

Control and flexibility are seemingly two conflicting goals in enterprise security management. Azure AD revolutionizes how enterprise administrators manage and enforce security policies. On one hand, Azure AD facilitates automatic SaaS application discovery and usage analysis so that administrators can bring SaaS application consumption into a centralized view. On the other hand, self-service mode relieves administrators from trivialities. With this in mind, answer the following questions:

1. How would you decide what activities can be carried out in a self-service mode?

2. Do you need governance over self-service activities?

Objective summary

- Azure AD provides a series of services and tools to help administrators cope with the challenges of access management in modern enterprises.

- Self-service is an effective way to bring flexibility into an RBAC strategy, making security policies more adaptive to changes. Azure AD supports a number of self-service features, including resetting and changing user passwords, creating groups, managing group memberships, requesting access to resources, and inviting external users to access protected resources.

- Azure AD Access Portal provides a centralized access panel to all SaaS applications to which the administrator has granted access.

- Using Azure AD Device Registration Service, you can register consumer devices with your Azure AD tenants so that administrators can monitor and design access policies for these devices.

Objective review

Answer the following questions to test your knowledge of the information in this objective. You can find the answers to these questions and explanations of why each answer choice is correct or incorrect in the "Answers" section at the end of this chapter.

1. To join a device to workplace, which Azure service should you use?

   A. Device Registration Service

   B. Azure AD Access Panel

   C. Azure RMS

   D. Key Vault

2. Select all Azure AD self-service features (when turned on by the administrator).

   A. Reset user password

   B. Manage group members

   C. Request to join a group

   D. Invite external users

3. Which of the following entities are resource scopes to which you can apply RBAC?

   A. Azure Subscription

   B. Tenant

   C. Resource Groups

   D. Resource

4. Which of the following Azure AD features help system administrators to discover and monitor possible security policy violations in an enterprise?

   A. Cloud App Discovery

   B. Audit reports and activity logs

   C. Automated email notifications

   D. Automatic anomalous activity detection

Answers

This section contains the solutions to the thought experiments and answers to the objective review questions in this chapter.

Objective 2.1: Thought experiment

1. A simple analogy is this: To lock a door, do you want to buy a padlock or make a padlock yourself? Buying a padlock is obviously a better choice, especially if the lock maker is reputable with a proven track record. With Azure AD, your identity data will be secure and the authentication service will be available. Azure AD handles billions of authentication requests every day, and it supports some of the largest SaaS applications in the world, such as Office 365.

2. The Internet is a hostile environment. When you provide services over the Internet, you need to ensure that only authorized users can access your services. However, designing and implementing a robust authentication system isn't an easy task; it requires deep knowledge of network security and rich experience in antihacking techniques. Taking on such tasks requires significant investment without a guarantee that the home-grown solution will actually work. It also distracts developers from implementing core business logics.

Objective 2.1: Review

1. **Correct answer:** D
   A. **Incorrect**: ws-Federation is one of the supported protocols.
   B. **Incorrect**: SAML 2.0 is one of the supported protocols.
   C. **Incorrect**: OpenID Connect is one of the supported protocols.
   D. **Correct**: Kerberos is not supported.

2. **Correct answers**: A, B, C, and D
   A. **Correct**: This is correct because HTTPS provides communication confidentiality. It protects message exchanges from certain attacks such as eavesdrops and man-in-the-middle attacks.
   B. **Correct**: This is correct because digital signature ensures the authenticity and non-repudiation of security tokens.
   C. **Correct**: This is correct because it ensures that only parties with corresponding keys can decrypt and read messages.
   D. **Correct**: This is also correct because it helps to reduce risks of threats such as playback attacks.

3. **Correct answers**: A and B

   A. **Correct**: Azure AD provides a RESTful Graph API for interactions with directory objects.

   B. **Correct**: Azure AD provides a client library to further simplify developments.

   C. **Incorrect**: LDAP is used to access Active Directory, which is different from Azure AD.

   D. **Incorrect**: X.500 is an older directory protocol that is not supported.

4. **Correct answer**: A

   A. **Correct**: An identity provider authenticates users and issues security tokens.

   B. **Incorrect**: A relying party reads from security tokens, but it doesn't issue security tokens.

   C. **Incorrect**: A user agent doesn't handle security tokens, although they do pass the tokens around.

   D. **Incorrect**: A user is the entity to be authenticated.

Objective 2.2: Thought experiment

1. Using Azure AD Application Proxy is a great way to securely expose on-premises applications to the cloud. In this case, the application is still hosted on local servers but accessible to users over the external network.

2. Using AAD Sync, you can project your on-premises Active Directory objects to the cloud so that enterprise users can continue to use their existing Active Directory credentials to access on-premises resources as well as cloud resources by using SSO.

Objective 2.2: Review

1. **Correct answers:** A, B, and C

   A. **Correct:** DirSync is an existing directory synchronization solution.

   B. **Correct:** AAD Sync is an existing directory synchronization solution.

   C. **Correct:** Azure AD Connector is an existing directory synchronization solution.

   D. **Incorrect:** Azure AD Graph API is a REST API for accessing directory objects, not for synchronization.

2. **Correct answers:** A, B, and D

   A. **Correct:** AD FS is a standards-based service that allows identity information to be shared across an extranet.

   B. **Correct:** AAD Sync is a service that synchronizes on-premises directory objects with Azure AD objects.

C. **Incorrect:** ADAL is a client library that facilitates accessing Azure AD objects. It doesn't help to make on-premises identities available to extranet.

D. **Correct:** Using Azure AD Connector, you can connect to one or multiple Azure ADs from Microsoft Forefront Identity Manager.

3. **Correct answer:** B

A. **Incorrect**: A user might have multiple accounts in different forests for legitimate reasons. Deleting one account can affect the user's ability to perform usual business activities.

B. **Correct:** With User Matching rules, you can match the two accounts by their email addresses so that you have a single account in you Azure AD tenant.

C. **Incorrect:** Renaming an account is a bad choice because now the user must remember two different account names as well as which account belongs to which forest.

D. **Incorrect:** This will cause conflicts during synchronization.

Objective 2.3: Thought experiment

1. In many cases an identity provider is selected not based on technical merits, but for business reasons. For instance, an application that extends Twitter functionalities might want to choose Twitter as the identity provider. For enterprise-oriented applications, Azure AD as an identity provider is a good choice, because Azure AD provides built-in support to federate with on-premises Active Directory, providing an SSO experience to enterprise users.

2. For a SaaS application that provides a consumer service, allowing new users to log on by using their existing social network credentials is a great way to tap into the massive user bases of popular social networks. Azure ACS brings more flexibility in identity provider selection. You can add new identity providers, and you can swap existing identity providers at any time without affecting the application itself. Moreover, ACS also supports claim transformation which makes it possible for identity providers and service providers to be matched together without modifications.

Objective 2.3: Review

1. **Correct answers:** A, B, C, and D

A. **Correct**: Microsoft account is a supported identity provider.

B. **Correct**: Facebook is a supported identity provider.

C. **Correct**: Yahoo! is a supported identity provider.

D. **Correct**: AD FS is a supported identity provider. Google is no longer supported by new ACS namespaces.

2. **Correct answers:** A, B, and D

   A. **Correct**: Claim types can be changed during token transformation.

   B. **Correct**: Claim values can be changed during token transformation.

   C. **Incorrect**: Combining two claims into one is not supported.

   D. **Correct**. Passing through is the default transformation.

3. **Correct answers**: A, B, and C

   A. **Correct:** ACS is an authentication broker that makes it possible for multiple relying parties and identity providers to work together.

   B. **Correct:** From the perspective of a relying party, ACS is its identity provider during the authentication workflow.

   C. **Correct:** From the perspective of an identity provider, ACS is its relying party to which it issues security tokens.

   D. **Incorrect:** ACS doesn't serve as an application server during the authentication workflow.

Objective 2.4: Thought experiment

1. For critical business applications, cross-region deployments are often used to ensure application availability. Some applications use an active–active scheme, wherein user traffic is routed to any of the deployments (often based on latency or proximity). Thus, when one of the deployments is down, all users are routed to the remaining deployment. Another common scheme is active–passive deployment, wherein users are routed to a primary site; they are routed to a secondary site only if the primary site is down.

2. Recovery from disaster includes recovering services as well as recovering data. If you've adopted backup solutions presented in this objective, you can recover your data from available backups or snapshots. Bringing services back online is often more complicated, because various applications and services have complex dependencies, and business and compliance requirements might require specific verifications to be conducted during restore. With Azure Site Recovery, you can conduct coordinated disaster recovery by executing recovery plans.

Objective 2.4: Review

1. **Correct answers:** A, B, and C

   A. **Correct:** Azure Backup provides data backup and recovery at the file level.

   B. **Correct:** StoreSimple provides data backup and recovery at the volume level.

   C. **Correct:** Site Recovery provides data backup and recovery at the machine and topology level.

   D. **Incorrect:** Azure RMS provides data encryption and key management.

2. **Correct answer:** C

   A. **Incorrect:** Azure Storage services provides a number of replication options such as LRS and GRS to ensure that data is safely stored.

   B. **Incorrect:** Azure SQL Database maintains three replicas of your database and provides automatic failover when the primary replica fails.

   C. **Correct:** When you configure SQL Database instances on Azure Virtual Machines yourself, you also need to configure and manage data replication.

   D. **Incorrect:** Azure AD uses multiple replicas of directory objects to ensure data availability.

3. **Correct answers:** A, B, C, and D

   A. **Correct**: LRS is a supported replication model supported by Azure Storage. LRS maintains three copies of your data within a single facility in a single region.

   B. **Correct**: ZRS is a supported replication model supported by Azure Storage. ZRS maintains three copies of your data across two or three facilities, either within a single region or across two regions.

   C. **Correct**: GRS is a supported replication model supported by Azure Storage. GRS maintains six copies of your data, with three copies residing in the primary region, and another three copies residing in a backup region.

   D. **Correct**: RA-GRS is a supported replication model supported by Azure Storage. RA-GRS provides all benefits of GRS, plus reading access to data at the secondary region when the primary region becomes unavailable.

Objective 2.5: Thought experiment

1. A key goal of self-service is to make it possible for enterprise users to conduct their day-to-day business without friction. A user (or a group of users) should be able to control accesses to resources he owns, as long as there are certain mechanisms to ensure that enterprise-wide policies are followed. For example, a user should be able to reset his own password. The credential is owned by him, and he's the only entity that is affected by the change.

2. Self-service actions require governance, as well. All security-related operations should be traceable and auditable to ensure that enterprise-wide polices are not violated.

Objective 2.5: Review

1. **Correct answer:** A

    A. **Correct:** With Device Registration Service, you can register consumer devices with the company directory.
    B. **Incorrect:** Azure AD Application Access Panel provides a centralized access to SaaS applications.
    C. **Incorrect:** Azure RMS helps you to manage data encryption and key distribution.
    D. **Incorrect:** Key Vault protects your security keys with HSMs in the cloud.

2. **Correct answers:** A, B, C, and D

    A. **Correct**: Resetting a user password is a self-service action that can be allowed by the tenant administrator.
    B. **Correct**: Managing group members is a self-service action that can be allowed by the tenant administrator.
    C. **Correct**: Requesting to join a group is a self-service action that can be allowed by the tenant administrator.
    D. **Correct**: Inviting external users is a self-service action that can be allowed by the tenant administrator.

3. **Correct answers:** A, C, and D

    A. **Correct**: Azure Subscription is the top resource scope.
    B. **Incorrect**: Azure AD tenant isn't a resource scope, although you can apply RBAC to it.
    C. **Correct**: Resource Group is the second-level resource scope.
    D. **Correct:** Resource is the lowest level of resource scope.

4. **Correct answers:** A, B, C, and D

   A. **Correct**: Cloud App Discovery is a feature by which SaaS application consumptions can be automatically discovered.

   B. **Correct**: Audit reports and activity logs help administrators to review and analyze possible security policy violations in an enterprise.

   C. **Correct**: Automated email notifications notify administrators about key security-related events and possible policy violations.

   D. **Correct**: Automatic anomalous activity detection is automatic activity pattern analysis based on machine learning.

## CHAPTER 3

Design an application storage and data access strategy

Data is a huge business today. The amount of data collected and used at present is astonishing. Walmart handles over 1 million transactions per hour, which are all stored in databases. More than 5 billion people are calling, texting, tweeting, and browsing on mobile phones worldwide. Facebook has 100 TB of data uploaded daily. Today, there is a projected 40 percent yearly growth in data generated globally, whereas corporate spending on IT is only growing at 5 percent per year. (You can find this data and more Big-Data statistics at *http://wikibon.org/blog/big-data-statistics/*.) Companies are looking for better and faster ways to store, analyze, and protect all of this information. Tools for handling large data sets and performing analysis on that data are growing, as well. Microsoft Azure helps companies to enhance their ability to handle data in secure ways. In this chapter, you'll learn about handling data in Azure, how to include data that is still on-premises, and how to design the data architecture for systems.

Objectives in this chapter:

- Objective 3.1: Design data storage
- Objective 3.2: Design applications that use mobile services
- Objective 3.3: Design applications that use notifications
- Objective 3.4: Design applications that use a web API
- Objective 3.5: Design a data strategy for hybrid applications
- Objective 3.6: Design a media solution

Objective 3.1: Design data storage

Companies are always looking to ensure that their information is safe and secured while being able to provide tools for customers and other businesses to access that data in a safe and secure way. This section looks at the various storage systems and database options that are available today in Azure.

Designing storage options for data

Azure offers many options for storage. Various storage needs have different requirements, from structured data to unstructured data.

Storage account

Azure Storage supports multiple types of storage: Queue, Table, Binary Large Objects (Blobs), and Files. The Storage account is the top level. This makes it possible for you to have all of the others under them. You can set up multiple Storage accounts, but each is limited to 20,000 input/output operations per second (IOPS) and a total of 500 TB of storage. The Storage accounts have a replication setting that you can set to one of three options: Locally Redundant, Geo-Redundant, and Read-Access Geo-Redundant. Locally Redundant replicates data in the same region. Geo-Redundant replicates it in a secondary region. Read-Access Geo-Redundant replicates a read only copy in a secondary region. The replication setting affects the cost of the Storage account. Each of the storage types has specific advantages and should be used for different scenarios. Figure 3-1 shows the various storage systems within a Storage account.

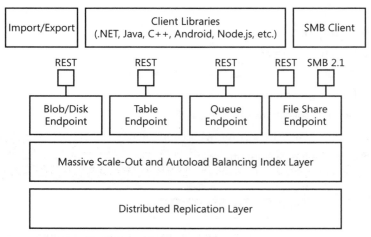

FIGURE 3-1 Azure Storage architecture

Table storage is a massively scalable NoSQL storage system that you can use to keep structured, nonrelational data. Each row has a PartitionKey and as RowKey with which you can perform index searches. Each row can contain different data fields, as well. This means that there could be rows containing five fields, and other rows that contain four totally different fields, all in the same table. This is very different than a standard relational database. Auto-load balances partitions to meet traffic needs. You can use the OData protocol to access the data (AtomPub or JSON).

The code snippet that follows adds a new row to an Azure Table. The *CustomerEntity* class is a basic class with properties to set the *First, Last, Email,* and *PhoneNumber* settings.

```
// Retrieve the storage account from the connection string.
CloudStorageAccount storageAccount = CloudStorageAccount.Parse("<ConnectionString>");

// Create the table client.
CloudTableClient tableClient = storageAccount.CreateCloudTableClient();

// Create the table if it doesn't exist.
CloudTable table = tableClient.GetTableReference("people");
table.CreateIfNotExists();
// Create a new customer entity.
CustomerEntity customer1 = new CustomerEntity();
{
    First = "Walter",
    Last = "Harp",
    Email = "Walter@contoso.com",
    PhoneNumber = "425-555-0101"
}
// Create the TableOperation that inserts the customer entity.
TableOperation insertOperation = TableOperation.Insert(customer1);

// Execute the insert operation.
table.Execute(insertOperation);
```

Blob storage is a service for storing large amounts of unstructured data such as text or binary files. You can think of this as similar to just storing files. Blob files are stored in Containers. You can access the blobs in these containers by using a standard HTTP/HTTPS call to download the file. There is also a simple Representational State Transfer (REST) interface by which you can access the Blobs (Put, Get, Delete).

The following code snippet demonstrates uploading a local file to a Blob storage account.

```
// Create the blob client.
CloudBlobClient blobClient = storageAccount.CreateCloudBlobClient();

// Retrieve reference to a previously created container.
CloudBlobContainer container = blobClient.GetContainerReference("mycontainer");
// Create the container if it doesn't already exist.
container.CreateIfNotExists();

// Retrieve reference to a blob named "myblob".
CloudBlockBlob blockBlob = container.GetBlockBlobReference("myblob");

// Create or overwrite the "myblob" blob with contents from a local file.
using (var fileStream = System.IO.File.OpenRead(@"path\myfile"))
{
    blockBlob.UploadFromStream(fileStream);
}
```

Blob storage is used to keep the images from a website, streaming audio and video, storing data for access on-premises or from Azure, and so on.

You can save files in Blob storage in either of two ways: *block* and *page* blobs. Block blobs can store up to 200 GB of data and are optimized for streaming. This is the type by which most blobs are stored. Page blobs can store up to 1 TB and are optimized for random read/write operations. They provide the ability to write to a range of bytes in a Blob. Virtual Drives in Azure Virtual Machines use page blobs because they are accessed randomly.

Queue storage is a messaging system built in to the Storage account. It is a reliable, low-latency, high-throughput messaging system. With it, you can decouple your components or roles. A web role can put data in a Queue for a worker role to perform. This makes it possible for the roles to scale independently. You can also use Queue storage to schedule asynchronous tasks and for things such as WebRoles.

The following code snippet adds a new message to an Azure Queue:

```
// Create the queue client.
CloudQueueClient queueClient = storageAccount.CreateCloudQueueClient();

// Retrieve a reference to a queue.
CloudQueue queue = queueClient.GetQueueReference("myqueue");

// Create the queue if it doesn't already exist.
queue.CreateIfNotExists();

// Create a message and add it to the queue.
CloudQueueMessage message = new CloudQueueMessage("Hello, World");
queue.AddMessage(message);
```

File storage is a shared storage that uses the standard Server Message Block (SMB) 2.1 protocol. Azure VMs and cloud services can access the File storage account using the SMB protocol, and on-premises devices can access the File storage account using the File Storage API from the Azure .Net Storage Client Library. There is no limit to the number of Azure resources that can connect to the File storage and access the file share.

This makes File storage very useful in many situations. Applications that are running within a company that access a File storage will not have to be rewritten to use a new storage type, such as Blob storage. The standard file I/O commands work just like they did before. File storage supports REST and SMB protocol access to the same file share.

EXAM TIP

Know the various storage types and their uses. For example, many times you can use Queues to decouple components of a system.

Azure SQL Database

There are two ways to create SQL Server databases in Azure. The first way is to use Azure SQL Database (Platform as a Service [PaaS]). The second method is to create a VM that implements SQL Server (Infrastructure as a Service [IaaS]). Each method has some advantages, and the choice depends on what is needed in the database.

SQL Database is a PaaS in Azure with which you can create a database with most of the functionality of running your own SQL Server in a VM but without having to worry about the VM part of it. You can create databases in SQL Database up to 500 GB in size. There are a few things that are not available in SQL Database: There is no SQL Agent, SQL Profiler, Native Encryption, Service Broker, Common Language Runtime (CLR), Use command, distributed transactions, or distributed views. If you need any of these things or a larger database size for the solution, you will need to look at running SQL Server in a VM (IaaS).

SQL Server running in a VM is very similar to running SQL Server on a VM on-premises. Databases can be up to 16 TB in size, and you have total control over what size of VM the database is using. The only real difference with this and running the data on-premises is where the physical server is located. Running SQL Server in a VM also means that you need to provide a license key for SQL Server. SQL Database, which is a PaaS service, does not need this.

EXAM TIP

Azure might update to change feature availability. The exam is updated over time, as well, to reflect these changes. However, because of the way Azure is steadily being updated, the newest features might not be on the exams.

MongoDB

MongoDB is an open-source NoSQL, JSON-like document–based storage system. Azure supports this in multiple ways. You need to use the Azure management portal to get to the Azure Marketplace to create a MongoDB database. There, you will find two options that you can use: creating a MongoDB in Azure Linux VMs (IaaS), or creating an account on MongoLab servers (SaaS). Creating the MongoDB in the Azure Linux VMs creates a cluster of three-node replica sets on which to run. The various plans that are available for this increase the size and speed of the Linux VMs as well as provide more storage space. Multiple plans are available for setting up an account on MongoLab. These plans range from a free 0.5 GB sandbox to use as a testbed, to a plan that provides 700 GB of storage. This service is separate from the Azure servers and is available in a limited number of regions around the world. You can also download MongoDB directly from *http://www.mongodb.org/.* You can then set up the database on a VM running Windows or Linux yourself. Figure 3-2 shows the Marketplace option for adding MongoDB to your Azure account.

FIGURE 3-2 Adding MongoDB to your Azure account

DocumentDB

DocumentDB is a data storage system also of the NoSQL variety. This system was developed from scratch, not adapted from any open-source JSON-based systems. Being a JSON document–based system means that each row in the database is a complete JSON document. This is quite a bit different from a traditional relational database. The data stored in the JSON document typically will be not normalized, and it will have everything needed to do the task for which the data is intended without having to query multiple times or joining tables.

A single DocumentDB account can support multiple databases and a store up to 10 GB per single Capacity Unit purchased. Each database unit also has a given amount of throughput; for example, each Capacity Unit can support up to 2,000 reads per second. If you need more storage or more throughput, you can add supplementary Capacity Units to the DocumentDB account.

MySQL

MySQL is a database system that is popular for many uses. Azure supports MySQL using ClearDB from the Azure Marketplace. To add a MySQL database, you need to go to the management portal and then into the Marketplace. From there, search for ClearDB MySQL Database. The wizard that opens will take you through the steps to set up the database on the ClearDB system. There is a free plan that supports a 20 MB database, and a larger plan that supports a database up to 10 GB. Keep in mind that this data-as-a-service is not running on your Azure's servers. ClearDB runs on its own clusters inside of Azure, which means that there are a limited number of regions around that world that it supports. Figure 3-3 shows the Marketplace option for adding MySQL to your Azure account.

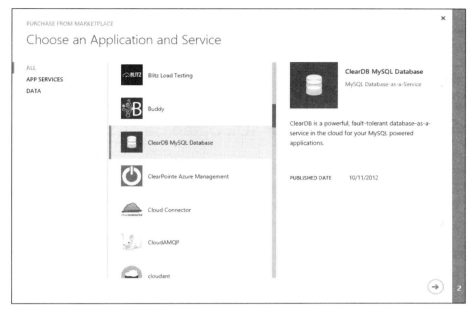

FIGURE 3-3 Setting up MySQL

The second option for having MySQL in Azure is to set up a VM and then install MySQL directly on that VM. You must configure everything yourself, but it is an option. You could use MySQL Cluster CGE to run on multiple VMs, which would afford a better Service Level Agreement (SLA).

Tools and libraries

There are multiple methods by which you can interact with the various storage systems and accounts that have been discussed thus far. There are client libraries that support .NET, Java, C++, Android, Node.js, Python, PHP, and Ruby, with more languages being added. Storage systems can also use a RESTful interface for interaction. This means that any language or platform that can call a RESTful service can use the storage systems.

You can use Windows PowerShell cmdlets to access features of Azure, as well. These are important to know because many system administrators use Windows PowerShell in their day-to-day activities, and knowing that similar commands are available to use in Azure helps these administrators to use it better. AzCopy 3.0 is another tool that you can use to copy Blobs and drives to Azure. Other storage types are being added to AzCopy, such as Tables and Files.

The final option for getting your company data into Azure is to use the Azure Import/Export service. Using this service, you can move terabytes of data into or out of Azure Blob storage by shipping physical drives. This gives you the means to move amounts of data that would not be practical to upload or download over an Internet connection. All of the drives created are encrypted by using BitLocker for added security.

> **MORE INFO** **AZURE STORAGE**
>
> You can learn more about Azure Storage accounts at *http://azure.microsoft.com/en-us/documentation/services/storage/.*

Designing security options for SQL Database or Storage

Security is an important issue when designing a solution for data storage. Companies do not want their data at risk of a breach or to fall into the wrong hands. Azure has systems in place to help with security of the aforementioned data storage systems. The two that you will look at in this section are for Azure SQL Database and for Azure Storage.

SQL Database employs multiple security strategies. The first is an allow list of all of the IP addresses that are allowed to access the database. If the server that you are on is not on the list—even if you have a valid user name and password to the database—access will be denied. Even other Azure services such as web roles or VMs need to be listed on the allow list. In the management portal, in the Configure section of the database, there is a switch with which you can turn on access from Azure Services. If this is turned on, all of the services on your account can connect to the database.

By default, SQL Database also requires that you use Secure Sockets Layer (SSL) encryption at all times. Your application can explicitly request an unencrypted connection to the database, as well. To validate certificates with ADO.NET code, in the connection string, set Encrypt to True (*Encrypt=True*) and TrustServerCertificate to False (*TrustServerCertificate=False*).

Finally, ensure that you use roles properly. If a person does not need full permissions to edit the tables, he should not be given the permission. Create users in roles to be used in the applications that are read-only (*db_datareader*) or that can write (*db_datawriter*) instead of giving people administrator rights (*db_owner db_ddladmin*). This is not something that is just for databases in Azure; it is a standard practice in a SQL Server database, and it is one option to help secure the data.

Azure Storage does provide security for the data that is stored within it. The first level of security is that you must use an HTTPS connection to access every service in Azure Storage. You can also use a standard HTTP connection, but it is not recommended. The second level of security is that to access any of the various types of data, you need to have the account name and the Access Keys. This means that without both, you cannot access the data.

Azure Storage can also use a Shared Access Signature (SAS) to limit the time and permissions that a user has to a storage account. You can create these for clients that need temporary access to data but should not get the Access Keys. SAS is a vital part of security for Storage accounts. SAS can include the start time, expiration time, resource type, permissions, and the signature. The SAS can be generated programmatically using the Azure Storage

Client Library and an Access Key to the Azure Storage account. The example SAS that follows will be valid until the expiration time of the Blob container that was used to create it. The signature grants a client permission to list blobs in the container and to write a new blob to the container.

```
https://<storageaccount>.blob.core.windows.net/sascontainer?sv=2012-02-12&se=2015-04-
13T00%3A12%3A08Z&sr=c&sp=wl&sig=t%2BbzU9%2B7ry4okULN9SOwst%2F8MCUhTjrHyV9rDNLSe8g%3D
```

Azure Storage also can use a Shared Access Policy to set the access to the storage account. This is similar to SAS, but it gives you the ability to implement an online policy that can be changed to shut down access event if people have a valid key. This can be useful if you're giving access outside your company which might later need to be removed. A Table, Queue, or Blob container can have up to five access policies. Policies provide more control to the owner of the Storage account, and it is recommended that you use them. The following example SAS uses a policy that hides the start and expiration times and the levels of permissions that are available.

```
https://<storageaccount>.blob.core.windows.net/sascontainer/myblob?sr=b&si=<your policy
identifier>&sig=<base 64 encoded signature>
```

Blob storage does provide an extra level of security: Blob containers are created to be the top level of the storage. You can mark these containers as public or as private. This way, if you would like to use the Blob storage to store all of the images from your blob, a simple URL will allow direct access to the files.

> **MORE INFO**   **AZURE SQL DATABASE SECURITY**
>
> You can learn more about Azure SQL Database security guidelines and limitations at *http://msdn.microsoft.com/en-us/library/azure/ff394108.aspx*. You can learn more about Azure Shared Access Storage at *http://azure.microsoft.com/en-us/documentation/articles/storage-dotnet-shared-access-signature-part-1/.*

Identifying the appropriate VM type and size for the solution

Azure's various storage systems offer options for the size of the VM used and the size of the data solution. No organization wants to pay for extra capacity that will be sitting idle.

SQL Database offers three tiers of service: Basic, Standard, and Premium. Each service tier has various performance levels that a database can use. The performance levels define how many Database Throughput Units (DTUs) the level can support. DTUs are based on a blended measure of CPU, memory, reads, and writes. As DTUs increase, the power offered by the performance level increases. For example, a performance level with 10 DTUs has two times the power of a performance level with 5 DTU. Each service tier also has a maximum allowed database size: 2 GB for Basic, 250 GB for Standard, and 500 GB for the Premium tier. Table 3-1 shows the SQL Database levels and their associated performance levels. The maximum database size can be set lower if needed, as well. A client might need a certain number of sessions connected to the database or require a certain level of transaction speed. For example, a tax preparation company might need more database power over the first four months of the year, and then less for the remainder of the year. By scaling the SQL Database up and down for the needs of the company, its overall costs are lowered but the required service level is still provided.

TABLE 3-1 SQL Database performance levels

Service tier/ performance level	DTU	Maximum database size (GB)	Maximum worker threads	Maximum sessions	Benchmark transaction rate
Basic	5	2	30	300	16,600 trans/hour
Standard/S0	10	250	60	600	521 trans/minute
Standard/S1	20	250	90	900	934 trans/minute
Standard/S2	50	250	120	1,200	2,570 trans/minute
Standard/S3	100	250	200	2,400	5,100 trans/minute
Premium/P1	100	500	200	2,400	105 trans/second
Premium/P2	200	500	400	4,800	228 trans/second
Premium/P3	800	500	1,600	19,200	735 trans/second

MongoDB and MySQL databases also have various performance and size settings that you can configure. These are defined in the service that is supporting those database types. The ClearDB website is where you can change from a free 20 MB database that can support 4 connections, up to a 10 GB database supporting up to 50 connections. You can adjust Mon-goDB running in VMs in Azure from the management portal. Linux is set as the operating system for the VMs in Azure which run as a cluster of 3 VMs. MongoDB can be scaled from each node of the cluster having 1.75 GB of RAM and 40 GB, up to 56 GB of RAM and 1,000 GB of storage. This makes it possible for you to configure a larger VM in the clusters to perform the tasks needed by the database.

EXAM TIP

Performance levels of the database are important to a company, and the ability to change this at times is equally important. The limits of each level of SQL Database can help the architect to determine the minimum level needed to satisfy those needs.

Thought experiment

Making the switch

In this thought experiment, apply what you've learned about this objective. You can find answers to these questions in the "Answers" section at the end of this chapter.

Contoso Suites is looking at the possibility of moving its existing SQL Database to a new storage type, such as a NoSQL database, to help with both speed and costs. The SQL Database is 5 years old and currently around 500 MB in size, growing by approximately 100 MB each year. This database has changed over time, adding new fields to support new features. The database is currently accessed by the client's mobile apps using a WCF web service that is hosted in Azure.

You have the following goals for the changes:

- The new storage platform needs to be able to support growth for the next five years.
- Existing users and new users of the mobile apps need to be supported.
- The company also wants to be able to have files or blobs in Azure so that the users can get at new data files without having to update the client apps each time.

With this information in mind, answer the following questions:

1. Which of the NoSQL solutions in Azure would best support the conversion of the SQL Database?

2. Would DocumentDB be a good solution to which to move the data, keeping in mind the speed and cost constraints?

3. The data to be downloaded is planned to be added to Blob storage to allow the clients to download the files, but they need to be able to protect the files so that other unauthorized users cannot get at them. What can be done to protect the files?

Objective summary

- Table storage supports structured data that uses a partition key and a row key for searches.
- Blob storage supports unstructured data files such as text or binary data.
- DocumentDB is a NoSQL, JSON document–based storage system that by default has every field indexed.
- MongoDB and MySQL databases are supported through the Azure Marketplace.

- SQL Databases need a "white list" of the IP address of machines that can access them directly, including Azure resources.
- You can set up Blob storage to have public containers.
- Different VM sizes have additional features that you can use for the various storage solutions.

Objective review

Answer the following questions to test your knowledge of the information in this objective. You can find the answers to these questions and explanations of why each answer choice is correct or incorrect in the "Answers" section at the end of this chapter.

1. Your client needs to be able to have 1,000 connections to the SQL Database server in Azure. Which level of database should you use to provide the correct level of service while still incurring the lowest costs?

   A. S1

   B. Basic

   C. P2

   D. S0

2. A title company needs to provide access to storage for people to upload scans of documents that they signed. There are time limits to when the documents are needed. Which approach should be used to provide access?

   A. Create a mobile service and set up the valid dates in a database that will be read in. Store the documents directly in the database.

   B. Use an SAS and set the expiration time and date for the user

   C. Set up Azure AD with permissions for the user that limit the time in which she can upload documents.

   D. Open up the Blob storage container to public access so that the user can add the document even if she is late.

3. A company is looking to move its existing system from on-premises to Azure and it is using MySQL. Which of the following are valid statements?

   A. MySQL is not a Microsoft product, so it cannot be used in Azure.

   B. MySQL can be set up in its own VM.

   C. Convert all of the data to SQL Azure to save time and money.

   D. There is a MySQL option in the Azure Marketplace.

Objective 3.2: Design applications that use Mobile Services

Since the release of the iPhone, mobile app development has taken off in dramatic fashion. Users have been collecting data in their apps and games at an extraordinary pace. Many people now get their email exclusively from their phones, and some do not even have computers anymore. Every platform is trying to add more features each year, and developers need to not only be able to keep up and have a consistent platform to support the devices that are available today, but also the ones that are being developed for tomorrow.

> **This section covers the following topics:**
> - Azure Mobile Services
> - Consuming Mobile Services
> - Offline Sync
> - Extending Mobile Services by using custom code
> - Implementing Mobile Service
> - Securing Mobile Services

Azure Mobile Services

Mobile Services is a cloud-based PaaS for apps that makes it possible for you to quickly implement online data storage for a mobile application. Companies do not need to design, build, test, deploy, manage, and upgrade the entire service structure. The first implementation of Mobile Services was implemented with Node.js, but there is also a .NET implementation. Mobile services work on iOS, Android, Windows, Windows Phone, and also HTML.

Mobile Services are not available in every region around the world. The older datacenters, such as North Central United States do not have Mobile Services as an option. Keep this in mind when setting up services in Azure; you'll want to keep things in the same datacenter.

Mobile Services provide many features to developers. One of the most used features of Mobile Services is to create a proxy to a data source. This creates classes for every table in a SQL Database. The connection to the data can also have collections that represent each table and can return each row of data. By default, services created tie into SQL Database, but you can change the code to store the data in many different locations, including using Hybrid Connection to an on-premises database. This makes sense when a data source cannot be moved to Azure so that it can still be used. Figure 3-4 shows the data flow from the mobile application using Mobile Services with a Data Transfer Object (DTO) using the Table Controller, and ending up in a Azure SQL Database.

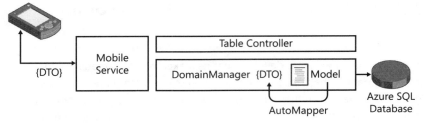

FIGURE 3-4 Mobile Services data flow

Mobile Services also includes the idea of a soft delete for data. Soft delete adds a _deleted field to the data being saved; then, when the data is deleted, it still exists in the storage, but it's marked as deleted. This can be useful for systems in which the data is taken out of general use, but the fact that it existed in the first place is still needed. For example, even though a medical professional has left the hospital, the activities of that person while in the employ of the hospital still need to be reported and maintained.

Mobile Services also have built-in support for all of the social-networking providers as well as Azure AD. This provides the application that uses Mobile Services a method to tie in to an authentication system that makes sense for the application. The tables and custom APIs can then be set to give access only for users who are authenticated.

The backend script or code for the mobile service makes it possible for you to perform data validations, logical flows, or tasks such as specifying a query to return data only for the current authenticated user. You can code the backend in Node.js or by using .NET.

Mobile Services also has a basic push notification system that can tie in to some of the mobile platforms. Mobile Services also can tie connect to the Notification Hubs to provide a more enhanced experience and support more platforms.

Mobile Services that are running at a Basic or Standard level also operate under an SLA that specifies 99.9 percent availability. A web API running in an Azure website could provide similar services to a .NET-based mobile service. The code is pretty much identical. But to achieve a 99.95 percent availability with a website, you would need a Basic or Standard hosting plan. For a fair comparison, you need to look at the amount of traffic that the mobile service will encounter in a month. If the Basic level of Mobile Services can provide the number of API calls and push notifications, it can be a more cost-effective solution. Even if the mobile service needs to scale up to three instances, Mobile Services is more cost effective than a website running a single Basic instance. These aspects will need to be analyzed based on the situation for the architecture being evaluated. Table 3-2 compares some of the Mobile Services hosting options.

TABLE 3-2 Mobile Services hosting options

Hosting method	SLA	Cost	API calls	Push
Free mobile service	N/A	Free	500 KB	Included (1 MB)
Basic mobile service	99.9%	~$15/month	1.5 MB	Included (10 MB)
Standard mobile service	99.9%	~$140/month	15 MB	Included (10 MB)
Free website	N/A	Free	N/A	Free (1 MB)
Basic website	99.95%	~$56/month	N/A	$10/month (10 MB)
Standard website	99.95%	~$74/month	N/A	$10/month (10 MB)

> **MORE INFO**   **MOBILE SERVICES**
>
> You can learn more about Azure Mobile Services at *http://azure.microsoft.com/en-us/ documentation/services/mobile-services/.*

Consuming Mobile Services

After your mobile service has been created, you now can add code to your project to access the mobile service and retrieve data from it. You can do this on all platforms, including: Windows, iOS, Android, HTML/JS, and Xamarin. Xamarin is a platform that uses C# to develop iOS and Android apps.

The pattern for consuming Mobile Services on any platform is for all intents and purposes the same. First, you add the reference to the Mobile Services Client Library to the project. The next step is to create an instance of the *MobileServiceClient* that points to the URL of your service and uses the Application Key. The instance of the client can then be used to get references to tables or custom APIs. With the reference to the table, items can be inserted, read, updated, or deleted. For most of the implementations (Windows, iOS, and Android), you will also need to create a class for each table in your project, but with JavaScript, you can use raw JSON. When you have classes referenced within other classes, the database will create a relationship between the two tables, as well. An example of the classes and the raw JSON are in the code that follows.

When you go to the Mobile Services page in the management portal, it shows examples of how to tie in the mobile service to an existing project. The page also has links to download a new project, and it offers links and instructions for Windows, Windows Phone, Android, iOS (Objective-C, and Swift), Xamarin, and HTML/JS.

For implementing a connection to Mobile Services using Windows or Windows Phone, there are two languages that you need to look at: C# and JavaScript.

For developing in C#, the first step is to right-click your client project, select Manage NuGet Packages, search for the WindowsAzure.MobileServices package and add a reference

to it. Add "using Microsoft.WindowsAzure.MobileServices;" and then copy and paste the following code into your App.xaml.cs file:

```
public static MobileServiceClient MobileService = new MobileServiceClient(
    "https://<mobile service name>.azure-mobile.net/",
    "<Application key>"
);
```

Add a sample *TodoItem* class to your project:

```
public class TodoItem {
    public string Id { get; set; }
    public string Text { get; set; }
    public bool Complete { get; set; }
}
```

Use the Mobile Services Client Library to store data in the mobile service:

```
TodoItem item = new TodoItem { Text = "Awesome item", Complete = false };
await App.MobileService.GetTable<TodoItem>().InsertAsync(item);
```

For developing with JavaScript, right-click your client project, select Manage NuGet Packages, search for the WindowsAzure.MobileServices.WinJS package, and then add a reference
to it. Then, add a reference to MobileServices.js in the default.html file.

WinJS is an open-source JavaScript library written by Microsoft that you can use to create
Windows Store applications. This has grown to a library that you can use in any web browser
for standard websites. WinJS is now available on GitHub under the Apache License.

Next, copy and paste the following code into your default.js file to connect your application to your mobile service:

```
var client = new WindowsAzure.MobileServiceClient(
    "https://<mobile service name>.azure-mobile.net/",
    "Application key");
```

Use the Mobile Services Client Library to store data in the mobile service:

```
var item = { text: "Awesome item", completed: false };
client.getTable("TodoItem").insert(item);
```

Other platforms, such as Android, iOS (Objective-C and Swift), and HTML/JS, implement
Mobile Services in a similar way to Windows. The Mobile Service section in the management portal provide the exact steps to add this to each platform. These steps are constantly
updated, and this is exemplified by the fact that Swift was included soon after it was released.
Figure 3-5 shows an example of the management portal, in this case, we're configuring iOS to
use the Mobile Service. Notice the tabs at the top of the page that you can click to connect to
the code for the other platforms.

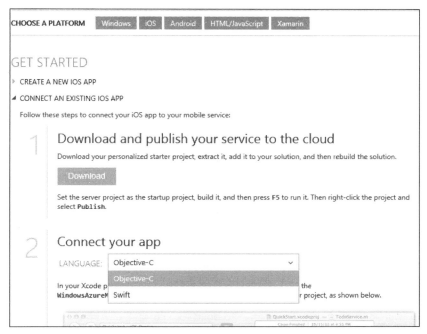

FIGURE 3-5 Setting up Mobile Services for iOS

MORE INFO **CROSS-PLATFORM SUPPORT**

You can learn more about Azure Mobile Services in iOS apps at *http://azure.microsoft.com/ en-us/documentation/articles/mobile-services-ios-how-to-use-client-library/*. For more information about Azure Mobile Services in Android apps, go to *http://azure.microsoft.com/ en-us/documentation/articles/mobile-services-android-how-to-use-client-library/*.

Offline Sync

When you design for a mobile platform, you need to consider that there might be times when the user does not have a connection to the Internet. Many people have limited data plans, and some might be using a device that is only connected to the Internet via Wi-Fi. To ensure that users can still use your mobile app and the mobile service, you can use a feature called Offline Sync. Figure 3-6 shows a data flow for offline data synchronization in which SQLite is added to the mobile app for performing the offline synchronization.

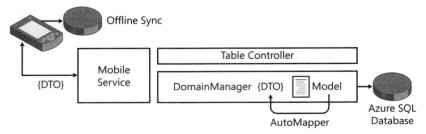

FIGURE 3-6 Mobile Services offline architecture

Offline Sync uses a local SQLite database within the app itself, which makes it possible for data to be stored locally. This means that an app could run using only local data with no network connection at all. From here, new data is stored in the SQLite database and can be pushed up to the Azure mobile service when network access is restored. After this, data can be pulled down from the server to populate the tables locally.

You can add Offline Sync capability to any platform that supports mobile services. To add Offline Sync capability to a Windows 8 or Windows Phone 8.1 app, you need to add references to SQLite for the platform and also add the WindowsAzure.MobileServices.SQLiteStore NuGet package. You will need to change the project to build for x86, x64, or ARM. The Any CPU option is not supported by the SQLite runtime. Each reference to *IMobileServiceTable* will need to change to *IMobileServiceSyncTable* to use *App.MobileService.GetSyncTable* to get the reference to the table.

```
var store = new MobileServiceSQLiteStore("localsyncdata.db");
store.DefineTable<TodoItem>();
await App.MobileService.SyncContext.InitializeAsync(store, new
MobileServiceSyncHandler());
```

When you are trying to pull data from a table or synchronize all of the changes that are stored locally, you can use the following calls. Keep in mind the push up to the server is done at the mobile service level so that all of the tables are pushed at the same time. Pulling data down is done at the table level.

```
todoTable.PullAsync();
App.MobileService.SyncContext.PushAsync();
```

The Azure documentation site has step-by-step instructions on how to set up the Offline Sync feature for other platforms.

> **MORE INFO** **OFFLINE SYNC**
>
> You can learn more about Mobile Services Offline Sync at *http://azure.microsoft.com/en-us/documentation/articles/mobile-services-windows-phone-get-started-offline-data/.*

Implementing Mobile Services

You can create a mobile service in one of two ways: by using .NET or Node.js. Each one offers certain benefits. Like many other parts of Azure, this makes it possible for developers who are skilled in either language to implement Mobile Services without having to learn a new language.

When creating a mobile service that is implemented by using .NET, you can reserve the service name directly in the management portal, but you create the service itself by using Microsoft Visual Studio. A .NET mobile service project is built on top of a Web API project. To create a .NET mobile service, create a new ASP.NET Web Application. When you see the list of templates, choose the Azure Mobile Service template, as shown in Figure 3-7. This provides a simple RESTful interface with which many .NET developers are familiar. Access to the data that is stored in the SQL Database is achieved through the /tables route. You can also create custom APIs here in a different controller, and they will use a /api route by default.

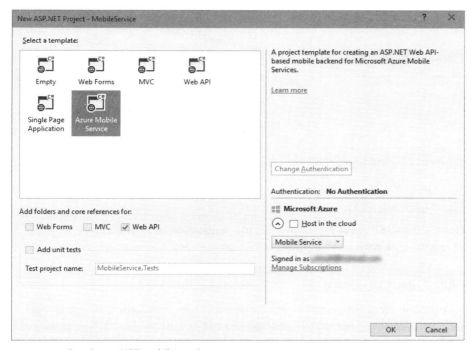

FIGURE 3-7 Creating a .NET mobile service

To implement a mobile service that uses Node.js as the backend, go to the management portal. The service generates Node scripts for each table action, and the scripts intercept the Create, Read, Update, Delete (CRUD) requests. These requests are then passed on to SQL Database by default, but you could change this by writing your own step to save the data to another location. This is also where you can add other business logic. You edit scripts directly in the management portal. In the Configure section for the service, there is a GIT URL from which you can download all of the scripts locally to edit. JSON files are available to describe the configuration and the security setting for each script, and JavaScript files for the scripts themselves are also available. Figure 3-8 shows how to create a JavaScript mobile service in the management portal.

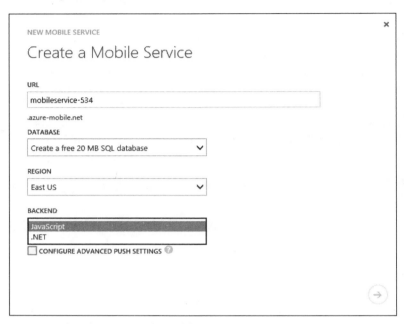

FIGURE 3-8 Creating a JavaScript mobile service

> **MORE INFO**   **USER AUTHENTICATION**
>
> You can learn more about Azure Mobile Services user authentication at *http://azure. microsoft.com/en-us/documentation/articles/mobile-services-how-to-use-server-scripts/.*

Secure Mobile Services

You can set up Mobile Services to authenticate the user and only allow calls to be made that use the system that you set up for security. The identity systems that are available in Mobile Services are Microsoft account, Facebook, Twitter, Google, and Azure AD. You can set up multiple systems to validate the user based on the business need of the application. Azure AD is one solution that a company can use to validate against an on-premises Active Directory by synchronizing the corporate Active Directory to the Azure AD. Figure 3-9 shows the data flow for the authorization, in which the call is made from the device to get credentials and then the identity is returned through the mobile service.

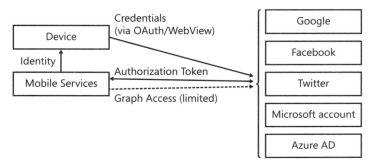

FIGURE 3-9 Mobile service authorization

You can configure all calls into the mobile service to use a data authorization setting that limits the use of the calls by people who are not set up with permissions. You can do this in four modes: Application Key Required, Everyone, Authenticated Users, and Admins And Other Scripts. Following is a description of each mode:

- **Application Key Required**   This mode allows access into the mobile service to anyone with the Application Key. This is useful during prerelease, but it's not as useful for production.

- **Everyone**   Calls can be made by anyone even if they do not have an Application Key. This means that the mobile service could be called directly from a web interface without the mobile applications at all.

- **Authenticated Users**   All requests to the mobile service need to have a user ID and a matching authorization token. Users must be logged on using one of the networks mentioned earlier and accept the terms of the application with that network.

- **Admins And Other Scripts**   This last option requires a Master Key from the mobile service to be allowed to use that call. If the authorization for the call fails, the Mobile Service will return a 401 Unauthorized response.

After the mobile service is set up with the identity system(s) that you want to include, the application needs to send a request to be authorized. You can do this by using the following code:

```
private MobileServiceUser user;
user = await App.MobileService.LoginAsync(MobileServiceAuthenticationProvider.Facebook);
```

After the call is made to *LoginAsync*, the user variable will have the user's level (Admin, Authenticated, or Anonymous) as well as the *userId* which includes the provider that was used for authorization. Other basic information, such as name, username, locale, picture, or a link, could be included based on the authentication provider used.

> **MORE INFO   USER AUTHENTICATION**
>
> You can learn more about Azure Mobile Services user authentication at *http://azure.microsoft. com/en-us/documentation/articles/mobile-services-windows-phone-get-started-users/*.

Extending Mobile Services by using custom code

You can extend Mobile Services by using a custom API to add yet more functionality beyond just getting the data from the database. A custom API is an endpoint in your mobile service that is accessed by one or more of the standard HTTP methods: GET, POST, PUT, PATCH, and DELETE. You can define a separate function for each HTTP method supported by the custom API.

Extending Mobile Services is done differently if you are using a Node.js or a .NET mobile service. For a Node.js–based mobile service, you do this directly from the management portal. For mobile services created with .NET, you can include an additional custom API controller to add a new custom controller to the Web API. This involves the same steps that are used to add custom code to a Web API website, which you can see in Objective 3.4, later in this chapter.

In the client apps, the custom code can be called by using the code that follows. This code demonstrates using the *MobileServiceClient* object to invoke the custom API asynchronously. You get to call the method and set how you are calling it, and you also can any parameters for the call itself. This means that you do not need to do all of this manually.

```
string message;
try
{
    // Asynchronously call the custom API using the POST method.
    var result = await App.MobileService
        .InvokeApiAsync<MarkAllResult>("completeAll",
        System.Net.Http.HttpMethod.Post, null);
    message =  result.Count + " item(s) marked as complete.";
}
catch (MobileServiceInvalidOperationException ex)
{
    message = ex.Message;
}
```

Thought experiment
Time to move

In this thought experiment, apply what you've learned about this objective. You can find answers to these questions in the "Answers" section at the end of this chapter.

Humongous Insurance has been using Azure for years to supply data for its mobile phone apps. The system is currently using an older WCF Web Service in a north-central United States region. The service is a proxy into the SQL Database that is in the same region. The Windows 8 and Windows Phone 8.0 apps that are in the market are being moved into a single universal app. To do this, a new mobile service is being looked at to replace the WCF Web Service. Android and iOS versions of the app are also available as well as a Facebook page that calls the WCF Web Service. Push notifications are currently being done inside of the WCF Web Service to tell the users that there is new data for them to view.

You have the following goals for the changes:

- The Windows 8 and Windows Phone 8.0 apps need to be changed to universal apps and need to have a data service that supports this change.
- The database is not very large (100 MB), but it might change to a different storage method to save on costs.
- The WCF Web Service wrapped methods around the existing tables. Mobile Services will provide direct access to classes for each table.

With this information in mind, answer the following questions:

1. Does the database that the apps are using also need to move into the same region as the new mobile service?
2. How can the company ensure that users who are still on older versions of the app can still use it when the new mobile service is up and running?
3. Will a custom API be needed for the mobile service or will the direct table access be all that is needed?

Objective summary

- Azure Mobile Services is a PaaS with which you can connect mobile apps and some type of data storage (typically SQL Server).
- You can carry out authentication by connecting to social network providers or Active Directory by using the built-in support for these systems.
- Push notification is available for all major mobile platforms.
- You can write custom scripts (.NET or Node.js) to provide data validation, logical flows, or custom data storage.

Objective review

Answer the following questions to test your knowledge of the information in this objective. You can find the answers to these questions and explanations of why each answer choice is correct or incorrect in the "Answers" section at the end of this chapter.

1. Your application uses Azure Mobile Services and your manager is worried about users losing connection to the Internet. What two steps would support offline data? (Each answer is a complete solution.)

   A. The users will need to have a network connection for the application to run; there is nothing else you can do.

   B. Use the Offline Sync capability of Mobile Services and store data locally until there is a connection available. When the connection is restored, push local changes up and pull new data down.

   C. Serialize to a local data file if there is no network connection.

   D. Use the Data Sync feature on SQL Server to synchronize the data to the devices.

2. Your company, Blue Yonder Airlines, is making a mobile app on all platforms for employees only. What two steps are needed validate the users, and which steps supports every platform?

   A. Use Mobile Services authentication and tie in to the user's Facebook accounts.

   B. Use Mobile Services authentication and tie in to Azure AD.

   C. Set up Azure AD and tie in to the corporate Active Directory.

   D. Set up Azure AD and tie in to all social networks to cover everyone.

3. The mobile app that you are working on needs to be able to handle a large amount of users quickly. The app uses Mobile Services to get to the SQL Database. How can you ensure that the service scales to handle the traffic and minimizes your expenses?

   A. Use Mobile Services running at the Free tier and turn on the Auto-Scale feature.

   B. Run the mobile service in two separate VMs that are at least sized Medium.

   C. Use Mobile Services running at the Standard tier and turn on the Auto-Scale feature.

   D. Watch the usage of the mobile service and then call a Windows PowerShell script to adjust the number of instances that are running.

4. You are setting up Mobile Services to be the backend of your mobile application. The requirements are that the system must support SQL Database today but might move to use MongoDB or another NoSQL solution in the future to lower costs. Which of the following are true?

   A. Changing the data storage on the backend of Mobile Services is only allowed if it were implemented in .NET.

   B. Changing the data storage on the backend of Mobile Services is only allowed if it were implemented in Node.js.

   C. Mobile services can support Azure Table storage as a NoSQL storage platform.

   D. Mobile Services can only support SQL Databases.

5. You are moving an older WCF Web Service in the north-central United States region into a new mobile service to use. The WCF Web Service is not going to be changed as well to support this transition. Which of the following steps are required?

   A. Convert the applications that tie in to the WCF Web Service to call the new Mobile Service.

   B. The database will need to be moved to the region where the mobile service is created.

   C. Create the mobile service in the north-central United States region to be near the existing database.

   D. The mobile service will need to be created in a different region than the original WCF Web Service.

Objective 3.3: Design applications that use notifications

Many applications available today will notify the user at times. This could be when it is the user's turn in a game, there is breaking news to display, or even when a stock has been bought or sold. Push notifications are transforming business and increasing employee productivity and responsiveness to issues that need to be taken care of immediately.

Each mobile platform employs a different Platform Notification Service (PNS). There are commercial systems to help implement a single system, which makes it simpler for the developer. In Azure, you can use something such as an Azure Cloud Services to create your own system for pushing to all of the mobile systems. Mobile Services, however, comes with a push notification system of its own, so this is something that you no longer need to create manually. You can send data by using a standard template for the PNS to which you are sending data, or in a raw format, as well.

This section covers the following topics:
- Implementing push notification services in Mobile Services
- Sending push notifications

Implementing push notification services in Mobile Services

Mobile Services implements push notification for Windows Store Apps, Apple Push Notification, and Google Cloud Messaging. This is the default for Mobile Services. You can see the basic pattern for setting up and implementing push notification in Figure 3-10. The client app retrieves a handle from the PNS. Then, the app takes that handle and passes it to a service that controls the notifications. This could be implemented in a cloud service in Azure. When the server code sends out a notification to the PNS, it uses the credentials that it was sent to authenticate with the service. The PNS then sends the notification to the device itself. The server does not actually do the communicating to the devices to send a notification. If the handle for the device has expired, the PNS will reject the notification and the service that is processing the pushes will need to remove the rejected address from the list of devices that it maintains.

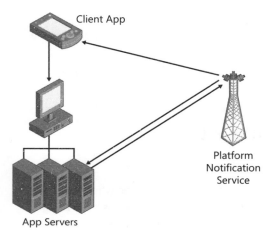

Client App

Platform
Notification
Service

App Servers

FIGURE 3-10 Basic push notifications

When you create the mobile service, there is an option to configure advanced push settings. The advanced push settings configure a notification hub to do the push notification for the mobile service. This adds additional devices and features to the push notification.

A key difference between push notification directly in Mobile Services and using a notification hub is scale. Notification hubs are optimized to broadcast millions of push notifications within minutes. Mobile Services push notification is good for simple event-driven events, such as notifying a a participant in a game that it is her turn.

Each platform for pushing needs a certificate, API Key, or a client secret to direct the system to push to that system. You can obtain these keys and certificates from the developer store account for the app itself. After all of this is set up, the mobile service, a website, or even a console app that you run manually can initiate a push to all, one, or a group of people. Keep in mind that when you push notifications, each PNS handles data differently and each system has a different call in the notification hub *Client* class that can be called if you want to send to just that platform. So, calls to each system can be made, but this work is offloaded to the notification hub and is now no longer part of your website, web service, or console app to handle each push separately. This will scale much better when large numbers of users need to be notified.

Each platform has libraries that you can include in a project to provide the calls to tie in to the notification hubs to carry out the push notification. As an alternative to calling the notification hub with the connection to the push service for the platform, you could add that logic to another application or service. This way the existing cloud service that you use to do notifications could just add the device to the notification hub. The application would need to handle the addition and removal of the device to the notification hub, but this is a possibility. This means that existing applications would need to still only pass their PNS connection to your service just as they have done in the past, and the new notification hub can still be used. You can use this to minimize changes to existing applications, but for new applications, directly connecting to notification hubs is the preferred method.

Implementing your push notification by using notification hubs has some advantages. The first is that it does support more device types and includes iOS, Android, Windows Phone, Windows, and Kindle. Also, by using notification hubs, you can avoid storing device information in your mobile service or the cloud service that you use. Devices can also register tags to determine the unique device as well as areas of interest for the user. These tags make it possible for the notification hub to work with large groups down to individual devices. You can also use templates to push down specific data that is needed for that user; for example, a stock price could be sent out in United States dollars as well as euros. A template for a user could be that he just wants to see the price in dollars, whereas a different template only shows the price in euros. By using a single push with both sets of data, you can do this more efficiently.

Another use of push notifications would be to create a secure notification system. For example, suppose that an application needs to send some sensitive data to a user. Raw data could be pushed to the user and the application on the device could use that raw data to pull sensitive data down over a secure connection. This way the sensitive data does not need to go through the PNS, because the PNS might not support secure connections. Having this type of trigger to inform the application that there is new data to retrieve is the best practice instead of adding the data directly into the payload.

You could even use push notifications to trigger synchronizing of offline data. If there are changes to a database that you would like to push to the offline synchronization capabilities of the application, it can listen for the push and use the data to trigger retrieval for any or all of the data tables that it is keeping locally.

> **MORE INFO**   **PUSH NOTIFICATION**
>
> You can learn more about Azure Mobile Services push notification at *http://azure.microsoft. com/en-us/documentation/articles/mobile-services-javascript-backend-windows-phone-get-started-push/.*

Sending push notifications

Sending a push notification to the users of your app is something that you can do from a variety of places. It could be something that is directly in the mobile service scripts to let users know that data was changed in the system. A company could develop an internal application to push out new offers to all of the users of the app. Keep in mind that many PNSs will limit the use of push for advertising purposes, so it is not a good design to put advertisements into the notifications themselves. You could create a website that connects to the Azure Service Bus and talks to the notification hub to send out notifications to devices.

Pushing to individuals or to groups of individuals is something that is available in notification hubs. As was mentioned earlier, notification hubs are designed and optimized to send out millions of notifications in minutes. When a device is registered with the notification hubs, it can also register tags to help identify the data in which the person is interested. You could create a tag that indicates what city the person is in so that offers for hotels or restaurants are sent only to the people who are in those cities. You can use tags for any purpose in your application to determine what push notifications it wants to receive. You also can create a unique tag to send user-specific notifications, such as alerting the user that a stock has reached the price she was waiting for, or that a new task has been assigned to her.

The following code snippet registers the device for a list of categories:

```
var hub = new NotificationHub("<hub name>", "<connection string with listen access>");

var channel = await PushNotificationChannelManager.
CreatePushNotificationChannelForApplicationAsync();

var categories = new HashSet<string>();
categories.Add("World");
categories.Add("Politics");
categories.Add("Business");

await hub.RegisterNativeAsync(channel.Uri, categories);
```

> **MORE INFO** **ENHANCED PUSH**
>
> You can learn more about getting started with notification hubs at *http://azure.microsoft. com/en-us/documentation/articles/partner-xamarin-notification-hubs-android-get-started/*.

 Thought experiment

Updating your notifications

In this thought experiment, apply what you've learned about this objective. You can find answers to these questions in the "Answers" section at the end of this chapter.

Margie's Travel has developed a mobile app that runs on all mobile platforms. The app distributes coupons for local restaurants and stores for cities around the United States. Users can sign up to receive coupons for multiple cities and also particular stores. The app uses an old WCF Web Service in Azure today that it had running for other tasks. The web service is manually doing the push notification to two out of three mobile platforms.

You have the following goals for the app:

- Users need to be able to sign up for multiple locations and stores.
- For apps on certain platforms, the icon for the app needs to display a count of the number of coupons available.
- All mobile platforms will have push notification.

With this information in mind, answer the following questions:

1. People do not always update their apps. How can the push notifications be moved over to Mobile Services push notification for those users with older apps.

2. The company wants to ensure that the new push notification service has an availability higher than 99 percent. What can you do to ensure that the push notifications are also at an SLA higher than 99 percent?

3. Push notifications are included in Azure Mobile Services directly. You also can implement push by using notification hubs, which is an extra cost. Which would be simpler for this application?

Objective summary

- Push notification supports Android, iOS, Windows, and HTML client apps.
- Push notification accommodates pushing all native types of notifications for each mobile platform, such as toast, tiles, and raw data.
- Notification hubs have enhanced features for push notifications to handle millions of devices.

Objective review

Answer the following questions to test your knowledge of the information in this objective. You can find the answers to these questions and explanations of why each answer choice is correct or incorrect in the "Answers" section at the end of this chapter.

1. For the app that is being created, the managers would like you to be able to do push notification to only certain groups of people. What is the most cost-effective way to implement this to perform the notification the fastest?

   A. Keep track of all of the users who are signed up for push notifications and then only push to those who need the data.

B. Utilize a notification hub to push to only the users who have the tag for the data that is to be sent.

C. The basic push notification in Mobile Services supports pushing to any group.

D. Implement the SignalR channel in Mobile Services to push data to the devices in real time.

2. Which statements are true for push notification?

A. The push notification system in Azure will directly connect to the devices and push data to it.

B. Push notification only supports pop-up or toast-types of notification.

C. Push notification uses the standard push system for each platform to communicate to the devices.

D. You can create custom templates to afford greater flexibility in the data being pushed.

3. Which of the following are architecturally sound uses of push notification?

A. A follower on Twitter posted a reply to one of your posts.

B. Every data point (thousands/second) for a temperature-monitoring system sending to thousands of users.

C. Notifying users of a stock market target–price hit.

D. Notifying a game player that he was sent a chat message.

Objective 3.4: Design applications that use a web API

ASP.NET Web API is a framework that makes it easy to build HTTP services that reach a broad range of clients, including browsers and mobile devices. ASP.NET Web API is a platform for building RESTful applications on the .NET Framework.

> **This section covers the following topics:**
> - Implementing a custom Web API
> - Scaling by using Azure Websites
> - WebJobs
> - Securing a web API

Implementing a custom Web API

You can create custom Web APIs in Visual Studio 2013 using C# or Microsoft Visual Basic (VB). Begin by clicking Cloud and then ASP.NET Web Application. From there, you can select the ASP.NET template to create the new project. Figure 3-11 shows the New ASP.NET Project dialog box with the template selections. Select the Web API template. In the lower-right corner of the dialog box, in the Microsoft Azure section, there is an option to host the new project in Azure. You can always publish the Web API application later. There is also an option to publish to a website or to a VM.

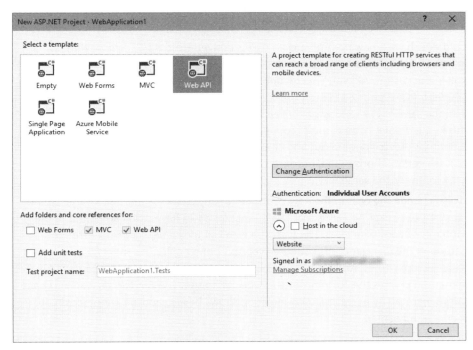

FIGURE 3-11 Creating a Web API application

If you selected the Host In The Cloud check box, after you select the template and how to publish to Azure, a dialog box opens in which you can configure the Azure publishing settings. Here, you will need to set up the website or the VM.

After the basic project is configured, you can run and test it locally before publishing it to Azure. The basic project provides a help page that you can access by clicking the API link in the menu at the top. The pages use a Model-View-Controller (MVC) pattern, which you can change depending on the requirements for your project.

To add a new custom controller to the project, perform the following steps:

1. In Solution Explorer, right-click the Controllers folder.

2. On the menu that appears, point to Add, and then select New Scaffolded Item.

3. A dialog box opens in which you specify the options for what type of Scaffolded Item you would like to add. To do this, in the Common section, from the menu, select the Web API option; you will see all of the Web API controllers that are available.

4. You can select any of the controllers, but for this example, select the Web API 2 Controller – Empty option.

5. Click Add. A dialog box opens in which you will create the name for the controller.

Do not remove the "Controller" name from the name of the new class. The Web API architecture uses that to determine what classes implement a controller. You can test this by renaming the class later. You can place the new controller anywhere in the solution, but it does help for consistency to keep them all in a single folder.

You should now have a new controller class that is derived from *ApiController* with no methods in it at all. Using Web API, you can add any method to the class and have it be a RESTful call in the custom API you are creating. RESTful calls use the standard HTTP requests—GET, PUT, POST, and DELETE—to perform standard database CRUD actions. With a custom API, the same HTTP requests are used for your own custom calls. There is a great example of this in the default code in the AccountController.cs file. There are methods for registering accounts as well as logging out and changing passwords. In a WCF web service, these would have just been methods in the interface that were created. In this Web API project, you can create the methods the same way.

You can also change the calls in the new controller to any route for the URL instead of the standard /api/Values or /api/Accounts that the premade classes have. You can do this in the attributes of the new controller class. The first step is to call the *config.MapHttpAttribute Routes()* method in the *Register* method in the WebApiConfig.cs file. This makes it possible for you to use the custom routes. Adding a *RoutePrefix* attribute to the class and a *Route* attribute to the method creates the custom route for the call to use. The *RoutePrefix* can also have multiple parts separated by a "/". The following code shows how to add a custom routing to the controller created earlier:

```
[RoutePrefix("Account")]
public class AccountController : ApiController
{
    …
    [Route("Logout")]
    public IHttpActionResult Logout()
    {
        …
        return Ok();
    }
    …
}
```

> **MORE INFO CUSTOM WEB API**
>
> You can learn more about the custom Web APIs using SQL Server at *http://azure.microsoft. com/en-us/documentation/articles/web-sites-dotnet-rest-service-aspnet-api-sql-database/*.

Scaling by using Azure App Service Web Apps

You can run Web API services in both VMs running Internet Information Services (IIS) and as an Azure website. You can scale-up Azure websites to increase performance and throughput of the service. You can do this several ways. The first option is to scale-up the Web Hosting Plan to a higher level. The levels are Free, Shared, Basic, and Standard. Different levels offer different sets of features and capabilities. Plans in the Free and Shared modes run on a shared infrastructure with sites managed by other customers. These sites will have strict quotas for resource utilization. (Plans in the Basic and Standard modes run on resources that are dedicated to your sites and have fewer restrictions.)

The second way that a website can scale is at the Basic and Standard levels. At these levels, you can select the Instance Size to run; this is referred to as *scaling up*. This provides more memory and CPU power for the website to use. Table 3-2 shows the values for each Instance Size as well as the sizes of the Free and Shared levels against which to compare.

TABLE 3-3 Website scaling

Instance size	Cores	Memory
Free	Shared	1 GB
Shared	Shared	1 GB
Small	1	1.75 GB
Medium	2	3.5 GB
Large	4	7 GB

Basic and Standard-level web hosting plans can scale the website to multiple instances. This is referred to as *scaling out*. Basic instances can be scaled to three instances, whereas Standard instances can be scaled to ten instances. You can carry out scaling manually by using a slider. Figure 3-12 shows the Instance Range slider that you can use to increase the number of instances. This is also where you turn on Autoscaling for Standard plans.

FIGURE 3-12 The blade for scaling websites

The Standard level offers an autoscaling feature. This means that when the metric being measured attains a certain level, another instance of the website is started to help with the work. When the metric falls below a certain threshold, instances are lowered again. This is only available at the Standard level, so if this is something that you require, you need to run the website at Standard. You can also set scheduled times so that you could scale differently during the day from the night or weekdays to weekends. The metrics that you can use to scale Azure websites are CPU, Memory Percentage, Disk Queue, Length, HTTP Queue Length, Data In, and Data Out. You can select these settings from the Azure Preview Management Portal, but not the management portal. In addition to the metric, you can set a time limit (Over Past) and a Cool Down time for the scaling. The Over Past setting is used to alert that the metric is over the threshold for more than a given number of minutes. The Cool Down value is the number of minutes to wait before applying any other scaling rules. The settings for Over Past and Cool Down help to prevent the service from getting into a circumstance in which it is continually scaling up and down because of spikes in the metric being measured. Figure 3-13 shows the blade that you use to add a new metric for scaling the website up or down.

FIGURE 3-13 Website scaling metrics

You also can set scaling functionality by using a Windows PowerShell script to create or remove instances as well as by using the management portal.

MORE INFO SCALING WEBSITES

You can learn more about scaling websites at *http://azure.microsoft.com/en-us/documentation/articles/web-sites-scale/.*

WebJobs

Azure WebJobs are executables or scripts that run in a website to handle long-running jobs. The WebJob system can use any of the following file types:

- .cmd, .bat, .exe (using Windows cmd)
- .ps1 (using Windows PowerShell)
- .sh (using Bash)
- .php (using PHP)
- .py (using Python)
- .js (using Node)

If the program or script needs to have additional files, such as data files or dynamic-link libraries (DLLs), zip all of the files that are needed to run the program and then upload the zip file.

You can configure WebJobs to run in three modes: continuously, on a schedule, or on demand. Figure 3-14 depicts the setup inside of the Preview Management Portal. If the WebJob is set up to run as a continuous job, it needs to be written in an endless loop or by using the WebJob SDK. Visual Studio 2013 Community edition does include an option uin the Cloud Project Templates section for creating an Azure WebJob. This will be an application that uses the WebJob SDK by default.

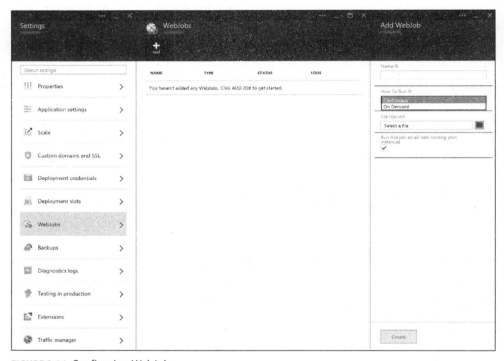

FIGURE 3-14 Configuring WebJob

For continuous tasks, it is recommended that you turn on the Always On feature on the Configure page for the website. This feature, available in Basic and Standard mode, prevents websites from being unloaded, even if they have been idle for some time. If your website is always loaded, your continuously running task might run more reliably.

WebJobs that are set to run continuously also will run on all instances of the website by default. This means that if you have two instances running, two copies of the WebJob will be running, as well. Using the preview portal, continuous jobs have the option of running on all instances or just on a single instance. WebJobs that are set to run on a schedule or on demand only run a single copy. Keep this in mind when planning WebJobs because the executable or script might be running more than one instance. Many applications cannot handle this type of usage and might need to be modified.

You can deploy WebJobs directly from the management portal, the Preview Management Portal, or even over FTP for the website. Each method is different. For example, using FTP, WebJobs are deployed in the App_Data/jobs folder under the root of the website. From there, WebJob will be in a folder using the name of the WebJob, in either a continuous or triggered folder based on how the WebJob is set up. One benefit of using FTP is that you can update the executable file or script without having to recreate the entire WebJob. The preview portal currently only supports creating WebJobs for continuous or on-demand deployment. To configure a WebJob on a schedule, you will need to use the standard management portal.

The WebJob will use the CPU and memory limits that you have set for the scale of the Web API/website. This means that if the WebJob is running too slowly, you could scale-up the website, and make more power available for it.

> **MORE INFO   WEBJOB SDK**
>
> You can learn more about the WebJob SDK at *http://azure.microsoft.com/en-us/ documentation/articles/websites-dotnet-webjobs-sdk-get-started/.*

Securing a Web API

There are several options to use when planning the security for a Web API. The authentication strategy should be planned to determine how users will be authenticated. You need to configure the Web API to use the authentication. The final step is to add the application to Azure AD so that it knows about the app and is aware that users need to be authenticated.

Planning the authentication strategy provides you with a few choices on how to secure it. Azure has multiple solutions for authentication, but you could always use custom solutions that you develop. It is recommended to use the standard authentication solutions, however, because they support many industry-standard methods. Each one has advantages depending on the needs for the strategy. Following are three Azure authentication solutions:

- **Azure AD Service**   A stand-alone directory or synchronized with an on-premises Active Directory.
- **Active Directory Federation Services (AD FS)**   Requests identity back to the on-premises Active Directory.
- **Azure Access Control Service (ACS)**   Can use multiple identity services to authenticate, including Active Directory.

The next step is to set up the Web API application to use authentication. In Visual Studio 2013, when you create the Web API application, there is a Change Authentication option. The two options that you want to look at are Organizational Accounts and Windows Authentication. If the application being developed is for your company Intranet only, use Windows Authentication. Intranet applications can also use the Organizational Account option and then set the authentication to be On-Premises. This will tie in to the on-premises Active Directory and perform similar to the Windows Authentication. The On-Premises option uses Windows Identity Foundation (WIF) instead of the standard Windows Authentication module. WIF allows access to query directory data and configure applications access in Active Directory. The Cloud – Single/Multiple Organization option allows for users to be authenticated using Azure AD or Windows Server Active Directory. These options also facilitate integration with Microsoft Office 365.

Figure 3-15 presents the steps to secure a website. When creating the website, you will need to register it with Azure AD, and you will need to include logic in the website to redirect a user to the sign-in page. The Azure AD tenant will give a token. That token is then given to the website to prove the user's identity.

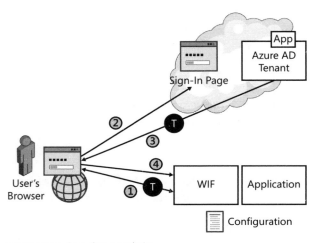

FIGURE 3-15 Securing a website

MORE INFO   **AZURE AD INTEGRATION**

You can learn more about Active Directory and Security in Chapter 2.

 Thought experiment

Moderation slowdown

In this thought experiment, apply what you've learned about this objective. You can find answers to these questions in the "Answers" section at the end of this chapter.

Nod Publishers has a website that offers a forum to which readers can post messages. The forum is an ASP.NET application. Each message is moderated before it is posted. The moderation is batched to notify people on the site when a number of new messages are available. The moderation step runs in a WebJob to go through all of the users and notify people of new messages and comments on their posts.

You have the following goals for the website:

- Employees who run moderation should not need to log on to the website, because they've already logged on to their work computer.
- Only employees should have access to the moderation system.

With this information in mind, answer the following questions:

1. The WebJob is taking two hours to run and the routine used to take three to four minutes. What can you do to speed up the WebJob?

2. To allow the employees to be able to use a Single Sign-On (SSO) logon, what will you need to do to the website?

3. The forum has gone viral on social media and adding new messages to the moderation process is taking longer than one minute. This is causing some of the messages to timeout. You can scale-up or scale-out the website. What are the benefits of each method?

Objective summary

- REST services are used by multiple platforms and devices for its simple usage over a standard HTTP connection. You can implement this in Azure by using ASP.NET Web API.
- You can use WebJobs on a Web API or Azure Websites to handle long-running tasks that need to be operate continuously, on a schedule, or on demand.
- Website scaling is available at Basic and Standard levels, but the Standard level is the only one to support autoscaling of the instances. The autoscaling feature can use CPU, Memory Percentage, Disk Queue, Length, Http Queue Length, Data In, and Data Out to determine if the website needs to be scaled up or down.
- You can use Azure AD security and for securing Web API applications running in Web Apps.

Objective review

Answer the following questions to test your knowledge of the information in this objective. You can find the answers to these questions and explanations of why each answer choice is correct or incorrect in the "Answers" section at the end of this chapter.

1. You want to configure a WebJob to run a job every morning. What two steps would you need to do to set up the WebJob?

    A. You can upload the WebJob using the management portal in the WebJob section for the website.

    B. Use the Azure Scheduler to set the dates and times for the WebJob to run.

    C. Zip up all of the files needed for the WebJob to run.

    D. WebJobs are only available on websites that run at the Basic level and above, so the website needs to be at the Basic level or higher.

2. You can install Web API applications on Azure websites. Which of the following is true for scaling the website on which it runs?

    A. Websites can scale up to a single 32-core instance for a single large site.

    B. Web API websites can scale-up to 4 cores.

    C. WebJobs on a website use the same CPU limit to which the website is set.

    D. If autoscaling is needed, the Standard plan level is required.

3. You develop a custom Web API called Orders for the Web API application. Which of the following are true?

    A. By default, the path for the Orders custom API will be http://<company>. azurewebsites.net/api/orders.

    B. You can modify the routing of the custom Web API.

    C. Custom Web APIs use SOAP protocols for communicating the data.

    D. You can use standard HTTP commands to route the calls to the correct functionality.

Objective 3.5: Design a data access strategy for hybrid applications

One feature that is very useful to many companies is the ability to connect to their on-premises network and servers. When this is implemented, VMs in Azure can access databases and other resources that are inside of the company's firewalls. You can use this when there are concerns with respect to keeping the data in Azure or if there is too much data to move up to Azure. No matter the reason for keeping the data on-premises, data can be accessed and used by other services in Azure.

Connect to on-premises data by using Azure Service Bus Relay

You can use Service Bus Relay to build hybrid applications that run in both an Azure datacenter and your own on-premises enterprise environment. Service Bus Relay facilitates this by enabling you to securely expose Windows Communication Foundation (WCF) services that reside within a corporate enterprise network to the public cloud. And it does this without your having to change incoming firewall rules or requiring intrusive changes to a corporate network infrastructure. Figure 3-16 shows the data flow using Service Bus Relay to access an on-premises WCF service.

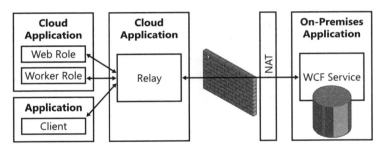

FIGURE 3-16 The Service Bus Relay architecture

Using Service Bus Relay, you can host WCF services within your existing enterprise environment. You can then delegate the task of listening for incoming sessions and requests to these WCF services to the Service Bus service running within Azure. This makes it possible for you to expose these services to application code running in Azure or to mobile workers or extranet partner environments. With Service Bus, you can securely control who can access these services at a detailed level. It provides a powerful and secure way to expose application functionality and data from your existing enterprise solutions and take advantage of it from the cloud.

Azure App Service BizTalk API Apps Hybrid Connections

Hybrid Connections provides an easy and convenient way to connect Azure Websites and Azure Mobile Services to on-premises resources. Hybrid Connections are a feature of App Service BizTalk API Apps. You must configure minimal TCP ports to access your network. Using BizTalk API Apps Hybrid Connections, you can make connections to on-premises resources that use static TCP ports, such as SQL Server, MySQL, Web APIs, and most web services. As of this writing, Hybrid Connections does not support services that use dynamic ports, such as SQL Express. Figure 3-17 shows the setup of a Hybrid Connection using BizTalk API Apps.

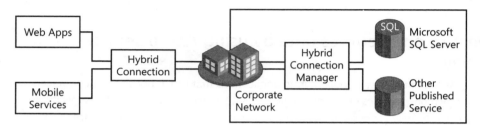

FIGURE 3-17 BizTalk API Apps Hybrid Connections

You can use Hybrid Connections with all frameworks supported by Azure Websites (.NET, PHP, Java, Python, and Node.js) and Azure Mobile Services (.NET, Node.js). A feature of using Hybrid Connections to work with resources that are on-premises is that when you move an application such as a website from on-premises to Web Apps, you do not need to change the connections string. Connecting to on-premises resources is exactly the same as if the web-site were running locally. This makes it possible for Web Apps to be moved to Azure faster because there are no changes required to access the needed data.

Enterprise administrators can keep control over what resources are available to the applications in Azure and can have access to other tools to help them monitor that access. Administrators can set up group policies to determine what resources applications can access through the Hybrid Connections. Event and audit logs can provide visibility into what resources are being accessed. Administrators also do not need to make changes to incoming firewall rules, because the traffic for the Hybrid Connections requires only outbound TCP and HTTP connectivity. Many administrators are reluctant to open up additional ports for security issues. Table 3-4 lists the ports that Hybrid Connections uses.

TABLE 3-4 TCP ports used by Hybrid Connections

Port	Why
80	HTTP port; used for certificate validation.
443	HTTPS port.
5671	Used to connect to Azure. If TCP port 5671 is unavailable, TCP port 443 is used.
9352	Used to push and pull data. If TCP port 9352 is unavailable, TCP port 443 is used.

To configure the BizTalk API Apps Hybrid Connections, follow these steps:

1. Sign in to the management portal.

2. On the left side, go to BizTalk API Apps.

3. Click the Hybrid Connections tab.

4. Select Add, or, if you do not already have a connection defined, click Create A Hybrid Connection.

5. Install the Hybrid Connection Manager on-premises but using the On-Premises Setup button in the taskbar while looking at the new Hybrid Connection.

6. Follow the steps for the Hybrid Connection Manager setup and connect it to the Biz-Talk service in Azure.

EXAM TIP

You can set up a Hybrid Data Connector in BizTalk API Apps to connect a mobile service or website to a database that is on-premises.

MORE INFO **HYBRID CONNECTIONS**

You can learn more about the .NET on-premises/cloud hybrid application using Service Bus Relay at *http://azure.microsoft.com/en-us/documentation/articles/cloud-services-dotnet-hybrid-app-using-service-bus-relay/.*

Web Apps virtual private network capability

Web Apps has the ability to integrate directly into Azure Virtual Network as well as to Hybrid Connections. This does not allow you to put the website into the Virtual Network, but it does allow for the website to reference other services in the Virtual Network. If the Virtual Network is connected to an on-premises network with a site-to-site virtual private network (VPN), the website can access all of the on-premises systems such as databases.

Azure ExpressRoute is another option that you can use to connect resources in Azure to the corporate network. This is a feature that uses an ExpressRoute Partner to set up a direct connection between your corporate WAN and Azure. This is the fastest connection to create a Hybrid Connection.

MORE INFO **WEB APPS VPN**

You can learn more about Web Apps Virtual Network integration at *http://azure.microsoft.com/blog/2014/09/15/azure-websites-virtual-network-integration/.*

Identify constraints for connectivity with VPN

When connecting via VPN to other networks, the maximum number of networks to which you can connect is 10. One Virtual Network can connect to six on-premises sites as well as four other virtual networks. This makes it possible for a company to connect to multiple sites around the world, and they can all share the Virtual Network.

Identify options for domain-joining Azure Virtual Machines and Cloud Services

You can add Virtual Machines and Cloud Services to a domain. These have different methods to join a domain even though a Cloud Service has a Virtual Machine underneath to run on.

You can add a cloud service—either a web or worker role—to an existing domain in a couple of ways: by using a Windows PowerShell script, or by adding code to the cloud service itself to connect to the domain. Windows PowerShell scripting is more secure, but adding the code to the cloud service itself is more flexible. For example, there is no way to remove a cloud service from a domain by using Windows PowerShell, but you can do it in the cloud service itself.

With the first method, you define the Windows PowerShell script as a Startup Task. This script runs in an elevated mode when the cloud service starts. This means that the cloud service does not need to be run in an elevated mode, because the script does it, which by extension makes the Startup Task method more secure.

Using the second method, you add code to the *RoleEntryPoint* of the cloud service to have it add itself to the domain. To do this step, the cloud service needs to be running in an elevated mode. This is not a great practice, because services like this typically do not run with administrator or elevated permissions. Giving elevated permissions is a practice that needs to be reviewed carefully to watch out for issues that a standard process could not perform.

You also can add Virtual Machines to a domain. You can do this in a couple of ways. You can log on to the VM and add it to the domain just like you would do with a local machine on the network. The second way is to use a Windows PowerShell script to add a VM to the domain during creation. The benefit of using this method is that there is no need for a second step to manually enter each VM into the domain. System administrators like to automate any process they can with scripting, and adding the VM to the domain at creation is something that lends itself well to scripting. If the company is creating many VMs, this will save a lot of time and effort.

MORE INFO **CONNECTING TO A DOMAIN**

You can learn more about the how to join web and worker roles to a domain in the same Virtual Network at *https://code.msdn.microsoft.com/windowsazure/How-to-join-web-and-worker-3a72db70*. To learn more about the domain joining Virtual Machines, go to *https://gallery.technet.microsoft.com/scriptcenter/Domain-Joining-Windows-fefe7039*.

Thought experiment
A sensitive move to the cloud

In this thought experiment, apply what you've learned about this objective. You can find answers to these questions in the "Answers" section at the end of this chapter.

Lamna Healthcare Company is looking to move some of its internal corporate web applications into Azure. Lamna is a small company, but it is growing in remote areas away from its main office. The web applications need to be available for use in the remotes offices as well as in its employees' homes.

You have the following constraints for the website:

- The database cannot be moved into Azure because of sensitive data.
- The corporate IT manager will not open any other ports to the Internet, except port 80 for web traffic.
- The IT group has been downsized over the years and cannot take the time to add each Azure VM to the domain, and they refuse to give developers the permissions to do this directly.

With this information in mind, answer the following questions:

1. One developer has the idea of using Service Bus Relay to get at the data within the firewall, the lead developer is not sure that this is the best approach. When would a Service Bus Relay be the best way and when would it not?
2. Can the services within Azure still use internal data over just port 80?
3. How can you add VMs to the domain, given these constraints?

Objective summary

- Service Bus Relay exposes a WCF service that is behind a firewall to services within Azure.

- BizTalk API Apps Hybrid Connections makes it possible for Mobile Services, Cloud Services, and Virtual Machines to have access to on-premises information directly over a VPN or ExpressRoute connection.

Objective review

Answer the following questions to test your knowledge of the information in this objective. You can find the answers to these questions and explanations of why each answer choice is correct or incorrect in the "Answers" section at the end of this chapter.

1. To expose a WCF web service from within your firewall, what service should you use in Azure?

   A. Service Bus Queue

   B. Service Bus Relay

   C. Service Bus Topics

   D. Service Bus Event Hubs

2. You need to add a cloud service to a domain. What steps would add the service to the domain? (Each answer is a separate solution)

   A. In the OnStart method of the cloud service, add code to add the cloud service to the domain. The cloud service needs to be running in a limited mode.

   B. In the OnStart method of the cloud service, add code to add the cloud service to the domain. The cloud service needs to be running in an elevated mode.

   C. Create a Startup Task and add the cloud service to the domain. Run this in elevated mode.

   D. Create a Startup Task and add the cloud service to the domain. Run this in limited mode.

3. Using BizTalk API Apps Hybrid Connections, to which of the following can Azure connect utilizing their standard setups?

   A. SQL Server

   B. SQL Server Express

   C. MySQL

   D. Web Services

Objective 3.6: Design a media solution

Azure Media Services gives you the ability to create solutions that can stream videos over the Internet. Video contributes up to 57 percent of all Internet traffic. People share or watch videos constantly. There are many different types of video traffic from companies such as YouTube that stream videos, or corporations like Microsoft that stream live events over the web. Each of these types of video services have different features, such as live streaming, saving existing progress in a program, and limiting the videos to authorized users. Using Media Services, companies can create the same type of systems without an in-house capability to support.

> **This section covers the following topics:**
> - Azure Media Services overview
> - Key components of Media Services

Azure Media Services overview

Media Services is an extensible PaaS offering that you can use to build scalable media management and delivery applications. With Media Services you can securely upload, store, encode, and package video or audio content for both on-demand and live streaming delivery to various device endpoints (for example, TV, PCs, and mobile devices).

You can build entire end-to-end workflows using Media Services. You can also choose to use third-party components for some parts of your workflow. For example, you could encode using a third-party encoder and then upload, protect, package, and deliver using Media Services. Figure 3-18 shows the major components in Media Services in the typical order in which they are used in a standard workflow.

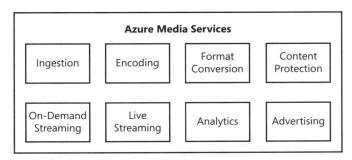

FIGURE 3-18 A sample Media Services workflow

MORE INFO AZURE MEDIA SERVICES

You can learn more about the Media Services at *http://azure.microsoft.com/en-us/develop/media-services/*.

Key components of Media Services

Media Services is a set of many components that function together to create workflows to serve your media. You can create workflows to provide video on demand, video streaming, or the ability to monitor the work being done. Figure 3-19 shows the various components that comprise Media Services.

Typically, video is encoded and stored in the format in which it will be streamed or downloaded. This means that more storage and processing is needed when the assets are uploaded to Media Services because they might be packaged with HLS for users on iOS and Android, but they might use Smooth Streaming on Xbox and Windows. Dynamic Packaging is a feature of Media Services by which you can skip the packaging step and package the asset on the fly, based on the platform that is requesting it.

For many companies, security of the media they are streaming is very important. Companies such as Netflix charge people to view its content, and it wants to prevent piracy, as well. For other companies, such as one providing a web broadcast of a free event, piracy is not as big of a concern. In either case, there needs to be protection from Man-in-the-Middle type attacks. With this type of attack, malicious individuals can inject their own data into what is being sent, or modify the original content. Media Services supports two types of security models: an AES Clear Key dynamic encryption, and a Digital Rights Management (DRM) technology.

AES Clear Key dynamic encryption is a basic "lite" encryption. This is done on-the-wire and is widely known as *symmetric AES encryption*. When using AES, there can be authentication restrictions in place. The first type is an *open restriction*. With an open restriction, the client asks for a clear key, and that is what is sent to the player and used to decrypt content. This means that it is a player and a client that is trusted. The second way is to use a *token restriction*. Media Services does not provide its own token system; instead, it uses other Secure Token Systems (STS) providers. Tokens can be in the Simple Web Token (SWT) format or the JSON Web Token (JWT) format. You can create a custom STS or use the Azure ACS to create the tokens. The tokens are then sent to Media Services, and the delivery service will then provide an encryption key if the token is valid for the content.

The second security option is to use a DRM technology, *PlayReady*. With DRM technology, you can define a restrictive licensing agreement to manage user access rights to the content. This can then support additional business models, such as a paid video streaming service. Before content is uploaded to Media Services, it is pre-encrypted by the PlayReady system using your license, content keys, and a Key ID. This is all done before the file is moved into storage. The client then asks for a license from the PlayReady server to allow the user access to the content. Media Services just serves up the encrypted file to the clients; it is decoded using the license from PlayReady. This security method uses common encryption scheme (CENC) to encrypt to the smooth streaming content.

Live Streaming

Another feature that Media Services supports is live streaming of content. This feature was used to stream the 2014 Winter Olympic games. This included live video encoding and streaming, access from web and mobile devices, and capacity for more than 100 million viewers. The United States versus Canada hockey game boasted 2.1 million concurrent HD viewers. One problem that many companies have when trying to create a live-streaming system is the capital expenses to purchase servers and other support systems. Media Services facilitates this without the crushing capital expenses, and companies can ramp up to a global scale quickly. There is yet one more benefit: When the need is over, the system can be removed from your Media Services platform immediately.

The first step to set up live streaming is to configure a channel to use to ingest the live stream. When a channel is created, it will provide two URLs to be used in the next steps. The first is an Ingest URL. You can set the protocol on this URL to either RTMP or to Fragmented MP4. The second URL is a Preview URL. With the Preview URL, you can preview what the stream is before it is published.

After the channel is set up, you must add a program to it. The program will specify the duration of an archive window as well as the encryption method for the streaming. When the program is configured and published, the live streaming can be viewed. The setting for the name of the asset for the live stream in the program will be created in the Content section of Media Services.

Azure Media Indexer

An additional service that is available in Media Services is the Media Indexer. Using the Media Indexer, you can make content of your media files searchable and generate a full-text transcript for closed captioning and keywords. You can also index files that are publically available on the Internet by specifying URLs of the files in the manifest file. You can run the Media Indexer on a single content file or you can batch it to handle large numbers of files.

An indexing job generates various output files, which include a score for the indexing job based on how recognizable the speech in the source video is. You can use the value to screen output files for usability. A low score would mean poor indexing results due to audio quality. Background music is something that could reduce how well the speech is recognized.

Monitoring Services

To monitor the data and the Media Services, you first need to turn on monitoring for the Blob container. After you do this, you can use the dashboard for the Media Services to keep an eye on information such as Encoder Data In, Encoder Data Out, Failed Tasks, Queued Jobs,

Streaming Data Out, Streaming HTTP Errors, and Streaming Requests. You can view the last six hours up to the last seven days of data.

> **MORE INFO**   **AZURE MEDIA SERVICES LIVE STREAMING**
>
> You can learn more about Azure Media Services live streaming at *http://azure.microsoft. com/blog/2014/09/10/getting-started-with-live-streaming-using-the-azure-management-portal/*.

 Thought experiment

Streaming to the world

In this thought experiment, apply what you've learned about this objective. You can find answers to these questions in the "Answers" section at the end of this chapter.

Southridge Video is covering a worldwide competition and would like to stream the finals live around the world. It also has existing videos of the competitors from previous rounds that it would like to have available for users to stream from its website. Southridge Video does not have a large IT staff and is unfamiliar with what it takes to stream this event or the videos. It is looking to Azure to help set this up.

You have the following goals for the broadcast:

- The broadcast needs to be available around the world.
- The company would like to have the stream saved for future use on its website and in marketing material for future events.
- The target audience for streaming the event should be any mobile or desktop system.

With this information in mind, answer the following questions:

1. When creating a live-streaming system for this, the program has the option for encoding with no encryption, AES, or PlayReady DRM encoding. Would there be any benefits for using a lower level of security?

2. You are looking at either packaging the videos for multiple platforms and formats or using the Dynamic Packaging system. What would be a benefit for each?

3. Because this is going to be a global broadcast, Southridge would like to have close captioning and a full text transcription available in multiple languages. How can Azure facilitate this?

Objective summary

- You can use Media Services to deliver video for download or for streaming.
- You can use Media Services to encode and stream live video.
- Media Services supports dynamic encoding to any output needed.

Objective review

Answer the following questions to test your knowledge of the information in this objective. You can find the answers to these questions and explanations of why each answer choice is correct or incorrect in the "Answers" section at the end of this chapter.

1. For companies delivering large quantities of digestible media, which is the best way for them to organize and classify media?

    A. Using the Media Indexer

    B. Searching by job IDs

    C. Using the Content pane in the Media Services subscription.

    D. Using channels to organize the media content

2. Dynamic packaging is an indispensable feature in Media Services because it provides: (Choose all that apply.)

    A. On-the-fly encryption for media assets

    B. Support for multiple platforms

    C. On-the-fly encoding for media assets

    D. A cheaper way of supplying media by requiring less space.

3. Dynamic Encryption supports which encryption methods that are built in to Media Services? (Choose all that apply.)

    A. AES

    B. PlayReady DRM

    C. RMTP

    D. FairPlay

4. What must companies consider when estimating cost with Media Services?

    A. Encoding, streaming, content protection, dynamic packaging

    B. Encoding, streaming, content protection

    C. Encoding, streaming, data storage

    D. Encoding, data storage, streaming, content protection

Answers

This section contains the solutions to the thought experiments and answers to the objective review questions in this chapter.

Objective 3.1: Thought experiment

1. To pick the correct NoSQL platform for the conversion, the data and how it is looked at needs to be evaluated. Table storage accommodates a partition and row for pulling in data, whereas DocumentDB can provide indexing on any and all fields. Table storage will be cheaper, but DocumentDB can provide more flexibility.

2. DocumentDB can operate at a speed of 2,000 reads/second. From a speed standpoint, this might be able to support the existing platform. DocumentDB does scale-up linearly by purchasing more capacity units. But, given the current size of the database, a SQL Database running as a Basic plan would work for the data amount and growth for years to come. A Basic plan SQL Database runs at the cost of $5/month, whereas each DocumentDB capacity unit costs $45/month. Speed will probably work, but cost would not be improved by moving to DocumentDB.

3. Blob storage can be totally open for anyone to use any of the files, but this is exactly the opposite of what the company wants. To really stop access to the files, you can create and use an SAS. The nice thing about this is that you can generate a new access key, rendering the previous SAS invalid. This way the data can be protected and controlled from the corporate side.

Objective 3.1: Review

1. **Correct answer:** C

    A. **Incorrect:** S1 supports a maximum of 900 connections.

    B. **Incorrect:** Basic supports a maximum of 300 connections.

    C. **Correct:** P2 supports up to 4,800 connections, and even though it is the most expensive option listed, it is the only one that will provide the needed performance.

    D. **Incorrect:** S0 supports up to 600 connections.

2. **Correct answer:** B

    A. **Incorrect:** A mobile service could handle access to this type of data and be used for uploading of data such as a document; however, uploading the document to a Storage account into something like Blob storage is preferred to having the documents inside of a database.

    B. **Correct:** SAS can provide permissions and time limits for access to a Storage account.

    C. **Incorrect:** Azure AD can provide users with permissions for things, but there is no option to set time limits for Storage accounts.

D. **Incorrect:** Opening the container does not impose time limits on the Storage account. This is not a good practice when people are uploading documents that others could then read.

3. **Correct answers:** B and D

A. **Incorrect:** MySQL is not a Microsoft product, but you can still use it with in Azure.

B. **Correct:** Azure VMs are just like on-premises VMs, and you can install anything on them, including your own database solution, such as MySQL.

C. **Incorrect:** Converting all of the data and access to the database from MySQL to SQL Database might be an option, but it will take time and effort to perform the conversion.

D. **Correct:** ClearDB is an option in the Azure Marketplace to provide MySQL services.

Objective 3.2: Thought experiment

1. Mobile Services can use any database in any region as a data-storage solution. The issue is that if it is not in the same region, there can be performance degradation and possibly various costs. So, it does not need to be moved, but it might be the best choice to move it to help with performance.

2. You can change the WCF service to call the new mobile service to get all of the data. This way all traffic is going through the mobile service. Then, each mobile application can be updated to use the new mobile service instead of the WCF service. The WCF service might need to be up for a while after the conversion to support the users who have not upgraded. You can monitor this service and scale it down in size over time, and then eventually remove it.

3. To determine if custom APIs will be needed in the new mobile service, you will need to review the WCF service to see if it has things that are not just data storage, but perform functionality, as well. You could move these to a custom API. However, when you review the dataflows for the service, it might be that the calls that would be in a custom API could be methods called inside of the standard CRUD calls to the database itself.

Objective 3.2: Review

1. **Correct answers:** B and C

A. **Incorrect:** Forcing a mobile-device user to have a network connection before it will function correctly is not the best answer. You could store data locally first and synchronize it with the online database later.

B. **Correct:** With the offline synchronization capabilities in Mobile Services, the application can save data as if it were connected, even if it is not. When a network connection is restored, data can be uploaded and downloaded as needed.

C. **Correct:** Serializing the data to a local file has always been an option on a mobile device when there is no connection. This method would need additional code to do all of the serialization and management of the local data compared to the online data. This could be a complex solution depending on the data.

D. **Incorrect:** The Data Sync feature on SQL Database makes it possible for you to copy data from one SQL Database to another, including on-premises. This has nothing to do with offline mobile data.

2. **Correct answers:** B and C

A. **Incorrect:** You can tie Mobile Services into Facebook for authentication, but the app is for internal employees only, and not everyone will use Facebook.

B. **Correct:** Mobile Services can tie into social networks as well as Azure AD for authentication. This is part of the solution for working with corporate users.

C. **Correct:** By tying Azure AD to the company's Active Directory, corporate users can be validated.

D. **Incorrect:** You can tie Mobile Services into social networks for authentication, but the app is for internal employees only, and not everyone uses social networks.

3. **Correct answers:** C

A. **Incorrect:** The Free tier of Mobile Services does not support autoscaling.

B. **Incorrect:** Mobile Services are not set up to be run in a VM like this.

C. **Correct:** The Standard tier of Mobile Services has support for autoscaling the service based on API calls.

D. **Incorrect:** Manually adjusting the size of the service is what had to be done before the autoscaling features were in place.

4. **Correct answer:** C

A. **Incorrect:** Changing the backend of a .NET-based Mobile Service is supported; however, Node.js scripts can be modified to also change the Node.js version.

B. **Incorrect:** Changing the backend of a Node.js-based Mobile Service is supported, but when changing the scripts, however, code can be modified to also change the .NET version.

C. **Correct:** You can set up Mobile Services to have SQL Database, Table storage, or MongoDB as a data storage.

D. **Incorrect:** You can set up Mobile Services to have SQL Database, Table storage, or MongoDB as a data storage.

5. **Correct answers:** A and D

   A. **Correct:** Because the WCF web service cannot be changed to use the mobile service, you will need to change the applications to point to the new mobile service.

   B. **Incorrect:** The database can be in a different region than the mobile service, so it is not a required step. Performance characteristics of the mobile service might mean that it must move, but not just to connect to the database.

   C. **Incorrect:** The north-central United States region does not currently support Mobile Services.

   D. **Correct:** The mobile service cannot be created in the north-central United States region; it will need to be created in a different region.

Objective 3.3: Thought experiment

1. The WCF web service can actually register devices for them by using the push connection string from the service for their platform. This means that the app itself will not need to register or unregister; the existing service will do it for them.

2. Mobile Services include access to the notification hubs at the same level; for example, the Free tier of Mobile Services include the free level of notification hubs, Basic Mobile Services include Basic notification hubs, and Standard includes Standard. To achieve higher than 99 percent availability in the mobile service, you need to use a Basic instance or higher. The same holds true for notification hubs. This does not mean that 99.9 percent of the push notifications will be received. Notifications can fail for multiple reasons, such as the device is turned off or the application was removed from the device but the app developer forgot to turn off notifications during the uninstall process. The SLA is for the availability of the service.

3. The push notification in Mobile Services would be a cheaper solution, but all of the tags to say what location and stores need to be sent to a user are then stored in your backend code. Using notification hubs, tags are set with the service, and then sending is much simpler.

Objective 3.3: Review

1. **Correct answer:** B

   A. **Incorrect:** Manually tracking the users in a group and pushing to them separately will stress the resources and time for running the Mobile Service.

   B. **Correct:** Notification hubs can push to tags that the users have signed up to monitor.

   C. **Incorrect:** The basic push notifications in mobile services do not support tags to define the groups of users.

   D. **Incorrect:** You can add SignalR integration .NET-based Mobile Services, it has nothing to do with push notifications to groups.

2. **Correct answers:** C and D

   A. **Incorrect:** The push notification and notification hub systems talk to the separate notification systems of each platform.

   B. **Incorrect:** The notifications can also be badge and raw data. Notifications are not limited to just pop-ups or toast.

   C. **Correct:** The push notification and notification hub systems talk to the separate notification systems of each platform.

   D. **Correct:** You can create custom templates in XML or JSON for extra flexibility.

3. **Correct answers:** A, C, and D

   A. **Correct:** Sending a single notification that a reply was made is a good use of push notifications.

   B. **Incorrect:** Sending every data point as a notification would be too much data to send. You could wrap this up to tell the user that there is new data to review, but not for every point.

   C. **Correct:** Notifying a group of users who are waiting for a stock price to hit a certain level is a good use. Notifications are grouped by stock and the price they are looking for.

   D. **Correct:** An individual push notification to a game player that they were sent a chat message is how many games use this feature today.

Objective 3.4: Thought experiment

1. To make a WebJob run faster, remember that it uses the CPU and memory that the website is set to use. You could scale-up the website to use a larger plan or you could scale-out to let it run on more instances. Continuous WebJobs run on every instance on which the website is running. You will need to ensure that if you scale-up to more instances, your WebJob can handle being run more than once at a time. If you are running the WebJob on demand or on a schedule, it only runs in a single instance selected for load balancing by Azure. The only way to speed that up is a larger plan for the website.

2. The easiest way to add a Single Sign-On (SSO) capability to a website is to configure it when you create it the website. You can change the security settings during creation and point to an organizational account for authentication. A dialog box opens, in which you can turn on SSO capability.

3. You can scale-up Web Apps running a Web API application to a larger data plan and also scale to multiple instances. WebJobs behave differently when scaling up or scaling out, and if these are used, you will need to determine which method is best for your Web API application. You will need to test your application to ensure what size works best for the Azure website. You can monitor the CPU and memory usage as well as network traffic. This can lead you to the size to use. Keep in mind that the Standard

level of Web Apps includes autoscaling to add new instances based on a metric. Scaling up and down automatically to handle your traffic is one benefit of having a larger plan for the website.

Objective 3.4: Review

1. **Correct answers:** A and C

    A. **Correct:** The management portal has a WebJobs section under Websites in which you can set up a new WebJob.

    B. **Incorrect:** You cannot use Azure Scheduler for configuring WebJobs.

    C. **Correct:** All of the needed files must be included in the Zip file that is uploaded.

    D. **Incorrect:** You can run WebJobs on the Free, Shared, Basic, and Standard plans for Web Apps.

2. **Correct answers:** B, C, and D

    A. **Incorrect:** Azure websites can scale up only to a large-sized instance (four cores). To scale beyond four cores, you could set up the website as a Web Role that can scale beyond four cores.

    B. **Correct:** You can scale website instances from one core to as many as four cores per instance.

    C. **Correct:** WebJobs share the CPU that the website is set to and can perform at a limited speed when at the Free or Shared level.

    D. **Correct:** Standard level is the only level to have autoscaling. The Basic level can scale, but you must do it manually.

3. **Correct answers:** A, B, and D

    A. **Correct:** The default path for a custom Web API is /api/Controller name, so this is true.

    B. **Correct:** Using the *RoutePrefix* and *Route* attributes, you can change the route to anything that is required instead of the default values.

    C. **Incorrect:** Custom Web API creates a RESTful service that uses JSON and not a SOAP protocol.

    D. **Correct:** The standard HTTP commands, GET, PUT, POST, and DELETE, are used to access the customer Web API.

Objective 3.5: Thought experiment

1. Service Bus Relays allow access to data behind the firewall through a WCF web service. This does not provide a direct connection to any database. WCF services can talk to an enterprise database within the firewall, but this is an extra step and would need to be maintained. Changes to database schemas might affect the service, as well.

2. Using port 80 will not use an HTTPS connection. Because security is critical for this application, HTTPS should be required. The IT manager would have to open at least port 443 as well as port 80.

3. The developers should ask the IT group to write a Windows PowerShell script to allow creation of a new VM in Azure to automatically be tied to the domain. The IT group can manage the Windows PowerShell so that the developers do not get access to the passwords via the script. This also allows the IT group to change the passwords and still manage the VM creation.

Objective 3.5: Review

1. **Correct answer:** B

   A. **Incorrect:** Service Bus Queues broker message communication from multiple clients to a single receiver. The receiver gets the messages in the order in which they were received in the queue. This is not a WCF service.

   B. **Correct:** With Service Bus Relay, you can securely expose a WCF service from behind a firewall.

   C. **Incorrect:** Service Bus Topics support a pub/sub messaging communication model, not a WCF web service.

   D. **Incorrect:** Service Bus Event Hubs provide an AMQP communications channel to send messages. This is not a WCF service.

2. **Correct answers:** B and C

   A. **Incorrect:** The cloud service would need to be running in elevated mode to have permission to add the service to the domain.

   B. **Correct:** Elevated mode is needed for this to work correctly.

   C. **Correct:** Elevated mode is needed for this to work correctly.

   D. **Incorrect:** The Startup Task would need to be running in elevated mode to have permissions to add the service to the domain.

3. **Correct answers:** A, C, and D

   A. **Correct:** SQL Server uses static ports for communications. You can use this over the Hybrid Connection.

   B. **Incorrect:** SQL Server Express uses dynamic ports for communications. You cannot use this over the Hybrid Connection. Names instances of SQL Express can use a static address if TCP is turned on first.

   C. **Correct:** MySQL uses static ports for communications. You can use this over the Hybrid Connection.

   D. **Correct:** Web Services use static ports for communications. You can use this over the Hybrid Connection.

Objective 3.6: Thought experiment

1. Lower levels of security would be a cheaper solution; however, the live stream is then susceptible to a Man-in-the-Middle attack, wherein malicious users can add their own content or change your content. Using AES encoding is a lower-cost solution to prevent this type of hacking.

2. Using a Dynamic Packaging system will save on storage costs because the asset will be converted to the size and platform that is being requested. With traditional encoding and packaging, you can have the needed sizes already converted and waiting for consumption. Multiple sizes will be stored and available. You can use the free version of the encoder to reduce costs. You will need to have at least one reserved streaming unit to enable Dynamic Packaging.

3. For translating the event, there are a number of options that Southridge has available. Videos could be sent to a translation service directly for a translation. The other option that can help is using Media Indexer. The Media Indexer can provide a full transcript and closed captioning files for the event. A translation service could use this transcript to provide any language needed. The same can be done for the closed captioning files.

Objective 3.6: Review

1. **Correct answer**: A
   A. **Correct:** Using the Media Indexer is the most comprehensive way to organize and classify media. It is provided as a feature within Media Services.
   B. **Incorrect:** Searching by Job ID is not a way to organize because jobs are volatile.
   C. **Incorrect:** Although it is possible to use the Content pane to view media, it is not a way to organize it.
   D. **Incorrect:** Channels are a good way to determine where media is displayed and through which outlets.

2. **Correct answers:** B, C, and D
   A. **Incorrect:** This is a feature of dynamic encryption.
   B. **Correct:** Dynamic Packaging, by definition, offers support for multiple platforms.
   C. **Correct:** Dynamic Packaging functions by encoding for the platform on demand on the server end.
   D. **Correct:** Dynamic Packaging makes cheaper storage possible by requiring only one copy of the media asset to cast to multiple protocols.

3. **Correct answers:** A and B

   A. **Correct:** AES Clear Key encryption is supported. The method trusts the end user with a key.

   B. **Correct:** PlayReady DRM encryption is supported. This is much more secure and decrypted at a very low level (on the operating system).

   C. **Incorrect:** RMTP is not an encryption method; it is one of many streaming protocols.

   D. **Incorrect:** Fairplay is DRM encryption that is not supported but is used in iTunes.

4. **Correct answer:** D

   A. **Incorrect:** Dynamic Packaging does not incur cost.

   B. **Incorrect:** It lacks Data Storage as a feature.

   C. **Incorrect:** It lacks Content Protection as a feature.

   D. **Correct:** All these features are ones that should be considered when estimating the cost for Media Services.

Design an advanced application

The cloud has revolutionized the software industry by making tremendous amounts of compute and storage resources readily available to developers. Countless resource-demanding scenarios are becoming reality. And, the scale of compute and storage is increasing exponentially. The cloud movement brings new opportunities as well as great challenges to developers and enterprises alike. To effectively take advantage of these resources at scale is becoming a day-to-day challenge that all organizations must face.

A successful cloud-based application is built on top of a successful partnership between the application author and the cloud. The application author brings quality of code, and the cloud brings Quality of Service (QoS). The combination of the two makes possible reliable, scalable, efficient, and innovative applications.

This chapter focuses on application design, which is essential for application architects to avail themselves of the QoS opportunities brought by cloud. You often hear about how the cloud is scalable and available. However, this doesn't mean that an application automatically will be available and scalable on the cloud. You need to design applications to take advantage of these offerings. This chapter covers several key scenarios as well as some important design patterns that can help you to design your applications for the cloud. The discussions will be focused mostly on creating high-quality services such as compute-intensive applications and long-running services. You'll also learn how to pick different Microsoft Azure services such as storage service and incorporate them in your solutions.

Objectives in this chapter:

- Objective 4.1: Create compute-intensive applications
- Objective 4.2: Create long-running applications
- Objective 4.3: Select the appropriate storage option
- Objective 4.4: Integrate Azure services in a solution

Objective 4.1: Create compute-intensive applications

As the name suggests, the purpose of *Big Compute* is to perform a lot of computational tasks in a distributed yet coordinated fashion. Typical Big Compute workloads include simulation (such as fluid-dynamics simulation), analysis (such as genome search), and modeling (such as risk modeling), and so on. These often require a large number of compute hours.

Microsoft Azure provides both hardware and software resources with which you can run large-scale batch jobs in parallel in the cloud. Instead of managing expensive infrastructure yourself at your own datacenters, you can dynamically request compute resources at any time, perform compute tasks on them, and then release them to avoid extra costs.

> **This section covers the following topics:**
> - Using Azure in a high-performance computing environment
> - Using Azure Batch
> - Understanding Azure Batch Apps
> - Implementing the Competing Consumers pattern

> **MORE INFO** **BIG COMPUTE AND BIG DATA**
>
> Big Compute and Big Data are often mentioned together, and the boundary between the two isn't always clear. Indeed, many applications need to perform complex operations on large amounts of data. To distinguish the two, you need to remember that they have different focus. Big Compute is concerned with using raw computing power to perform complex computing tasks, whereas Big Data is about an entire data pipeline that includes data ingress, transform, storage, analysis, and presentation.

Using Azure in a high-performance computing environment

Azure brings raw computing power to your high-performance computing (HPC) applications with high-performance servers, storages solutions, and networks. On the other hand, if you already have computing clusters on-premises, with Azure you can dynamically extend these clusters to the cloud when you need additional resources to handle more complex computing tasks.

Compute-intensive instances

Azure's A8, A9, A10, and A11 virtual machine (VM) sizes are tailored specifically for HPC workloads. They combine high-speed, multicore CPUs and large amounts of memory, and they are connected by extremely fast networks. Table 4-1 shows the specifications of these four VM types.

TABLE 4-1 A8, A9, A10, and A11 compute-intensive instance specifications

Attribute	CPU	Memory	Network
A8	Intel Xeon E5-2670 8 cores @ 2.6 GHz	DDR3-1,600 MHz 56 GB	10 Gbps Ethernet 32 Gbps backend, RDMA capable
A9	Intel Xeon E5-2670 16 cores @ 2.6 GHz	DDR3-1,600 MHz 112 GB	10 Gbps Ethernet 32 Gbps backbone, RDMA capable
A10	Intel Xeon E5-2670 8 cores @ 2.6 GHz	DDR3-1,600 MHz 56 GB	10 Gbps Ethernet
A11	Intel Xeon E5-2670 16 cores @ 2.6 GHz	DDR3-1,600 MHz 112 GB	10 Gbps Ethernet

Each A8 and A9 instance is equipped with two network adapters; one connects to a 10 Gbps Ethernet backbone for accessing external services and the Internet, and another connects to a 32 Gbps backbone (through Mellanox QDR InfiniBand) with Remote Direct Memory Access (RDMA) capability for instance communication. A10 and A11 instances are designed for so-called *parametric*, or *embarrassingly parallel*, applications that don't require constant, low-latency communication among nodes.

Another way that Azure handles HPC environments is through its support for Intel MPI Library. Intel MPI Library is designed to boost the performance of applications running on clusters that are based on Intel architecture. It is widely used by many HPC applications and takes advantages of Azure's low-latency network and RDMA capabilities.

Constructing an HPC cluster

An HPC cluster comprises a head node and a number of compute nodes. The head node is responsible for managing the cluster, and the compute nodes run compute jobs. The nodes in a cluster are often connected to one another on a private, low-latency network because they need frequent network communications to coordinate the workloads on the cluster.

You can use Microsoft HPC Pack to create, manage, and run HPC applications on an HPC cluster. The cluster can be made up of dedicated on-premises servers, part-time servers, VMs in the cloud, and even workstations. As of this writing, the latest version of HPC Pack is HPC Pack 2012 R2 Update 1, which you can download from the Microsoft Download Center.

Figure 4-1 shows a simple HPC cluster deployment on Azure.

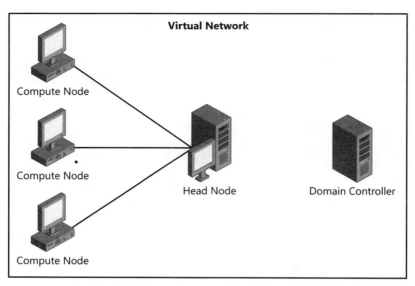

FIGURE 4-1 A simple HPC cluster on Azure

The following is a list of high-level steps for configuring an HPC cluster head node in Azure:

1. Create a virtual network.
2. Create a domain controller on the virtual network.
3. Create a domain user account that you'll use to configure the cluster.
4. Create a VM as the head node.
5. Add the domain user account to the local Administrators group.
6. Install and configure HPC Pack on the head node.
7. Complete the Deployment To-Do List in the HPC Cluster Manager.

Azure Premium storage and large VM instances

There are many existing compute-intensive applications that enterprises would like to migrate to the cloud. However, these enterprises don't want to take on the extra cost and risk to redesign and reimplement these applications. For such lift-and-ship scenarios, Azure provides faster storage options and bigger VM sizes so that you can deploy and scale-up these applications on Azure without any code changes.

Premium storage is designed to provide sustained high I/O performance using solid-state drives (SSDs). Premium storage drives provide up to 5,000 I/O operations per second (IOPS) with 200 megabits per second (Mbps) throughput. With the 16-core DS series VMs, you can attach up to 32 TB of data disks and achieve more than 50,000 IOPS.

For compute workloads, Azure provides several series of VM sizes, which make it possible for you to choose what fits best. In addition to the A-series servers just mentioned, Azure also provides a D-series with SSD temporary drives and higher memory-to-core ratio, a DS-series that can use the Premium storage capability, and a G-series with Xeon E5 V3 family processors, high memory and CPU core numbers. For example, G5 VMs have 32 cores, 448 GB of memory, and can attach up to 64 TB of data drives.

NOTE **DIFFERENCES BETWEEN D-SERIES AND DS-SERIES**

D-series is designed for applications with high demand in compute power and temporary drive performance. D-series uses SSDs as temporary drives. DS-series is designed for I/O intensive workloads. DS-series uses SSDs for both hosting VM drives and local caches.

Using Azure Batch

If you don't want the trouble of managing a compute cluster yourself, you can use Azure Batch service. Using Batch, you can schedule and manage large-scale parallel workloads on Azure-managed compute resources without the need to manage any infrastructure details.

Overview

Batch is designed to run a large number of parallel tasks on a set of allocated compute resources. Because all compute resources are managed for you by Azure, you simply prepare the input data as well as the processing program, and then Azure takes cares of the rest for you.

You have two ways to programmatically interact with Batch: a higher-level Batch Apps API, or a lower-level Batch API. When using the Batch API, you are directly scheduling computational tasks onto a pool of resources. You need to manage task scheduling and execution yourself. On the other hand, with Batch Apps API, you can wrap an existing application and run it as parallel tasks. Batch will handle all the details for you, such as task scheduling, managing execution pipelines, and partitioning workloads.

Before going into more detail, take a few moments to ensure that you understand the following terms:

- **Batch account** To interact with Batch, you need a Batch account, which you can create via the Azure management portal. All Batch service requests must be authenticated with a Batch account and its associated security key.

- **Task virtual machine (TVM)** A TVM is a dedicated VM that is allocated to run your tasks. A collection of TVMs form a resource pool. You don't directly manage the underlying infrastructure, but you can control the characteristics of these pools by using Batch API. For example, you can specify the number, size, operating system, as well as scaling rules of TVMs in a resource pool.
- **Work items, jobs, and tasks** Work item is the description of how an application runs on a TVM pool. When a work item is scheduled, it becomes a job, which consists of a number of tasks, as shown in Figure 4-2.

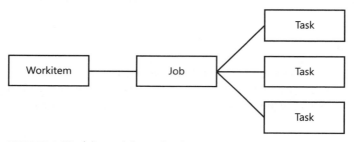

FIGURE 4-2 Work items, jobs, and tasks

- **File** A file is the input data that a task processes. You need to upload input data files to Azure Storage, and then Batch will transfer them to TVMs for processing.

Sample scenario: face detection with Batch

There are two stages to working with Batch: preparation and execution. During preparation, you upload to an Azure Storage account all input data files as well as program binaries and dependencies. During execution, you schedule tasks on the TVMs by creating a work item. After the tasks are scheduled, you can use Batch API to monitor task status and collect task results.

In this sample scenario, you'll run face detection on a number of images by using Emgu CV, which is a .NET wrapper of the OpenCV image processing library. The sample scenario assumes that you already have an Azure Storage account, and you've already uploaded a number of images to a container named Images.

1. Sign in to the management portal. On the command bar, create a new Batch account by clicking New, Compute, Batch Service, and then Quick Create. Pick an account name and a region for the account, and then click the Create Account link.

2. In Microsoft Visual Studio 2013, create a new C# Console Application named **FaceDetection**.

3. Add a reference to the Azure.Batch NuGet package.

4. Modify the *Main()* method by adding the code in Listing 4-1.

   As with using many other Azure services, the first step to use Batch is to create a client reference, as shown in the first two lines in Listing 4-1. Then, the code uses an *IPool-Manager* to create a pool of three small VMs. Your batch workloads will be carried out on this pool of machines.

   LISTING 4-1 Creating a batch client and resource pool

```
BatchCredentials credential = new BatchCredentials("[account]", "[account key]");
IBatchClient client = BatchClient.Connect("https://batch.core.windows.net",
credential);
const string PoolName = "fdpool";

using (IPoolManager pm = client.OpenPoolManager())
{
    var pools = pm.ListPools();
    if (!pools.Select(pool=>pool.Name).Contains(PoolName))
    {
        Console.WriteLine("Creating pool " + PoolName);
        ICloudPool newPool = pm.CreatePool(
            PoolName,
            osFamily: "3",
            vmSize: "small",
            targetDedicated: 3);
        newPool.Commit();
        Console.WriteLine("Pool created.");
    }
}
```

5. Define a work item and then schedule a job based on this work item.

   After a job is created, the code uses a task state monitor to wait for all tasks to complete. And finally, the code reads output from tasks by using their standard output streams. With this design, the actual processing program doesn't need to know anything about Batch—it simply generates outputs to the standard output stream. And, it can also use the standard error stream to return error messages. Listing 4-2 presents the code to define a work item and to schedule a job.

   LISTING 4-2 Defining a work item and scheduling a job

```
string WorkItemName = string.Format("detection-{0:yyyyMMdd-HHmmss}", DateTime.
Now);
string JobName = "job-0000000001";
using (IWorkItemManager vm = client.OpenWorkItemManager())
{
    ICloudWorkItem workitem = vm.CreateWorkItem(WorkItemName);
    workitem.JobExecutionEnvironment = new JobExecutionEnvironment() { PoolName =
PoolName };
```

```
    workitem.Commit();
    Console.WriteLine("WorkItem created.");

    var job = createJob(WorkItemName, JobName, vm);

    job = vm.GetJob(WorkItemName, JobName);
    client.OpenToolbox().CreateTaskStateMonitor().WaitAll(job.ListTasks(),
        TaskState.Completed, new TimeSpan(0, 30, 0));
    Console.WriteLine("All tasks completed. Terminating WorkItem...");
    vm.GetWorkItem(WorkItemName).Terminate();
    foreach(var task in job.ListTasks())
    {
        Console.WriteLine(string.Format("Task {0} returns: {1}",
            task.Name,

            task.GetTaskFile(Constants.StandardOutFileName).ReadAsString()));
    }
}
```

6. When everything is finished, you can remove the resource pool and the work item.

```
using (IPoolManager pm = client.OpenPoolManager())
{
    pm.DeletePool(PoolName);
}
Console.WriteLine("Pool is deleted.");
using (IWorkItemManager wm = client.OpenWorkItemManager())
{
    wm.DeleteWorkItem(WorkItemName);
}
Console.WriteLine("WorkItem is deleted.");
```

7. Now, you need to focus on the method to schedule the job. Listing 4-3 provides the complete code.

   This code might look a little complex, but all it does is enumerate all of the images in your Images container and generate a task for each image. For each of the tasks, the code downloads necessary binary files from a binary file container, which you'll prepare in the next steps. Finally, the code specifies the task command line before it submits the task to Azure Batch.

LISTING 4-3 Scheduling a job

```
private static ICloudJob createJob(string WorkItemName, string JobName,
IWorkItemManager vm)
{
    var job = vm.GetJob(WorkItemName, JobName);
    CloudStorageAccount storageAccount = CloudStorageAccount.Parse("[azure storage
account connection string]");
    CloudBlobClient storageClient = storageAccount.CreateCloudBlobClient();
    var container = storageClient.GetContainerReference("images");
    var blobs = container.ListBlobs().OfType<CloudBlockBlob>();
    string blobPath = "[URL or SAS of binary file container]";
    foreach (var blob in blobs)
```

```
    {
        IResourceFile programFile = new ResourceFile(blobPath + "FaceDetector.
exe", "FaceDetector.exe");
        IResourceFile downloadFile = new ResourceFile(blobPath + "EmguDownloader.
exe", "EmguDownloader.exe");
        IResourceFile batchFile = new ResourceFile(blobPath + "FaceDetection.bat",
"FaceDetection.bat");
        IResourceFile dataFile = new ResourceFile(blobPath + "haarcascade_
frontalface_default.xml", "haarcascade_frontalface_default.xml");

        string commandLine = string.Format("FaceDetection.bat {0}", blob.Uri.
ToString());
        ICloudTask task = new CloudTask(blob.Name.Replace('.', '_'), commandLine);
        task.ResourceFiles = new List<IResourceFile>();
        task.ResourceFiles.Add(programFile);
        task.ResourceFiles.Add(downloadFile);
        task.ResourceFiles.Add(batchFile);
        task.ResourceFiles.Add(dataFile);

        job.AddTask(task);
        job.Commit();
        job.Refresh();
    }
    return job;
}
```

8. Create a new FaceDetector console application.

This application doesn't hold reference to any Batch libraries. It downloads an image for a URL, runs face detection on it, and then prints the number of detected faces to the standard output. Listing 4-4 shows the complete implementation of the *Main()* method.

LISTING 4-4 Face detection

```
if (args.Length >= 1 && !string.IsNullOrEmpty(args[0]))
{
    WebClient client = new WebClient();
    var srcImage = Image.FromStream(new MemoryStream(client.
DownloadData(args[0])));
    Emgu.CV.CascadeClassifier classifier = new Emgu.CV.CascadeClassifier("haarcasc
ade_frontalface_default.xml");
    Image<Bgr, byte> image = new Image<Bgr, byte>(new Bitmap(srcImage));
    Image<Gray, byte> grayImage = image.Convert<Gray, byte>();
    var faces = classifier.DetectMultiScale(grayImage, 1.1, 3, new System.Drawing.
Size(20, 20), System.Drawing.Size.Empty);
    Console.WriteLine("# of faces: " + faces.ToList().Count);
}
```

9. Create a new EmguDownloader console application.

   This application downloads and installs Emgu 2.9 on TVMs. The code in Listing 4-5
   demonstrates how to include a third-party library in your solution.

   LISTING 4-5 Emgu downloader

```
WebClient client = new WebClient();
client.DownloadFile("http://sourceforge.net/projects/emgucv/files/emgucv/2.4.10/
libemgucv-windows-universal-2.4.10.1940.exe",
    "libemgucv-windows-universal-2.4.10.1940.exe");
string path = Directory.GetCurrentDirectory();
ProcessStartInfo info = new ProcessStartInfo("libemgucv-windows-
universal-2.4.10.1940.exe", "/S /D=" + path);
var process = Process.Start(info);
process.WaitForExit();
File.Copy("bin\\Emgu.CV.dll", "Emgu.CV.dll");
File.Copy("bin\\Emgu.Util.dll", "Emgu.Util.dll");
Directory.CreateDirectory("x64");
foreach(var file in Directory.GetFiles("bin\\x64"))
{
    FileInfo fileInfo = new FileInfo(file);
    File.Copy(file, Path.Combine("x64", fileInfo.Name));
}
```

10. Compile all projects. Then, upload EmguDownloader.exe, FaceDetector.exe, as well as
    haarcascade_frontalface_default.xml to the Binary Large Objects (Blob) binary con-
    tainer (see Listing 4-3). You also need to create and upload a FaceDetection.bat, which
    invokes *EmguDownloader* if Emgu hasn't been installed, and then calls face detection.

```
@ECHO OFF
IF NOT EXIST "x64" EmguDownloader
FaceDetector.exe %1
```

11. Run the FaceDetection program. Figure 4-3 shows the output of a sample run with five images.

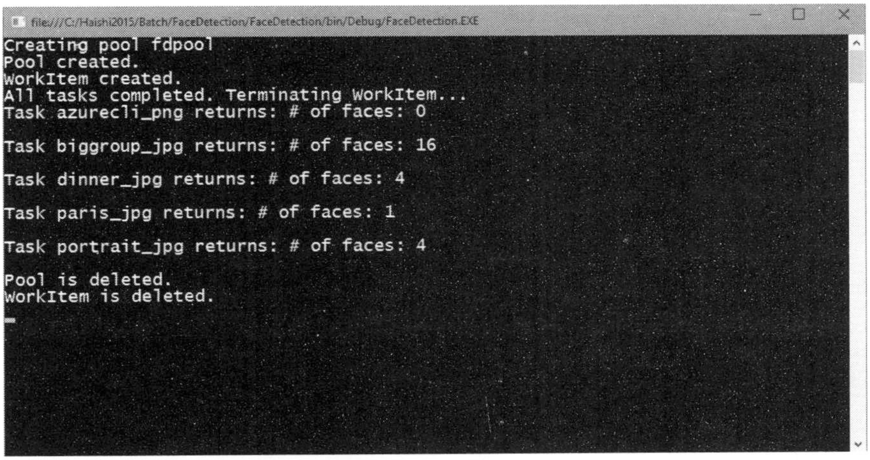

FIGURE 4-3 Sample Azure Batch run

Understanding Azure Batch Apps

Batch Apps is a feature of Azure Batch with which you can manage, run, and monitor repetitive batch jobs. More often than not, a batch job is repeated with different inputs over time. So, instead of defining work items and scheduling jobs through code as you've seen in the previous example, you probably want to set up a job that can be easily repeated with different inputs. For example, a business that does frequent video rendering might want to set up a rendering job that can be executed with different inputs, as needed.

Batch Apps provides a management portal where you can submit and monitor your batch jobs. Figure 4-4 shows an example of a job-run that renders a high-definition image in small tiles, and then merges the tiles together into a final picture. This is one of the simplest cases of MapReduce, which splits a big job into small, parallel tasks to be carried out independently, and then summarizes task results into high-level results.

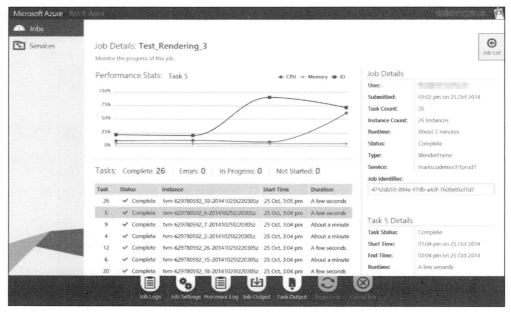

FIGURE 4-4 Sample image rendering batch job on Batch Apps portal

Preparing a Batch Application

With Batch Apps, the repeatable job is called a *Batch Application*. You create a Batch Application by submitting two packages to Batch, an Application Image and a Cloud Assembly, described here:

- **Application Image** This is a zip file that contains application executables along with all support files.
- **Cloud Assembly** This is a zip file that contains implementations of several methods, including a method to break down the job into tasks, and a method to invoke application executables.

When you have the packages ready, you can create a new Batch Application on the Batch Apps portal, and then schedule jobs on this application.

Implementing the Competing Consumers pattern

Competing Consumers is a design pattern by which you can implement a simple parallel task execution engine. With this pattern, one or more task creators generate tasks to a common task queue. That queue is monitored by one or many task processors. These processors compete with one another for new tasks, hence the pattern's name. The pattern has several desirable characteristics:

- **Scaling-out as needed** You can have as many task processors as needed. And, you can adjust the number of processors at any time without affecting other components. Be aware that for a massive-scale application, the job queue itself might become a bottleneck. In this case, you need a scalable queue, such as a queue that supports partitions.

- **Failover** When a task processor retrieves a task, it places a lock on it. The lock is released when the processor finishes with the task. If the processor crashes before it can release the lock, the lock is released after a predefined amount of time so that the task is available for other processors.

- **Hybrid compute** As long as the queue is accessible, you can have a mixture of task processors of different capabilities at different locations, either in the cloud or on-premises.

- **Dynamic load balancing** Because a task processor only takes on a new task after it finishes with the current task, loads are dynamically balanced among processors. As a processor is handling a complex task, other processors can handle smaller tasks without centralized coordination.

Azure Cloud Services makes implementing Competing Consumers easy, which you'll see in the next objective.

Thought experiment
Choosing between Azure Batch and competing consumers

In this thought experiment, apply what you've learned about this objective. You can find answers to these questions in the "Answers" section at the end of this chapter.

Batch brings you comprehensive support for running parallel compute tasks. On the other hand, it's not hard to implement a simple parallel execution engine yourself. With these in mind, answer the following two questions:

1. When would you choose Batch over implementing your own engine?

2. When would you choose to implement your own engine?

Objective summary

- Azure provides raw compute power for your HPC needs with instance sizes optimized for compute-intensive workloads.
- With Azure, you can transfer on-premises applications to the cloud and scale them up by using larger VM sizes and Premium storage.
- Batch is a hosted Azure service that supports running parallel tasks at large scale. Batch provides flexible programming models as well as comprehensive management and monitoring capabilities to manage your tasks.
- You can implement a simple parallel execution engine by using the Competing Consumer pattern.

Objective review

Answer the following questions to test your knowledge of the information in this objective. You can find the answers to these questions and explanations of why each answer choice is correct or incorrect in the "Answers" section at the end of this chapter.

1. Which of the following instance sizes are optimized for compute-intensive workloads?
   A. A8, A9, A10, and A11
   B. D-series
   C. DS-series
   D. G-series

2. Which two programming models does Batch support?
   A. Azure Batch API
   B. Azure Service Management API
   C. Azure Batch Apps API
   D. Azure API Management

3. What are the benefits of using Batch to execute parallel tasks at scale?
   A. Automatic compute resource management
   B. Management portal for job submission, management, and monitoring
   C. Scale-out to thousands of cores as needed
   D. Flexible programming models

Objective 4.2: Create long-running applications

Long-running applications refer to applications that run continuously over a long period of time. Although the concept sounds simple, it has several implications. First, the application needs to be reliable, which means that it can consistently provide functionalities as designed. Second, the application needs to be available such that it can continuously deliver services to its consumers. Third, the application needs to be scalable; that is, it can easily adapt for workload changes, either planned or unexpected.

Helping developers to create and host high-quality service has been a primary focus of Azure as a cloud platform. Azure affords you opportunities to improve the QoS of your application via various tools and services. However, this doesn't mean your applications on Azure will be automatically available, reliable, and scalable. A successful Software as a Service (SaaS) solution is based on a healthy partnership between the developer and Azure. You need to design your application with the cloud in mind in order to take full advantage of the benefits that Azure provides.

This section covers the following topics:

- Designing available applications
- Designing reliable applications
- Sample scenario: using Application Insights
- Designing scalable applications
- Using Azure Autoscale
- Using Azure Cloud Services
- Sample scenario: Cloud Services basics

Designing available applications

You can define availability as a ratio between the system available time and total subscribed time. For example, a service that remains available for 9 out of 10 hours has an availability of 90 percent. Service availability is often backed by a Service Level Agreement (SLA), which guarantees the level of service availability. Most Azure services are backed by SLAs. Table 4-2 summarizes SLAs for some of the Azure services.

TABLE 4-2 SLAs for some of the Azure services

Service	SLA	Comment
Active Directory	99.9%	Applies to Basic and Premium services
API Management	99.9%	Applies to Standard tier
Automation	99.9%	Jobs will start within 30 minutes of their planned start time
Backup	99.9%	Availability of backup and restore functionality
BizTalk API Apps	99.9%	Connectivity to Basic, Standard, and Premium tiers
Cache	99.9%	Connectivity between cache endpoints and Azure's internal gateway
CDN	99.9%	Respond to client requests and deliver contents without error
Cloud Services	99.95%	Requires two or more instances in different fault and upgrade domains
Virtual Machines	99.95%	Requires two or more instances in the same Availability set
Virtual Network	99.9%	Gateway availability

A key technique to improve service availability is to use redundancy, which means to deploy multiple instances of a service so that when one or several instances fail, there are still healthy instances to provide continuous service. Be aware, however, that redundancy incurs additional cost. Before you set up an availability goal for your own application, you need to evaluate the availability requirements and decide how much redundancy you need to build into your deployments. When you've determined that level, you can begin to consider different strategies to improve service availability. First, you'll go over a couple of basic strategies for a single component or a single service. Then, you'll discover some strategies that apply to multicomponent systems.

Single-component availability

Single-instance availability is achieved by using multiple service instances. Many Azure services have built-in redundancy for high availability. For instance, if you use Azure SQL Database, the database instance is backed by multiple secondary instances to ensure availability.

Generally speaking, the two most common deployment strategies are homogeneous instances and primary–secondary instances.

HOMOGENEOUS INSTANCES

In such a multi-instance deployment, all instances are identical. They often have similar processing power, and they are joined behind a load balancer, which distributes workloads evenly to them.

These instances are often autonomous, as well, which means that they don't have dependencies on one another. Autonomous ensures that a failing instance won't have a ripple effect that might take down all instances. In other words, when some of the instances fail, the level of service might degrade due to reduced capacity, but the completeness of functionality is unimpaired.

A practical challenge of using homogeneous instances is session state management. Because services' requests are distributed by the load balancer, requests within a user session are likely to be routed to different instances. There are a couple of ways to deal with this challenge:

- **Session affinity** All requests of a session will be routed to the same instance. You can achieve this by some routing mechanisms such as a gateway or cookie-based session affinity. Session affinity is also referred as *sticky sessions*.
- **External state store** All session states are externalized and saved in a separate data store that is independent from the service instances. Using this design, requests can be freely distributed among instances. But, it comes with a performance penalty because of the overheads of accessing the external state store. When the states are externalized, the instances become *stateless*.

> **NOTE   STATELESS VERSUS STATE-FUL**
>
> Using stateless instances is definitely not the only way to design scalable applications. In many cases, state-ful instances have preferable characteristics in terms of simplicity and performance, and there are fascinating programming models such as the Actor pattern to help you to write scalable, distributed applications. Further discussion on the Actor pattern is beyond the scope of this book.

PRIMARY–SECONDARY INSTANCES

A primary–secondary deployment designates a primary instance that handles all incoming requests, with one or more secondary instances as active backups. When the primary instance fails, a secondary instance is promoted to primary to handle requests. The original primary instance is repaired and brought back online as a new secondary. If the original primary is unrecoverable, you can provision a new instance as a new secondary to restore the number of instances to the desired level.

You can predetermine primary selection. In this case, each instance is assigned a priority level. When an instance fails, the instance with the next highest priority level is elected as the primary. Another scheme of primary selection is to use a dynamic voting process among running instances.

System-level availability

A more complex system is made up of multiple components. For example, an *n*-Tiered application might have a presentation layer, a business layer, and a database layer. To make the overall system available, you must make each component of the system available. The following is a general rule of system availability:

A system is less available than its least available component.

This rule states that when designing a system, you need to ensure that *all* components are available, because any unavailable components will bring down the availability of the entire system.

AVOID SINGLE POINT OF FAILURE

A Single Point of Failure (SPoF) refers to a component that renders the entire system unavailable if it fails. For example, if an entire system relies on a single database instance to function, the database instance is a SPoF of the system.

You should aim to eliminate SPoF from your system design. Although centralized components might be easy to design and implement, they bring a high risk to your system's availability. As a matter of fact, you can avoid many centralized components by using some innovative design. For example, you can replace a centralized job dispatcher with a job queue. With a job queue, jobs are published to the queue, and multiple job processors compete for jobs by reading jobs from the queue. Because Azure queue services such as Service Bus queue has ensured availability, such design is much more robust than a job dispatcher at application level.

ALTERNATIVE SERVICES

As the aforementioned rule-of-thumb states, a system is less available than its least available component. This rule assumes that there is a single dependency chain among components. You can overcome the constraints of this rule by introducing branches in dependency relationships. If you know a component is naturally unavailable, you should introduce alternative services so that when the component is inoperative, the system can continue to function by using alternative services. For example, when designing a notification system, you might want to implement multiple channels to ensure that a message is delivered, even when the preferred channel is unavailable.

CROSS-REGION DEPLOYMENTS

Although rare, region-wide outages do happen as a result of catastrophic events such as hurricanes and earthquakes. For mission-critical systems, it's advisable to have key services deployed across multiple geographic regions so that the system remains available.

Azure Traffic Manager provides automatic failover capabilities for critical applications. You can configure Traffic Manager to route your customers to a primary site, but redirect them to a backup site if the primary site continuously fails to answer health probe signals. Your customers don't need to remember different addresses of the various deployments. They simply access the service through endpoints provided by Traffic Manager. All health probes and traffic routing occur behind the scene. Furthermore, you also can associate custom domains to Traffic Manager endpoints to provide your customers more friendly service addresses.

> **NOTE LOAD-BALANCING POLICIES**
>
> Failover is one of the supported load-balancing policies. You also can set up round-robin load balancing and performance-based load balancing.

Designing reliable applications

Reliability is the probability that a system functions correctly during any given period of time. Obviously, an application rife with bugs is less reliable. A comprehensive discussion of best practices and techniques of reliable engineering is beyond the scope of this book; nonetheless, here we'll focus on several additional challenges that come with developing applications for the cloud, and how Azure helps you to handle these challenges.

Fault domains and update domains

Cloud datacenters are made up of commodity hardware. With hundreds or even thousands of servers running at any given time, hardware failures are unavoidable. To help you to cope with such failures, Azure introduces two concepts: *fault domain* and *update domain*.

- **Fault domain** This is a group of resources that can fail at the same time. For example, a group of servers on the same rack belong to the same fault domain because they share the same power supply, cooling, and network routing systems. When any of these shared devices fail, all servers on the same rack are affected. When you deploy a service to Azure, you can distribute service instances evenly to multiple fault domains so that all service instances won't fail at the same time due to hardware failures.

- **Update domain** An update domain is a logical group of resources that can be simultaneously updated during system upgrades. When Azure updates a service, it doesn't bring down all instances at the same time. Instead, it performs a rolling update via an update domain walk. Service instances in different update domains are brought down group by group for updates.

Both fault domain and update domain help you to guarantee your service has at least one running instance at any given time during hardware failures and software updates.

Transient errors

Transient errors are caused by some temporal conditions such as network fluctuation, service overload, and request throttling. Transient errors are quite elusive; they happen randomly and can't be reliably re-created. A typical way to handle transient error is to retry a couple of times. Many Azure SDK clients have built-in transit-error handling so that your code won't be cluttered by retry logics.

When your applications have dependencies on external services, you need to plan for throttling. You should clearly understand quotas imposed by these services and ensure that you don't exceed such limits. On the other hand, when you provide your services to the public, you might want to implement throttling yourself so that you can sustain enough resources for fair service consumption.

> **NOTE TRANSIT-FAULT HANDLING APPLICATION BLOCK**
>
> Microsoft Patterns & Practices provides a transient-fault handling application block that helps you to cope with transient errors.

Loose coupling

When a service fails, all services with direct dependencies on the service are affected. Because of such dependencies, a single error can generate a chain of failures that ripple through multiple layers of the system. Loosely coupled components don't have direct dependencies on one another. Loose coupling has many benefits, such as dynamic scaling and load leveling. More important, loose coupling facilitates different components having separate lifecycles. You can maintain, host, and update the components independently without affecting other components. Architectures such as Service Oriented Architecture (SOA), Microservices, and Message-Based Integrations all advocate for loose coupling among system components. With loose coupling, a failing component won't produce the ripple effect on the entire system.

Loosely coupled components are often integrated by using a reliable messaging system such as an Azure Service Bus queue. In terms of reliability, the messaging system serves as an intercomponent buffer that helps to contain errors.

Health monitoring

It's very important to monitor a long-running application continuously to ensure that it's functioning normally, at a sustained performance level. Some problems such as resource leakage and bugs under stress only reveal themselves after the system has been running for a period of time. Having an efficient, reliable, and secure telemetry collection system is a necessity for most modern web applications.

A health-monitoring system can also help you to analyze the usage patterns of your application. It can assist in monitoring and analyzing how customers are accessing your service so that you can focus on the areas that are of greatest concern to your customers.

Azure supports various diagnostics, tracing, and monitoring solutions such as Azure Diagnostics and Application Insights.

Azure Application Insights is a hosted service that helps you to detect issues, solve problems, and analyze usage patterns of your applications, including ASP.NET and Java applications, WCF services, Windows Phone, and Windows store apps.

Azure also supports third-party solutions such as New Relic and AppDynamics. To help you to understand how health monitoring works on Azure, we'll go through a sample scenario of using Application Insights to monitor usage of a website.

Sample scenario: using Application Insights This scenario walks you through the steps you need to follow to set up Application Insights to monitor an ASP.NET application. You'll learn how to turn on Application Insights, how to use its data, and how to perform a distributed load test of your website.

1. Sign in to the Azure Preview Management Portal (*https://portal.azure.com*).

2. Click New, and then click Application Insights to create a new Application Insights instance.

3. Type a name for the instance. Then, for the Application Type, choose ASP.NET web application. Select/create resource group, subscription and location, and then click the Create button to create the instance.

4. In Visual Studio 2013 Update 3 or above, create a new ASP.NET Web Application. As you create the project, you'll notice an Add Application Insights To Project check box (see Figure 4-5). Select the checkbox, and then select the Application Insight instance that you just set up. If you want to add Application Insights to an existing application, you can right-click a web project in Visual Studio and select the Add Application Insights Telemetry menu.

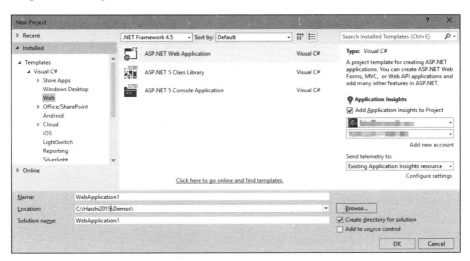

FIGURE 4-5 The New ASP.NET Project Wizard

5. After the site is created, press F5 to open the website locally. A message box appears, displaying the notice, "Your first Application Insights event has been sent!"

   Now, your web application is automatically collecting a rich set of telemetry data, which you can view and analyze on the Preview Management Portal, as shown in Figure 4-6.

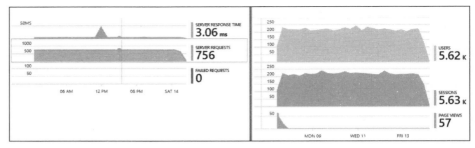

FIGURE 4-6 Application Insights reports on the Preview Management Portal

6. Create a web test to ensure high availability of the website around the world. On the website page, click the tile labeled "Creating webtests helps you to ensure high availability around the world".

7. Provide a name for the test and then select URL Ping Test as the test type. Alternatively, you can use Multi-Step Test, which requires you to upload a web load test. You can record a load test by using Visual Studio.

8. Click Test Locations.

    You can select from a dozen available test locations around the globe. Test agents from these locations will carry out specified test cases against your websites. Traditionally, setting up such a distributed test requires a lot of work. Now, Azure makes it easily accessible with just a few clicks.

9. After the test is created, you'll begin to see test results in several minutes, as shown in Figure 4-7.

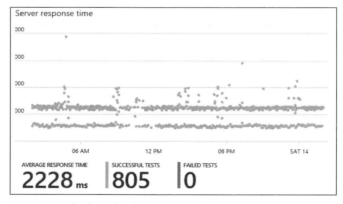

FIGURE 4-7 Distributed web test results

Designing scalable applications

The workload of an application tends to change over time, and the application needs to be able to adapt to such changes. There are two typical workload change patterns: gradual changes and spikes.

Some applications have relatively stable workloads. For such applications, you can plan server capacity in advance. As the workload slowly grows beyond that capacity, you can gain more by *scaling up* or *scaling out* the application.

- **Scaling up** This refers to raising system capacity by increasing the processing power of service instances. For example, you can scale-up a CPU-bound or memory-bound instance by increasing the number of cores or amount of memory on the server. In most cases, scaling up doesn't require application changes, meaning you can do it with low cost and low risk. However, you can't infinitely increase the processing power of service instances. All VMs and physical servers have upper limits regarding how many cores and how much memory they can accommodate. When the workload exceeds what a single service instance can handle, you'll need to scale out.

- **Scaling out** This refers to expanding system capacity by increasing the number of instances. All workloads will be distributed among all the instances. In theory, you can add as many instances as you can afford. In other words, you can increase the capacity of your system infinitely by adding more and more instances. The downside of scaling out is that the application must be designed to accommodate it, which might call for architectural changes to legacy applications. Such changes can be expensive and risky. If you are designing a new application for the cloud, you should have scaling-out in mind from the beginning so that you can avoid the inherent risks of redesigning it later.

Dynamic scaling

Workload spikes come in two flavors. Some workload changes are predicable. For example, an online store likely expects increases in traffics during weekends and holiday seasons, and a gaming site might need to prepare for increased download requests when a new release for a popular game is made available. On the other hand, some workload changes are difficult to predict. For example, a news website might experience unexpected spikes when breaking news occurs, and a wiki page might collect more views when the covered subject becomes a public interest for various reasons.

The best way to cope with workload spikes is to deploy some sort of autoscaling solution. Autoscaling dynamically adjusts a system's capacity when workloads change. Such dynamic adjustments reduce the operational cost of your hosted applications. For most of the time, you need to keep only enough resources to handle regular workloads. When a spike occurs, the application's capacity can be dynamically adjusted by acquiring more resources and deploying more service instances.

Two major autoscaling methods are *scheduled scaling* and *reactive scaling*, as detailed in the following:

- **Scheduled scaling**   This is suitable for expected workload changes. In such cases, the system administrators can schedule to increase system capacities in preparation for a busy time, and then reduce the capacity when the busy period is over. A class registration system at universities is a perfect example. It's very easy to predict that the system will be extremely busy at the beginning of a semester, but it will experience very little traffic during a semester. In this case, the system administrator can schedule to scale the system to great capacity at the beginning of the semester, and to release most of the resources after the first few weeks.

- **Reactive scaling**   Reactive scaling is suitable for unexpected workload changes. It monitors certain system metrics and adjusts system capacity when those metrics attain certain thresholds. A common performance counter used as a scaling trigger is CPU usage. Some other common triggers include length of request queue, drive stress, and memory stress. Because system telemetries such CPU usages are elusive, you don't want to react whenever those values change. Instead, you would commonly use average values spanning a time interval.

A practical challenge of reactive scaling is the latency in provisioning new resources. Provisioning a new VM and deploying a new service instance need time. So, when you design your reactive-scaling solution, you need to leave enough space for new resources to be brought online. For even more advanced controls, you might want to employ some sort of predictive analysis on top of the simple reactive mechanism.

Container technologies such as Docker make it possible for you to package workloads in light-weight images, which you can deploy and activate very quickly. For example, many Docker containers can be started in less than a second, because launching a new container is equivalent to starting a new process. Such agility affords new possibilities to reactive scaling by eliminating the needs to account for latencies.

Workload partitioning

As mentioned earlier, one way to scale-out a service is to use homogeneous instances. In this case, all instances join the same load balancer as peers, and the load balancer distributes workloads evenly to these instances.

Another way to scale out is to use *workload partitioning*. In this case, the total workload is sliced into small portions, and each portion is assigned to a number of designated instances. There are several advantages to using workload partitioning compared to homogeneous instances, among them is tenant isolation.

With workload partitioning, you can route workloads for a certain tenant to a designated group of instances instead of being randomly routed to any instances in a bigger instance pool. Tenant isolation presents new scenarios such as per-tenant monitoring, tiered service offerings, and independent updates to different tenants.

You can configure either static or dynamic partitioning. For cases in which workload distribution is predetermined, you can use static partitioning. For example, a ballot system can partition its workloads by states or provinces. It can thus assign more resources to bigger states or even create multiple subpartitions for those states. On the other hand, it can choose to combine multiple smaller states into a bigger partition.

Dynamic partitioning ties to dynamic scaling. When a new node is joined to a cluster, the new node takes on a fair share of the workload without impacting more running nodes than is necessary. Techniques such as consistent hashing are commonly used to facilitate such workload relocation. In some other cases, dynamic scaling can be relatively easy. For example, for a system partitioned by customer IDs, adding or removing a partition rarely has any impact on other instances because of the tenant isolation.

Using Azure Autoscale

Azure provides autoscaling capability to applications, regardless of whether they are running as Azure App Service Web Apps, Cloud Service Web Roles, Cloud Service Worker Roles, or VMs. In addition, Azure Autoscale supports planned scaling as well as reactive scheduling.

Managing scaling via the management portal

You can configure autoscaling settings easily in both the management portal (*https://manage. windowsazure.com*) and the new Preview Management Portal (*https://portal.azure.com*). Figure 4-8 depicts an example of autoscaling settings for a website on the Preview Management Portal.

FIGURE 4-8 Autoscaling settings on the Preview Management Portal

> **NOTE IMPARITY BETWEEN THE TWO MANAGEMENT PORTALS**
>
> As of this writing, certain imparities have been observed between the two versions of Azure's management portals. For example, in the new Preview Management Portal, you have more metric choices in addition to CPU usage and queue length. On the other hand, there is no facility in the new portal for scheduled scaling. There is also no Cloud Services management at all.

Configuring autoscaling is straightforward in both portals, each providing intuitive interfaces to help you with the process. In the interest of brevity, I'll skip specifics here. Instead, Figure 4-9 presents the current portal, in which you can set up different scaling rules for different times of the day, different days of a weeks, and data ranges.

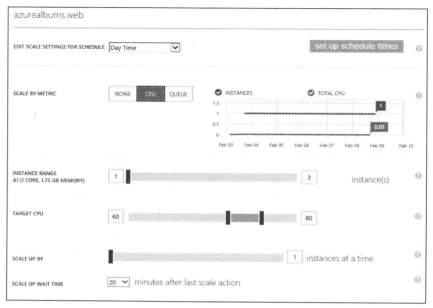

FIGURE 4-9 Autoscaling settings on the current management portal

Virtual Machine Availability Set and autoscaling

Applications directly deployed on VMs rely on those VMs to scale their capacities. There are many ways to provision and destroy VMs, including manual operation, Windows PowerShell and CLI scripts, and automated solutions such as Azure Automation, Chef, and Puppet. A full discussion of all automation options is beyond the scope of this chapter. Instead, I'll briefly introduce Virtual Machine Availability Set and how it ties in with autoscaling.

Virtual Machine Availability Set is essentially an availability mechanism. You can join multiple VMs into the same availability set to provide high availability. As a matter of fact, if you want to take advantage of the Azure SLA for VM availability, you are required to have at least two instances in the same availability set. You can define autoscaling rules to Virtual Machine Availability Sets. These rules work the same way as do the scaling rules for Cloud Services and Web Apps.

Scaling a system

Before wrapping up the discussion of scalability, I have to mention that scaling an application involves scaling compute, storage, and communication. So far, this discussion has been focused on the compute component. However it's important to realize that other components need to be scaled accordingly so that they don't become system bottlenecks. In Objective 4.3, you'll explore some scaling considerations when choosing among different storage options.

Using Cloud Services

Cloud Services is Azure's Platform as a Service (PaaS) offering for building and hosting cloud-based applications. It's designed for building *n*-Tiered applications in the cloud. A typical multitiered cloud service includes a presentation layer, a business layer, and a database layer. When the application is deployed to Azure, it might become a SaaS application that is accessible to all authenticated users across the globe.

The major benefit of developing applications in a PaaS environment is that it unburdens you of cumbersome resource management tasks such as managing VMs and load balancers. Instead, you can focus on implementing business logics and let Azure handle the infrastructural details for you. All you need to do is to build your service package and hand it over to Azure. Then, Azure will take care of creating, managing, and monitoring instances of your services.

Roles and instances

A cloud service is made up of one or multiple roles. Cloud Services supports two types of roles, Web Roles and Worker Roles, which are described here:

- **Web Role**   An ASP.NET project, which constitutes the presentation layer of your application.
- **Worker Role**   This is a long-running process. What it does is really up to you, but a common pattern is for a Worker Role to listen to a job queue, to which the Web Role sends requests for the Worker Role to handle.

When a cloud service is deployed to Azure, its roles are instantiated according to its configuration file. Web Roles and Worker Roles are loosely coupled by design. This design makes it possible for you to deploy and scale them separately. For instance, if your application has a high demand on UI interaction, you can scale-out your Web Roles to more instances as needed. Or, if your application does mostly processing in background, you might want to increase the number of Worker Role instances.

Cloud Services assumes that role instances are homogeneous, which means to scale out, you need to make role instances stateless because any new request can be routed to any available instances. If you need session affinity, you'll need to implement some sort of gateway or routing solutions yourself.

Endpoints and load balancing

Roles provide access to their services via endpoints. There are three types of endpoints, Input Endpoints, Internal Endpoints, and Instance Input Endpoints, each described here:

- **Input Endpoints** These can be accessed openly over the Internet. The Input Endpoints of a role point to an Azure-provided load balancer. User requests are distributed to role instances by the load balancer. An Input Endpoint has both a public port and a private port. The public port is what the load balancer exposes to service consumers; the private port is what the load balancer uses to communicate with role instances. Input Endpoints support HTTP, HTTPS, TCP, and UDP.

- **Internal Endpoints** Internal Endpoints are private to the cloud service. They are used for role instances to communicate with one another. Internal Endpoints are not load-balanced. Internal Endpoints support HTTP, HTTPS, TCP, and ANY.

- **Instance Input Endpoints** These are publicly accessible endpoints with port ranges. A service consumer can directly access different instances by choosing different ports in the given range. For instance, an Instance Input Endpoint with port range from 8008 to 8012 corresponds to 5 instances, with 8008 mapped to the first one, 8009 mapped to the second one, and so on. Instance Input Endpoints support TCP and UDP.

By default, all cloud services are deployed to the cloudapp.net domain. For example, a cloud service with name "service1" will have the address service1.cloudapp.net. When you have multiple roles in a cloud service, which role will be assigned to this address? The answer is the role that has an Input Endpoint that matches with the protocol and the port. For example, http://service1.cloudapp.net will be mapped to the role that has an HTTP-based Input Endpoint at port 80.

Availability, reliability, and scalability of Cloud Services

Cloud Services provide many of the availability and scalability mechanisms that were discussed earlier in this objective. Cloud Services availability features include the following:

- **Built-in load balancer** Multiple instances of a cloud service's role with Input Endpoints are joined to a built-in load balancer for load balancing as well as high availability.

- **Rolling updates** When Azure deploys a new version of Cloud Services, it performs an update domain walk to update service instances group by group so that at any moment you have at least a subset of service instances running.

- **Swap deployment** During rolling updates, there is a risk of multiple versions of your application running at the same time. If the new version is incompatible with the older version, you can deploy the new version to a different staging slot and swap the production environment and the staging environment by a quick virtual IP swap.

As for reliability, Cloud Services provides the following:

- **Automatic instance recovery**   Cloud Services monitors instance health by monitoring the instance process. It will automatically restart the instance process if the process crashes.

- **Built-in diagnostics**   You can use Azure Diagnostics to collects various logs, such as application logs, Windows event logs, and crash dumps. These logs are offloaded from instance VMs to Azure Storage periodically so that even in the case of total instance failure, you can still access these log files.

- **Integration with Application Insights**   Use this to monitor your service health.

- **Multiregion deployment with Traffic Manager**   Use this to fail-over from a primary site to a secondary site when needed.

For scalability, you can take advantage of the following features:

- Planned or reactive autoscale.

- Independent adjustments of instance numbers of different roles.

Inter-role communications

Role instances can directly communicate with one another via Internal Endpoints. However, a more common pattern is for the roles to communicate over a messaging system such as a Service Bus Queue. The message queue ensures that different roles are completely decoupled from one another. The next sample scenario demonstrates how to construct a basic cloud service, and how a Web Role sends a job to a background Worker Role. This scenario is also a basic implementation of the Competing Consumer pattern.

Sample scenario: Cloud Services basics

In this sample scenario, you'll implement a "Hello World" cloud service with a Web Role and a Worker Role. The Web Role submits a string to a job queue, and then the string is retrieved by the Worker Role from the same queue.

Prerequisites

- Visual Studio 2013 with Update 3 or above, with Azure SDK for .NET 2.4 or above.

- An active Azure subscription.

- A Service Bus Queue. Managing a Service Bus Queue is beyond the scope of this objective. For details, refer to the relevant documentation.

Creating a cloud service

1. Start Visual Studio, click File, and then click New Project.

2. In the New Project dialog box, click Cloud, Azure Cloud Service Project.

3. In the New Microsoft Azure Cloud Service dialog box, add an ASP.NET Web Role and a Worker Role with Service Bus Queue to the project, as shown in Figure 4-10.

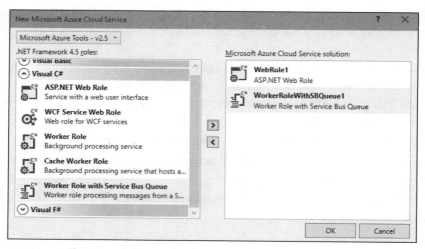

FIGURE 4-10 The New Microsoft Azure Cloud Service Wizard

4. Click OK to create the Cloud Service Project.

5. In the New ASP.NET Project dialog box, pick the MVC template, and then click OK to continue. Note that this dialog box is triggered by ASP.NET project creation. This is not specific to Cloud Service.

   Your Visual Studio solution now has three projects: one Cloud Service project, one Web Role project, and one Worker Role project.

6. In the Cloud Service project, double-click WorkRoleWithSBQueue1 to open the properties page for the Worker Role. Click the Settings tab, and then modify the Microsoft. ServiceBus.ConnectionString to the connection string of your Service Bus queue. Save your changes.

7. Double-click the Web Role to open its properties page. Define a same Microsoft. ServiceBus.ConnectionString setting with the same Service Bus connection string, and then save your changes.

8. Add a reference to WindowsAzure.ServiceBus NuGet to the Web Role project.

9. Replace the *About()* method of *HomeController* with the following code:

```
public ActionResult About()
{
    QueueClient Client;
    string connectionString = CloudConfigurationManager.GetSetting("Microsoft.
ServiceBus.ConnectionString");
    Client = QueueClient.CreateFromConnectionString(connectionString);
    Client.Send(new BrokeredMessage("Hello World!"));
    return View();
}
```

10. Open WorkRole.cs of the Worker Role project.

11. Set a breakpoint at the *OnMessage* callback of the *Run()* method.

12. Press F5 to start the application.

    Visual Studio will start a simulated compute environment and a simulated storage environment for you to test your Cloud Services locally.

13. When the webpage opens, click the About link and observe that the breakpoint is reached upon arrival of the message.

EXAM TIP

We intentionally left out many details so that we could focus on architecture topics in this chapter. However, sometimes the exam can be very specific. You might be asked about Azure Service Definition Schema, which is commonly referred to as *service definition file* (see *https://msdn.microsoft.com/en-us/library/azure/ee758711.aspx*). This is an XML file with a .csdef extension. It defines the service model of an application, including roles, endpoints, and configurations. Similarly, there is Azure Service Configuration Schema, or as it's more commonly known, *service configuration file*. This is another XML file with a .cscfg extension that supplies configuration values for different environments (see *https://msdn. microsoft.com/en-us/library/azure/ee758710.aspx*). When you create a new Cloud Services project, you can observe both files in the project folder. Follow the attached links to familiarize yourself with these two schemas in case some specific schema questions are asked.

Thought experiment
Choosing among web application hosting options

In this thought experiment, apply what you've learned about this objective. You can find answers to these questions in the "Answers" section at the end of this chapter.

Azure provides several options to host a web application: Web Apps, Cloud Services Web Roles, and web servers hosted on VMs. As a system architect, you need to make a choice of which hosting options to use.

With this in mind, answer the following questions:

1. Which hosting options would you choose, and under what circumstances?

2. How would you scale the application?

Objective summary

- The cloud provides QoS opportunities for your cloud applications. However, you need to design your application for the cloud to take advantage of these offerings.

- Availability is commonly realized by redundancy, but redundancy has its associated costs. So, you should pick a realistic availability goal.

- To ensure system-level availability, you need to ensure that all components are available. SPoF has significant negative impacts on system availability.

- You can increase system-level availability by using multisite deployments. You can also increase system-level availability by introducing alternative service paths.

- Azure uses Update Domains and Fault Domains to help you to keep at least a number of service instances running during system failures and software updates.

- Scaling-up is when you increase processing power of a single instance. Scaling-out is when you increase system capacity by using more service instances.

- Autoscale helps you to reduce operational cost by adjusting the system capacity as workloads change.

- Web Roles and Worker Roles can directly communicate with each other. However, a more common pattern is to use a reliable messaging system such as Azure Service Bus Queue to pass messages between them.

Objective review

Answer the following questions to test your knowledge of the information in this objective. You can find the answers to these questions and explanations of why each answer choice is correct or incorrect in the "Answers" section at the end of this chapter.

1. Azure brings QoS opportunities to your applications. Which of the following QoS benefits can you get by designing your application for the cloud?

   A. Availability

   B. Scalability

   C. Reliability

   D. Security

2. When you need to increase system capacity, what scaling options can you use?

   A. Scaling up

   B. Scaling out

   C. Primary–secondary deployment

   D. Loose coupling

3. Which of the following are valid endpoint types of Cloud Services roles?

   A. Input Endpoint

   B. Internal Endpoint

   C. Instance Input Endpoint

   D. Output Endpoint

4. What are the benefits of the Competing Consumers pattern?

   A. You can adjust number of consumers at any time.

   B. Consumers are deployed in a hybrid environment.

   C. Failover to ensure each task is handled.

   D. You can avoid a centralized job dispatcher or scheduler.

5. What tools and services can you use to monitor your cloud applications?

   A. Application Insights

   B. New Relic

   C. AppDynamics

   D. Azure management portal

Objective 4.3: Select the appropriate storage option

When it comes to data storage, relational databases have been a dominating choice for many years. In more recent years, NoSQL databases have become popular in many large-scale systems for their scalability and performance. Furthermore, with the amount of data that is collected, transmitted, stored, and analyzed increasing exponentially, large data warehouses such as Hive and multidimensional databases have found their places in many modern solutions.

Because Chapter 3 covers different data storage options, we'll not focus on introducing these services here. Instead, in this objective you'll look at how to pick appropriate storage options for your applications. Note that in this objective we are excluding Big Data–related solutions, which is covered briefly in the next objective. Instead, you'll focus on generic applications such as web applications and Line of Business (LoB) applications.

> **This section covers the following topics:**
> - Understanding data access patterns
> - Selecting a data storage solution
> - Evaluating data storage qualities

Understanding data access patterns

Before you make a choice regarding which storage to use, you first need to understand how your application accesses data. Does the application do mostly reads or mostly writes? What kind of queries does the application run against data? How much data does the application handle? What types of data does the application process? What are the performance requirements? Finding answers to these questions will help you to make a smart choice when you design your data access solutions.

Read/write patterns

The level of complexity involved when an application accesses data increases dramatically when there are multiple readers and/or multiple writers. Tradeoffs between performance and consistency often need to be made so that these readers and writers can work together in harmony. Depending on the number of readers and writers, the frequency of data operations, and concurrency requirements, you'll need different strategies.

IMMEDIATE CONSISTENCY VS. EVENTUAL CONSISTENCY

Immediate consistency, or *strong consistency*, means that when an entity is updated, all observers of this entity will have a consistent view of the updated entity. In other words, these observers will either see updated data at the same time or none of them will see the update. Strong consistency is very familiar to developers who have been relying on relational databases for data storage. However, to ensure strong consistency, some sort of locking method needs to be used, preventing the application from accessing the data for the duration of data updates. And, if the system performs a large amount of updates, there will be many locks, hence more delays in the system. Furthermore, when there are multiple replicas of data, maintaining consistency across the replicas needs extra processing cycles before the update is available for reading across all of the replicas.

Eventual consistency relaxes the consistency constrains by allowing certain replicas of data to be updated ahead of others, and updates are eventually propagated across the entire replica set. This means that at any given time, a reader might have accessed a "dirty" copy of the data. Such propagations are very fast in some systems, such as a well-connected Redis cluster. On the other hand, propagations in some systems can take much longer, such as eventual consistency of Domain Name System (DNS) records.

For many transactional applications, strong consistency is highly desirable because many parties operate based on the universal truth of the data. On the other hand, for reading-heavy applications, eventual consistency is often desirable for improved performance.

OPTIMISTIC CONCURRENCY VS. PESSIMISTIC CONCURRENCY

Pessimistic concurrency, as the name suggests, holds a quite pessimistic view of possible update conflicts. So, it asks the database to lock the item during its update operations. *Optimistic concurrency*, on the other hand, considers the probability of conflicts being relatively low. When it reads data for update, it keeps a revision number of the original data but it doesn't hold a lock. Then, as it writes back, as long as the latest revision number on the database is still the same as it has read, the update will succeed.

If your application does a large amount of writes, pessimistic concurrency usually provides a better performance, because optimistic concurrency will lead to many failed operations in this case. On the other hand, you can use optimistic concurrency when your application has mostly reads and fewer writes.

For some applications, you can use an even simpler method: *last-write wins*. With last-write wins, all writers are free to update the entities at will; whichever happens to be the last writer, wins the competition.

SEQUENTIAL ACCESS VS. RANDOM ACCESS

This pair of patterns doesn't require much explanation. *Sequential accesses* are efficient to read data within a continuous range. *Random access* directly addresses data points. A data point can be addressed either by location or by content. A typical case of addressing by location is to read a file by its path. Conversely, addressing by content uses a hash code of the data as its address. In this case, a data reader doesn't need to worry about locating where the data is physically stored. Instead, it locates data by looking up the hash, which is very efficient.

Data query patterns

Data queries can be very simple (such as recalling an entity by its key), or they can be very complex (such as using multiple steps of correlations, filters, and transformations to construct desired result sets).

STATIC SCHEMA VS. DYNAMIC SCHEMA

A *static schema* defines an explicit data contract. An *explicit schema* makes data integrity check and data exchange simple because all participating parties know exactly how the data is structured. The fixed schema also makes certain automations possible such as autogenerated UIs. A schema being static doesn't mean that you can't change it. Most relational database support lossless schema updates. However, you need to apply such updates across all participating parties for consistency.

You can construct complex queries based on static schemas. I believe most developers are no strangers to record filters and table joins. Using techniques such as populated views and compiled stored procedures can make such queries more efficient. No matter what databases you use, eventually the data is preserved on drives as files, with the exception of memory-based databases. When you query a range of data, the database engines needs to locate these data files and load the required data in memory. Such location-based addressing is not always efficient. To deal with this, many databases have built-in indexing mechanisms to optimize different data-access scenarios. However, having more indexes means you have more overhead to rebuild these indexes when data is changed.

Dynamic schema, or *schema-less*, or NoSQL databases don't have enforced schema. Data is saved in the database as key–value pairs. Complex queries are often difficult on such databases. Most data retrievals are done by providing specific keys or key ranges. Some schema-less databases support additional levels in data hierarchy, such as partitions in Azure Table storage. Many developers prefer schema-less databases for their agility because you don't need to worry about schema mismatches. You can add data fields, change them, and remove them as needed, without having to maintain uniformity of data structures in the table.

To enable complex queries on NoSQL databases, you can use advanced indexing techniques such as full-text indexing. In some cases, schemas can be inferred from data to support complex queries. For example, you can infer a schema from JSON documents by treating each property as a field.

REPETITIVE QUERIES

Many systems have *repetitive queries*. For example, when a blog site presents the latest posts, the underlying query is invariant to all of the users. In this case, it doesn't make sense to repeatedly query for the same set of data. Instead, the result can be cached and directly served within a certain Time-To-Live (TTL) specification.

Caches are good fits for storing repetitive query results. Many cache solutions, such as Azure Cache, provide auto-evictions of least-accessed data. This provides a natural solution to put the most frequently used data in memory for faster access. Furthermore, if you can predict with certainty that specific query results will be used, you can prime the cache in advance to avoid performance penalties when there are cache misses.

Caching repetitive query results can bring significant performance improvements to your application, especially when the original queries are complex. However, using cached results means that the latest updates are not always reflected, which can lead to inconsistency issues. So, caching is most suitable for cases in which data is updated infrequently.

Selecting a data storage solution

It's difficult to provide a definitive guideline of data-store selection, because each application can have its unique requirements in terms of data storage. In this section, you'll look at a couple of general guidelines that can help you to make sensible decisions when choosing data stores.

Combination of data stores

Modern applications often need to deal with different types of data, such as transactional data, Blobs, and log files. Although many relational databases have extended their capacities to save Blobs, it's often advisable to use the most appropriate storage options for specific types of data.

Traditionally, there weren't many alternatives for saving data beyond a few database and storage options. Today, there are abundant choices. In addition, you can often provision new storages by using various PaaS and SaaS offerings on the market.

Some might argue that centralized databases can simplify backups and disaster recovery. However, this is not necessarily true in many cases. First, different types of data usually have different backup requirements. It's wasteful to back up static data at the same frequency as that of volatile data. And, large amounts of unnecessary backups can lead to increased storage cost and prolonged data recovery time. Second, a centralized database is a potential SPoF, or a bottleneck for the overall system.

So, the best choice will be to use the most appropriate tools for different types of jobs. Although having multiple data stores increases management complexity, you'll achieve optimized performance and reduced cost in return. For example, you can use SQL Database for your transactional data, Azure Blob for large binary files, DocumentDB for loosely structured data, and Azure Search for indexing free-text files.

Keep data close to compute

Keeping data close to where it's needed greatly improves system performance, especially when there are a lot of interactions between the compute and the data.

When you use hosted databases, you should ensure that the databases and the compute instances are hosted in the same geographic region to reduce network latency. If you host a database in Azure Virtual Machines, you should consider deploying your compute instances and database instances to the same Azure Virtual Network. If your compute is on-premises, you'll probably want to use a local database, as well. However, you can use data replication to back up your data to Azure for disaster recovery.

The ultimate way to keep the data close to compute is to co-locate the data and the compute. Actor Pattern, or Actor Model, is a good example of an entity keeping its status close to itself. An actor can access and update its states quickly because its state is kept local. There's no external service calls or additional network hops to go through. Moreover, because an actor is the only writer to its own state, you can achieve maximum parallelism without locking.

Cost matters

Developments in storage technologies are constantly driving down the cost of storage. However, at the same time, the rate at which data is collected is growing even faster. Layered storage and periodic data reduction can help you to control of your storage costs.

You can reduce data size by using compression and periodic trimming. In some systems, avoiding saving multiple copies of the same data significantly reduces data size, as well. For example, a backup system often periodically backs up certain files and folders. Because not all files and folders are updated all the time, there will be a considerable amount of duplicate files in the system. If the system adopted a mechanism to avoid duplicated copies, the system could provide more efficient backup solutions with smaller backup sizes and cheaper storage costs to its customers.

Layered storage keeps "hot" data in a more capable storage to provide rich interactions, such as complex queries and faster accesses, whereas it keeps "cold" data in cheaper storage to reduce overall costs. Some compliance policies require certain retention periods for data. In this case, choosing a more cost-effective storage is the key to keeping the cost down while still satisfying compliance requirements.

Evaluating data storage qualities

Most applications require data stores to be scalable and reliable. In this section, we'll briefly discuss what you should consider to ensure that the selected data stores provide such QoS characteristics.

> **NOTE** **SECURITY**
>
> Security is also a very important service quality. However, it's too big a topic to be covered here. For some related discussions in this book, refer to Chapter 2 and Chapter 3.

Reliability

A common method for data stores to provide reliability and availability is to use replicas. For example, by default Azure Storage keeps three copies of your data automatically. And you can turn on geo-replication that keeps two 3-copy replicas across different geographic regions that are hundreds of miles apart. Such replication and clustering exist in third-party data stores such as Redis, MongoDB, and MySQL.

When you provision a new SQL Database in Azure, the database is backed by multiple active secondaries. When the primary fails, a secondary automatically steps in without the need for you to perform any explicit actions.

If you choose to host data stores yourself, you need to ensure that they are configured with redundancy. For example, when you configure MongoDB, you probably want to set up a replica set with a primary and two secondaries.

Scalability

A common practice in the industry to scale data stores is *data sharding*. If the data store you chose doesn't support sharding natively, you'll need to perform it yourself at application level, which is quite difficult to do.

Azure SQL Database Elastic Scale (currently in preview) provides native data sharding support. From an application developer's perspective, SQL Database Elastic Scale provides a series of .NET APIs for various sharding-related tasks:

- **Shard map management (SMM)**   Defines groups of shards for your application and manages mapping of routing keys to shards. With Elastic Scale, you can dynamically reallocate tenants to different shards as loads from particular tenants change. You can monitor the performance of each shard and split busy shards, or merge idle shards dynamically as needed.

- **Data dependent routing (DDR)**   Routes incoming requests to the correct shard (such as routing by tenant ID) and ensures correct routing as tenants move. DDR makes writing queries against shared databases easy. For example, you can use the following query to check the sales numbers of a particular tenant:

```
SELECT * from SalesData WHERE TenantID = 123
```

DDR helps you to route the query to the appropriate shard where the tenant data resides. To avoid repetitive queries to SMM, the Elastic Scale client library also provides a route map cache so that the client application doesn't need to continuously utilize SMM to look up shards.

- **Multishard query (MSQ)**   Interactively processes data across multiple shards. For example, you can execute the same statement on all shards and get results in a T-SQL UNION ALL semantic.

> **NOTE   MIGRATION FROM SQL DATABASE FEDERATIONS**
>
> If you've been using Azure SQL Database Federations, there's a tool named Federation Migration Utility that can help you migrate Federation applications to Elastic Scale without any data movement. You can get a copy of the tool at *https://code.msdn.microsoft.com/vstudio/Federations-Migration-ce61e9c1*.
>
> The federation feature will retire with Web and Business editions in September 2015.

> **NOTE   ADOPTING MULTITENANCY**
>
> Adapting a single-tenant application for multitenancy is a serious architectural change that should not be taken lightly. Such change often needs modifications across all application layers, so it's a high-risk change. More important, multitenancy often has profound impacts on business processes, such as sales strategy, support workflow, and version managements. For example, because all customers are moved to new versions at the same time, a customer can't elect to keep using a known working version to reduce the risk of breaking changes. Another example is that at business level, the company often needs to adapt from licensing or installation-based sales to subscription-based sales, which deeply affects sales prediction, cash flow management, and even sales team building.

Thought experiment
Data storage changes when adapting an application for multitenancy

In this thought experiment, apply what you've learned about this objective. You can find answers to these questions in the "Answers" section at the end of this chapter.

When on-premises applications are migrated to the cloud, one common challenge is to change the application architecture from single-tenant to multitenant. Traditional on-premises deployments often have a one-to-one relationship between service deployments and customers. When deployed to the cloud, it's desirable to bring in multitenancy support for several reasons. First, multitenancy affords more effective usage of compute and storage resources because resources can be repurposed for different tenants as needed. Second, multitenancy simplifies application management. For example, you can roll out an update to all tenants at the same time. Third, multitenancy creates additional opportunities for new features and additional business intelligence across the customer base. With this in mind, answer the following questions:

1. What changes do you need to make to data stores in such cases?

2. How do you control the risks of such changes?

Objective summary

- Immediate consistency ensures that all readers read the same version of data all the time. Eventual consistency means that readers will get the same version of data some time thereafter.
- Pessimistic concurrency requires a data lock to avoid update conflicts. Optimistic concurrency use revision numbers to detect conflicts in updates.
- Sequential data access is suitable to read continuous ranges of data. Random data access is suitable to address individual data points.
- Relational database is suitable for transactional data and complex queries.
- Complex queries on NoSQL databases can be enabled by inferred schemas and full-text indexes.
- Data cache is an effective way to reduce the cost of repetitive queries.
- You should pick data stores that are most suitable to save specific types of data.
- Keeping data stores close to compute components can improve overall system performance.
- A layered data storage strategy can help you to achieve balance between performance and cost.
- Data sharding is a common practice to scale-out data stores.
- Data replication is a common practice to improve data store availability.

Objective review

Answer the following questions to test your knowledge of the information in this objective. You can find the answers to these questions and explanations of why each answer choice is correct or incorrect in the "Answers" section at the end of this chapter.

1. What is a common practice to scale-out data stores?

   A. Data replication

   B. Data sharding

   C. Use NoSQL databases

   D. Use more powerful database instances

2. For a read-heavy application, what are the possible techniques to improve data-read performance?

   A. Optimistic concurrency

   B. Data cache

   C. Read-only replica

   D. Prepopulated views

3. For a write-heavy application, what are the possible techniques to improve data-write performance?

   A. Pessimistic concurrency

   B. Data sharding

   C. Use more powerful database instances

   D. Eliminate unnecessary database indexes

Objective 4.4: Integrate Azure services in a solution

Azure provides a rich set of application services to help developers implement various typical scenarios. However, it's unrealistic to cover all the application services in a single objective, even just briefly, not to mention the new services that are being added all the time. In this objective, we'll go through several common application types and introduce some of the application services that you can use to realize these scenarios.

> **This section covers the following topics:**
> - Creating data-centric web applications
> - Working with Big Data and the Internet of Things
> - Building enterprise mobile applications
> - Creating media applications
> - Managing related services

Creating data-centric web applications

Modern web applications use high-performance architectures, are convenient to use, and are often visually pleasing. Another characteristic of modern web applications is that they are frequently used to present large amounts of data. The traditional page-based navigation doesn't work for these types of applications. Instead, flexible queries and searches become necessities.

Ingredients

In the past, most data queries were carried out on relational databases. Today, most data is saved in NoSQL databases and Blob storages, making structured queries nearly impossible. One possible solution is to automatically abstract schemas out of data sets to re-enable structured queries. Another possible solution is to use full-text indexes, which makes it possible for information to be recalled by using key words or key phrases.

Another piece to complete the puzzle of scalable data presentation is the strategic use of caches. For example, you could keep more frequently accessed "hot" data in memory for faster accesses. Another example is to cache repetitive query results to preclude frequent, expensive queries. Furthermore, Content Delivery Networks (CDNs) can significantly reduce system loads by serving cached content directly from CDN edge nodes.

Sometimes, even flexible searches are not enough, especially when it's difficult to ensure precision of query results. In this case, users still need to navigate through a large set of recalled data to find the optimum answer. Automatic ranking of data can significantly improve user satisfaction by presenting the most relevant entries at the top. To push even further, a recommendation brings the most interesting data to the users without the need for explicit search operations. Recommendations are commonly made based on entity popularity, similarity, purchase histories, and so on.

Table 4-3 lists how a number of Azure services are used to realize different application features in this scenario.

TABLE 4-3 Map between Azure services and application features

Web component	Azure services
Search and query	DocumentDB, Azure Search
Cache	Azure Cache, CDN
Recommendation	Azure Search, Azure Machine Learning

AZURE DOCUMENTDB

DocumentDB is a NoSQL database for JSON documents. It automatically indexes all documents for relational and hierarchical queries. DocumentDB is optimized for frequent writes so that you can push documents into DocumentDB quickly and update documents as frequently as needed. And, it automatically maintains all indexes for you. Finally, if data is written in bursts that are too big to be indexed synchronously, you can change the indexing mode from consistent (synchronous) to lazy (asynchronous).

You can create a new DocumentDB database by using the Preview Management Portal. In each DocumentDB, you can create multiple collections of documents. You can also scale-out DocumentDB by *capacity units*. Each capacity unit includes 10 GB of database storage and reserved throughput. Then, you can use DocumentSQL, which is quite similar to SQL syntax, to query your documents. For example, the following query returns children of a JSON document with a family-children structure:

```
var items = client.CreateDocumentQuery<dynamic>(documentCollection.DocumentsLink,
    "SELECT f.id, c.FirstName AS child " +
    "FROM Families f " +
    "JOIN c IN f.Children");
```

AZURE SEARCH

Popularized by leading search engines, the ubiquitous search tool has become an expected method of navigation for most users. Instead of trying to manually locate the correct page to view, users can easily acquire the most relevant data by performing simple searches.

Search is a hosted service that helps you to easily incorporate search capabilities into your websites. In addition to full-text search, Search also affords advanced search behaviors such as autosuggestion, autocompletion, faceted searches, results highlighting, spell corrections, and geospatial searches.

You interact with Search through REST APIs or the Azure Search Client Library (as a NuGet package). For example, the query that follows searches on the term "lamp" and returns color, category, and price facets. The query returns the top 10 results.

```
https://my-app.search.windows.net/indexes/furnitures/docs
?search=lamp&facet=category&facet=color&facet=price,values:50|10|150|200&$top=10
&api-version=2014-07-31-Preview
```

AZURE CDN

CDN is a global high-bandwidth content delivery solution. It caches static compute contents and Blobs such as images, stylesheets, and script files on its physical nodes across the globe. As of this writing, there are more than 30 CDN point-of-presence (POP) locations in the United States, Europe, Asia, and Australia.

Contents are cached and served from POP locations. When the original contents become unavailable (because of deletion or restricted access), it is removed from POP locations after TTL expires.

CDN improves site performance in two ways: First, it provides faster response time by serving contents from locations closest to the end user, and second, it removes a large portion of content serving workloads from the service servers. Some sites report that more than 90 percent of the traffic is served from POP locations.

Sample architecture

In this sample scenario, users can access an online album website to create albums and to upload pictures and video clips to these albums. In the background, the system runs some image analysis algorithms to tag the pictures to indicate their features, such as number of people on the picture, location where the picture is taken, and the tone of the picture. For video clips, the system runs speech-to-text analysis to extract scripts. All the features and scripts are indexed for searching.

Figure 4-11 shows the system architecture.

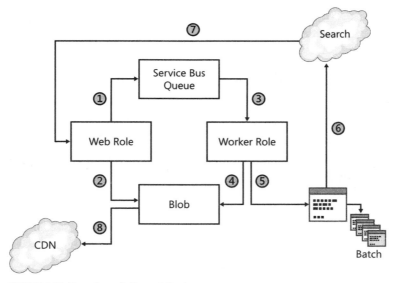

FIGURE 4-11 Sample website architecture

Here's what's happening in Figure 4-11:

1. The web frontend is provided as a Cloud Services Web Role. When a user uploads a picture or a video clip, a job is sent to a Service Bus Queue.

2. The media itself is saved to Blob storage.

3. A Worker Role reads jobs from the job queue.

4. The Worker Role offloads speech-to-text tasks to Batch.

5. The Worker Role runs image analysis locally and augments Blobs with metadata tags.

6. Batch feeds abstracted transcripts to Search.

7. Search features are made available on the Web Role.

8. The CDN is configured to serve contents more efficiently.

Working with Big Data and the Internet of Things

Analyzing data in motion has becoming increasingly important for many businesses in order to gain competitive edge, maintain customer satisfaction, and seek opportunities for continuous improvements and innovation. Big Data is applicable to many scenarios, such as financial sales tracking, smart grid, connected cars, click-stream analysis, data and identity protection, fraud detection, and customer relationship management (CRM). However, due to the sheer volume of data and demanding time constraints, Big Data solutions need to provide data ingress, transform, storage, analysis, and presentation at large scale with great efficiency. Open-source solutions such as Kafka, Storm, and Hadoop have gained great popularity in recent years. However, it requires considerable effort to assemble them into an end-to-end and easily maintainable solution. Now, Azure provides a fleet of Big Data–related services with which you can construct your Big Data and Internet of Things (IoT) solutions easily and host them on Azure.

Ingredients

A canonical Big Data pipeline comprises several components, including data producers, data collectors, data ingestors, data transformation, long-term storage, analysis, and presentation and action. The following describes each of these components:

- **Data producers** These are the entities that generate the original raw data. They can be various types of devices and applications deployed in the field.

- **Data collectors** These can be either in the field or in the cloud. They collect data by either actively retrieving it from the data producers or by providing an interface for data producers to send in data. An explicit data collector isn't always necessary. Many IP-capable devices can directly send data to data ingestors such as Azure Event Hub.

- **Data ingestors** Data ingestors take data into the cloud at great scale. They are the starting points of the data processing pipeline in the cloud.

- **Data transformation**   This transforms data into a consumable format for down-stream processors.
- **Long-term storage**   This maintains the data.
- **Analysis**   This can be done either in real time or at a later time. Real-time analysis sometimes is integrated with data transformation, and non-real time analyses are often done in batches based on aggregated data, instead of based on live streams.
- **Presentation and action**   These present data processing results, including (trans-formed) data streams and analysis results. Then, you can build solutions on top of this data to provide Business Intelligence (BI), monitoring, search, query, alert, command and control, and so on.

There are quite a few Azure services that are designed to enable Big Data and IoT sce-narios. Table 4-4 presents an overview of how these Azure services map into the canonical components in the preceding architecture.

TABLE 4-4 Map between Azure services and Big Data pipeline components

Big Data pipeline component	Azure services
Data ingestor	Event Hubs
Data transformation	Stream Analytics
Long-term storage	HD Insight, Azure Storage, SQL Database, DocumentDB
Analysis	Stream Analytics, Machine Learning, Batch
Presentation and action	Power BI, Excel
Orchestration	Azure Data Factory

EVENT HUBS

Event Hubs facilitats efficient data ingress at scale. An event hub can connect to more than one million data producers, with over 1 Gbps aggregated throughput. You can send data to Event Hubs through either HTTP or AMQP.

Event Hubs provides such scale by means of several partitioning mechanisms in the system.

First, you can create multiple partitions that work in parallel. When a publisher sends data to an event hub, it can directly address a partition by its partition ID. Or, it can use hash-based distribution or random distribution. Each partition needs to be associated with a *Throughput Unit*, which controls the quota and billing of your throughput on that partition. A Throughput Unit can be shared among multiple partitions.

Second, on the consuming side, consumers are organized into *Consumer Groups*. Con-ceptually, Consumer Groups are different views of the same data stream, and consumers in the same group share the same view of data. You can receive data by using either .NET API or a generic AMQP 1.0 client. Supporting AMQP enables great interoperability with existing queue clients of other platforms.

STREAM ANALYTICS

Stream Analytics provides a hosted, reliable, and scalable solution for real-time data analysis. It provides both high throughput and low latency without the need to worry about setting up any underlying infrastructures. Stream Analytics takes in millions of events per second, and it transforms, augments, and correlates data as needed as it works through streams of data. In addition, it can detect patterns and abnormalities in streaming data. Finally, it can correlate streaming data with reference data.

As for reliability, Stream Analytics is designed to preserve data order on a per-device basis without any data loss. The service also has built-in fast recovery to recuperate from failures and maintain high availability.

Stream Analytics provides a SQL-like language for you to easily filter, project, aggregate, and join data streams by using familiar SQL syntax. You can implement advanced scenarios such as pattern detections with a few lines of SQL code. The service also provides a built-in debugging experience as well as real-time monitoring through the management portal to expedite development processes. For example, a query to count the number of tweets by topic takes only the following two lines of code:

```
SELECT count(*), Topic from Tweets
GROUP BY Topic, TumblingWindow(Second, 10)
```

This statement is self-explanatory to developers with even basic understanding of SQL language. The only foreign clause is the *TumblingWindow* function, which creates a tumbling window with fixed time length along your data stream (for more information, go to *https://msdn.microsoft.com/en-us/library/azure/dn834998.aspx*).

AZURE MACHINE LEARNING

Essentially, machine learning is about building systems that can learn from their experiences and adapt their behaviors when confronted with a similar problem later. For example, a typical handwriting recognition system based on machine learning is often trained with a large amount of data, and the system will formulate a detection algorithm that it can apply to future data sets. Machine learning is widely used in many classification, ranking, clustering, and prediction scenarios.

Machine Learning makes machine learning more approachable to not only data scientists but also business analysts. It provides a web-based drag-and-drop UI for you to build and test models, with minimum coding required. In addition, it provides a rich set of best-in-class machine learning algorithms out of the box. And, you can extend it by using R.

When a model is ready, you can easily make it operational through an API service so that web or mobile applications can easily consume the model.

Sample architecture

In this sample scenario, telemetry from a fleet of trucks is collected and monitored on a map. The system also tracks several behaviors of the drivers, including how they follow the posted speed limits, how often they take breaks, and how they plan out their routes. Then, the results are posted on a custom portal.

Figure 4-12 illustrates one possible architecture.

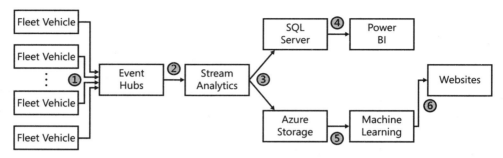

FIGURE 4-12 Sample Big Data architecture

Here's the sequence of events:

1. Data ingestion is handled by Event Hubs.
2. The data stream is pumped into Stream Analytics.
3. Stream Analytics writes data to SQL Server and Azure Storage.
4. Power BI presents and analyzes data in SQL Server.
5. Machine Learning analyzes driver behavior.
6. The Machine Learning model is exposed as a Web API for consumption.

Building enterprise mobile applications

With the increasing popularity of mobile devices, more and more people rely on them to carry out day-to-day business. Many enterprises are motivated to create mobile applications with which their employees can access data and business functionalities at any time, from any place. Enterprise administrators also face the challenges of Bring Your Own Devices (BYOD). They need effective ways to enable mobile devices while at the same time ensuring enterprise data security.

Ingredients

An enterprise mobile application needs several building blocks, including identity, security, connectivity, notification, and integration with other systems.

Most enterprise applications require authentication with the enterprise's Active Directory. Microsoft Azure Active Directory (Azure AD) provides an Azure AD Authentication Library (ADAL) that you can use in your mobile client applications to authenticate with Azure AD. As soon as a user is authenticated with Azure AD, she can access other enterprise applications such as Microsoft SharePoint and Microsoft Office 365 through Single Sign-On (SSO).

Enterprise mobile applications often need to access on-premises data and services, as well. One way to achieve this is to make on-premises services available in the cloud by using services such as Azure Application Proxy and Service Bus Relay. The other way is to connect to on-premises services using connectivity enablers such as Azure App Service BizTalk API Apps Hybrid Connections.

Push notification is a common feature of mobile applications. You can use Azure Notification Hub to push messages to mobile users.

Finally, Azure Mobile Services is a turn-key solution with which you can build mobile applications with a data server, scheduled jobs, push notifications, and so on.

Table 4-5 lists how a number of Azure services are used to realize different application features in this scenario.

TABLE 4-5 Map between Azure services and enterprise mobile applications

Mobile app component	Azure services
Identity	Azure AD
Security and compliance	Workplace Join, Key Vault, Azure Rights Management
Notification	Notification Hubs
Application server	Mobile Services
On-premises integration	BizTalk API Apps Hybrid Connections, Application Proxy, Service Bus Relay

AZURE APP SERVICE BIZTALK API APPS HYBRID CONNECTIONS

With BizTalk API Apps Hybrid Connections, Mobile Services and Azure Websites can connect to on-premises resources that use static TCP ports, such as SQL Server and Web API. Hybrid Connections requires only outbound TCP or HTTP connections. It uses standard HTTP and HTTPS ports. It also uses port 5671 for connecting to Azure, and port 9352 for data exchange when these ports are available.

AZURE NOTIFICATION HUBS

Applications can use Notification Hubs to push messages to any device platform, such as Windows Phone, iOS, Android, and Kindle Fire.

Push notifications are delivered through platform-specific Platform Notification Systems (PNS). For example, Microsoft Windows devices use Windows Notification Services (WNS). For iOS devices, the service is Apple Push Notification Service (APNS). Notification Hubs abstracts all platform-specific details so that you can send messages to different platforms easily.

You can broadcast messages to millions of devices through Notification Hubs. Alternatively, you can push messages to a user, or specific devices of the user. You can also push messages to a group of users; for example, users at a given geographic location.

Sample architecture

In this sample scenario, an enterprise mobile application is designed for enterprise users to access both Office 365 documents and on-premises SharePoint documents as well as on-premises SQL Server database, as well.

Figure 4-13 shows a possible architecture using Mobile Services as the center piece of the solution.

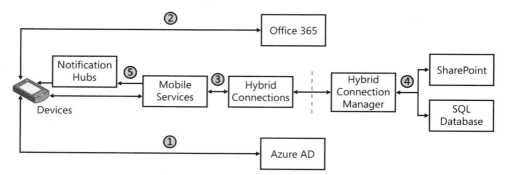

FIGURE 4-13 Sample enterprise mobile application architecture

Here's what the architecture in Figure 4-13 does:

1. A user authenticates with Azure AD.
2. The user accesses Office 365 documents.
3. Mobile Services uses BizTalk API Apps Hybrid Connections.
4. The user connects to on-premises SharePoint and SQL Database.
5. Mobile Services uses Notification Hubs to push messages to mobile devices.

Creating media applications

Delivering media to various types of devices is a very complex problem. You need to deal with not only different encoding and decoding requirements and fluctuations in network conditions, but also security and copyright protections. Fortunately, you don't need to cope with any of these issues yourself. Instead, you can use services such as Azure Media Services.

Ingredients

A media application needs large-scale storage, effective encoding and decoding, flexible streaming, as well as robust content and copyright protection.

AZURE MEDIA SERVICES

Media Services is designed for implementing advanced media applications. It supports high-availability encoding, packaging, and streaming. And, it natively supports all kinds of delivery endpoints including Flash, iOS, Android, HTML5, and Xbox.

Media Services also provides everything you need to implement a live streaming solution. This is the same set of services behind events such as English Premier League broadcasts, FIFA World Cup coverage, and the streaming of the 2014 Winter Olympics in Sochi. Now, your applications can use the same stable, scalable, and efficient services for your own purposes.

In terms of content protection, Media Services provides industry-leading content protection with Microsoft PlayReady Digital Rights Management (DRM) or AES encryption.

Sample architecture

Using this application, you can broadcast a live event to a group of authenticated users, all of whom might be using different mobile device platforms.

Figure 4-14 depicts a possible Media Services architecture.

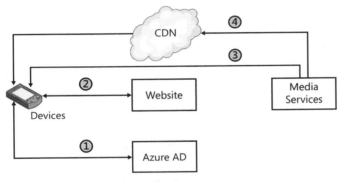

FIGURE 4-14 Sample media application

Here's what the architecture in Figure 4-14 does:

1. Users sign in to Azure AD using ADAL.
2. Users interact with the website to create and manage event metadata.
3. Media Services streams, encodes, and serves video.
4. Media can also be served from through CDN.

EXAM TIP

The key to designing a complex system is to determine how the system should be separated into individual components. More components often bring more flexibility in system design and more agility in development process. However, the increasing number of components also means more complex communication patterns among components. When choosing which services to use in your system, you need to evaluate the services to ensure that they can indeed provide, or can be extended to provide, solutions to the specific problems you need to address. Although some exam questions might ask you to do a simple problem-to-service match, you need to keep in mind that in reality the decision process is often much more complex.

Managing related services

When an application uses many external services, how to manage these services as a logical unit becomes a practical challenge. Before closing this chapter, let's briefly review some of the tools and services that help you to manage a group of related Azure resources.

Resource groups

Using Azure resource groups, you can manage all resources in an application as a logical unit. This logical unit provides a lifecycle boundary and a security context across all resources in the application.

- **Lifecycle boundary**   You can describe all resources of an application in a single JSON-based template. You can provision or de-provision all resources at the same time.

- **Security context**   You can apply Role-Based Access Control (RBAC) policies to a resource group. All resources in the group inherit the group-level policies.

The Preview Management Portal

The new Preview Management Portal focuses on application-centric views instead of resource-centric views provided by the existing portal. With the new portal, you also can customize your views to bring in all application-related information into the same window. Figure 4-15 shows an example of a customized view that contains billing, service health, performance, visit statistics, and load test results, all in the same view.

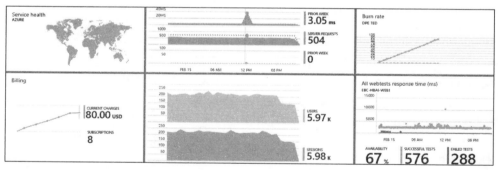

FIGURE 4-15 A sample custom view on the new Preview Management Portal

Scripting options

You can also manage a group of Azure resources programmatically by using Azure Management API, Azure PowerShell (including DSC), and Azure cross-platform CLI. Furthermore, you can automate configuration tasks by using Azure services such as Azure Automation, or third-party services such as Chef and Puppet.

Thought experiment

Dealing with service dependencies

In this thought experiment, apply what you've learned about this objective. You can find answers to these questions in the "Answers" section at the end of this chapter.

With more and more SaaS offerings available on the market, you'll find that in many situations when you need a specific functionality, there's already a proven service out there providing exactly what you need. As an architect, you need to evaluate different services and incorporate them into your applications.

With this in mind, answer the following questions:

1. What are the evaluation criteria that you would use?

2. How do you prepare for the case in which a service can no longer satisfy your requirements?

Objective summary

- DocumentDB is a NoSQL database for JSON documents.
- Azure Search is a hosted service with which you can incorporate search capabilities into your application.
- Search, ranking, and recommendation are common features of modern web applications.
- CDN serves static content directly from its edge nodes for faster access.
- A canonical Big Data architecture includes data producers, data ingestors, data transformation, long-term storage, analysis, presentation and action.
- Event Hubs is a highly scalable service for data ingestion to Azure.
- Stream Analytics provides live data-stream transformations and analysis with high scale and low latency.
- Machine Learning makes machine learning approachable through an intuitive UI and built-in models.
- Cloud applications can use BizTalk API Apps Hybrid Connections to connect to on-premises data and resources.
- You can use Notification Hubs to send push notifications to large numbers of devices of different types.
- Media Services provides a comprehensive set of media streaming, encoding, decoding, publication, and protection services.

Objective review

Answer the following questions to test your knowledge of the information in this objective. You can find the answers to these questions and explanations of why each answer choice is correct or incorrect in the "Answers" section at the end of this chapter.

1. Azure provides a number of NoSQL data stores. Which of the following are such stores?

    A. Blob storage

    B. Table storage

    C. DocumentDB

    D. MongoDB

2. A Big Data solution is a pipeline that involves many components. Which of the following components belong to this pipeline?

    A. Event Hubs

    B. Stream Analytics

    C. Machine Learning

    D. Power BI

3. If you want to push messages to a large number of devices, which Azure services should you consider?

    A. Web Apps

    B. Event Hubs

    C. Notification Hubs

    D. CDN

4. What features of modern websites can help users to navigate through large amounts of data?

    A. Search

    B. Data ranking

    C. Recommendation

    D. Input auto-completion

5. Which of the following services can help you to connect to on-premises resources?

    A. BizTalk API Apps Hybrid Connections

    B. Service Bus Relay

    C. Azure Application Proxy

    D. Azure Virtual Network

Answers

This section contains the solutions to the thought experiments and answers to the objective review questions in this chapter.

Objective 4.1: Thought experiment

1. In most cases, Azure Batch should be a clear choice when you need to execute many tasks in parallel. Batch provides a flexible programming model as well as comprehensive management and monitoring capabilities to manage your tasks. Batch also has built-in MapReduce support.

2. If you want tasks to be executed in Linux environments, you'll need to implement your own solution, because as of this writing Batch doesn't support Linux TVMs.

Objective 4.1: Review

1. **Correct answer:** A

   A. **Correct:** A8, A9, A10, and A11 are optimized for compute-intensive workloads. They have high-speed multicore CPUs and large amounts of memory. A8 and A9 are also equipped with fast network connections.

   B. **Incorrect:** D-series is designed for workloads with high demand on compute power as well as temporary disk performance.

   C. **Incorrect:** DS-series can use Premium storage, which gives you sustainable, high-performance IO operations.

   D. **Incorrect:** G-series provides the largest VM sizes in the industry. These VMs make it possible to scale-up legacy applications in the cloud.

2. **Correct answers:** A and C

   A. **Correct:** With Azure Batch API, you can directly schedule computational tasks onto a pool of resources.

   B. **Incorrect:** Azure Service Management API is for programmatically managing Azure resources. It's not specific to Batch.

   C. **Correct:** Using Batch Apps API, you can wrap an existing application and run it as parallel tasks.

   D. **Incorrect:** Azure API Management is a service that helps you to develop, host, and manage APIs. It's not related to Batch.

3. **Correct answers:** A, B, C, and D

   A. **Correct:** Batch manages all the underlying infrastructures for your compute tasks. You don't need to manage compute resources yourself.

   B. **Correct:** Batch provides a management portal for you to submit, manage, and monitor your batch jobs.

C. **Correct:** Batch is a hosted service on Azure, which is backed by a tremendous amount of compute resources. You can scale-out to a very large number of cores as needed.

D. **Correct:** Batch supports both Batch API and Batch Apps API for you to interact with Batch as different levels.

Objective 4.2: Thought experiment

1. App Service Web Apps is designed specifically to host web workloads. Not only can you host ASP.NET applications, you can also easily host PHP, Java, and Python-based websites. Azure Websites also has built-in support of WebJobs, which are periodic jobs triggered on the server for routine tasks. Furthermore, you can pick from a wide variety of website templates to create common websites.

   Azure Cloud Services is designed for multitiered applications. If your web tier is a presentation layer of a larger system, you can consider Cloud Services Web Roles.

   Finally, Azure Virtual Machine gives you the most flexibility in building highly customized environments, including Linux-based environments. Of course, if you choose to use Virtual Machines, you are taking on the responsibility of managing infrastructures yourself.

2. Both Web Apps and Cloud Services have built-in support for scaling up and scaling out. For websites hosted on Virtual Machines, you can scale up by using bigger VM sizes. When you scale out VMs, you can join the machines into the same cloud service so that you can take advantage of Azure load-balancing to distribute workloads among multiple VM instances.

Objective 4.2: Review

1. **Correct answers:** A, B, C, and D

   A. **Correct:** With Azure, you can deploy multiple instances of your service behind a load balancer for high availability.

   B. **Correct:** With Azure, you can adjust number of your service instances either manually or automatically.

   C. **Correct:** Azure supports concepts such as automatic role recovery to help you improve your application's reliability.

   D. **Correct:** Azure provides services such as Azure AD and RBAC for your authentication and authorization needs.

2. **Correct answers:** A and B

   A. **Correct:** Scaling up increases the processing power of individual service instances.

   B. **Correct:** Scaling out increases system capacity by introducing more service instances to share the workload.

C.   **Incorrect:** Primary–secondary deployment is for availability instead of scalability. The secondaries don't take on any workloads. Instead, a secondary is promoted to primary to take on the workload if the primary fails.

D.   **Incorrect:** Loose coupling is a design pattern. Although loose coupling makes it possible for you to scale different components independently, it doesn't have a direct impact on system capacity.

3.   **Correct answers:** A, B, and C

A.   **Correct:** Input Endpoints are public, load-balanced endpoints that service consumers can access.

B.   **Correct:** Internal Endpoints are private endpoints for roles within a cloud service to interact with each other.

C.   **Correct:** Instance Input Endpoints are public endpoints through which you can address individual service instances by choosing corresponding ports in the port range.

D.   **Incorrect:** Output Endpoints do not exist.

4.   **Correct answers:** A, B, C, and D

A.   **Correct:** You can add or remove consumers at any time without affecting task generators or other consumers.

B.   **Correct:** You can deploy consumers in the cloud or on-premises. You can have a mixture of consumers written in different languages and hosted in different environments.

C.   **Correct:** A consumer locks on a task until it finishes with it. If the consumer crashes before it unlocks the task, the lock expires after a predefined amount of time so that the task can be picked up by another consumer. The Competing Consumer pattern ensures that a task is handled at least once (a task might be handled multiple times, though. The task developer should ensure idempotence of the task).

D.   **Correct:** By using a high-availability messaging system, Competing Consumer patterns can eliminate the need to use a central job dispatcher or scheduler.

5.   **Correct answers:** A, B, C, and D

A.   **Correct:** You can use Application Insights to monitor various types of your Azure resources, including compute services such as Web Apps and Cloud Services.

B.   **Correct:** New Relic is a supported third-party monitoring solution.

C.   **Correct:** AppDynamic is a supported third-party monitoring solution.

D.   **Correct:** Azure management portal provides customizable views, charts, and reports for you to monitor your application statuses.

Objective 4.3: Thought experiment

1. Adapting a data store for multitenancy has three different levels of requirements: accommodation, isolation, and federation.

   Accommodation is the most basic requirement, which means tenant information needs to be captured and stored. Whether the existing data schema needs to be extended to include a tenant as an additional key depends on the application requirements and design. However, it's usually not a good idea to perform such radical changes, especially when database keys need to be redefined. Accommodation also means that the data store needs to be scalable to accommodate data for not only one customer, but potentially for hundreds or even thousands of customers. As discussed in the objective, a common practice is to use data sharding to scale-out data stores for increased storage demands.

   Isolation is a security requirement. Customer data must remain isolated, either physically or logically, from one another. This is to ensure that one customer won't gain access to another customer's data, either intentionally or accidentally. Isolation is a key compliance requirement for most multitenant systems.

   Federation refers to queries and features across multiple tenants. Although certain scenarios can be implemented at application level, a strong data-store support such as Azure SQL Database Elastic Scale can greatly simplify implementation of such scenarios.

   You can also design a system in a mixed mode, in which a pool of resources is multitenant but limited to a certain number of tenants. This mode introduces flexibilities in version controls so that some customers can be kept on the last known working version to reduce the risk of breaking changes.

2. In traditional layered architectures, modifying databases often leads to rippling changes across all layers. Sometimes, deploying a separate database per customer is not necessarily a bad choice. Then, new tenants can be hosted with modified data stores where multitenancy is natively supported. This arrangement affords a controlled, step-by-step approach to migrate all customers.

Objective 4.3: Review

1. **Correct answer:** B

   A. **Incorrect:** Data replication is for data availability.

   B. **Correct:** Data sharding is a common practice to scale-out data stores.

   C. **Incorrect:** Although you can scale-out many NoSQL databases, it doesn't necessarily mean that NoSQL databases provide more scalability than relational databases or other data storage options.

   D. **Incorrect:** Using more powerful instances is to scale up instead of scaling out.

2. **Correct answers:** A, B, C, and D

    A. **Correct:** Optimistic concurrency works the best with less frequent database up-dates by avoiding locks.

    B. **Correct:** Caching is an important technique to reduce workloads on a database by directly serving cached results to applications.

    C. **Correct:** Read-only replicas, especially cross-region read-only replicas, make it possible for users from different geographic regions to access data from the rep-lica that is the closest to them, thus gaining the best read performance.

    D. **Correct:** Some database queries could be complex. Prepopulated views (or materi-alized views) make result sets available in advance.

3. **Correct answers:** A, B, C, and D

    A. **Correct:** Although pessimistic concurrency uses locks, it avoids possible write con-flicts by implementing optimistic concurrency. The benefit is most apparent when rolling back a failed transaction is expensive.

    B. **Correct:** Data sharding facilitates more parallel writes because different shards can handle write requests from different tenants independently.

    C. **Correct:** Scaling up is an easy and effective way to boost database performance. This had been the go-to solution prior to the cloud era.

    D. **Correct:** Rebuilding indexes incurs additional overheads. You should examine your database to eliminate unnecessary indexes to avoid such overheads, which can seriously affect write performance.

Objective 4.4: Thought experiment

1. QoS is an obvious metric for evaluating services. When evaluating a service, its scalabil-ity, availability, reliability, manageability, and security need to be evaluated to verify that the service matches with your application requirements. In addition, its simplicity and extensibility are also important aspects to consider in terms of productivity. On the business side, the service's price, SLA agreements, and even level of customer sup-ports should also be examined. The bottom line is that using an external service takes effort. As a manager, you should budget enough time and resources to ensure that the service is a real match. As a technical lead, you should not be over-optimistic just because some prototype works.

2. Adopting an external service has its inherent risks. There's no guarantee that the chosen services will have the same lifespan of your own applications. Although an exit strategy isn't always practical, some architecture patterns such as loose coupling, MicroServies, and SOA can help to control such risks.

Objective 4.4: Review

1. **Correct answers:** A, B, and C

   A. **Correct:** Blob storage is a NoSQL storage designed to hold large amounts of binary or text data files.

   B. **Correct:** Table storage is a key-value store that can save large amounts of unstructured data.

   C. **Correct:** DocumentDB is a NoSQL database for JSON documents.

   D. **Incorrect:** MongoDB is not a Microsoft product. However, it's provided through Azure Store.

2. **Correct answers:** A, B, C, and D

   A. **Correct:** Notification Hubs is a scalable data ingestion component.

   B. **Correct:** Stream Analytics is a data transformation component.

   C. **Correct:** Machine Learning is a data analysis component.

   D. **Correct:** Power BI is a data presentation component.

3. **Correct answer:** C

   A. **Incorrect:** Websites is designed to host various kinds of web workloads.

   B. **Incorrect:** Event Hubs is for scalable data ingestion.

   C. **Correct:** Notification Hubs is designed to push messages to mobile devices at scale.

   D. **Incorrect:** CDN is for static content distribution. However, it doesn't proactively push content to clients.

4. **Correct answers:** A, B, C, and D

   A. **Correct:** Search helps users to locate data quickly via key words and key phrases.

   B. **Correct:** Data ranking brings the most relevant data to the top of result sets for easier access.

   C. **Correct:** Recommendation helps users to discover relevant data without explicit user actions.

   D. **Correct:** Input autocompletion provides on-the-spot hints to help users narrow down appropriate search terms to use.

5. **Correct answers:** A, B, C, and D

    A. **Correct:** Using BizTalk API Apps Hybrid Connections, cloud applications can connect to on-premises data and services.

    B. **Correct:** With Service Bus Relay, on-premises services can register a publically accessible endpoint for service consumption.

    C. **Correct:** You can use Azure Application Proxy to securely make on-premises web applications available in the cloud, securely.

    D. **Correct:** Azure Virtual Network supports Point-to-Site connection as well as Site-to-Site connection that can bridge your on-cloud virtual networks and your local network segments.

## CHAPTER 5

Design Web Apps

Websites are the identities that an individual or company presents to the rest of the world. And the pervasiveness of technology in general and advances in the web in particular have made sophisticated users out of nearly everyone. People now reflexively use web resources to gather information, whether it's to learn about a company and its products or services or simply to connect with friends via social media. At the same time, users' expectations regarding performance and design have become more exacting. Today, a slow website is something that most people will not tolerate, and they will quickly move on to another site without hesitation. This means that websites must be designed to support features such as scalability as well as maintenance features such as backup and restore.

When looking at this topic against the backdrop of certification exams, you need to keep in mind that Microsoft Azure and the Azure management portal as well as the Azure Preview Management Portal change frequently. The exams are based on the portals and features that are available when the exam was written. The screenshots and features might be slightly different from what you see in the portals when you are studying for the exam.

For example, the portals reflect the recent name change from Azure Websites to Azure App Service Web Apps. However, the information in the topic has not changed much from what is needed for the architecture exam.

Objectives in this chapter:

- Objective 5.1: Design Web Apps for scalability and performance
- Objective 5.2: Deploy websites
- Objective 5.3: Design websites for business continuity

Objective 5.1: Design web applications for scalability and performance

When a website is slow or unresponsive, people are quick to think that it is unavailable or is just a poorly constructed site, and they will move on to another one. So, performance is an important issue that you need to address and keep in mind when designing the web application. Azure Web Apps provides options to scale and debug a website to help developers find issues that can cause slow performance. Azure has multiple ways to host websites and to support moving existing websites or generating a new one. Web Apps also support any type of web development language and not just websites developed with Microsoft Visual Studio. Azure Web Apps were built to be used for any type of website and to support the operation of the site.

> **This section covers the following topics:**
> - Globally scale websites
> - Create websites using Microsoft Visual Studio
> - Debug websites
> - Understand supported languages
> - Websites, VMs, and cloud services

Globally scale websites

More companies are doing business globally and need to have their website support scaling globally. App Service Web Apps supports scaling globally to help decrease load times for accessing a website, which translates to a better experience for users.

One option to scale a website globally is to use a Content Delivery Network (CDN). This caches the static content of a website to other regions around the world, placing the website physically closer to the various locations from which people are trying to access it. You can configure the CDN with the domain name itself and have it point to a web application as its *origin domain*. When requests then come into the CDN for the website, it ensures that the site is copied over to a region closest to the user. There are very few settings for the CDN. You can add a custom domain name to the website, and you can enable HTTPS and query string forwarding. Figure 5-1 shows the configuration in the management portal.

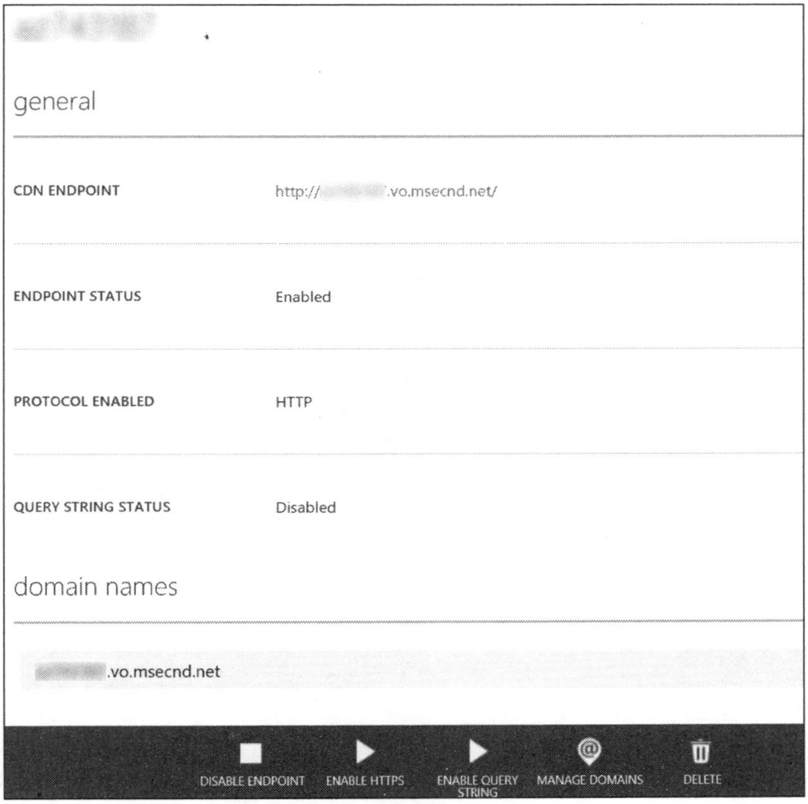

general

CDN ENDPOINT	http://███████.vo.mscnd.net/
ENDPOINT STATUS	Enabled
PROTOCOL ENABLED	HTTP
QUERY STRING STATUS	Disabled

domain names

███████.vo.msecnd.net

DISABLE ENDPOINT   ENABLE HTTPS   ENABLE QUERY STRING   MANAGE DOMAINS   DELETE

FIGURE 5-1 CDN setup in the management portal

The second option to scale a web application globally is to use Azure Traffic Manager. You can deploy web applications around the world and then, via Traffic Manager, you use a single URL to reference all of them. This means that the web application that is closest possible geographically will be used when a person visits the website. Using the Traffic Manager invloves more configuration work to handle the traffic load and entails more manual effort than the CDN solution if new traffic patterns come up, but it provides better control on where the other web applications are being deployed around the world. CDN will deploy when it is called from a location, whereas by using a Traffic Manager, the locations are all planned out carefully at the beginning.

> **MORE INFO   SCALING WEB APPLICATIONS**
>
> You can learn more about scaling web applications at *http://channel9.msdn.com/Events/ TechEd/NewZealand/2014/DEV320*.

Create websites using Microsoft Visual Studio

Visual Studio Community Edition 2013 is a great tool to create websites for hosting in Azure. Your first task in the setup is to ensure that the latest Azure SDK is installed. If you have Azure SDK 2.5 or earlier installed, the App Service Web Apps features will show up as Azure Websites. Keep this in mind for the exam because the wording in the questions could be different than what you see in the portals currently.

To create a new web application for Azure using Visual Studio, click File, and then choose New, Project. (You can use the File, New, Website, but that is an older template to create a website.) In the New Project dialog box that opens (Figure 5-2), in the tree on the left, select your favorite language, and then select Web for the project type. Notice the arrow indicating that there are more Templates. These are also older templates for Visual Studio 2012. I recommend that you work with the ASP.NET Web Application option in Web. You also can select Cloud because the same template for ASP.NET Web Application is available there, as well. On the right side of the dialog box, select the Add Application Insights To Project check box. (We will talk more about this later in the chapter).

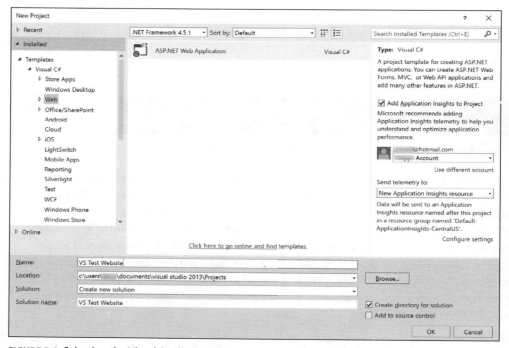

FIGURE 5-2 Selecting the Visual Studio Template

The next step is to pick what type of ASP.NET project will be created. Figure 5-3 shows the New ASP.NET Project dialog box with the options that are installed by the Azure SDK. In the lower-right corner of the dialog box, notice the Microsoft Azure section. If you select the Host In The Cloud check box, the dialog box that would then open is where you would set up the Web App into Azure and select the region and Service Plan to use. If you do not select Host In The Cloud, the publishing step is where all of this can be tied to Azure.

The available templates at this step show Web Forms, MVC, Web API, Single Page Applications, Azure Mobile Service, as well as the new Azure API App.

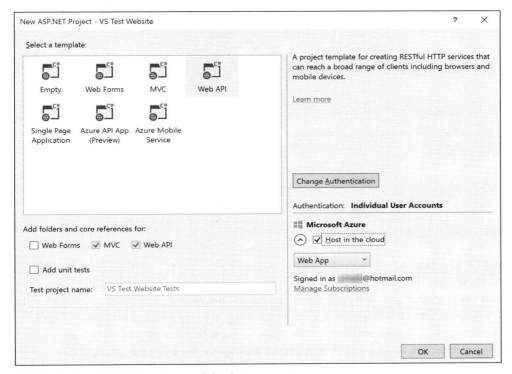

FIGURE 5-3 The ASP.NET Project setup dialog box

If you selected the Host In The Cloud check box, the Configure Microsoft Azure Web App dialog opens, as shown in Figure 5-4. The dialog box provides default selections for the Azure subscription, location, and service plan for the new site. It also provides a random name; change this to the name that you would like to use for the site.

FIGURE 5-4 Azure Web App settings

Click OK to create the new web application, which you can run from within Visual Studio for development and testing. When you've completed development and testing, there are multiple methods that you can use to move and publish the web application to Azure. The first is to use an Azure PowerShell script. The second way is to right-click the main Web App project within Visual Studio, and then, in the shortcut menu that opens, choose Publish. This should already be set up against the Web Deploy settings for the web application. If there are parts of the web deploy that are missing, you can remove the settings and download the publish profile from Azure again. From within the Publish dialog box, you can also publish the web application using FTP. This is a quick process that will ensure you have the correct settings. The final way that you can publish websites to Azure is to use Continuous Deployment using a source repository. You can read more about using a source repository in Objective 5.2.

> **MORE INFO   CREATING WEBSITES USING VISUAL STUDIO**
>
> You can learn more about creating websites using Visual Studio at *http://azure.microsoft. com/en-us/documentation/articles/web-sites-dotnet-get-started/*.

Debug websites

Of course, there are times when something goes wrong on the website that you are developing, and it needs to be debugged. The best way is to first debug the website locally to verify that it functions correctly. Still, developers know that just because a site works in their browser on their desktop, that doesn't mean it will function flawlessly in the production environment, if it functions at all.

Monitor

One of the most basic ways to troubleshoot your site is to use the Monitor component that is built into the blade for the web application. You can use the Monitor to view data such as requests and errors that have occurred on the server. You also can add alerts to notify you when certain conditions are met (for example, Http Server Errors > 0). Other metrics that you can add include CPU Time, Data In, Data Out, and more. Figure 5-5 shows the Monitor Chart.

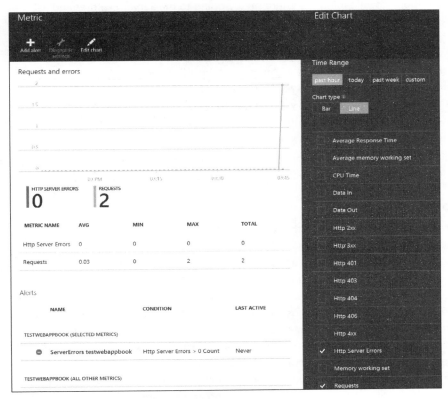

FIGURE 5-5 Setting up the Monitor component

Azure Application Insights

Application Insights is a system in Azure by which any website can send telemetry data to the Preview Management portal. There are many different versions of the Application Insights SDK that you add to your site based on the platform, language, and the IDE being used. By default, Visual Studio specifies a new ASP.NET application. To add Application Insights to any website running on any server, on the Application Insights blade, click the Quick Start button (a cloud and a lightning bolt graphic). This provides a script to add to the pages that you would like to monitor. First, however, you need to create Application Insights, but you can use this to add a monitor from any webserver, not just Azure. The data is stored in Azure, and the charting in the Application Insights blade displays various captured data elements.

Visual Studio

Visual Studio provides you with the ability to remotely debug the web application in Azure. You can do this without downloading the entire site by going to the Server Explorer and opening the Azure item. Websites are listed in the App Service section and then organized by the Resource group. To debug a web application using Visual Studio, right-click its name, and then, in the shortcut menu that opens, select Attach Debugger. If you have the Python tools installed, the shortcut menu will also have an option to Attach Debugger (Python). Visual Studio will load the page in a browser window and attach the debugger to the process running in Azure. A DOM Explorer opens in which you can debug the site itself. The DOM Explorer includes a pane that shows the styles, computed data, layout, events, and changes to help you to determine the source of any issues with the website.

Visual Studio also gives access to the log files in the Azure section of the Server Explorer. You can double-click any of the logs to read them within Visual Studio.

Site Control Manager

The Site Control Manager (SCM) is a tool that you can use to debug your website. You can run it from the *https://<webapp>.scm.azurewebsites.net/* for a site. The Site Control Manager site runs Project Kudu, which is an open-source project for managing deployments, WebJobs, and other features for Web Apps. You can find the project at *https://github.com/projectkudu/kudu*. By default, the Site Control Manager shows currently running processes, system information, application settings, connection strings, environment variables, PATH, HTTP headers, and server variables. Site Control Manager also has the ability to launch a remote CMD or PowerShell window so that you can perform commands directly. These windows also provide a graphical representation of the file structure for the current folder. From this portal, you can add in site extensions to carry out tasks such as watching the Event Log, or you can add a direct editor using Visual Studio Online. You can create and add custom Site Extensions to the site, as well, which you can read about in Objective 5.2.

The Site Control Manager also has the ability to stream log files for display. There are also site extensions in the gallery to view the log files.

Understand supported languages

One of the biggest benefits of Azure is that it supports the use of many different open-source languages for developing applications and websites. The supported languages are .NET, Java, Node.js, PHP, and Python. Let's take a look at each of them.

.NET

.NET is used in many applications to develop websites, including ASP.NET Web Forms, MVC apps, Single Page Applications, or Web API sites. You can publish ASP.NET Web Applications to Azure Web Apps even if they were not originally built for Azure. The publishing dialog boxes can use the publishing profile files from Azure to set up all of the fields for the Web Deploy or FTP transfer of all of the files needed to run on Azure. Visual Studio includes templates that you can use with C# or Visual Basic .NET. To support older ASP.NET websites, App Services Web Apps also supports .NET 3.5 as well as .NET 4.5. This makes it possible for companies that have not upgraded to the newest version of .NET to still use and transfer websites to Azure. Figure 5-6 shows the ASP.NET templates that you can deploy in Azure.

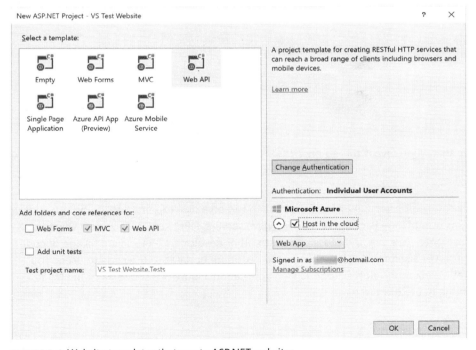

FIGURE 5-6 Website templates that create ASP.NET websites

Java

By default, in App Services Web Apps, Java is turned off when you create a new website. To use Java on the website, you need to turn this on in the Application Settings section of the website in the Preview Management Portal or in the Configure section in the management portal. Figure 5-7 shows the setting to turn on Java. When you turn on the Java runtime, the second option for the Web Container becomes active. This is the container that will host the Java runtime. You can set this to Tomcat or Jetty.

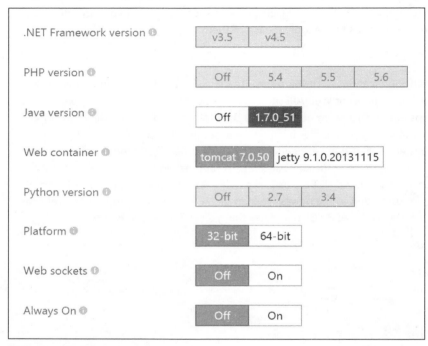

FIGURE 5-7 Turning on Java

Observe that when Java is turned on,.NET, PHP, and Python are all dimmed.

Node.js

Node.js is a server-side version of JavaScript. It can run on a desktop or a server and provides many plugins using Node Package Manager (NPM) servers. NPM servers provide a way for JavaScript developers to share and reuse code with other developers. Putting a package of code on an NPM server also provides a simple way to distribute updates to the code to users. You can use WebMatrix to develop a Node.JS web application. Figure 5-8 shows all of the Node.JS websites in the Azure Martketplace.

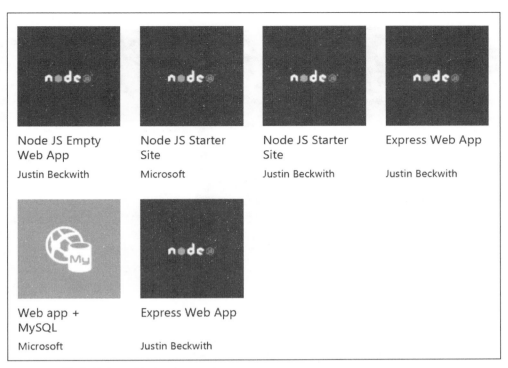

FIGURE 5-8 Node.JS Azure Marketplace options

PHP

PHP is a popular language with which to create websites. Systems such as WordPress use PHP for developing their software and for the plugins that others develop. The Azure Marketplace has many sites in the Web App gallery that are all built using PHP, such as Joomla! and the aforementioned WordPress. Figure 5-9 shows the Azure Marketplace options. You also can use WebMatrix to create websites using PHP. First, confirm that the correct version of PHP is configured for the website; Azure supports versions 5.4, 5.5, and 5.6.

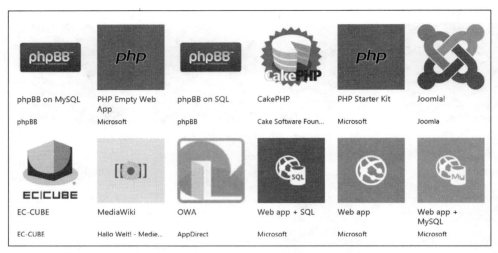

FIGURE 5-9 PHP Azure Marketplace options

Python

Python is a free, open-source programming language that runs everywhere. It is a popular language among a broad swath of users, from beginners to experienced programmers. Python can run websites, desktop applications, and perform networking programming. You can even use it for software and game development. To use Python on your own computer, you must install the Python SDK, which you can download from *https://www.python.org/*. You also will need the tools to tie Python into Visual Studio, which you can get at *https://pytools.codeplex.com/*. When you use the tools for Visual Studio, you can create websites using Python and deploy them to Azure by using the standard Publish menu option. You can develop a web application using the Azure Marketplace, as well. There are three samples using various bootstrapping options to provide the user with a sample project with which to begin development. Figure 5-10 shows the options that are currently in the Azure Marketplace. You can edit websites that you develop in Python by using Visual Studio, WebMatrix, or your favorite IDE. When publishing the Python site to Azure, verify that the Azure settings are set up for the correct version of Python. As of this writing, the only versions that Azure supports are 2.7 and 3.4. As new versions are created and used by the public, Azure will add them to this list.

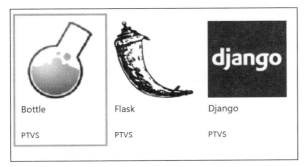

FIGURE 5-10 Python Azure Marketplace options

MORE INFO **SUPPORTED LANGUAGES**

You can learn more about supported languages in Azure at *http://channel9.msdn.com/ Shows/Azure-Friday/Making-multi-language-Azure-Web-Sites-with-PHP-nodejs-NET-and- more.*

App Service Web Apps, Azure Virtual Machines, and Azure Cloud Services

Websites can be deployed in Azure in multiple ways. App Service WebApps, Azure Virtual Machines, and Azure Web Roles can all host a website. Each solution for hosting a website offers various features and benefits. Originally, Web Roles were the only means by which you could create a website. Virtual Machines were added, which made it possible to host websites in a virtual machine (VM). The latest solution that you can use to host in Azure is Web Apps.

Cloud Services

Cloud Services, such as Web Roles and Worker Roles, were the first way to create a website in Azure. Web roles could be created using Visual Studio and provided access to running websites, Web API sites, and Windows Communication Foundation (WCF) Services. You can create Cloud Services in Visual Studio or using the management portal. To create them in Visual Studio, select the Cloud project template, and then select Azure Cloud Service. The New Microsoft Azure Cloud Service dialog box opens in which you can configure options such as what language and what types of services can be created, as illustrated in Figure 5-11. You also can use this dialog box to add multiple projects to the new solution, and you can publish each project to Azure separately. Using the C# templates, the only options for making a website is an ASP.NET Web Role or a WCF Service Web Role; however, a Worker Role could also self-host a site or a WCF service, as well. The Web Role templates create websites with public endpoints.

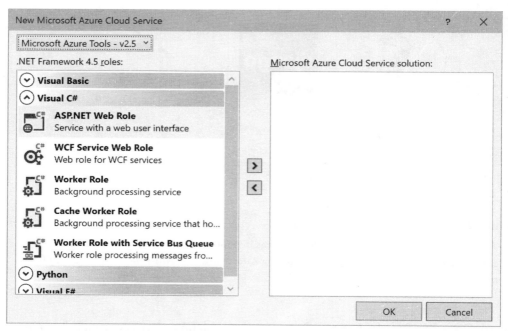

FIGURE 5-11 Setting up a new Cloud Service

These Visual Studio templates create the Web/Worker Role projects, but also the configuration project files that describe the Cloud Service, such as the size of the pricing plan and the number of instances that will be run. The .cscfg file defines the number of instances and the configuration settings for the service to be uploaded. If remote desktop is turned on, the logon information is stored in the .cscfg file, as well. The .csdef file defines the name of the Web Role Service and the EndPoints for the service.

Virtual Machines

Virtual Machines was created in Azure as an Infrastructure as a Service (IaaS) offering that has the capability to host websites. Virtual Machines can run Windows Server, Linux, or even consumer operating systems such as Windows 8.1. You can set up Websites using Internet Information Services (IIS) on Windows or Tomcat on Linux. This is similar to how a website would be hosted on an on-premises server.

A benefit that you get by running your own VM to host a website is that you have total control over all setting for the hosting system. If you understand and feel comfortable with managing the hosting software, this is a great choice.

Another benefit is that a single VM can host multiple websites, which helps to keep a cap on costs.

VMs can scale larger than Cloud Services or Web Apps. Virtual Machines have options for running with up to 32 cores with 448 GB RAM. There are also options that are optimized for network traffic with a 40 GB network card.

VMs can also run any language; they are not limited to using only .NET, or JavaScript, or the other open-source languages that Web Apps support. If you want to create a website that is developed and hosted using Ruby on Rails, or even a language such as D, a VM is your best choice. You also can use VMs to run a Node.JS site, Python, or any of the supported languages. If you experience any issues creating a web application in one of the open-source languages, but the application runs perfectly well in your own environment, moving to a VM is an option for publishing.

Another reason why you might use a VM is that a company might be just moving their existing VMs to Azure instead of running them locally. Many companies already virtualize their websites and this would be a simple change for an IT group to move it to a new host.

In addition to Windows operating systems, you can set up Azure VMs to run Linux. Some websites are configured to run in Linux and are not able to run in Windows. Figure 5-12 shows some of the websites that are in the VM Depot that run Linux only.

FIGURE 5-12 Linux VMs running websites

Web Apps

Web Apps is a Platform as a Service (PaaS) method for hosting websites. You can configure the website from the management portal, using the RESTful API, or by using Azure Power-Shell cmdlets. The Azure Marketplace has many different prebuilt web applications that you can install directly into Web Apps. This is one of the key benefits for using Web Apps over the other methods of hosting a website. Figure 5-13 shows various web applications that are available in the Azure Marketplace.

EXAM TIP

Until recently, App Service Web Apps was called Azure Websites, and that might be what you see on the exam or in Visual Studio if you have an older Azure SDK installed.

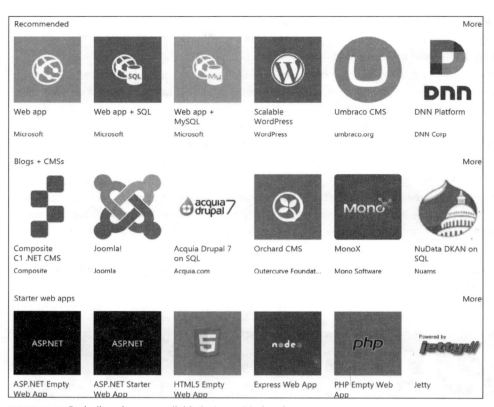

FIGURE 5-13 Prebuilt web apps available in Azure Marketplace

Comparison

Most of the characteristics among each of these service types are quite similar. However, as Table 5-1 shows, there are some key differences that you need know about when deciding which to use.

TABLE 5-1 Comparison of service characteristics

Feature	Websites	Cloud Services	Virtual Machines
Automatic OS updates	X	X	
Multiple deployment environments	X	X	
Deploy with GIT, FTP, Web Deploy	X		X
Startup tasks		X	X
Remote desktop		X	X
Traffic Manager support	X	X	X
Secure Sockets Layer (SSL) support	X	X	X

MORE INFO **WEB APPS, CLOUD SERVICES, AND VIRTUAL MACHINES**

You can learn more about all three services at *http://azure.microsoft.com/en-us/ documentation/articles/choose-web-site-cloud-service-vm/*.

EXAM TIP

Web Apps and Websites are the same thing. The new name is what is used in the management portal and in the latest Azure SDK for Visual Studio.

Thought experiment
Moving your website

Adventure Works Cycles wants to move to Azure its internal corporate websites that it uses in its manufacturing process. The current websites are all running on IIS on Windows servers. The current configuration has the Windows Server running as a VM on one of its existing large servers. Remote offices have been added to the company over the past few years, and staffers at these offices have reported that accessing the internal websites has been slow. In the past seven years, the climate control for the server room has failed four times. During these times, servers needed to be taken out of service to lower the temperature in the server room.

You have the following goals for the changes:

- The websites need to move to Azure for scaling and stability.
- The websites are needed for manufacturing, thus they are required to be available 24 hours each day.
- OEM companies that sell equipment to Adventure Works Cycles need to be able to use some of the websites to generate license keys at any time.

With this information in mind, answer the following questions:

1. What benefits will the company gain by moving the websites to Azure?

2. The IT group does not have much experience with coding. Would it be best for them to use Cloud Services, Virtual Machines, or Web Apps to move the existing websites?

3. When the websites are moved to Azure, how difficult will it be for developers to make changes to the sites?

Objective summary

- You can deploy websites in Azure to Web Roles, Virtual Machines, or Web Apps.
- You can create web applications by using .NET, Java, Node.JS, PHP, or Python.
- You can tie Web Apps to Application Insights to save information and telemetry for the website.
- You can use Visual Studio to create ASP.NET Web Applications that you can then deploy to Azure Web Apps.
- You can use a CDN to distribute web applications to datacenters around the world.

Objective review

Answer the following questions to test your knowledge of the information in this objective. You can find the answers to these questions and explanations of why each answer choice is correct or incorrect in the "Answers" section at the end of this chapter.

1. Azure supports what language(s) to develop websites?
   A. .NET – C#
   B. JavaScript
   C. Python
   D. Ruby

2. When creating a website in Azure, which Azure services can you use?
   A. Cloud Services
   B. Virtual Machines
   C. Web Apps
   D. Only using on-premises servers

3. Which of the following are true when hosting a website in a VM?
   A. The website has multiple deployment environments.
   B. You can use a remote desktop to log on to the machine.
   C. Operating system updates are applied automatically.
   D. You can use Azure Traffic Manager.

Objective 5.2: Deploy websites

You need to copy websites to the server that is going to host them. There are many ways to deploy a Web App to Azure, ranging from simply copying file to using FTP, to just using a source code repository. However, this is but a single step in deploying the website and running it correctly in Azure.

Implement Azure Site Extensions

Site Extensions is a feature of App Service Web Apps with which you can create and deploy custom administrator functionality. You can add Site Extensions to your own site and also publish it to *http://www.siteextensions.net/.* Every web application has its own Site Control Manager that you use for administration and debugging. This is automatically created and available for all websites. Figure 5-14 shows the Site Control Manager website to manage a web application.

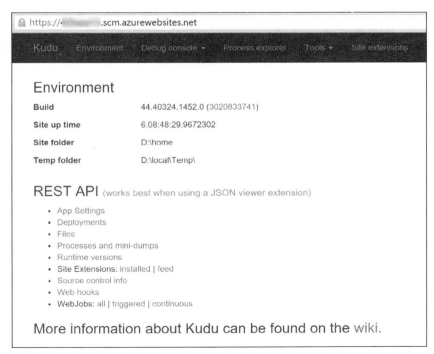

FIGURE 5-14 Site Control Manager site for Web Apps

Developing a new Site Extension involves a few extra steps beyond making a normal website. The biggest difference is in how you install the code into the Site Control Manager site. To begin, create a website that can provide the functionality that you would like to add to the administration/debugging Site Control Manager portal. This could be a standard ASP.NET MVC website created within Visual Studio. After you create the website, there are a few additional steps that you need to follow to get the website setup to be run within Site Control Manager portal:

1. At the root of the project, add an applicationHost.xdt file.

   This is used to transform the applicationHost.config so that it can be used on the Site Control Manager. The following example is a good starting point for this file:

   ```
   <?xml version="1.0" encoding="utf-8" ?>
   <configuration xmlns:xdt="http://schemas.microsoft.com/XML-Document-Transform">
     <system.applicationHost>
       <sites>
         <site name="%XDT_SCMSITENAME%" xdt:Locator="Match(name)">
           <application path="/<projectname>" applicationPool="%XDT_APPPOOLNAME%"
   xdt:Transform="Insert">
               <virtualDirectory path="/" physicalPath="%XDT_EXTENSIONPATH%" />
           </application>
         </site>
       </sites>
     </system.applicationHost>
   </configuration>
   ```

2. Add a build.cmd file to the root of your project, and then add the following code to it.

   ```
   if not exist ..\artifacts mkdir ..\artifacts
   "%windir%\Microsoft.NET\Framework\v4.0.30319\MSBuild.exe" <projectname>.csproj /p:
   webpublishmethod=filesystem;PublishUrl=..\artifacts /t:WebFileSystemPublish
   ```

   This will be used to compile the project and to publish it into a folder named artifacts. At this point run the build.cmd file and compile your project locally.

3. Add the new website to the Site Control Manager website. Go to the Debug Console, which you can go to directly at *https://<webapp>.scm.azurewebsites.net/debugconsole*, and create a new folder for the project files by typing **mk *<foldername>*** in the console.

4. Copy all of the files from your artifacts folder from step 2 into the new folder.

5. Restart your website. You can do this from within Visual Studio, from the Preview Management Portal, or directly from the Site Control Manager site itself. To restart the website from the Site Control Manager portal, go to the Site Extension tab, and then click the Restart Site button.

After the website has restarted, you can go to your new Site Extension and run it by going to *https://*<webapp>*.scm.azurewebsites.net/*<extension name>, where *<webapp>* is your site.

> **MORE INFO**   **WRITING SITE EXTENSIONS**
>
> You can learn more about writing your own site extensions at *http://blog.azure. com/2014/09/09/writing-a-site-extension-for-azure-websites/*.

Create packages

You can create web deployment packages by using Visual Studio. These packages will create a .cmd file with which users can customize where and how the website is installed on an IIS server. All of the files for the website will also be zipped up and referenced in the supporting files. There are also a couple of XML files that are created that include the ability to change parameters for the site being deployed. You can edit the .cmd and .xml files manually to change things if needed. When you create this package, a readme.txt file is also created that explains all of the command-line parameter options that users can configure when deploying the site.

To generate the package, first begin with the website that will be published. This website can be a standard ASP.NET website or a Python site (if you have installed the tools needed to run Python that were mentioned in Objective 5.1). The steps for creating the package for an ASP.NET or a Python site are the same. When you are ready with the website, in Visual Studio, in the Solution Explorer, right-click the project name, and then, in the shortcut menu that opens, select Publish. A dialog box opens that shows the options for how the website should be published, as depicted in Figure 5-15. (This screenshot shows the new Web App naming; if you have the Azure SDK 2.5 or earlier installed, the options will show up as Websites, instead.) Click Custom to create a custom installation package. You can select any of the other options, but in the end it will turn into a custom package.

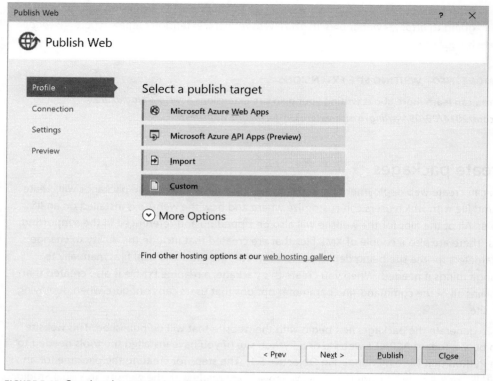

FIGURE 5-15 Creating the custom installation package

The next step is to select the folder in which you want the package to be created. The name of the website is also set at this time, but you can edit it later in the parameter XML file. The final step is to select the settings for the package. At this point, you can select which configuration to deploy, Release or Debug. This will show all of the configurations that you created in the project. You can use the File Publish Options to precompile the website during publishing and exclude the files from the App_Data folder. You might want to exclude the App_Data folder on websites where the database strings will be changed on the production site. If the project has a link to a database, it will be listed here as well. You can see the options for this in Figure 5-16.

The newly created package can then use the Web Deploy tool to perform the actual deployment to any IIS server including Web Apps.

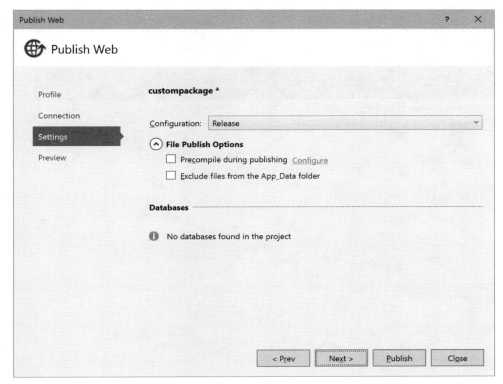

FIGURE 5-16 Custom package settings

MORE INFO   **CREATING DEPLOYMENT PACKAGES**

You can learn more about web deployment packages at *https://msdn.microsoft.com/en-us/library/dd465323(v=vs.110).aspx.*

App Service Plan

App Service Plan is the new name for App Hosting Plan. This is a way to logically group Web Apps and other App Services together so that they can be scaled and managed together. If an App Service Plan is changed to a different pricing tier, all of the websites and other App Services that are under that plan are moved to the new pricing tier, as well. In addition, the scaling and autoscaling for all of the services can be set together. Figure 5-17 shows an App Service Plan that is set at the free pricing tier.

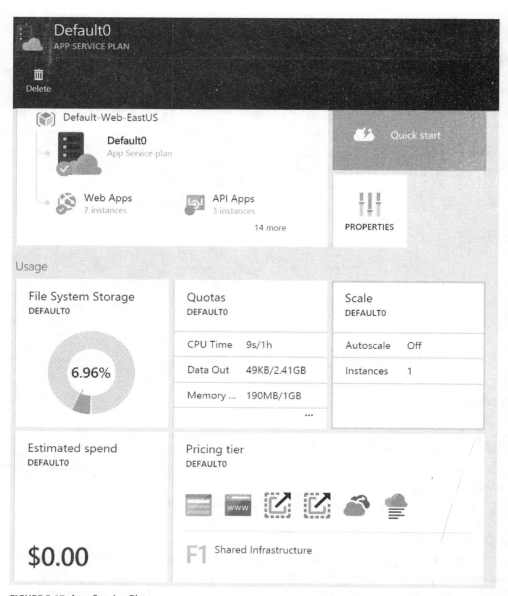

FIGURE 5-17 App Service Plan

MORE INFO APP SERVICE PLAN

You can learn more about App Service Plan at *http://azure.microsoft.com/en-us/ documentation/articles/azure-web-sites-web-hosting-plans-in-depth-overview/*.

Deployment slots

A deployment slot is a feature of App Service Web Apps with which you can publish your code to Azure and have it running in the actual environment in which it will be used in production. The benefit of using a deployment slot is that you are not uploading to the live site; instead, you're uploading to a separate deployment slot. You can test the website in the deployment slot with it connected to either a test or production database to verify that everything is in place for the update to a new version of the website. Uploading code directly to the production site will cause errors for the users of the site causing a bad experience. Figure 5-18 shows adding new deployment slots to a web application.

FIGURE 5-18 Setting up a deployment slot

After the website in the deployment slot has been tested and everything is working properly, you use the Swap button in the Preview Management Portal to exchange the production site with the staging site in the deployment slot. This does not copy over files, but instead swaps the names and the pointers to the website to bring up when a user accesses it. The previous production site is still available and becomes the staging site in the deployment slot. This way if there is a problem, you can bring the original site back quickly without having to restore a backup or redeploy from older source code. Note that you can swap between any deployment slots in the Preview Management Portal. This means that you can set up multiple testing slots and then have one swap over into the production staging slot. Figure 5-19 shows swapping between any slot types.

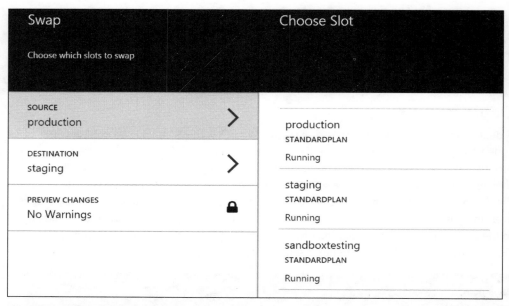

FIGURE 5-19 Swapping deployment slots

One feature that is available in the Preview Management Portal is that you can set the connection strings and app settings to be *sticky* with the slot for which they are defined. This way, a test site can use a connection string that points to a test database instead of the live database. When the test site is swapped into production, it will use the connection string that is set up to be used only in production. This feature is available only in the Preview Management Portal. By default, the sticky feature is turned off in the connection strings and app settings, so you would need to turn it on. This makes it possible for you to use the settings that are in the web.config file when testing on-premises and then use the one in the website configuration in the Preview Management Portal when it is uploaded to Web Apps. Figure 5-20 shows the settings in the Preview Management Portal.

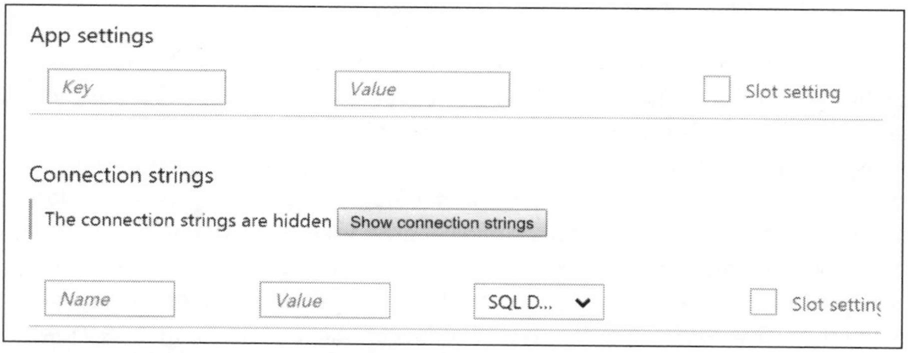

FIGURE 5-20 App settings and connection strings

You can add deployment slots to a web application two ways: by using the Preview Management Portal, using a RESTful API call, or by using a Azure PowerShell cmdlet. You can remove a deployment slot by using the same methods. The following code shows how to add and remove a deployment slot using Azure PowerShell.

```
New-AzureWebsite <webappslotstestname> -Slot staging -Location "West US"
Remove-AzureWebsite -Name <webappslotstestname> -Slot staging
```

> **MORE INFO**   **STAGING ENVIRONMENTS FOR WEB APPS**
>
> You can learn more about staging environments for Web Apps at *http://azure.microsoft. com/en-us/documentation/articles/web-sites-staged-publishing/.*

Resource groups

Resource groups make it possible for you to show how all of the various parts of a system are connected, such as a website, database, and Application Insights for the website. Figure 5-21 shows how you can add more resources to an existing resource group. The list for new resources does not include everything that's available, but it provides the ability to connect most common resources to the resource group.

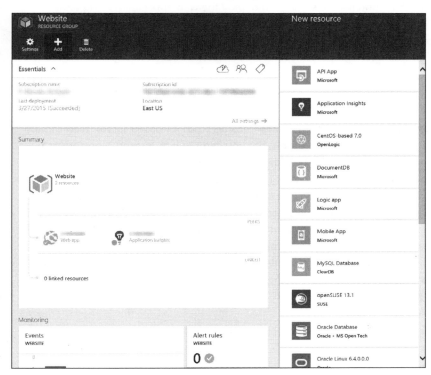

FIGURE 5-21 Adding a resource to a resource group

At the bottom of the Resource Group blade, a list shows all of the billing data for the resources in the group. This is a quick way to determine the costs for that system based on the resources that are assigned to the group. This can be useful when doing specific projects for which cost tracking is important.

> **MORE INFO** **RESOURCE GROUPS**
>
> You can learn more about resource groups at *http://azure.microsoft.com/en-us/ documentation/articles/azure-preview-portal-using-resource-groups/.*

Publishing options

You can publish App Service Web Apps in many ways. You can create and use custom packages with Web Deploy, you can copy files directly using FTP, you can set up source control systems to deploy using continuous integration, or you can even use a folder in Dropbox.

On the blade for your website, at the top, is the Get Publishing Profile button. Click this to download the publishing profile and save it on your computer. If you are doing things with Azure PowerShell, you will need the publishing profile. Also, when publishing using Visual Studio, one of the options to publish is to import the publishing profile file. The publishing profile is an XML file that contains the settings to deploy the web application using either Web Deploy or FTP. The usernames, passwords, publishing locations, databases strings, and publishing method are all defined in this file. If the publishing profile is ever inadvertently reset on the Preview Management Portal, you can download it again and deploy the site with new credentials.

Web Deploy

Web Deploy is a system that simplifies deploying websites to an IIS-based server. Web Deploy is built in to Visual Studio and WebMatrix tools, but you can run it as a stand-alone application from a command prompt, as well. The publishing profile files, which you can download from the Web App blade on the Preview Management Portal, contain all of the settings to use Web Deploy within Visual Studio, and you can load them when you're publishing a web application. You use the stand-alone application when you're running the Web Deploy Package .cmd file from a command prompt. To turn on Web Deploy, in the Publish Web dialog box, set Publish Method to Web Deploy, as shown in Figure 5-22. This shows the Server, Site Name, User Name, Password, and the Destination URL settings. If something changes, in the pane on the left of the dialog box, select the Profile option to import the settings from a publishing profile file or directly from Azure.

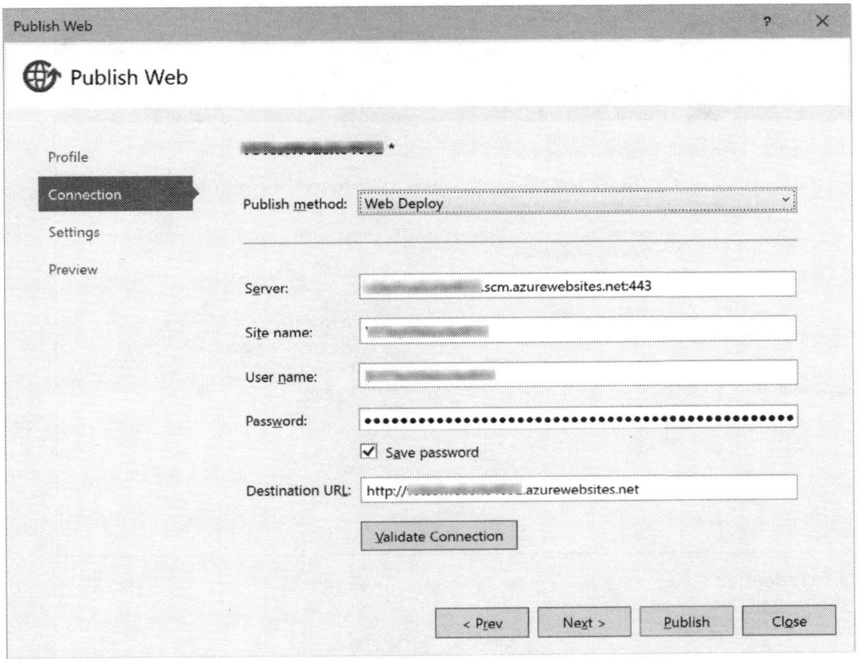

FIGURE 5-22 Web Deploy settings

> **MORE INFO   WEB DEPLOY**
>
> You can learn more about Web Deploy at *http://www.iis.net/downloads/microsoft/ web-deploy.*

FTP locations

A common way to deploy a website files to most hosting systems is to use FTP. Windows Explorer offers direct FTP support and FTP software packages.

To set up FTP, first create a set of credentials with which to log on. To set up the credentials, go to the Settings blade for the web application. Select the Deployment Credentials setting, and then add a user name and password. This user name and password are not for logging into the site, just for FTP and GIT. This will be used for logging on with your favorite FTP software, but is also used for the local GIT publishing. Figure 5-23 shows the setup of the deployment credentials.

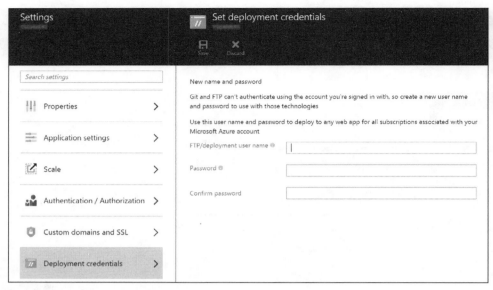

FIGURE 5-23 FTP/GIT credentials

MORE INFO   **MANAGE WEB APPS**

You can learn more about managing App Service Web Apps at *http://azure.microsoft.com/en-us/documentation/articles/web-sites-manage/*.

Source Control

Web Apps offers a number of ways by which you can use source control systems such as Team Foundation Server or GIT to publish websites. GIT is the documented method for deploying websites built by using PHP, Python, Node.js, or Java. Figure 5-24 shows the list of systems that you can use to publish Web Apps.

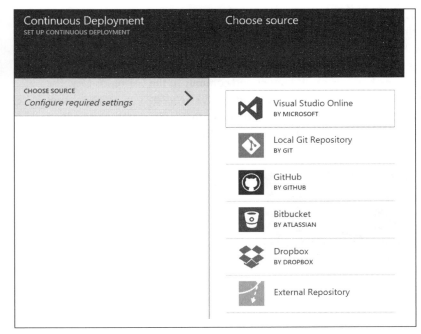

FIGURE 5-24 Supported sources for continuous deployment

When tying a web application to a source control system, one of your options is to select what branch of code to use for publishing the website. By setting up a separate branch in the source-code repository, you will need to update the code in that branch before you publish it. This prevents every check-in from publishing automatically. Figure 5-25 shows how to configure this for a GitHub repository.

Continuous Deployment
SET UP CONTINUOUS DEPLOYMENT

Authorization

CHOOSE SOURCE GitHub	>
AUTHORIZATION Configure required settings	>
CHOOSE PROJECT Configure required settings	🔒
CHOOSE BRANCH Configure required settings	🔒

Azure needs your permission to access your GitHub account.

Authorize
[Authorize]

FIGURE 5-25 GitHub setup for website deployment

Web Apps also has the ability to create its own local GIT repository in Azure to which you can synchronize locally. This means that for smaller companies without their own source-control system, Azure will create a GIT repository and control your source code for you. This is a huge benefit because then there is no need to use a third-party system for hosting the code. Plus, Azure provides online backups of all changes and commits to the GIT repository. The local GIT Clone URL is in the format of https://*<username>*@*<webapp>*.scm.azurewebsites. net:443/*<webapp>*.git. This is available only if you configure the deployment to use a local GIT repository. Figure 5-26 shows the setup to use a Local GIT Repository that is hosted in the web application.

FIGURE 5-26 Setting up Local GIT Repository

MORE INFO **DEPLOYING A WEB APPLICATION**

You can learn more about deploying web applications at *http://azure.microsoft.com/en-us/ documentation/articles/web-sites-deploy/.*

Dropbox

Another way to deploy a website is to tie it to a folder in a Dropbox account. Many small businesses use Dropbox as a repository for things such as source code and websites so that they can be shared with the developers that are working on the site for the owner.

You can tie a Dropbox folder to a web application in the Preview Management Portal by performing the following steps:

1. On the blade for the web application, select the Deployment option—you might need to scroll down the blade to see it.

    The Continuous Deployment blade opens, offering several options.

2. Click Choose Source and then select Dropbox.

    The Continuous Deployment blade opens, as depicted in Figure 5-27.

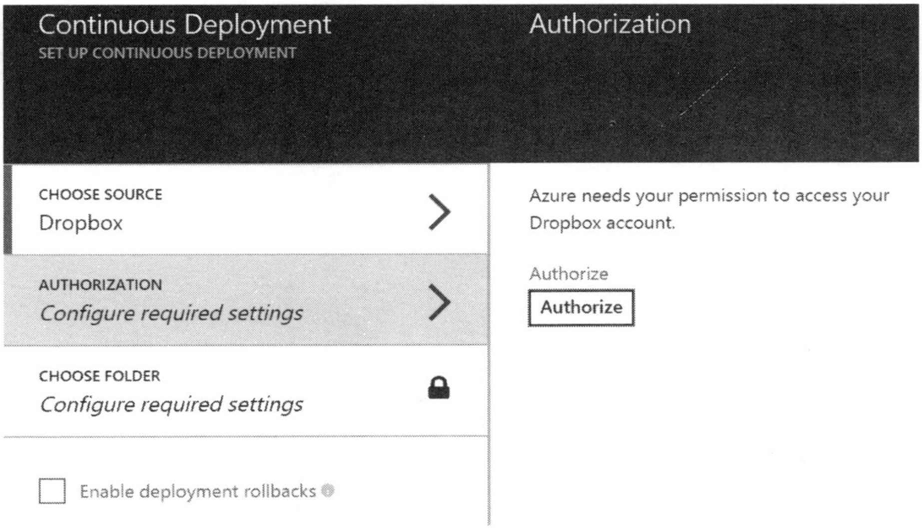

FIGURE 5-27 Dropbox Deployment Setup

3. Authorize your Dropbox account to give Azure the permissions to use it.

4. Select the folder in the Dropbox account.

5. The default location in your Dropbox account is in the Apps/Azure folder.

When files are added to this folder, you can deploy them by clicking the Sync button at the top of the Deployments blade. If you do not click the Sync button, the files are not automatically sent to Azure. Because file uploads to Dropbox can take some time, this method has the added the benefit of giving you an opportunity to ensure that everything is in the Dropbox before the Sync operation is started.

One additional feature that is available with Dropbox integration is the ability to turn on deployment rollbacks. The Deployments blade lists all of the deployments for the website. You can select one and then instruct the portal to redeploy and it will copy and put all of the files back to the way the previous state. The files in the Dropbox account will not be changed back, just the files that are deployed to the website. You can see a sample of a website that was redeployed in Figure 5-28.

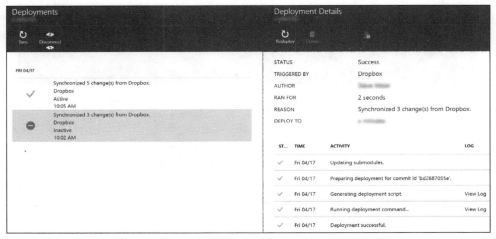

FIGURE 5-28 Dropbox redeployment

MORE INFO **USING DROPBOX TO DEPLOY WEBSITES**

You can learn more about website deployment using Dropbox at *http://azure.microsoft.
com/en-us/documentation/articles/web-sites-deploy/.*

Thought experiment
Moving a site

Tailspin Toys is a small game development company that a group of college friends
started while still in school. None of the people in the company actually had any
website experience when the company launched, so they contracted out the development to someone else. This contractor has worked for the company for around
six months and decided to move to Boston for a new job. The contractor has been
using Dropbox to put all of the work that he has been doing into a folder that the
founders of the company share with him. This is the only source repository that is
used for the website. For the games being developed, a GitHub account is used to
store all of the game assets and source code. The company is looking to use Azure
for its website because it is in the BizSpark program and has a certain amount of
Azure credits each month to use. In the past, changes to website actually crashed
and caused many issues and there was no way to restore the old site.

You have the following goals for the changes:

- Move the existing website to Azure to reduce operational costs
- Place the website under source control as is already the case with the game
- Other website developers will be hired and worked might not be performed onsite

With this information in mind, answer the following questions:

1. The entire existing site is stored in a folder on Dropbox. By moving to Azure, does the source for the site need to move to a different place?

2. How can the move to Azure help the company with issues such as the website crashing on an update?

3. The company is becoming very popular around the world, but users are complaining that the website for the game runs very slowly. How can the move to Azure help with this, given that the people in the company are not web developers?

Objective summary

- App Services Web Apps support many different deployment methods including source-control systems and Dropbox.
- Using deployment slots, you can deploy websites to a staging location where you can perform testing in the production environment.
- Using Service Plan, you can scale multiple web applications while still using the same pricing tier.
- You can use Azure Site Extensions to help administer or debug a web application. You can install site extensions into the Site Control Manager site for the web application.
- You can create Web Deploy Packages using Visual Studio. These make it possible to deploy web applications to multiple locations.

Objective review

Answer the following questions to test your knowledge of the information in this objective. You can find the answers to these questions and explanations of why each answer choice is correct or incorrect in the "Answers" section at the end of this chapter.

1. Which of the following can you use to deploy to Web Apps?

    A. Dropbox

    B. OneDrive

    C. GitHub

    D. Visual Studio Online

2. Which of the following statements about Azure Site Extensions are true?

    A. You can install Site Extensions within Site Control Manager.

    B. Site Extensions are standard websites that add administrative or debug functionality.

    C. Site Extensions are only able to be created using HTML5/JS.

    D. Site Extensions are able to be published to the siteextensions.net website.

3. Which of the following are true?

    A. Deployment slots are available for any pricing tier in Web Apps.

    B. You can swap staging deployment slots with each other.

    C. You can reverse deployment slot swapping if problems are found.

    D. It takes a minimum of one minute to swap deployment slots.

4. Which of the following are true for Web Deploy Packages?

    A. Web Deploy Package creates a zip file with the files that need to be uploaded.

    B. The deployment is set for a single location that cannot be changed.

    C. A .cmd script file is generated that calls the Web Deploy application.

    D. You can exclude the App_Data folder from the deployment.

Objective 5.3: Design websites for business continuity

Websites that are used for business needs must be available and have the security of backups in case of problems, which can range from the catastrophic (the datacenter being consumed by fire) to the more mundane (loss of power in the server room). Today, companies need their data and websites to be up and available as close to 100 percent of the time as possible. This might be to perform work-related activities, but also might be an industry requirement that data is available for the last seven years of manufacturing. No matter the reason for designing and setting up the websites for backups and security, Azure can help perform these functions to help with your business needs.

> **This section covers the following topics:**
> - Scale-up and scale-out with App Service Web Apps and Azure SQL Database
> - Configure data replication patterns
> - Update websites with minimal downtime
> - Backup and restore data
> - Design for disaster recovery
> - Deploy websites to multiple regions for high availability
> - Design data tier

Scale-up and scale-out with App Service Web Apps and Azure SQL Database

There are two ways to scale an Azure website: scaling up and scaling out. Scaling-up means using a larger instance for hosting; for example, moving from a one-core plan to a four-core plan. Scaling-out means running multiple instances of the Web Apps service.

You can manually scale-out Web Apps running at the Basic tier and above. Basic tier can scale-out to three instances, Standard can scale-out to 10 instances, and Premium can scale-out to 20 instances, subject to availability. The scaling can be done from the management portal, from the RESTful interface, or from Azure PowerShell commands. As mentioned, manual scaling is available, but you risk not scaling for those times when more instances are needed.

Web Apps offers autoscaling at the Standard and Premium levels, which is based on rules that are defined for the Service Plan. You can set up the autoscale rules to scale web applications to run more or less instances based on a specific monitored metric that that you choose. For example, if the CPU is running at more than 80 percent capacity, the site can scale to add one or more instances. There is also a "cool down" time, which is a predefined waiting period before the web application scales down after the monitored metric falls back below the autoscale threshold. The rules for reducing the number of instances run similarly but in the opposite way. For example, you could set a rule that states if the CPU is running at less than 60 percent capacity, the site can scale down by shutting down one or more instances. Figure 5-29 shows the settings for configuring the autoscaling features.

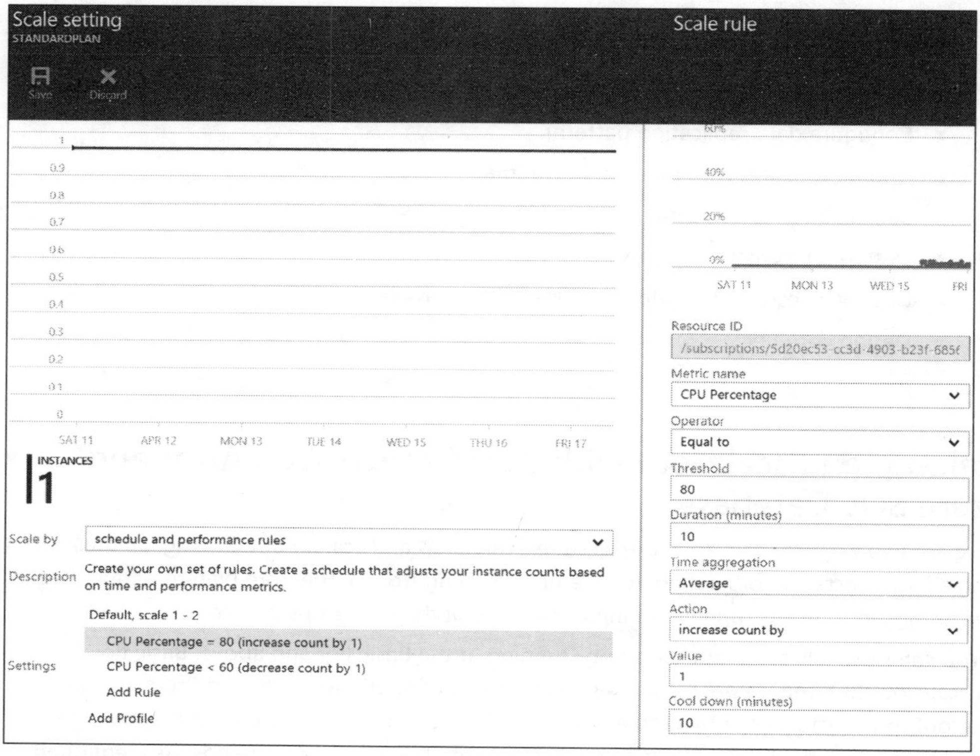

FIGURE 5-29 Autoscaling Service Plan

In the Service Plan for the web application, the pricing tier can be changed to scale-up to use a larger machine. The pricing tier can also be moved up from Free, Shared, Basic, Standard, and all the way up to Premium. Each higher level of pricing provides additional features and capabilities. When designing the plan for your web application, keep in mind which features you need to help determine what pricing tier to use. Within a pricing tier, you also can set the size of the plan so that more CPU cores and more RAM are available. To determine the size that you need, use the monitor for the site and watch the CPU and memory usage. If you are using multiple instances of one resource, it might be more cost effective to increase the size of the plan instead of the number of instances that are running. For example, a WebJob runs using the same CPU and memory that a web application uses. Increasing the size of the Service Plan to a higher level can increase the speed of the WebJob instead of having multiple instances of that WebJob.

SQL Database offers a scaling feature called Elastic Scale. You can scale databases horizontally to *shard* the database into multiple databases based on the data. Sharding a database means to split it and partition the different parts to multiple drives. For example, you might split a database that contains employee names into two separate databases, one with employees whose last names begin with A through M, and the second with data for employees with names beginning with N through Z. Another example would be to split out financial data based on fiscal quarter. This would divide the data into four separate databases.

The other way is to scale a database is vertically. Vertical scaling moves the database from a Standard pricing tier, for which the size of the database is limited to 250 GB, to a Premium pricing tier, which can support up to 500 GB. It might be that you use both methods of scaling to support a database size larger than the normal size of 500 GB. Database sharding is not a new concept for database administrators. With Elastic Scale, you can implement scaling much more easily.

> **MORE INFO** **ELASTIC SCALE**
>
> You can learn more about Elastic Scale at *http://azure.microsoft.com/en-us/documentation/articles/sql-database-elastic-scale-introduction/*.

Configure data replication patterns

When you reference and set up a website to run from around the world, you can configure the data behind the website to be available closer to the users, as well.

Content Delivery Network

The Azure Content Delivery Network (CDN) is one way to replicate data to other geographic locations. When you create a CDN, you can tie it to an Azure Blob storage account, a web application, or a cloud service. The system that the CDN points to is referred as the *origin domain*. The CDN will be given its own address, but you can set it up to use any other address, as well, by adding those domain names to the setting. When the items in the origin domain are addressed, the address for the CDN is used instead. This will cache the files that are needed to a location that is closest geographically to the person requesting the data. The bigger issue with this system is that to access the files, the address for the CDN needs to be used in a web application instead of the direct address to the items from the origin domain, such as a Blob Storage account.

SQL Sync

A feature of the managed SQL Database system is SQL Sync. You can use this to set a time interval at which the database synchronizes its data to one of more other databases. You also can use this feature to synchronize data to an on-premises SQL Server database. SQL Sync is not a replacement for actual data replication, because it is not being run against the transactions, but it does move the data to where it needs to go. You can configure SQL Sync to synchronize selected tables and columns with other databases. You specify one as a host, and the other databases then get the data from the host. You can also specify to allow data to flow from the destination database back to the source (called HUB) database. This can be useful when you are slowly moving websites or other apps over to a new database, but there might still be people who are using the older database. Figure 5-30 presents the setup for the

SQL Sync feature. This is available on the management portal, not on the Preview Management Portal.

FIGURE 5-30 SQL Sync setup

SQL geo-replication

You can configure geo-replication in the Standard and higher pricing tiers for Azure SQL Database. Geo-replication sets up replica databases on other SQL Servers or in other datacenters that can be used in a disaster recovery scenario. With the Standard tier, you can configure an offline secondary. This means that the database will be replicated, but it is not readable. To create a readable backup, you need to use the Premium tier. With the Premium tier, you can create up to four readable backups. Figure 5-31 shows the configuration for a geo-replicated database for a Standard tier SQL Database.

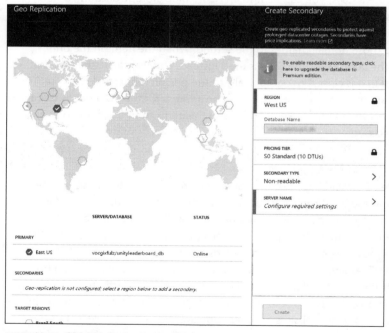

FIGURE 5-31 SQL Database geo-replication setup

MORE INFO **GEO-REPLICATION FOR SQL DATABASE**

You can learn more about geo-replication for SQL Databases at *https://msdn.microsoft.com/en-us/library/azure/dn741339.aspx*.

Update websites with minimal downtime

To do their job properly, websites need to be up and running. When sites are updated, some companies display temporary page to notify its users that maintenance is being performed. For a business, this is not the best scenario because your customers will go to a competing site to get the information or product that they are looking for. Web Apps has features to help keep websites up and available.

Deployment slots are one of the best features to use to minimize downtime. New files are copied to the staging slot, and then, when testing is complete and the website in the staging slot has been verified as up and running, you swap the staging slot with the production site. There is no downtime for the file copies and there is minimal time when the site is switched from staging to production.

Another feature to help to minimize Web Apps downtime is to run multiple instances and put the instances into *Upgrade Domains*. This will make certain that when one instance is being upgraded the other is available.

MORE INFO **AZURE STORAGE**

You can learn more about Azure Storage accounts at *http://azure.microsoft.com/en-us/documentation/services/storage/*.

Backup and restore data

The backup and restore features for Web Apps is only available in the Standard tier. If you are using the Free or Basic tiers, you can still backup the website manually using FTP/FTPS or the GIT Clone URL that is available in the Properties section of the settings for the web application. The Premium tier for Web Apps provides up to 50 backups each day, whereas the Standard tier provides a single backup per day. When planning your backup strategy, you need to determine how often backups are needed. For a site that does not update frequently, you might find that a single daily backup is sufficient.

To start a backup or restore an existing web application, in the Preview Azure Management Portal, go to the web application, and then go to the Settings blade. From the Settings blade, scroll down to Backups and select it. The first step to backing up data is to select where the backup will be stored. Backups are created and placed into an Azure Storage account into Blob storage. You need to select a Storage account and an existing container for the location. After the Backup Destination is specified, at the top of the blade click the Backup Now button to back up the current web application and place it in the Blob storage container.

When the backup is complete, it will create two files in the Blob container: an XML configuration file and a zip file with all of the files from the site. These names for these files are a combination of the website's name and the date and time at which the backup was made. If the database was backed up as well, the backup file for that will be in the content zip file at the root level. This gives you everything that you need for the site. Figure 5-32 depicts the display for the backup and restore.

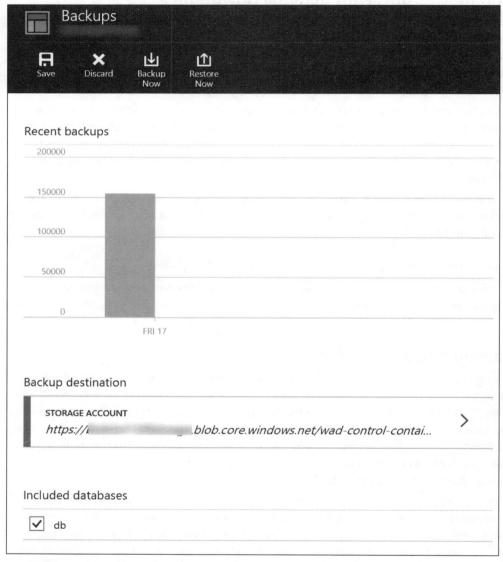

FIGURE 5-32 Web Apps Backup and Restore blade

When you restore a website, there are several settings that you must specify (see Figure 5-33). The first is the location to which to restore the web application. By default, the restore process selects the Web App on which the backup was based, but you have the option at this point to select a different Web App to be used during the restore, or you could create a new one, as well. This is a quick way to make a copy of a web application. Next, you need to specify which deployment slot to which to place the restored files. You also need to indicate whether the data needs to be restored (the database might not need to be restored). The final setting determines whether the connection strings should be updated. If you are restoring to a staging slot, the connection strings might be set up just for that staging slot, so be careful with the setting.

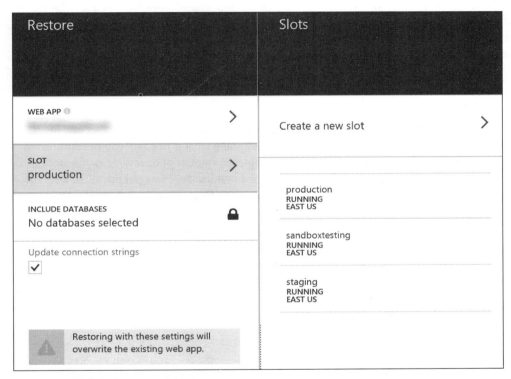

FIGURE 5-33 Web App restore settings

MORE INFO   **BACKING UP A WEBSITE**

You can learn more about website backups at *http://azure.microsoft.com/en-us/ documentation/articles/web-sites-backup/.*

Design for disaster recovery

Unfortunately, disasters do strike and catastrophic events do occur which can knock out your servers to the point that you're not able to bring them back online. These are the times when you'll want to have a well-considered disaster recovery plan in place. Proper disaster recovery preparation is essential for mission-critical websites and services that you need to run your business.

Azure offers multiple systems that can help with a recovery for a web application, but you first need to set them up. The first line of defense is to maintain current backups of the web applications and databases used by the website. The backups are stored in Azure Blob storage, but to ensure that they are available in the event of a region-wide disaster, you should set the Storage account to a Geo-Redundant or Read-Access Geo-Redundant pricing tier instead of just locally redundant. This means that if there is something catastrophic occurs at the original datacenter, your backups would still be available in a different datacenter.

You also can set up databases to automatically replicate to other regions. Keep in mind, though, that active replication with readable databases is only available at the Premium tier for Azure SQL Database.

So overall, the upper tiers for Web Apps, Storage accounts, and SQL Databases provide various levels of backups and replication. When designing what is needed, you need to review your web applications to determine what the acceptable amount of downtime is. If restoring a database of the web application files can tolerate a manual step, you can use lower levels of service. For internal business web applications, this might be acceptable, but for something like an ecommerce site, the potential for lost revenue would make it unacceptable.

Azure also has the ability to back up Microsoft Hyper-V–based machines that are running on-premises. Using Azure Site Recovery, you can back up on-premises VMs to Azure Storage and then restore them into Azure. This is also handy to have available so that if there is a disaster on-premises, internal web applications are also protected. If a server rack or the server room air conditioning fails, you can use Azure for the recovery to run the VM. This is also a way to protect against disasters such as losing an entire server room due to fire.

> **MORE INFO**   **DISASTER RECOVERY**
>
> You can learn more about disaster recovery planning and strategies at *http://blogs.msdn. com/b/rockyh/archive/2013/06/15/whitepaper-disaster-recovery-and-high-availability-for-windows-azure-applications.aspx.*

Deploy websites to multiple regions for high availability

Websites today are visited by people around the world. Even internal business sites need to run from various remote locations to be effective. No one likes waiting for a website, especially if it is an internal one, to load in their browser. Azure supports websites in multiple regions for high availability in a number of ways.

One method that was discussed earlier is to use a CDN that automatically deploys the web application as close as possible geographically to the users requesting the site. The URL for the website is set to the CDN system, and the website is set as the origin domain.

You can deploy websites to multiple regions; for example, East US and West US. Then, you can set up Azure to use the Traffic Manager to expose the websites via a single URL. Each endpoint website is added to the Traffic Manager. Keep in mind, though, that to connect a web application to the Traffic Manager, you must be running in Standard pricing tier. The other limitation is that you can include only one web application from any given Azure Region, meaning, for example, that you cannot add two web applications from East US. Figure 5-34 shows the configuration settings for the Traffic Manager. The Load Balancing Method has three possible options, Performance, Round Robin, and Failover. The default setting is Performance, which uses locations geographically closest to the request. Round Robin distributes traffic evenly between all of the endpoints. Failover specifies that the main website is used for all traffic and then the backups are used if the primary site goes offline. The Performance option will be the best for improving the performance around the world.

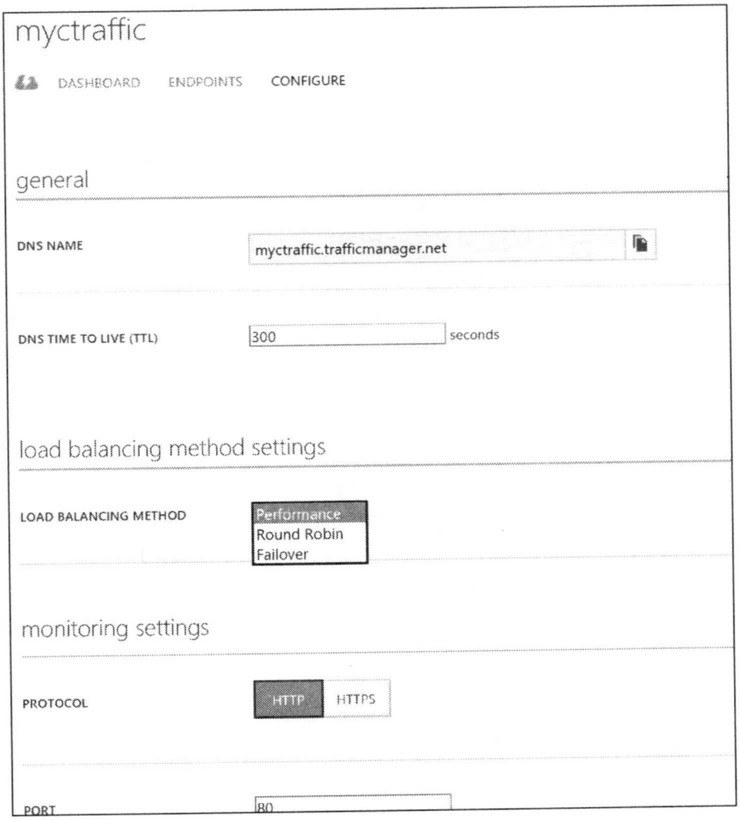

FIGURE 5-34 Configuring the Traffic Manager

MORE INFO   **AZURE TRAFFIC MANAGER**

You can learn more about Azure Traffic Manager at *http://azure.microsoft.com/en-us/documentation/articles/web-sites-traffic-manager/.*

Design data tier

When designing the data tier for your website, there are many things that you need to consider. First you need to decide what database system to use, a relational database (RDBMS) or would something such as a NoSQL database be more appropriate. Another topic to look into is how much the database will need to scale-up to handle the traffic that you anticipate supporting. Another element to think about is the actual database schema for the data that is being saved. Finally, you need to look at strategies regarding backup and sharding. Let's explore all of these a bit deeper.

What type of database should you use? RDBMS and NoSQL databases differ considerably in how they store data and facilitate querying of that data. A standard RDBMS system uses Transact-SQL (T-SQL) or maybe command-line interface (CLI) functions defined to get or manipulate data. For a NoSQL system, each one could have different ways of getting to the data; for example, Azure Table storage uses a Partition Key and a Row Key to separate the data and for searching, but Azure DocumentDb indexes every field that is stored in the JSON documents that are added to the system. Thus, DocumentDb operates closer to a standard RDBMS, but it is still a JSON document storage system. Many database administrators feel that using a stored procedure is the best method because they can fine-tune those procedures to optimize access to any needed data. Many NoSQL systems do not support the concept of a stored procedure for defining the commands to be used. DocumentDb does allow JavaScript routines to be used as stored procedures. So, all of these things need to be considered when planning your data tier and picking which system is going to be used.

Web Apps websites can automatically scale when the thresholds of their autoscaling rules are met, but this scales only the website, not the database behind it. A database might need to handle a certain amount of data or an amount of traffic. Using the managed SQL Database provides a means for the database to scale up in size, whereas using SQL Server in a VM will require management by the administrators. However, the managed SQL Database can only scale up to 500 GB for a single database; many corporate databases are larger than this. NoSQL databases are built for large amounts of data. For example, the MongoDB offering in Azure scales-up to 1,000 GB of storage. DocumentDb scales linearly based on how many units are purchased, with each unit supporting up to 10 GB of data. Each of these systems have limitations for how it scales and if it can scale automatically or just manually. These options need to be considered when designing your data tier.

Typically, in a standard RDBMS system, the schema that was designed is based on the classes that can be developed or generated for each table. Many database are normalized to the third normal form (3NF). This means that redundant data is minimized and that data might be stored in a separate table to reference. For example, a purchase-order system that needs to get the shipping address for an order would find that information stored with the customer information, not for each order separately. This reduces data entry errors and ensures that the data is accurate. One problem with a perfectly normalized database, however, is that more tables are used, and those tables will need to be joined in queries to extract all of the requested data. An example of this was a contest website that I was working on for which a professional database expert made a perfectly normalized database. The problem was that the otherwise simple process of a user logging on required joining more than 12 tables to gather all of the account information. The database was far too slow because of this and the website could not be made to perform as needed. As a result, the project was eventually canceled.

If left unchecked, databases can grow to enormous sizes. When designing your data tier, you should develop a plan to back up the database or shard data that no longer needs to be in the database. As a side benefit, moving data to a backup after a transaction is completed can also help to protect customer information. For example, if the main database is hacked, only the most recent information can be stolen, not the entire history of your company and its customers. Thus, for a SQL Server database through which people are placing orders, you might want to move the completed orders to a NoSQL system such as DocumentDB for long-term storage and reporting. In this manner, queries against the normal database are executed against less data, which also makes it possible for you to create a fixed reference of the data being saved. If the price or description of an item in the order changes, the data stored in the NoSQL system will not have a direct connection to the normal database and will keep the data that was there when the order was completed. This system does not work for every instance, however. If a social-media system used a NoSQL system to save of all of the messages and posts for your user page, this then might not have any updates if your friends changed their names or profile pictures because of the databases being disconnected.

> **MORE INFO** **AZURE DOCUMENTDB**
>
> You can learn more about Azure DocumentDB at *http://azure.microsoft.com/en-us/services/documentdb/*.

 ## *Thought experiment*
Merger

Northwind Electric Cars uses multiple custom websites to manage its customer base and orders that need to be fulfilled. It recently acquired a competitor and needs to combine all of the competitor's data, as well. The websites being used are running in Azure with SQL Database as the storage for the website. During the transition process, the developers learn that when the data from the two companies are merged, the total size will be just under the 500 GB limit that SQL Database can use. This means that there will not be enough room in the database for all of the data for the rest of the year.

You have the following goals for the changes:

- The competitor that was purchased is in Europe, whereas Northwind Electric Cars is on the West Coast of the United States.
- For a while, both company's websites will be used until everything is merged.
- Moving to a VM to run SQL Server is not an option, beacuse the chief technology officer wants to stay with SQL Database.

With this information in mind, answer the following questions:

1. How can you change the SQL Database to help with the amount of data?

2. The websites being developed to use the combined data need to be updated with minimal downtime, because both companies run their manufacturing 24 hours a day, 7 days a week. What can can you do to minimize the times that the sites are down?

3. The websites that are currently used by the company are already running slowly. What can you do to the new websites to help this when the new acquisition is also using the websites?

Objective summary

- Web Apps running at the Standard Pricing level and higher have the ability to auto-mate backups.
- SQL Database can use Elastic Scaling to scale-out to multiple databases or scale-up to a larger one.
- You can use deployment slots to minimize downtime when web applications are updated.
- You can use Traffic Manager to point to multiple Standard tier websites to increase performance for people around the world.
- You can use a CDN to copy websites or data storage to other regions around the world, putting them in closer geographic proximity to end users.

Objective review

Answer the following questions to test your knowledge of the information in this objective. You can find the answers to these questions and explanations of why each answer choice is correct or incorrect in the "Answers" section at the end of this chapter.

1. Which of the following are true?

   A. A web application cannot backup the database that it uses.

   B. A web applications can scale the database that it uses.

   C. You can scale-up and scale-out SQL Databases like you can a website.

   D. You can set up SQL Sync to synchronize all transactions to other databases.

2. Web App backup will save which of the following?

   A. Web App files

   B. A database tied to the web application

   C. Log files from the website

   D. WebJobs for the web application

3. Designing the data tier for a web application means that you should look at which of the following?

   A. The language and platform used for the web application

   B. The data storage type

   C. The scaling of the data used

   D. The backup strategy for the data

Answers

This section contains the solutions to the thought experiments and answers to the lesson review questions in this chapter.

Objective 5.1: Thought experiment

1. Moving websites to Azure will provide the IT department a few benefits. The first is that it will be simpler to support external offices and users without setting up a VPN or opening ports in the corporate firewall. The second benefit is the ability to have the websites up and running even if the air conditioning in the server room fails again.

2. The simplest way for the IT department to move things would be to create a VHD of the existing web server and then launch that VHD as a VM in Azure. To do this, you will need to run sysprep on the drive and generalize the operating system drive. If the websites need to have databases to support them, the connection strings could be changed to point to SQL Servers or other databases running in other VMs. If BizTalk API Apps is set up, connection strings could still point to the on-premises databases. Web Apps could be used, but then the IT department would need to transfer everything and set up all of the settings for the website. Using FTP to transfer the website over to Web Apps is something that the IT group is probably familiar with, but they might not know all of the things that are directly needed. Developers sometimes are bad at documenting their websites. Because Web Apps could be easy to move the files over, this is also a viable option to move the websites. Cloud Services would not be as simple to set up and transfer because of the Web Role description files

3. After the websites are moved to Azure, the developers will be able to edit and update the sites as easily as they did when the VM was running on-premises. The same tools can be used as long as they have the logon credentials to publish the sites. If the websites were also moved to Web Apps, additional features are now opened up to the developers, such as not having to worry about operating system patches, using tools such as Web Matrix or being able to edit the code by using an online version of Visual Studio. Tools such as Application Insights and Site Control Manager provide additional ways to debug the websites, as well.

Objective 5.1: Review

1. **Correct answers:** A, B, C, and D

   A. **Correct**: You can create web applications using C#.

   B. **Correct**: You can create web applications using Node.JS.

   C. **Correct**: You can create web applications using Python. If the Python tools are installed in Visual Studio, they can also be created and deployed from there.

   D. **Correct**: You can make websites on a VM using Ruby. Ruby is not available to create web applications, but this is valid for VMs.

2. **Correct answers:** A, B, and C

    A.   **Correct**: Cloud Services can host websites using Web Roles.

    B.   **Correct**: Virtual Machines can host websites using IIS in Windows Servers or using Tomcat in a Linux VM.

    C.   **Correct**: Web Apps hosts websites developed with .NET and many different open-source languages.

    D.   **Incorrect**: On-premises servers do not host Azure websites.

3. **Correct answers:** B and D

    A.   **Incorrect**: Websites hosted in a VM only have a single deployment environment. To get multiple environments, a website would need to be hosted using Cloud Services or Web Apps.

    B.   **Correct**: Remote desktop is available when using Virtual Machines and Cloud Services for hosting a website.

    C.   **Incorrect**: When running a VM, operating system updates are the responsibility of the administrator and are not automatically applied.

    D.   **Correct**: You can use Traffic Manager on Web Apps, Cloud Services, and Virtual Machines.

Objective 5.2: Thought experiment

1. Dropbox is not a source control system, so using it was a convenience when the company was starting out. Files could be acquired from the website developer, and that person did not need to have access to the corporate source code. This way, the game code is protected. This system works and could stay in place in the future. Moving the website to Azure does fix some of the things that the company is looking to support, however, without the need to perform major changes. The website can have rollbacks defined when using Dropbox as a source for the files. This way, if a new change is made that corrupts the site, the previous version can be put back online. The website could be moved to a new repository under the company's GitHub account. This could be an additional fee for the new repository. Azure would support this, as well, but there is no need to change to this new method.

2. Moving its website to Azure provides multiple ways to help with the issue that it has seen in the past where an update crashes the website. The first method is that by using the deployment from Dropbox, the setting can be enabled to allow for rollbacks of the code back to a previous working copy. The second possible way to resolve this issue is to use deployment slots. Changes to the website go directly to a staging slot and are tested online before going live. This method makes it possible for the developer/tester to see how it works on the real services before going live. If there is a problem, the websites can be swapped back to the previous one quickly using deployment slots. Deployment slots can be used even if the deployment method changes, as well.

3. When the website is ready to be updated, a deployment package could be created for the website. The deployment package could be run against multiple datacenters around the world where the users of the game are located. This way, the website that a users access is local to them.

Objective 5.2: Review

1. **Correct answers:** A, C, and D

   A. **Correct**: You can use Dropbox to copy files from a folder.

   B. **Incorrect**: OneDrive is not a source that you can use for deployment.

   C. **Correct**: GitHub source control can set up a project and a branch to be used for deployment.

   D. **Correct**: You can use Visual Studio Online to deploy a TFS project.

2. **Correct answers:** A, B, and D

   A. **Correct**: Site Extensions are installed and run from inside the Site Control Manager.

   B. **Correct**: The purpose of Site Extensions is to provide additional administrative and/or debug functionality.

   C. **Incorrect**: You can create Site Extensions from ASP.NET templates and HTML5/JS.

   D. **Correct**: *http://siteextensions.net* is a website that hosts Azure Site Extensions.

3. **Correct answer:** B and C

   A. **Incorrect**: Deployment slots are only available for Standard and Premium Web Apps

   B. **Correct**: You can swap staging slots with each other or with the production slot.

   C. **Correct**: The VIP swapping can be swapped back if problems are discovered.

   D. **Incorrect**: Deployment slots are used to make the swap practically instant. There is no minimum time to perform the swap.

4. **Correct answers:** A, C, and D

   A. **Correct**: The package includes all of the files inside a zip file. The files include the full path from your location computer.

   B. **Incorrect**: Optional settings in the .cmd file make it possible for you to install the web application on any server.

   C. **Correct**: The .cmd file that is generated has many options to call and it calls the Web Deploy application.

   D. **Correct**: During creation of the Web Deploy Package, you can exclude the App_ Data folder from the build.

Objective 5.3: Thought experiment

1. There are a few options to help with the issues with the SQL Database and the size limits imposed by Azure. The first option is to use Elastic Scaling to shard the database into multiple databases. This could be based on historical data that does not need to be in the live database. You could also put the data into shards based on which company had the data. The websites could then just use the data that they used previously. Another option is to look into the conversion of the SQL Database into a different type of database such as a NoSQL or even SQL Server running on a VM. You could perform an investigation and then present to management to determine the best approach moving forward.

2. Because all of the websites that are being developed are needed and used 24 hours a day, 7 days a week, downtime needs to be minimized. Using deployment slots for testing and then swapping over to production will be the best method to make this happen. Another thing that you can do is to make the original websites available while new versions that will support the new workflow for the combined company are being developed. The issue with this is that data might need to be duplicated from the older tables into the newer tables.

3. To help with the website that is already becoming slow, scaling the website will need to be reviewed. This will need to evaluate if larger instances or more instances will work better for the existing load. Because the new company is on the other side of the world, having the website use Traffic Manager will keep traffic for the other site to not use the same servers that are running in the West US datacenter. This means that if Traffic Manager is used, there might not be much of an impact on the existing websites.

Objective 5.3: Review

1. **Correct answer:** C

   A. **Incorrect**: Web Apps can back up the SQL Database if it is defined for the web application.

   B. **Incorrect**: Web Apps can autoscale the number of instances that are used, but this is only at the website level, it is not including the SQL Database side.

   C. **Correct**: SQL Databases have the ability to use Elastic Scaling to scale-out to multiple database or scale-up to a large database.

   D. **Incorrect**: SQL Sync copies data from one database to another, but it does not operate at the transaction level.

2. **Correct answers:** A, B, C, and D

    A. **Correct**: The Web App files are saved in a zip file that is kept in Blob storage.

    B. **Correct**: The database tied to the web application will be saved if the setting is enabled.

    C. **Correct**: The log files are stored in the folder that is saved.

    D. **Correct**: WebJob files are saved under the files for the site. These are backed up with the web application.

3. **Correct answers:** B and C

    A. **Incorrect**: Azure libraries are available to support most languages and platforms, so those are not really a factor in the design process.

    B. **Correct**: The data storage type is important to determine how to organize and set up the data.

    C. **Incorrect**: The scaling of the data storage is something that needs to be reviewed to ensure that it can be supported.

    D. **Correct**: The backup strategy for the data tie is an important option to review when creating the data tier so that the correct data storage system is used.

## CHAPTER 6

Design a management, monitoring, and business continuity strategy

Maintaining availability of our infrastructure is an important aspect of IT operations. To maintain availability, the systems must be designed and deployed with requirements and scope in mind. Systems must then be monitored for issues and potential issues. These issues need to then be mitigated and logged. Issues could be related to a particular element of the system or even, in the case of a major disaster, the complete outage of the entire data-center. Fortunately, you can design strategies and processes and deploy tools to take most of this massive burden off of you and put it onto automated systems.

In this chapter, you will learn how you can use tools to deploy an effective strategy to monitor and manage systems and even automate systems deployment and remediation of issues. We will look at automation tools that will help you to ensure that when systems are deployed or changed they maintain best practices or even company preferences.

To share these lessons, you will look at System Center, Azure PowerShell, the Azure management portal, and other capabilities that you can employ to keep systems humming and maintain uptime. As we look at the different components and tools that you can use, you will learn about what design elements you should deploy in various situations.

Objectives in this chapter:

- Objective 6.1: Evaluate hybrid and Azure-hosted architectures for Microsoft System Center deployment
- Objective 6.2: Design a monitoring strategy
- Objective 6.3: Design Azure business continuity/disaster recovery (BC/DR) capabilities
- Objective 6.4: Design a disaster recovery strategy
- Objective 6.5: Design Azure Automation and PowerShell workflows
- Objective 6.6: Describe the use cases for Azure Automation configuration

Objective 6.1: Evaluate hybrid and Azure-hosted architectures for Microsoft System Center deployment

In designing a platform to manage and monitor systems for maintaining uptime or to create a business continuity strategy, you need an introduction to the tools. You will learn the various System Center components so that you understand at an architectural level which components are supported in Microsoft Azure and what they do. You will learn the design considerations for managing Azure resources with System Center. You will also learn which scenarios would dictate a hybrid scenario.

> **This objective covers:**
> - Understanding System Center components supported in Azure.
> - Design considerations for managing Azure resources with System Center.
> - Understanding which scenarios dictate a hybrid scenario.

Understanding System Center components supported in Azure

System Center is far more than a tool. It is an entire suite of tools with which administrators can manage and monitor many different aspects of your systems. System Center components include the following:

- Operations Manager
- Configuration Manager
- Virtual Machine Manager
- Orchestrator
- Data Protection Manager
- Service Manager
- App Controller
- Endpoint Protection

Each of these components has a unique job. Some of these components have integration points with the others, and most components are directly supported in Azure. The components directly supported in Azure will receive the bulk of the focus in this Objective.

System Center Virtual Machine Manager

You can use Virtual Machine Manager to configure and manage your virtualization hosts, networking, and storage resources. It gives you a single view into all virtualization and cloud infrastructure and resources. This includes Microsoft Hyper-V, ESX, and XenServer hosts, as well as Azure cloud resources. You can use Virtual Machine Manager to deploy resources to any of these destinations. It can also create and manage private and public clouds and their resources. It uses template-driven workload deployment. In a private cloud or on-premises environment, Virtual Machine Manager can easily automate the task of moving virtual machines (VMs) from one host to another. Virtual Machine Manager has a built-in capability for doing basic monitoring of system resources. It also integrates very deeply with Operations Manager for a much deeper and detailed management solution for moving resources based on workload priority and resource availability. Virtual Machine Manager Integrates directly with Azure and is a conduit for other components to integrate with Azure.

System Center Orchestrator

Orchestrator is a workflow management solution for the datacenter. With Orchestrator, you can automate the creation, monitoring, and deployment of resources in your environment. You can create runbooks with which you can execute management tasks on and between systems. It uses integration packs for extensibility and integration. Orchestrator integrates with other System Center components so that it can be the execution arm, performing actions on behalf of other components. It features visual runbook authoring, and cross-platform workflow integration. Orchestrator integrates directly with Azure through the addition of the Azure Integration Pack. Through integration pack extensibility, it also integrates with many non-Microsoft solutions. Orchestrator is often the execution arm of moving and changing configurations of systems. You can extend any runbook through Azure PowerShell scripting.

System Center Data Protection Manager

Data Protection Manager is an enterprise backup system. You can back up data from systems to file locations and to tape. You also can send the backups to a secondary location. Using Data Protection Manager, you can back up data from Microsoft servers, workloads, and client computers. It supports full backups, incremental backups, and differential backups. It also supports bare-metal restores and restores to alternate systems. Data Protection Manager offers centralized backups for VMs and applications, item-level recovery for VMs, and archiving backup data to Azure. Data Protection Manager integrates directly with Azure by downloading, installing, and configuring the Azure Online Backup Agent on the Data Protection Manager server.

System Center Configuration Manager

You can use Configuration Manager to deploy software, drivers, and configuration settings to VMs. Starting with System Center 2012 SP1, there is a direct integration with Azure. You can now add a Cloud Distribution Point. This means that you can upload updates and software to Azure directly; you simply need to set up certificate authentication with Azure and configure the distribution point. Configuration Manager also directly integrates with Microsoft Intune. Intune is one of the Cloud Services in the Microsoft Software as a Service (SaaS) product offerings. It is, among other things, a software deployment and configuration management service. You can make configuration changes to systems running on Azure if those VMs are accessible through a technology such as VPN access. However, this is not considered direct integration; the cloud distribution point is considered direct integration. To learn more, go to *https://technet.microsoft.com/en-us/library/gg712321.aspx#BKMK_CloudDPCost*.

> **EXAM TIP**
>
> A Cloud Distribution Point is a Configuration Manager Site System Role in the Cloud. By using it, companies do not need to worry about size, performance, reliability, security, and access from all around the world.

System Center App Controller

App Controller provides a self-service environment that can help you easily configure, deploy, and manage VMs and services across private and public clouds. It offers cross-cloud provisioning as well as VM and application self-service. Using App Controller and Virtual Machine Manager, you can take a template of a machine that you have in your on-premises datacenter, stage it in App Controller, and then deploy it into Azure. App Controller integrates directly with Azure by configuring a Public Cloud Connector.

System Center Service Manager

Service Manager provides an integrated database management system (DBMS) platform for automating and adapting your organization's IT service management best practices, such as those found in Microsoft Operations Framework (MOF) and Information Technology Infrastructure Library (ITIL). It provides built-in processes for incident and problem resolution, change control, and asset life-cycle management. Service manager provides a service catalog, self-service request portal, release and Service Level Agreement (SLA) management, data warehousing and reporting, and incident and change requests. You use it as the central repository to track automations and tasks generated from other elements of System Center. Service Manager does not connect directly to Azure. All connectivity from Service Manager is done through other System Center components.

System Center Operations Manager

Using Operations Manager, you can monitor services, devices, and even some applications from a single console. It includes dashboard capabilities with rollup and drill-down for services running on a computer or device.

> **NOTE DEFINING A DEVICE**
>
> A device could be any computer (regardless of operating system) or network-attached component that has Internet Control Message Protocol (ICMP) or Simple Network Management Protocol (SNMP) capabilities built in. Examples would be a server, a desktop or laptop computer, network printers, firewalls, switches, Storage-Area Network (SAN), Network-Attached Storage (NAS), Network Load Balancing (NLB), or other.

You can carry out the monitoring with or without an agent. Agent monitoring provides much greater insight than agentless monitoring. Agentless monitoring, or monitoring via ICMP or SNMP, is run from an Operations Manager server querying the device. There are built-in dashboards and the capability to create your own dashboards to get a fully customized view of your environment. Operations Manager can show state, health, and performance information at a very detailed level. It can also generate alerts on availability, performance, configuration or even security situations.

> **NOTE   DEFINING AN ALERT**
>
> Alert types are defined by notification channels. Operations Manager supports Session Initiation Protocol (SIP). There are several channels including email notification, Instant Message (IM), and text message (SMS). In addition to the standard channel alerts, you can also run a command script or application to perform almost any action you desire. Alerts are sent to subscribers (users or group membership) based on their notification subscriptions, which makes it possible for the subscriber to define what channels he prefers for alert notifications.

Operations Manager can be very detailed in its monitoring capabilities. As an example, you can monitor disk availability on a server and when a threshold of a defined percentage—perhaps 80 percent—is reached, a warning alert can be triggered. If the issue is not resolved another critical alert could be set at 90 percent. Operations Manager also can also delve deeply into .NET or Java (JEE) applications to get very detailed performance and availability information, even behind logon screens. Operations Manager uses Management Packs for extensibility. Extensibility is the ability to integrate with other systems and services from Microsoft and third parties. Direct integration with Azure is available in Operations Manager by installing and configuring the Microsoft Azure Management Pack. By doing this, Operations Manager can monitor cloud services and resources in Azure.

System Center Endpoint Protection

Endpoint Protection is a security solution for the Microsoft platform that provides malware protection, identification, and remediation. There is no direct integration with Azure; however, the security capabilities built in to Endpoint Protection are available as a service in Azure VMs.

System Center deployment

You can install all System Center components individually through their primary setup routines. There is also a Unified Installer that you can use to automate its deployment. The Unified Installer uses Orchestrator to do most of the work. The PowerShell Deployment Toolkit is another tool that you can use to automate the installation and configuration of System Center.

System Center is a massive product with an enormous amount of capability. With this capability also comes some level of complexity. Because all of the components that make up System

Center are very tightly integrated, even after the components are installed, there is a considerable amount of configuration that you must do to get all the components working optimally with one another. This is where the PowerShell Deployment Toolkit comes in. Deploying and configuring System Center manually can take days. Using the PowerShell Deployment Toolkit can cut this down to a few hours. As the name implies, the PowerShell Deployment Toolkit uses Windows PowerShell to do all the work of creating the VMs (on Hyper-V hosts), installing the software for the desired components, and doing much of the work to configure the components to work together. To use the toolkit, you change variables in an XML file (VM Names, which components you want to deploy, and so on) and then simply execute a Windows PowerShell script. The toolkit will take care of downloading all the software needed, and then it performs the deployment on your hosts.

> **MORE INFO** **SYSTEM CENTER UNIFIED INSTALLER AND POWERSHELL DEPLOYMENT TOOLKIT**
>
> For more information about the Unified Installer, go to *https://technet.microsoft.com/en-us/library/hh751266.aspx*. To find the PowerShell Deployment Toolkit, go to *http://blogs.technet.com/b/privatecloud/archive/2013/02/08/deployment-introducing-powershell-deployment-toolkit.aspx*.

EXAM TIP

The PowerShell Deployment Toolkit is the fastest and easiest way to deploy all or most components of System Center.

Design considerations for managing Azure resources with System Center

There are many architectural considerations when designing a hybrid management solution with System Center. Most important is authentication and the bandwidth needed for the volume of data moving between systems.

When using System Center to connect with Azure, you must consider how authentication will transpire. Your options are to either use domain authentication with a VPN connection between Azure and your on-premises systems or public-key infrastructure (PKI) computer certificates with Internet Protocol Security (IPSec). Domain authentication is very easy to configure: you simply need to set up VPN connectivity and various domain credential accounts, and then grant those accounts the service or other access rights needed. If you do not want to use domain authentication, you can configure authentication via computer certificates. In this case you create computer certificates and import those certificates into the management servers. This is the only option for non–domain-joined machines. It is also the required method if you do not have or wish to maintain a VPN between your Azure and on-premises servers. Even if you do have a VPN between your networks, you might consider setting up

IPSec and certificates for authentication to increase the security posture of those communications. You can read more about authenticating through VPN and certificates in Objective 6.2.

Another element of authentication to consider is the amount of time it can take to connect to an on-premises Active Directory server from your Azure infrastructure. It would be best, to have a domain controller in Azure to do the authentication for the Azure machines locally instead of doing that authentication over the VPN. This adds some resiliency in the system because if the VPN goes down, the servers in Azure can still function and users that might be connected to them from external sources will still be able to authenticate and work. If security is a concern, you could set up a read-only domain controller in Azure to handle the authentication.

Network performance can be a concern when designing a hybrid management solution, especially for System Center components that deal with large amounts of data. Data Protection Manager will be sending large volumes of data across your Internet wire.

> **NOTE   HIGH BANDWIDTH**
>
> You can add high-bandwidth capabilities by installing and configuring ExpressRoute or other high-bandwidth technologies to handle very large network loads.

You should consider the amount of data being backed up and how long it will take to back up changes (also known as the backup window). Based on the bandwidth you have available, you should determine that you have enough capacity to perform the daily, weekly, or monthly backups. You will want to verify that you have enough performance on your Internet connection to handle the backup & restore load without detracting from other critical services.

> **REAL WORLD   BANDWIDTH PERFORMANCE BOTTLENECKS**
>
> Systems designed without proper consideration of the bandwidth needs of all systems communications—including backup, restore and replication, as well as users, servers, and other services connecting to cloud resources—often create bandwidth bottlenecks. It is important to evaluate all communications at the busiest time of day and year to ensure that you have all data transfers covered. Not doing so will end up costing money, time, and aggravation to fix it later on.

You also must consider your potential restore window. Leave enough spare bandwidth for high-volume days and for restores that might be needed. These same volume and performance concerns should be addressed with other components such as App Controller, Orchestrator, and Virtual Machine Manager. If they are moving services such as VMs into Azure regularly, you will need to have plenty of reserve to handle those jobs in the time desired. The location of the various components of System Center should be considered, as well.

It is generally best to have the management servers and the database servers that they are communicating with in the same location. If you deploy the management servers in Azure, the databases for them should also be in Azure. If they are deployed on-premises, it is best to have the database for them on-premises to minimize performance issues in managing and monitoring systems.

Understanding which scenarios dictate a hybrid scenario

There are scenarios for which a hybrid approach is necessary. Hybrid means that there are components or services on both sides of the firewall—some on-premises and some in Azure.

Extending storage to Azure is a very cost-effective hybrid scenario. Many of the things that are stored on-premises can be moved to the Azure cloud to offload the storage burden. If there are replica copies of systems for disaster recovery, you can move those easily to Azure. You can copy files by using Windows PowerShell or any number of Microsoft tools and third-party tools. You also can use REST API calls to create your own routines. For more details, see *http://blogs.msdn.com/b/windowsazurestorage/archive/2014/05/12/introducing-microsoft-azure-file-service.aspx*.

Operations Manager almost always requires a hybrid scenario. This is because you typically always want to monitor servers in your on-premises infrastructure and in your Azure infra-structure. The same is true for other components. With Data Protection Manager, you always want to protect your cloud servers. With Configuration Manager, you always want to config-ure and patch your cloud servers. With Virtual Machine Manager, you always want visibility into your cloud infrastructure, and so on. Let's dig a bit deeper into Operations Manager to illustrate.

The Operations Manager agents, that run on servers to report back to the management server, generate a lot of traffic. Deploying an Operations Manager gateway where you have the local Azure agents reporting to the gateway and the gateway reporting back to the on-premises environment would very much be a hybrid scenario. Often you will have applica-tions or databases that are running in Azure that need to be monitored. If you're using Azure SQL Database or Azure Websites, you do not have an option for an agent, so you would configure your management server to directly connect with those servers through Azure to grab statistics.

Companies that have many offices (branch offices or store locations) for which there is infrastructure spread out all over the country/region or all over the world are a perfect candidate for a hybrid deployment. You can significantly decrease the overhead of managing large and diverse organizations by using cloud services for the remote offices and an on-premises environment for the corporate headquarters or primary datacenters. This also holds true if there are only a few remote offices. It is usually much more economical to utilize cloud services for all scenarios in which there are multiple offices. Doing this can avoid having to maintain a large management infrastructures in each location.

For a growing company that only has one office but is considering opening others, it would be best to design a solution for the second office as though there will be more. Using cloud services in this environment can greatly decrease barriers to future expansion and de-crease capital expenditures for setting up the second office.

During mergers or acquisition of another company, it is often much easier to integrate systems by moving those workloads into Azure. There are plenty of tools available to easily move workloads into Azure. By doing this, your hybrid infrastructure can quickly bring these workloads and services into the organization with minimum effort. This one scenario alone can shorten the acquisition merger process by months or even years.

For a scenario in which you desire or are required to have a disaster recovery plan with a short recovery time, using Azure in a hybrid configuration can make short work and short cost of an otherwise daunting project. This is also true when you have multiple datacenters and want to use one datacenter as a backup or failover replica for each other. Taking advantage of Azure Site Recovery, you can coordinate, manage, and orchestrate the failover of one datacenter to the other in case of a site failure. Site Recovery manages replication of data by integrating with on-premises services such as Hyper-V Replica, System Center, and SQL Server Always On. You can configure each site to be a replica site of another. Azure can also be a site, so on-premises services can be replicated to Azure and failed-over with Azure Site Recovery.

EXAM TIP

You can use Azure Site Recovery to manage replication of a multisite organization for which systems from one site are replicated to another site. In event of a site failure, Site Recovery can orchestrate the recovery of the systems on the secondary or replica site. You also can use Azure as a replica site and configure it to be the failover destination.

Offsite backup is generally considered a requirement for businesses in their continuity plan. However, it can be an expensive and burdensome process for businesses. Typically, a business must hire a service provider to come in and pick up media after the backup if performed. Then, when the business needs to restore something from that media, it submits a request to have that media returned in order to restore it. This request can often take 24 hours or more. This long time frame can be incredibly burdensome for businesses if, due to a problem, some functions are out of commission until the restore can be performed. A hybrid scenario could solve this problem completely. In a hybrid scenario, you could still use your primary media for backup (disk, tape, and so on), but for the offsite delivery, instead of shipping the media, you send the data to Azure. This can limit the restore window to the time it takes to bring down the exact files that are needed to do the restore. Using a tool like System Center Data Protection Manager makes this entire process simple.

EXAM TIP

Using Azure with System Center Data Protection Manager to store offsite data in Azure can significantly decrease cost, complexity, and restore window time for data recovery operations. Even without Data Protection Manager, With Azure, you will still realize cost savings and benefit from a shorter restore window.

There are two key scenarios in which you can use System Center Configuration Manager to manage hybrid infrastructure.

- When you have workloads in an on-premises datacenter and in Azure, you can use on-premises Configuration Manager Infrastructure to manage Azure VMs (Windows and Linux) through a secure Site-to-Site connection via VPN or Azure ExpressRoute. (You can read more about setting up Site-to-Site connections and ExpressRoute in Chapter 1.) In this scenario, all of the management (including Azure VMs) is being done from your on-premises servers.

- You could also set up a single stand-alone primary site in an Azure VM to manage your Azure infrastructure. In this scenario, the Azure VMs are managed from Configuration Manager running on one of your Azure VMs, and your on-premises servers are still being managed from your on-premises servers. Table 6-1 lists the capabilities that are available. Notice that Network Access Protection is not available in this scenario unless you also have secure Site-to-Site configured.

TABLE 6-1 List of services Configuration Manager can provide for both Windows and Linux

For Windows Server	For Linux
Application management Compliance settings Endpoint protection Inventory—software, hardware, and asset intelligence Network Access Protection (with Security Site-to-Site only) Software updates deployment Software metering Remote control Reporting	Software distribution Endpoint protection Inventory—hardware, software Reporting

Thought experiment
Using System Center in a hybrid environment

In this thought experiment, apply what you've learned about this objective. You can find answers to these questions in the "Answers" section at the end of this chapter.

You are an administrator for Contoso, Ltd. You have 5 VMware ESX hosts and 12 Hyper-V hosts (including 3 replica servers) with more than 80 total VMs. You currently have no centralized management infrastructure. Significant changes are required in IT because budgets are being cut by 10 percent across the board; meanwhile, service delivery expectations are increasing. Your manager has asked you to find a way to streamline IT operations. She wants you to cut down deployment time for new VMs from the current process of 18 hours to a couple hours. As part of this initiative, she would like for you to configure it so that business units can deploy their own servers when needed. She would also like for business units to assist with basic administrative tasks such as rebooting their own servers. She wants text message alerts sent to her phone if systems go down. She also would like to streamline and automate the process of patch management and software distribution. Storage capabilities are being stressed by the explosion of new data your employees are creating. Purchasing a new SAN is simply not an option due to budget constraints. With this in mind, answer the following questions:

1. What management solution can provide all the functionality you need today and give you the capability of growing into the cloud later?

2. How should you implement self-service provisioning and self-management of servers for business units?

3. What tools are available for you to automate patch management and software distribution?

4. How can you clean up or improve your storage capabilities without significant hardware capital costs?

There is an incredible opportunity to save money and drastically increase productivity in this organization.

Objective summary

- System Center is made up of many components that can help you to manage, monitor, orchestrate, and protect systems.

- Designing solutions for a hybrid scenario can save time and money while simplifying and automating IT tasks

- The larger an enterprise, the more likely it needs automation, management, monitoring, and protection. However, the tools and use-cases for hybrid scenarios are relevant for businesses of any size.

Objective review

Answer the following questions to test your knowledge of the information in this objective. You can find the answers to these questions and explanations of why each answer choice is correct or incorrect in the "Answers" section at the end of this chapter.

1. Which System Center components have direct integration with Azure? (Choose all that apply.)

   A. Operations Manager

   B. Configuration Manager

   C. Virtual Machine Manager

   D. Orchestrator

    E.   Data Protection Manager

    F.   Service Manager

    G.   App Controller

    H.   Endpoint Protection

2.   What size or type of company can benefit from System Center and hybrid scenarios?

    A.   Small: less than 10 servers

    B.   Medium: greater than 10 servers but less than 100

    C.   Large: greater than 100 servers

    D.   Extra Large or multisite: greater than 1,000 servers or greater than 100 locations

    E.   All of the above

3.   How can administrators ensure secure access to cloud systems and data without loss of functionality? (Choose all that apply.)

    A.   It is not possible to enable secure access to cloud data

    B.   Secure data in a private Binary Large Object (Blob) stored on Azure

    C.   Limit all access to cloud services except Remote Desktop services, port 3389

    D.   Set up VPN for encrypting data in transit to Azure

    E.   Set up computer certificates for on-premises servers and services to communicate with cloud services.

Objective 6.2: Design a monitoring strategy

Operations Manager is the key component of System Center that is used to design a monitoring strategy. However, Operations Manager interfaces with many services and components, and understanding these is vital to designing an effective monitoring strategy.

> **This section covers the following topics:**
>
> - Identify the Microsoft products and services for monitoring Azure solutions
> - Understand the capabilities of System Center for monitoring an Azure solution
> - Understand built-in Azure capabilities
> - Identify third-party monitoring tools, including open source
> - Describe use-cases for Operations Manager, Global Service Monitor, and Application Insights
> - Describe the use-cases for WSUS, Configuration Manager, and custom solutions
> - Describe the Azure architecture constructs, such as availability groups and update domains, and how they impact a patching strategy

Identify the Microsoft products and services for monitoring Azure solutions

Azure has built-in monitoring capabilities for servers and services running in Azure. There are currently two portals, both built on HTML5: the current production portal, which is located at *http://manage.windowsazure.com*, and the new portal at *http://portal.azure.com*. The Azure Monitor and Diagnostic Service (built in the portals) provides various metrics on most azure services. You can also get monitoring information from the Azure Management APIs.

System Center Operations Manager is Microsoft's enterprise monitoring product. When you add the Azure Management Pack in Operations Manager, you can monitor Azure systems, configure alerts and perform other high-end monitoring capabilities. System Center Virtual Machine Manager and System Center App Controller also have dashboards that provide some monitoring capabilities. Configuration Manager along with WSUS can monitor and manage software updates and deploy new updates.

Understand the capabilities of System Center for monitoring an Azure solution

System Center Operations Manager is the primary component used for monitoring Azure. To use Operations Manager on-premises to monitor resources on Azure, you need to have authentication between the agents and the on-premises servers. You could use a gateway or direct IPSec. Most Azure services use certificate-based authentication by default, so if you are not already comfortable with Private/Public Key authentication, you could benefit from digging into it a bit. You can find more on creating and uploading a management certificate for Azure at *https://msdn.microsoft.com/library/azure/gg551722.aspx*.

To fully integrate and monitor Azure, you need to install the Azure Management Pack for Operations Manager. This management pack gives you insights from the monitoring infrastructure provided in Azure. In most cases, when it is possible to install an agent, you will want to run one. Running an agent gives you much more insight than just what is provided by connecting to the machine through Operations Manager with the Azure Management Pack. In Operations Manager, if you have many machines on Azure that you are monitoring, you will likely want to set up a gateway so that all the machines in Azure will report to the gateway. Then, information from the gateway will be sent collectively to the on-premises management server instead of constantly, as shown in Figure 6-1. This will minimize the constant traffic of updates from many agents. Direct connecting through a Site-to-Site VPN tunnel would be the easiest to set up.

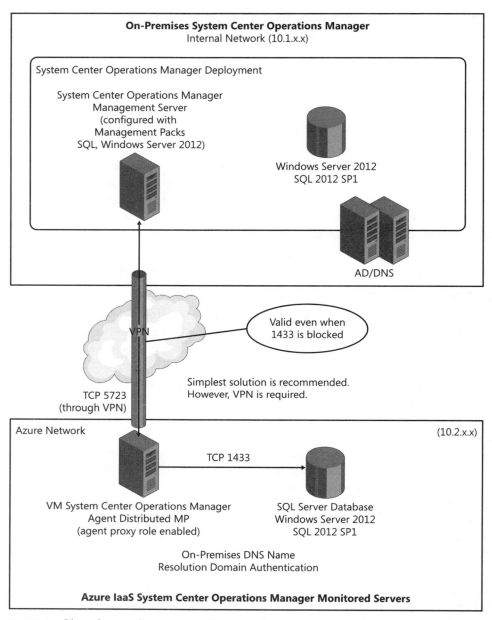

FIGURE 6-1 Direct Connect System Center Operations Manager proxy agent through a VPN Tunnel

However, you could also Use IPSec with an Operations Manager gateway. In this scenario, use certificate services to create PKI client-server authentication between the agent machine and the destination management machine. If you have multiple machines in the cloud, gateway communication would likely be best. By setting up an Operations Manager gateway, each agent running in the cloud would report back to the gateway, and then the data that changed would be sent to the main Operations Management server on-premises, as illustrated in Figure 6-2. By default the management server port on which the communication would occur is 5723. Each of the computer agents would need to connect to the gateway which would require two things. First, you would need to allow traffic out of the agent machine on 5723 and into the gateway machine by opening the firewall ports and endpoints. By default, outbound traffic is allowed, but inbound traffic to the gateway will need to be configured. Second, there must be authentication done between the machines, which, in this case, is done by a certificate.

This gives you a good overview about monitoring a VM, but monitoring other services such as Azure SQL Database and Azure Websites does not have the capability of installing an agent. In this case, you leverage the Azure Management Pack and the Azure Diagnostic Monitor to get information on the roles and services. In this case, a Proxy Agent is used to monitor the application. The proxy agent can be the operations management server or any agent that that is configured to be a proxy agent. The agent uses the .cloudapp.net DNS name, subscription ID, Azure certificate, and the certificate password account to connect to Azure for data collection. The more logging and monitoring you have turned on, the more you will be able to get out of the Azure monitoring platform. It is possible to set up your on-premises VMs and your Platform as a Service (PaaS) applications, roles, and services on the same network. By doing this, you can gain access to monitoring your cloud services with much less effort. Because the logs are placed on Blob storage, you will want to give System Center Operations Manager direct access to Azure Service through the public and private key certificates, as depicted in Figure 6-3.

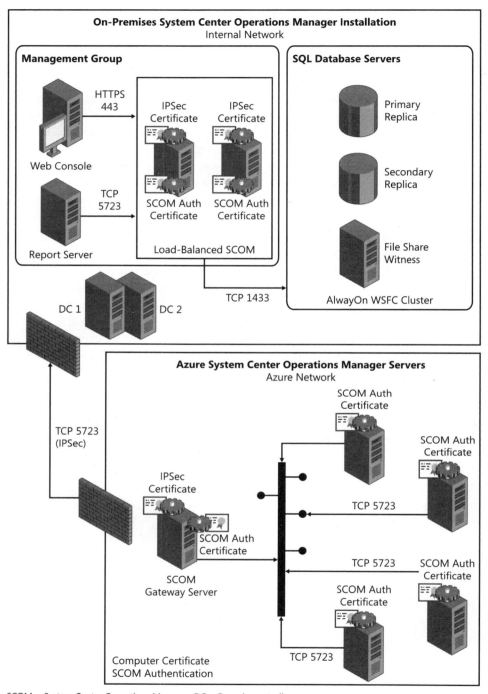

FIGURE 6-2 Monitoring System Center Operations Manager gateway in Azure, no VPN

SCOM = System Center Operations Manager; DC = Domain controller

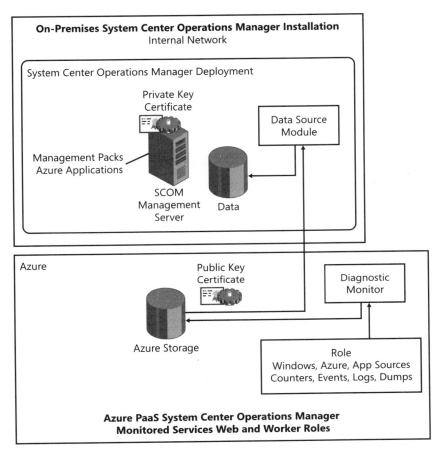

On-Premises System Center Operations Manager Installation
Internal Network

System Center Operations Manager Deployment

Private Key
Certificate

Data Source
Module

Management Packs
Azure Applications

SCOM
Management
Server

Data

Azure

Public Key
Certificate

Diagnostic
Monitor

Azure Storage

Role
Windows, Azure, App Sources
Counters, Events, Logs, Dumps

Azure PaaS System Center Operations Manager
Monitored Services Web and Worker Roles

SCOM = System Center Operations Manager

FIGURE 6-3 Monitoring a PaaS Solution

Azure uses the Public Key of the System Center Operations Manager Server, which is uploaded into Azure. The Management Server uses the Private Key of the Management Sever. This makes it possible to get events, logs, dumps, and other monitoring information collected by Azure. System Center Operations Manager uses Microsoft.WindowsAzure.Plugins.Diagnostics.ConnectionString to connect to the Azure SDK. The connection string for Windows Azure Diagnostics must be specified in the service configuration file (.cscfg)

Understand built-in Azure capabilities

Azure has built-in monitoring capabilities. By default, for virtual machines Azure will monitor the following:

- CPU usage
- Disk reads (bytes/second)
- Disk writes (bytes/second)
- Network in
- Network out

You can add additional endpoint monitoring with Azure using Global Service Monitor (discussed later in this Objective) from up to three different geo-distributed locations.

For web apps, default monitoring is turned on for the following (see Figure 6-4):

- CPU time
- Data in
- Data out
- HTTP server errors
- Requests

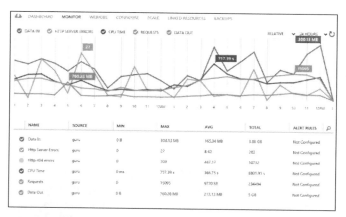

FIGURE 6-4 The Azure Website Monitor tab

You can then add additional endpoints by clicking Add Metrics. In addition to monitoring you can add application diagnostics and logging. These are not turned on by default. The diagnostics are as follows:

- **Application Logging (File System)**   The logs are collected by the file system of this web app. You can access these files from the FTP share for this web app.
- **Application Logging (Table Storage)**   The logs are collected in the Table storage that is specified under Manage Table Storage. You can access the traces from the specified table in the storage account.

- **Application Logging (Blob Storage)** The logs are collected in the Blob container that is specified under Manage Blob Storage. You can access the traces from the specified container in the storage account.

All of the web app (and site) metrics are available via API calls and through Windows PowerShell. This makes these internal Azure metrics very easy to expose. There are many third-party and open-source tools that are using these metrics. There are different metrics you can extract for different types of services in Azure.

> **NOTE** **ADDING MORE PERFORMANCE COUNTERS FOR CLOUD SERVICES**
>
> If you use verbose monitoring, you can add more performance counters at the cloud service role instance startup through a diagnostics configuration file. To be able to monitor these metrics in the management portal, you must add the performance counters before you configure verbose monitoring. For more information go to *http://azure.microsoft.com/documentation/articles/cloud-services-dotnet-diagnostics/*.

Identify third-party monitoring tools, including open source

There are many third-party and open-source monitoring tools. Some of these include the following:

- **CloudNinja Metering Block** This is designed to meter and track resource usage. You can find it on CodePlex at *http://cnmb.codeplex.com/*.
- **New Relic** APM provides real time .NET application monitoring. New Relic also provides SQL database monitoring. (*http://newrelic.com*)
- **AzureWatch** This provides autoscaling and monitoring service for Azure. (*http://www.paraleap.com/azurewatch*)
- **AppDynamics** Designed for Windows Azure and available in the Microsoft Azure Marketplace at *http://datamarket.azure.com/application/f9949031-b8b9-4da5-b500-c615f3f2a7cd*.

Describe use-cases for Operations Manager, Global Service Monitor, and Application Insights

Global Service Monitor is an Azure cloud-based service that monitors web applications from the perspective of an end user. It monitors for availability of the service from multiple global locations. Because it is an external service, it can see problems that are external to the web service it is monitoring. Some of these might include external Domain Name System (DNS) name resolution and external inbound network connectivity to the datacenter. You cannot easily monitor these cannot from inside the datacenter. Global Service Manager integrates with the Operations Manager console so that you have complete visibility of potential issues inside or outside your datacenter from a single dashboard. To use Global Service Manager, you must have System Center 2012 – Operations Manager installed and configured. Web application availability monitoring is checked by a public-facing URL where there is no authorization required. If you need to monitor behind an authentication, you will need to write an agent worker node to do the monitoring.

EXAM TIP

Global Service Monitor is an Azure cloud service used to monitor availability of a public website from multiple external points.

Application Insights gives deep insights into a web application and the infrastructure and services on which it relies. Services integrated into Application Insights include outside availability monitoring and application performance monitoring. As of this writing, there are two different versions of Application Insights. The first is Application Insights for Visual Studio Online works with Visual Studio Online as well as Visual Studio 2012 and 2013; this version will be discontinued at some point. The other is Application Insights Azure Preview. This is the future Application Insights, but now it only works with Visual Studio 2013 Updates 3 and 4, and Visual Studio 2015 and later. Application Insights gives developers deep analysis on what is going on inside their application, making it possible for them to pinpoint problems introduced as a result of application changes. This is a feature that came out of the Application Performance Monitoring (APM) feature (from AviCode acquisition) in System Center Operations Manager 2012 R2. You can embed it inside your .NET or Java application and look at performance every step of the way. It can analyze beyond logon screens and can see very detailed data, including, for example, the duration of a particular SQL call. It can work with applications running on a VM or applications running as a web role in Azure. It can also provide email alerts as events are triggered. Application Insights is used to get deep insight into your custom application.

System Center Operations Manager works with Global Service Monitor and Application Insights to provide a single view of the health of a system, service, or application. It takes the knowledge from many sources and presents a combined dashboard and alerting system. This system sees all of the interconnections between different services and infrastructure components to give a holistic view of any given server, service, or application and all its dependencies. With its robust dashboard customization capabilities and alerting systems, administrators, developers, business units, application team leaders, or anyone else can always know the health within the systems. You will need Operations Manager if you want or need to analyze different components of a system to understand how all of the interdependencies impact the health of any system.

Describe the use cases for WSUS, Configuration Manager, and custom solutions

Providing operating system and application patches to systems is an important job to maintain security and optimum performance of systems. WSUS gives you the capability to apply application updates and patches to Vms. The VMs are configured to obtain updates from the WSUS server (instead of Windows Updates), and the WSUS server provides the updates to the computer. The advantage of WSUS is that there is unified management and monitoring capabilities built in to the platform. Also, the administrator can fully control what updates are presented to the destination VM through an approval process. You do not need to approve updates. There is an auto-approve process for updates that can be configured.

Using WSUS can save a considerable amount of bandwidth and time for clients otherwise connecting directly to Windows Update for patches. This is because the update files are downloaded from the Internet only once by the WSUS server. They can then be distributed to all VMs over the local area network (LAN) instead of each client downloading them from the Internet. Because administrators have control over what patches go out and when, WSUS can provide administrators the ability to test updates and deny updates for patches that cause problems for applications or services being run by the company.

System Center Configuration Manager provides much better reporting and much more detail in how updates are managed, applied, and delivered to client VMs. With the quantity and risk of the many vulnerabilities in the market today, high-speed external connections from VPN clients, and partner networks, managing compliance of patching has become a critical priority for organizations. This is such an important problem for businesses that the term patch management is now often considered synonymous with *software vulnerability management*. Change management processes are often needed and required for regulatory and certification purposes. To meet all of these needs, a centralized monitoring and remediation process is needed for patching and software updates.

Configuration Manager centralizes all of this management and compliance. Configuration Manager Network Access Protection (NAP) interacts with Configuration Manager and Windows Network Access Protection to help protect the network. This protection is achieved by denying network access to machines that are not in compliance (through Windows Network Policy Server) with resources, except resources such as software updates that can be used to bring the machine into compliance. The centralized management also includes reporting and auditing to both monitor and show proof of compliance.

You can set up Configuration Manager with multiple sites that can synchronize. You carry out the initial download to the primary site from Microsoft update or a WSUS server in the Configuration Manager hierarchy. Within a site, Configuration Manager can have multiple software update points. The additional software update points use the first update point as the synchronization source; the other sites are configured as replicas. This replication is set in motion by the WSUS Synchronization Manager sending a request one at a time to WSUS running on other software update points at the site.

Custom patch management is often provided for individual applications. Sometimes, these solutions are embedded into the application so when the application is run, it checks online to see if there are updates available. If there are, it prompts you to install the updates. It could also be an agent that is always running, looking for updates. Again, if there are updates, the agent alerts you. This approach is especially relevant for applications that run in the background, particularly when the user does not often open the application. An example of this is antivirus. The major disadvantage to these types of applications is the overhead they consume running all day, every day. In some cases, updates are embedded with the Windows Update service. You, as the user or administrator, can then decide if you would like to apply application updates with Windows Update. Some examples of these are device drivers, device-specific applications, or even Microsoft Office.

For a relatively small organization, Windows Update is used where each client connects directly over the Internet for updates from Microsoft Update. As businesses grow larger and the network bandwidth is consumed by multiple updates, WSUS is often presented as the next evolution for protection. However, when a business reaches a certain size or as compliance, regulation, or auditing becomes a requirement, a more robust solution such as System Center Configuration Manager is deployed.

When designing a solution, it is important to look at the architecture and understand the advantages and disadvantages of these various systems. As an example, suppose that you are the administrator of a company that has 75 client computers and 30 servers in your corporate headquarters. You have an additional 350 remote users who connect via a VPN. You have begun moving all of your on-premises infrastructure to the cloud, so you have an additional 20 servers running in Azure. You decide that it is time to move your software distribution server into Azure.

No problem, right? Not so fast.

Once you move the Software Distribution Point to Azure, all of the servers and all of the clients, both on-premises and remote, will now download their updates from the software distribution point in Azure. This means that all the servers and users in your corporate headquarters will be downloading updates over the Site-to-Site VPN. It also means you will have an increase in egress (outbound) traffic from Azure. Have you accounted for this additional cost in your plan? A better approach is to keep that server at you on-premises datacenter until you have fully developed the plans for the additional expense and network overhead. On the other hand, if your on-premises Internet connection is saturated and becoming an unacceptable burden on your on-premises machines and VPN users, there is a better solution. You could split that workload with Configuration Manager to run a distribution point on-premises for the users and servers in the corporate office and another distribution point in Azure for all the VPN users and Azure servers. This could significantly lighten the burden of your Internet network and Site-to-Site VPN. In Addition, if you do want to cut your egress costs and you are not concerned about selectively releasing updates to your users, you can configure your remote users to grab updates from Windows Update. The checks to confirm compliance can still be done prior to granting full network access.

Describe the Azure architecture constructs and how they affect a patching strategy

Azure has several architecture constructs to ensure flexibility and availability of services during failures and planned downtime such as patching. These constructs work together to give you assurances that, if designed properly, will give you the availability you need for your services.

A *Fault Domain* is a construct to define the physical layer of a service or deployment. It includes everything that makes up a Single Point of Failure (SPoF) for a system. This includes things such as hosts, switches, racks, and power. There is no assurance or guarantee that a Fault Domain will remain up. In fact, the very nature and definition of a Fault Domain implies that it is either up or down. You do not have the ability to set or change a particular fault domain. However there is a way to force servers and services into different Fault Domains. This is done through an *Availability Set*.

An Availability Set is a logical grouping of like services which forces components into multiple Fault Domains. If there is only one component in an availability set, the Availability Set serves no purpose. The value of an Availability Set is realized as additional component services are added to it. These additional services are automatically split between Fault Domain. An Availability Set is designed to protect against underlying hardware or service outages. An additional value of an Availability Set is that when you have duplicate services within it, Microsoft provides an SLA that availability to the service will be maintained. For multiple services in an Availability Set, you will always have at least two Fault Domains.

With Azure Apps or App Service Web Apps, the availability concept is handled differently. When you deploy multiple instances of a service, it is managed by an *Update Domain*. Update Domain (also referred to as an Upgrade Domain) is a logical grouping of role services that defines separation between services. It is different from an Availability Set in that it has no impact on Fault Domain allocation. It is an additional grouping that you can use to limit underlying upgrades and outages to services caused by application or underlying service patches. Update Domains are configured in the service definition file (.csdef) by changing the *UpgradeDomainCount* variable. You can have a maximum of 20 update domains per role service; the default is set to 5 per service. When a new service role is deployed, it is automatically assigned an Update Domain. The assignment ensures that the fewest number of servers or services would be impacted by a system patch. Update Domains are logically separated across Fault Domains; however, there are usually more update domains than there are fault domains, so there will be multiple services on a single Fault Domain. Also, if the number of Update Domains is less than the number of services, you would have multiple services in a single Update Domain. As an example, if you have three services with Update Domain 0, 1, or 2 applied to them, only one would be brought down at the same time for updates. However, both Update Domain 0 and 2 might be on the same Fault Domain, so if there is a failure, two of the services could go down.

When patches or upgrades/updates are applied, they are applied within a single Update Domain. When that Update Domain is finished, Azure moves on to the next one, and so on until all systems updates are completed. As patches are applied, there is a possibility—indeed a likelihood—of service outage for the services in that Update Domain due to services being stopped or servers being rebooted. The more Update Domains you have, the less of a burden or probability of failure during an update. However, the more Update Domains you have, the longer it will take to perform the updates because they are done sequentially.

Fault Domains, Availability Sets, and Update Domains all work together to maximize availability of services during hardware failure and patching, as shown in Figure 6-5.

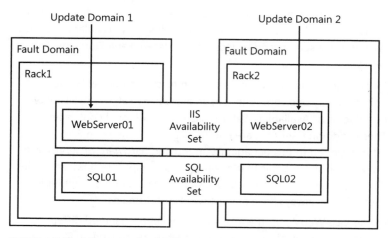

FIGURE 6-5 Fault Domains, Availability Sets, and Update Domains

If we were to build this out further, suppose that we had eight services in an availability set. If we kept the default of five Update Domains, in two of them we would only have one service, in the other three, we would have two. This means that when patches are applied to those three update domains, two role services would be unavailable at the same time. To avoid this, you can increase the number of Update Domains. Having multiple service outages for updates at the same time across a large set of services is not generally a problem, because the more services you have, the lower the probability of failure. Additionally, if you are auto-scaling services and the additional services are needed at the time of the update, additional services could be made available to handle the load while the update is under way.

When it is your application that you are updating, there is another method that you should consider: the virtual IP (VIP) swap. When upgrading your application, it is a best practice to use the VIP swap to deploy your application update, which gives you the opportunity to test your application. It also gives you the ability to roll-back the update very easily by doing the VIP swap again to bring back the prior version of the application.

Thought experiment

Building a comprehensive monitoring strategy

In this thought experiment, apply what you've learned about this objective. You can find answers to these questions in the "Answers" section at the end of this chapter.

In your organization, you do not currently have any monitoring systems in place. As a result, systems sometimes fail with no advance notice. Because you have some in-house applications developed by your company, you also hear different excuses from different departments as to why performance of applications is lacking. The database administrators are blaming the infrastructure people, who in turn are blaming the programmers, and the programmers are blaming the database administrators. Your manager needs to determine what is really going on and where the problems are so that they can be fixed. You have some infrastructure in your datacenter and some in the Azure cloud. Currently, these systems are managed separately. Your manager wants to know if there is a way to see what is going on across the entire organization, regardless of location.

With this in mind, answer the following questions:

1. How can you determine where the performance problems are for the in-house built applications?

2. How can you know in advance that systems are in jeopardy of failing?

3. Is there a way to see and manage all infrastructure, both that which is on-premises and that which in the cloud?

Objective summary

- Designing an effective monitoring strategy requires understanding many services that run on-premises and in the cloud. Some of these components include System Center, WSUS, management portal, Preview Management Portal, Azure Diagnostic Monitor, Global Service Manager, and Application Insights. It is only when all of these work together that you have a complete picture of the health of your applications, services, and systems.

- Azure has some monitoring capabilities built in to the platform. However, these capabilities are not enough to provide comprehensive and healthy systems.

- Uptime and system reliability is a key reason for monitoring. Monitoring alone is not enough to keep systems up. You are also required to understand the architectural constructs such as Availability Groups, Update Domains, and Fault Domains. You also need to understand how the architectural decisions you make can have a direct impact on performance, reliability, and even costs of systems and services.

Objective review

Answer the following questions to test your knowledge of the information in this objective. You can find the answers to these questions and explanations of why each answer choice is correct or incorrect in the "Answers" section at the end of this chapter.

1. If you have 14 role instances deployed in a highly available cloud service and you have the default of 5 update domains defined for the service, what is the maximum number of server instances that could be down due to updates?

   A. None, no instances should go down during updates

   B. One could go down

   C. Two instances could go down

   D. Three instances could go down

2. What tool is needed to gather deep application performance metrics, such as the amount of time it takes to carry out a particular SQL query? (Choose all that apply.)

   A. Azure PowerShell

   B. Operations Manager

   C. Configuration Manger

   D. Application Insights

   E. Global Service Monitor

3. What needs to be turned on and configured to gather Azure endpoint statistical information, event logs, and counters to be read by Operations Manager? (Choose all that apply.)

   A. Nothing, these are turned on by default

   B. Verbose monitoring

   C. Application logging

   D. Azure Storage Certificate Authentication

Objective 6.3: Design Azure business continuity/ disaster recovery (BC/DR) capabilities

Availability, scalability, and fault tolerance are key requirements of any business continuity and disaster recovery plan. To have availability, you need scalability to handle the workload as the needs of the workload increase. You need fault tolerance to overcome any issues that might arise. To incorporate these characteristics within your systems, you must have redundancy. Azure has redundancy built in to all aspects of the platform and offers SLAs to guarantee uptime. There are, however, things that must be done to ensure that your systems have the redundancy and fault tolerance needed to meet business requirements.

Understand the architectural capabilities of business continuity and disaster recovery

Azure is a great platform for adding redundancy to your on-premises systems. But, there are some things you must do to ensure redundancy is turned on at all levels. Chapter 1 covers networking and load balancing, but it is important to understand that all of these technologies are necessary to give you real business continuity and disaster recovery.

There are circumstances in your business continuity and disaster recovery (BC/DR) plan for which you do not need high availability. In these cases, you might simply want to have another copy of the data and services available should there be a problem. Here are some questions that you need to consider when planning:

- What is an acceptable amount of data loss? How many minutes, hours, or days of data can your business afford to lose in case of a disaster? The answer to this will determine your *Recovery Point Objective*.

- How long you are prepared to be down before the data and services are back online after a disaster? This is known as *Recovery Time Objective*.

Let's look at a few key terms you will need to understand in designing systems and in taking the exam:

- **Recovery Point Objective (RPO)**   RPO is the target maximum length of time that data loss can occur during a disaster—how many seconds, minutes, hours, or days, you can afford to lose data. This can be, and usually is, different for different types of data. From a planning standpoint, this is the amount of data (in time) that can be lost due to a disaster.

- **Recovery Time Objective (RTO)**   This is the amount of time that systems can be unavailable in the event of a disaster before unacceptable business loss occurs. From a planning standpoint, systems must be restored to functional levels within the RTO.

- **Data Loss**   Data loss is data that has been collected by systems but is not recoverable after a disaster. This could be in the form of lost data that was not saved or data that was saved but is now corrupt and no longer usable.

- **Disaster**   This is any event that causes system outages or data loss. It is generally a term that is used in only extreme cases such as natural disasters, but from a systems standpoint, any outage or data loss can be considered a disaster. This should also include accidental deletion of data.

EXAM TIP

RPO is the amount of data that can be lost (in time)—it is the amount of time between backup, replication, or synchronization. It answers the question, "What is an acceptable amount of data loss?" It is usually *much* smaller than RTO.

RTO is how long it takes to restore services after a disaster. It answers the question, "How long will it take to get service back up?"

Using the RPO and RTO, you can determine how much money and effort you should put into your BC/DR plan and your systems. It will impact and dictate costs, so calculate what the real numbers are based on the business; this is not just a stab in the dark. How much money does the company lose when systems are unavailable? How much money is lost when data is lost? It is only after you ascertain these answers that you can properly establish the RPO and RTO. If your RPO is short (minutes), you need to design high availability for services. If your RTO is short, you will likely need to use multiple geographies and synchronize your data so that the systems can be brought up quickly.

There are many different types of systems and services to consider when developing a BC/DR plan. The exam will not go too deeply into these. When you are designing systems for a living, you will likely need to learn all the aspects of the various types of workloads. Because this is an exam reference, I will focus on the types you are most likely going to see on the exam, which are SQL Server workloads and storage. Chapter 3 covers both SQL Server and storage, but here let's look more closely into high availability and replication.

Storage redundancy is provided for all storage components in Azure. When Azure writes a bit of data, it is automatically written three times to three separate drives. There is nothing you need to do or to turn on for this to work. It just happens. This is how Microsoft provides hardware redundancy. If you enable Geo Redundant Storage (GRS), the data is written an additional three times in a different geographic datacenter. Geo-replication is an asynchronous (opposite of synchronous) process, which means in the event of disaster, some data can be lost. The amount of data lost can vary based on the synchronization schedule. If the synchronization interval is five minutes, depending on when a failure occurs within that interval, you can lose up to five minutes of data.

EXAM TIP

An asynchronous operation is one that transpires sequentially: first one action, and then another. The operations do not take place simultaneously. This type of processing means that there is a time gap between the first operation and the second. An example would be writing data to primary and secondary storage. First data is written to the primary; data destined for the secondary is queued and must wait until the write operation to the primary is complete.

EXAM TIP

Synchronous means that operations are carried out at the same time (think of this as parallel processing). With this type of processing, there is no time gap between the first process and the second process. Both operations take place simultaeously.

The SLA between you and Microsoft determines the level of availability for your systems, which will vary based on service. Table 6-2 shows the SLA-specified availability for the most important services.

TABLE 6-2 Sample Azure service SLAs

Azure service	SLA	Minutes downtime per month
Compute (including VM)	99.95	21.6
SQL Database	99.90	43.2
Storage	99.90	43.2

EXAM TIP

You should learn the Azure service SLA table. At the very least, the Azure service and the Azure SLA for that service will be needed for the exam.

MORE INFO   AZURE SLA TABLE

For more information on SLAs, go to *http://go.microsoft.com/fwlink/?LinkId=309059*.

Microsoft honors these SLAs only if the systems are configured with high availability. For Azure Virtual Machine (IaaS), this means that the VM must be duplicated and in an Availability Set. If there is a hardware failure, drive failure or even a host operating system update or reboot, a failure could be triggered. To avoid this, your systems should be designed for redundancy, as demonstrated in Figure 6-6.

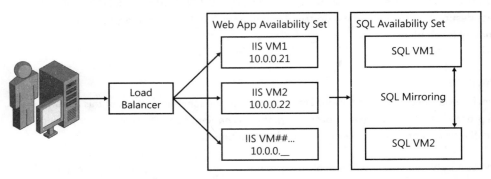

FIGURE 6-6 High-availability architecture is achieved through duplication of systems in an Availability Set and with a load balancer front end

You put a network load balancer in front of the VMs in the Availability Set so that if one VM fails, others are there to handle the load. For high-availability websites, you must configure them as always-on and make multiple instances of each website.

Because of the transactional nature of SQL Server, it is handled differently. To gain high-availability in a VM you need to replicate the database. There are multiple ways to do this. The most popular are SQL Mirroring and SQL Server AlwaysOn.

SQL Server AlwaysOn Availability Group is a capability built in to SQL Server that only works when SQL is configured properly and running in a cluster of VMs in Azure. To set up this configuration, you need a three-node cluster of servers, and then configure Windows Server Failover Cluster (WSFC) using the three VMs. You can use more, but three is the minimum: one for the primary database, one for the replica database, and one for the quorum or witness. All three VMs should be in the same storage container and in the same Availability Set, as shown in Figure 6-7. As you expand your cluster, you could stretch it across multiple networks to add redundancy at the network layer. You then configure SQL Server AlwaysOn and replicate the databases. You can configure the replica as just a replica or for read-only access.

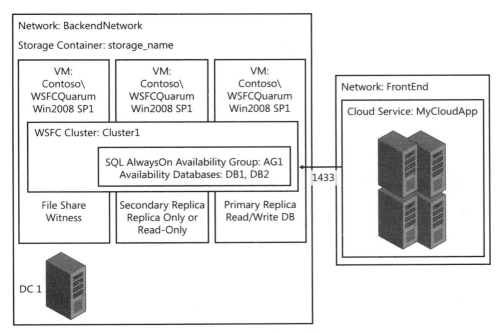

FIGURE 6-7 SQL Server AlwaysOn Configured in a 3-node VM Cluster

This (WSFC) configuration is considered a scale-out or horizontal scaling scenario. When you want to add more capability, you simply add additional nodes to the cluster.

Availability can be directly affected by scalability. If systems are not designed with scalability, the systems could fail if the workload on them is greater than can be handled by the VMs servicing the request. You can manage scalability in one of two ways: scaling out or scaling up. Scaling-out adds machines with the same characteristics (CPU, memory, bandwidth) to relieve some of the load from the existing machines. Scaling-up means to add additional resources (CPU, memory, bandwidth) to an existing machine.

Scaling-out is generally preferred when possible because applications do not need to be redeployed. When scaling out, for example web and worker roles, the state must be stored externally; it cannot be stored on the web server directly. You can—and should—scale-out storage. An example of this is using multiple storage units, so as the application server is scaled-out, the storage can keep up with the demand. The same is true for database access. You can partition data so that different tables of data are spread across multiple drives. This technology is referred to as *sharding*.

EXAM TIP

Sharding is when you split a database and partition the different parts of the database across multiple drives. A shard is a single horizontal partition of the database.

For very large workloads, this must be part of the design, and the application must be coded to utilize these scaling technologies. For a more in-depth look at scaling, read Best Practices for the Design of Large-Scale Services on Azure Cloud Services at *http://go.microsoft. com/fwlink/?LinkId=309060.*

Describe Hyper-V Replica and Azure Site Recovery

Hyper-V Replica is a feature that was introduced in Windows Server 2012 as part of the Hyper-V virtualization platform. With it, you can asynchronously replicate VM changes from one Hyper-V host to another Hyper-V host. At the primary site and replica site, you turn on replication. Then, on the VM's you wish to replicate, you configure replication and select the replica server. Because the replication is configured for the VM (instead of the host), a single Hyper-V host can replicate different VMs to different replica hosts. Communication is via HTTP. You can turn on encryption, if desired. You can do planned failovers, test failovers, or even unplanned failovers. Replication is asynchronous, meaning there can be some loss of data in the event of an unplanned failover. Data loss will be limited to the amount of changes that were made since the last successful replication. There is no shared storage required, and Replica does not rely on any external replication technologies. However, if you own SAN replication from some storage vendors such as NetApp, HP, and EMC, those can be used to simplify and improve recovery protection.

Azure Site Recovery works in conjunction with Hyper-V Replica to automate and orchestrate the recovery to a second site by monitoring all sites and executing workflows as needed to fail-over to the replica site. There are many different modes or setup recovery types in Site Recovery. Each performs the same action but in different ways.

Site Recovery setup

- Between an on-premises Virtual Machine Manager site and Azure (uses System Center)
- Between two on-premises Virtual Machine Manager Sites (uses System Center)
- Between an on-premises Hyper-V site and Azure
- Between two on-premises VMware sites (uses InMage Scout)
- Between Two on-premises Virtual Machine Manager sites and SAN array replication (uses System Center)

Site Recovery sometimes utilizes System Center to orchestrate on-premises workflows to activate and deactivate replica sites, as presented in Figure 6-8. In all cases, authentication is done by downloading and installing a registration key. The key is installed on whichever server is managing the replication (Hyper-V, Virtual Machine Manager, Scout). There are also other tasks such as creating storage accounts, virtual networks, and protection groups that must be done and configured for Site Recovery.

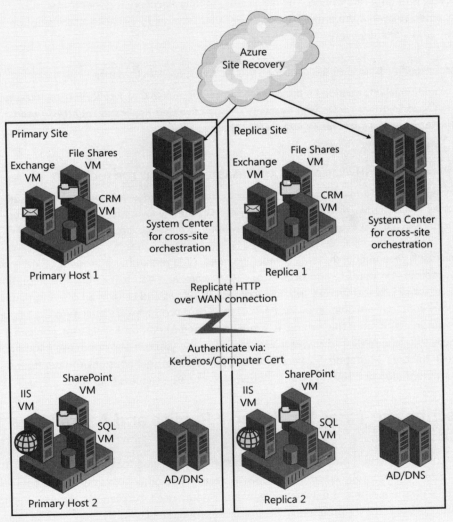

FIGURE 6-8 Site Recovery primary site and replica site

With Site Recovery, you also can configure Azure as the replica site. This can eliminate the need for large capital expenditures to establish and maintain a replica site for disaster recovery. All communications with Azure are encrypted. You also can choose to encrypt data at rest in Azure. Site Recovery constantly monitors protected systems from an Azure service. If a site fails, Site Recovery executes predefined Azure PowerShell scripts to automate the fail-over to the replica site. There are a couple dozen Azure PowerShell cmdlets that make creating recovery scripts easy to build. Recovery plans are created through the management portal. You can test plans without disrupting primary site services. A key concept of Site Recovery is remote monitoring. The monitoring for Site Recovery is done from outside the datacenter, so even if the firewall, Internet, or other external force causes the disruption, it will be caught by Site Recovery.

> **MORE INFO**   **DISASTER RECOVERY USING ACTIVE GEO-REPLICATION**
>
> For additional information on disaster recovery using Active Geo-Replication, read Designing Cloud Solutions for Disaster Recovery Using Active Geo-Replication at *https://msdn. microsoft.com/en-us/library/azure/dn741328.aspx* .

> **MORE INFO**   **HIGH AVAILABILITY AND DISASTER-RECOVERY FOR SQL SERVER**
>
> For additional information on high availability and disaster-recovery approaches for SQL Server in Azure VMs, read High Availability and Disaster Recovery for SQL Server in Azure Virtual Machines at *https://msdn.microsoft.com/en-us/library/azure/jj870962.aspx*.

Microsoft recently purchased a company named InMage that has a product called Scout. Scout replicates systems to and from Hyper-V, VMware, and Azure. It can handle migrations from virtual or physical servers. InMage Scout for Windows and Linux is an offering that is currently coupled with Site Recovery. Parts of the Scout product were built in to the Migration Accelerator, which, as of this writing, is in preview. Using Migration Accelerator, you can move physical, VMware, AWS, and Hyper-V VMs to Azure, and you can perform these migrations to Azure in minutes. Migration Accelerator also supports heterogeneous environments, and you perform migration and testing prior to cutover to assure a seamless migration.

Describe use-cases for Hyper-V Replica and Azure Site Recovery

Disaster recovery and business continuity is the primary use case for Hyper-V Replica and Azure Site Recovery. You can configure disaster recovery to other VMs in the same datacenter, other VMs in a different datacenter, or even to Azure itself. You can use Hyper-V Replica and Site Recovery for on-premises to on-premises protection. Using Hyper-V Replica in a single datacenter gives you the ability to bring a VM on a crashed host back online very quickly by activating a replica of that VM on another host. This does not require the use of Site Recovery or System Center.

Replicating to Azure can offer an additional layer of protection for single-datacenter environments. Replicating to Azure as the replica datacenter can give customers almost instant offsite recovery capabilities without expensive hardware purchases. When replicating to Azure, you can use Availability Sets can give high-availability workloads the uptime SLA they need.

If there is more than one datacenter, you can replicate between datacenters, increasing the protection available over that of a single datacenter. This capability will offer protection from not only the host failing, but also an entire site outage. In a dual-datacenter scenario, all data can be stored on-premises. A hybrid approach is also viable, in which you can replicate some VMs to another datacenter while replicating others to Azure.

You also can use Hyper-V Replica and Site Recovery as a migration mechanism to move workloads from one datacenter to another or from on-premises datacenters to Azure. In fact, these technologies are particularly advantageous for migration, especially considering they have built-in capabilities for testing deployments before the final move.

When there are multiple sites involved in the disaster recovery or migration plan, you need Site Recovery. And using Site Recovery in a datacenter has tremendous cost benefits, too; with Azure, you are charged a small fee for each instance that is configured and synchronized as well as the storage, but you are not charged for the Azure VM itself until it actually fails-over.

Thought experiment
Acquisition and migration of Fabrikam

In this thought experiment, apply what you've learned about this objective. You can find answers to these questions in the "Answers" section at the end of this chapter.

You are the administrator for Contoso. You have more than 100 hosts in your on-premises datacenter. You are replicating and using Site Recovery as part of your BC/DR plan. Contoso just acquired another company, Fabrikam, Inc. Fabrikam has 15 hosts and more than 60 VMs. It has a mix of operating systems, some running Linux but most running Windows Server. As a cost savings strategy developed prior to acquisition, the decision was made to close the Fabrikam offices and datacenter. Your leadership would like you to move the applications and services currently being provided at Fabrikam so that the datacenter can be decommissioned prior to the Fabrikam facility shutdown. The management team would like you to complete the migration as soon as possible. However, it is important to minimize system downtime of Fabrikam services. Management would also like to minimize capital expenditures wherever possible.

Objective summary

- High availability in Azure is handled by an Availability Set. Multiple services (Virtual Machine, App Service Web Apps) should be duplicated (scaled-out in an Availability Set) to provide redundancy.

- SLAs require services to be configured with high availability.

- Hyper-V Replica is a feature inside Hyper-V on Windows Server 2012 and above. When configured, it creates an asynchronous replica of data from one Hyper-V VM to another host, in the same or different location or to Azure Storage.

- Site recovery is a service that runs in the cloud that monitors availability of Hyper-V replicas and can initiate the orchestration of a failover to the replica should a VM fail.

- Using Azure for disaster recovery purposes is very easy and economical relative to setting up another site at which to hold the replicas.

- System Center can handle orchestration for a failover triggered by Site Recovery.

Objective review

Answer the following questions to test your knowledge of the information in this objective. You can find the answers to these questions and explanations of why each answer choice is correct or incorrect in the "Answers" section at the end of this chapter. You might not need to use all terms.

1. Match the term with the definition. On the exam, this type of question will have you drop the term onto a block in front of the definition. It's possible that you can have more terms than definitions.

   - Scaling up
   - Scaling out
   - Data Loss
   - Recovery Time Objective
   - Recovery Point Objective
   - Disaster

A. The amount of time systems can be offline in the event of a disaster before unacceptable business losses occur.

B. Adding additional resources (CPU, memory, and bandwidth) to an existing VM.

C. The target time frame in which acceptable data loss can occur during a disaster.

D. Adding additional machines with the same characteristics (CPU, memory, and bandwidth) to remove some of the load from the existing VMs.

2. What is the SLA for a highly available VM in Azure?

A. 99.90

B. 99.95

C. It is not possible to have an SLA with a VM

3. What tool does Microsoft have that makes possible seamless migration from a VMware ESX VM to Azure?

A. Hyper-V

B. Site Recovery

C. Migration Accelerator

D. Microsoft does not have a tool to move from VMware to Azure

Objective 6.4: Design a disaster recovery strategy

Any disaster recovery strategy must include systems backup to meet the defined RPOs. Azure has an integrated solution called Azure Backup by which an agent is deployed onto a protected machine and the data is backed up to Azure. This agent can run on a windows system as part of the backup service on the system or it can run in conjunction with System Center Data Protection Manager. Microsoft also has an offering called StorSimple that can store data locally, and if that data is not regularly used, it can be automatically scaled-out to Azure.

> **This section covers the following topics:**
> - Design and deploy Azure Backup and other Microsoft backup solutions for Azure
> - Understand use-cases when StorSimple and Data Protection Manager would be appropriate

Design and deploy Azure Backup and other Microsoft backup solutions for Azure

There are many things that you should expect to get out of your properly designed backup solution. Here are some of them:

- **Flexible capability**   The ability to back up various workloads, applications, servers, disks, files, and folders. Flexibility includes different levels of details for different types of data or data stored in different locations.

- **Resilient, nondisruptive, on-demand, and scheduled**   You should be able to run backups without any interruptions in accessing any of the underlying data. You should be able to schedule and run backups without any human interaction. There are also times when you might want to trigger a manual on-demand snapshot of your data; thus, the system should provide that, as well.

- **Scalable and secure offsite storage**   Storage needs within any company can and almost always do change regularly. Because of this, the backup storage capability should be able to scale as the volume of data to be backed up increases. This data should also be accessible outside the datacenter so that if there is a regional or datacenter disaster, the data can be retrieved outside the disaster zone. The data needs to be able to be encrypted while in transit as well as while it's at rest. The backup of the data should conserve retention space as well as transfer bandwidth.

- **Meet RPO and RTO**   Backup should, regardless of circumstances, be able to meet RPO. You should be able to recover the systems and data within the time allocated by the RPO, recognizing that different data or data types might have different RPOs. It should also allow for recovery of data and systems within the RTO designed for the data.

- **Simple data recovery**   The real reason for backup is to have the ability to restore data and systems. Backup solutions should easily be able to recover data, manually or automatically, and provide the ability to restore to the same location or a different location. It should provide the ability to restore entire systems of very small subsets such as individual files.

- **Simple management and monitoring**   You must be able to check the status of the backup and have the ability to easily modify or act on the status of the backup solution.

- **End-user capabilities**   In many cases, you might want to offer users the ability to recover their own files without having to open a ticket or place a call to the help desk. It might also be beneficial to provide costing so that individual departments can be charged for the IT servers that are being provided.

Microsoft backup solutions give you all of these capabilities. Some of these capabilities require Data Protection Manager, most do not. However, even the basic features that are available with Azure Backup are greatly enhanced by using Data Protection Manager.

Azure Backup

Backup encrypts and protects your backups in offsite cloud storage with Azure. This gives you scalable and secure offsite storage that complies with your RPO. You can manage cloud backups within Windows Server Backup, which means that you can use very familiar tools and benefit from simple scheduling, the ability to run on demand, and utilize its management and monitoring capabilities. Backup minimizes network bandwidth use, provides flexible data retention policies, and provides a cost-effective data protection solution that can be geo-replicated with ease. There is no bandwidth cost to move data into (ingress) Azure. You pay for the instance plus the storage consumed. Your data is encrypted before it leaves your premises, and remains encrypted in Azure, and only you have the key. You can use this key to recover to the server that made the backup or to any server to which you have provided the key. Incremental backups provide multiple versions of data for point-in-time recovery. Plus, you can recover just what you need with file-level recovery. Agent is supported on Windows client (version 7 or above) and server 2008 SP2 or above. One restriction is that data must be on an online local fixed disk, which must be an NTFS-formatted volume. Read-only volumes, network share volumes, and removable drives are not supported.

For VMs running in Azure, you can perform a snapshot of the Blob to capture the drives kept in Blob storage in Azure. This works for both Windows and Linux machines. However, to get the system state, the VM must be stopped or shut down. To perform this task, use the Azure PowerShell *Export-AzureVM* and *Import-AzureVM* cmdlets. To register VMs for backup and manage jobs right from the management portal, you must first discover them. A better option for backing up VMs is to use the agent. This gives you the detailed capabilities most customers need.

To deploy and configure Backup, perform the following steps:

1. **Recovery Services – Create Vault** In the navigation pane, create a new vault by using Recovery Services, and then create a new Backup Vault. Provide the vault a name and select the location.

EXAM TIP

When you create a recovery vault for Backup, use a different region than that of the servers and services you will be backing up. This will provide a level of protection against a regional disaster such as the failure of an Azure datacenter or hurricane that can take out an entire region including your on-premises datacenter.

2. **Download Vault Credentials** From the vault Quick Start page, click the link to download the vault credentials certificate, and then save it to a location where you will have access to it from the server that you want to back up.

3. **Download The Agent**   Also on the Quick Start page is a link to download the agent. There are two agents:

   A. For Windows Server or System Center Data Protection Manager or Windows Client

   B. For Windows Server Essentials (use for Essentials Only)

4. **Run The Install Of The Agent**   Installation requires .NET framework 4.5 and Windows PowerShell. Then, click Proceed To Registration.

5. **Upload Vault Credentials**   On the Registration Wizard, click Browse and go to the location where you stored the downloaded vault credentials. Open the credential file, and then, on the Encryption Settings page of the wizard, enter a passphrase (minimum 16 characters) into both Passphrase boxes, or click the Generate Passphrase button. Browse or select a location to save the passphrase file. Ensure that this file is kept in a safe location. Without it, you will not be able to decrypt the data. The preferred method is to store it on an encrypted USB drive or network drive. Also of note, the data in the file is not encrypted. The passphrase can be read by any text editor. A link to the file created will be provided on the final page of the wizard.

6. **Launch "Microsoft Azure Backup"**   The first thing you will likely notice is that the agent is managed through the Windows or Windows Server Microsoft Management Console (MMC) [obsadmin.msc]. Also, the agent is fully embedded into the standard backup that is built in to Windows.

7. **Microsoft Azure Backup Properties**   In the Actions pane, you can set work hours, work days, turn on bandwidth throttling, configure proxy settings, and change the passphrase.

8. **Schedule Backup**   In the Actions pane, you can schedule jobs. Click Schedule Backup to launch the wizard.

   A. Select the files that you want to back up. You have access only to files for this backup. You do not have access to SQL, Microsoft SharePoint, Microsoft Exchange or other applications. You can create application snapshots or backups onto drives for these applications and then back up those dumps with Microsoft Azure Backup. There is much more flexibility with Data Protection Manager, which we will cover later.

   B. Specify the schedule (daily, weekly) and what days/times (up to three times per day). This setting will be dictated by your RPO.

   C. Select the Retention Policy (Daily, Weekly, Monthly, Yearly) for a maximum total of up to 366 backups, as shown in Figure 6-9.

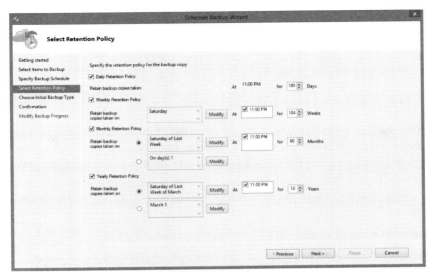

FIGURE 6-9 The Select Retention Policy wizard page

D. Choose initial backup type (Automatically over the network or Offline). If you choose offline for your initial backup, you can save to a USB drive that can then be shipped to Microsoft to import into to your storage account. Followed by all of the information needed by Microsoft to gain access to your account and storage and place the files where you want them.

EXAM TIP

If you choose Offline for your initial backup, you can save to a USB drive that can then be shipped to Microsoft to import into to your storage account. You select the staging location (USB or Network), Import Job Name, Azure Publish Settings File, Azure Subscription ID, Azure Storage Account, and Azure Storage Container. Microsoft needs all of this to gain access to your account and storage and place the files where you want them.

NOTE BACKUP SIZE LIMITS

Backup imposes a limit of 1,700 GB of data per volume that that you can back up in one backup operation.

NOTE PERFORMING A MANUAL BACKUP

Even after you have created a scheduled job, you can still manually initiate a backup operation. To do so, on the Action pane, click Backup Now!

You can monitor the job status and job history from both the Backup application and from the management portal, in the Recovery Services section. The management portal displays a list of all protected items in the Protected Items section. The dashboard displays an overview along with success and failure counts.

To recover data, click the Recover Data option. A wizard starts, offering the the following options:

- **Restore To**   On the getting started page select "this server" or "another server" for the restore. If you are restoring to another server, provide the vault credentials which you can get from the management portal. Credentials only have a shelf-life of two days, so there is no need to keep them around. Just regenerate them as you need. In a disaster, your recover destination can have a significant impact on your RTO.

- **Select Recovery Mode**   Browse or search for files.

- **Select Volume And Date**   Select the volume from the drop-down list box, and then pick a date and time.

- **Select The Files**   Select the individual files or folders that you want to recover. You can select multiple individual files within a single folder.

- **Recover Options**   Your options include Original Location or Another Location; Conflict Resolution: Create Copy, Overwrite Existing, Do Not Recover; and Restore Access Control List.

- **Confirmation**   Review your settings and then click Recover.

You can use Azure PowerShell to perform tasks in Backup. Following are some examples:

Create New Policy:

```
$policy = New-OBPolicy
$filespec = New-OBFileSpec -FileSpec <C:\Documents\Contracts>
$sched = New-OBSchedule -DaysofWeek Wednesday -TimesofDay 12:00 -
WeeklyFrequency 2
$ret = New-OBRetentionPolicy -RetentionDays 20 -RetentionWeeklyPolicy -WeekTimesOfDay
12:00:00 -WeekDaysOfWeek Sunday,Monday -RetentionWeeks 20 -RetentionMonthlyPolicy
-MonthDaysOfMonth 30 -MonthTimesOfDay 12:00:00 -RetentionMonths 11
-RetentionYearlyPolicy -YearMonthsOfYear January,March -YearWeeksOfMonth Second
-YearDaysOfWeek Sunday -YearTimesOfDay 12:00:00 -RetentionYears 11
```

Assign variables to policy

```
Add-OBFileSpec -Policy $policy -FileSpec $filespec
Set-OBSchedule -policy $policy -schedule $sched
Set-OBRetentionPolicy -policy $policy -rententionpolicy $ret
Set-OBPolicy -policy $policy
```

Backup Now

```
$policy = Get-OBPolicy
Start-OBBackup -Policy $policy -Force
```

In the Azure PowerShell command, OB stands for Online Backup. If you get an Azure PowerShell exam question on backup, make sure that your answer is using the Online Backup or OB version of the command; for example:

- *Get-OBPolicy* retrieves the current backup policy, which includes the schedule.
- *Start-OBBackup –Policy $policy –Force* executes a Backup Now.

To run Azure PowerShell modules for Online Backup, you must be running with Administrative permissions (elevated).

Backup with Data Protection Manager

Backup with Data Protection Manager works much the same way as Backup and performs all of the functionality and much more. The agent is installed on the Data Protection Manager server. Then, you register your Data Protection Manager server with the vault credentials. Data Protection Manager is a full-featured backup and recovery solution. The Backup agent on a Data Protection Manager server, does not back up individual files from the Data Protection Manager–protected servers; instead, it backs up the data stored on the Data Protection Manager backup volumes. If you have multiple Data Protection Manager servers, Backup operates only from the Primary.

Data Protection Manager does support bare-metal recovery. With Data Protection Manager, you can configure Role-Based Access Controls (RBAC) so that you can delegate backup and restore tasks. Data Protection Manager uses Changed Block Tracking to identify what blocks on a particular file have changed and only needs to transfer and store those blocks. However, when doing a restore, you can do point-in-time restore of an entire file. If that file is a Hyper-V VHD, Item Level Restore (ILR) allows you to restore individual files inside the VHD. This increases performance and significantly reduces the overall load on the protected servers, the Data Protection Manager server, and destination storage while maintaining optimal restore capabilities.

To connect Data Protection Manager to Azure, in the Data Protection Manager client, click Management–Online, Register, and then click Register A Recovery Service, which is your Azure Backup Vault, just as you did with Azure Backup.

After you have registered your Data Protection Manager server, you can configure and turn on online protection groups. The protection group is the configuration of the backup set. Within that is the option to turn on online protection. If you do turn it on, you can then set your online protection goals, which include the schedule, retention, and so on. You use this to specify how often your Data Protection Manager data store is uploaded to Azure. You can also manually set recovery points. To do so, in the Data Protection Manager client, in the Protection section, right-click a protected item, and then, in the context menu that opens, select Create Recovery Point. You can store data with Azure for up to 3,360 days (9.2 years).

To recover Data Protection Manager data, in the Data Protection Manager console, in the navigation pane, click Recovery. Next, click the data set to be restored, select the date, select the time of the backup to be used for the restore, and then click Recover. The Recovery Wizard starts, in which you can change location, type, options, and other specifications.

You can deploy Data Protection Manager on-premises (physical or virtual) or in Azure. Data Protection Manager can back up many Microsoft workloads, including Hyper-V, SharePoint, SQL, Windows File Shares, and Exchange. It can back up to local drives, to tape, and replicate to other Data Protection Manager servers in other locations or in a partner-hosted facility. When deployed in Azure, you can offload storage to Azure, which makes it possible for you to scale-out by storing older data in Azure Backup and new data on a local drive, as illustrated in Figure 6-10.

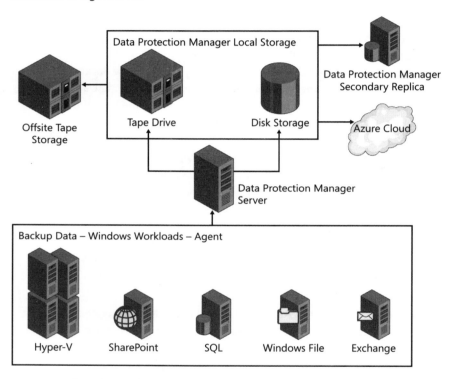

FIGURE 6-10 Data Protection Manager data flow

The Azure Backup of Data Protection Manager data is a copy of the data stores that has been performed by Data Protection Manager since the last online backup. Each online backup is a single recovery point. Remember, the number of recovery points can't exceed 366, so you need to design your online recovery points (daily + weekly + monthly + yearly) to ensure that they do not exceed this limit. Data Protection Manager is a much more robust platform for backup than Azure Backup alone. Table 6-3 shows the workloads and versions that Data Protection Manager supports when running on-premises or in Azure.

TABLE 6-3 Workloads and versions supported by Data Protection Manager 2012 R2, Update Rollup 5 or higher

Workloads	Supported versions
Server backup Back up and recover server volumes, files, folders, and shares	Windows Server 2012 R2, Windows Server 2012, Windows Server 2008 R2 SP1, Windows Server 2008 R2, Windows 2003 Server
Client backup Back up and recover client files, folders, shares	Windows 8.1, Windows 8, Windows 7
SQL Server backup Back up and recover SQL Server data-bases	SQL Server 2012, SQL Server 2008 R2, SQL Server 2008
SharePoint backup Back up SharePoint farms, databases, and frontend web servers Recover farm or SharePoint databases	SharePoint 2013, SharePoint 2010
Hyper-V backup Host-level backup of Hyper-V host server or cluster. Recover VM, Item-level recovery of files and folder, volumes, and virtual hard drives	Windows Server 2012 R2, Windows Server 2012, Windows Server 2008 R2 SP1
Guest-level backup of VM Back up and recover at applica-tion-level	
Exchange backup Exchange 2013 and Exchange 2010: Back up stand-alone Exchange server, database under a Database Availability Group DAG. Recover mailbox databases	Exchange 2013, Exchange 2010
Exchange 2007 Back up storage group. Recover storage group	

For exam purposes, you do not need to memorize Table 6-3, just recognize that there is support for these applications. However, if you are running Data Protection Manager in an Azure Virtual Machine, you need to be aware that you are limited to 16 volumes on a drive. This will have a very significant effect on your ability to set many recovery points because recovery points are stored as volumes. The way around this is to use Backup to protect the Data Protection Manager server in Azure. You can then just save a couple of days in Data Protection Manager and the rest in Backup. However, Backup does not have the detailed restore capabilities of Data Protection Manager, because it is backing up the backup data file, not the actual files. Performing restores would then be a two-step process: restore the Data Protection Manager volume, and then restore the data needed. Another thing to consider as you design system backups that use Azure Storage is there is a 500 TB limit per storage account. Another key limitation to emphasize is that Data Protection Manager is for Microsoft work-loads (with DPM 2012 R2 there is limited support for Linux if it is running in a VM).

> **MORE INFO** **ADDITIONAL INFORMATION ONLINE**
>
> For a more in-depth look at deploying Data Protection Manager backup and recovery for business continuity, go to *https://technet.microsoft.com/en-us/library/dn621063.aspx*.

StorSimple

StorSimple is a complete turnkey hybrid storage solution. It is a physical device that you install in your datacenter and has the capability of performing storage tiering. StorSimple has both spinning media as well as solid-state drives (SSDs). It can automatically move data between tiers based on how much the data is used. "Hot data," or data that is most active, is sent to SSD. Other working data is stored on spinning media. StorSimple also has the capability to add a third tier, which is Azure cloud storage. StorSimple uses cloud storage for inactive data ("cold data"), snapshots, archive folders, and backup data from on-premises drives. Pushing data into Azure does not carry any bandwidth charges (ingress); however, pulling data out of Azure (egress) does have associated costs.

In addition to built-in high performance and redundancy, StorSimple boasts many other useful features, including the following:

- Cluster service to provide high availability for any data or services using the device for storage.

- Cluster aware updating, so cluster loads on the StorSimple device are not affected by updates to the system.

- Multiple network interfaces for redundancy or connectivity for multiple systems.

- Deduplication and compression capabilities to reduce storage needs and increase storage utilization.

- You can use automated cloud snapshots as part of your disaster recovery strategy to cut or significantly reduce replication and tape management.

- You can perform disaster recovery testing without interruption to primary systems availability.

- Data uploaded to Azure can very easily be accessed by other sites for recovery or data migrations.

- StorSimple uses the Internet Small Computer Systems Interface (iSCSI) protocol to link data storage. This gives remote cloud storage the appearance of being stored locally.

- StorSimple provides a Microsoft Management Console (MMC) snap-in for managing backup and restore functions.

These functions can also be managed from the Azure management portal.

EXAM TIP

StorSimple uses iSCSI protocol to link data storage. This means that the storage that is in Azure is presented as locally attached iSCSI volumes.

One of the best features of StorSimple is the ability to restore on demand. Because of the system architecture, an Azure volume can be attached to a new location with zero restore time. In this scenario, as files are used, they are simply downloaded from the cloud storage and cached locally. Additionally, VM hard drives running in Azure can be mounted as Azure StorSimple virtual devices, giving you access to data for test or recovery purposes.

New as of Jan 2015, StorSimple has an adapter for SharePoint which gives you the capability to move Blob content from content databases to StorSimple data storage. StorSimple now also has the capability to have a virtual device. This is an Azure Virtual Machine, which provides much of the capabilities of the on-premises StorSimple device.

> **MORE INFO**   **STORSIMPLE ON TECHNET**
>
> You can learn more about StorSimple on TechNet at *https://msdn.microsoft.com/en-us/ library/dn772442.aspx.*

Understand use-cases when StorSimple and Data Protection Manager would be appropriate

StorSimple can provide backup, but that is not the best use-case for it. You should use StorSimple when you want local storage that is very fast and scalable to give you seemingly limitless expansion into Azure. It is designed more for tiering data than for backup. It is great for storing file shares, when you want very fast access to files that are used regularly but want to take infrequently used data off the expensive internal storage and put it on cloud storage.

StorSimple can replicate data through the cloud and across sites, so setting up another site or recovering to another site is very simple. This is another prime use-case, particularly if you have a very low RPO and a low RTO. With StorSimple, it is not necessary to do a full system restore to begin using the data, so the RTO is greatly reduced. However, the data that can be backed up and restored is limited to Exchange, SharePoint, Hyper-V, or virtual hard drive data and files or file shares.

Data Protection Manager has much more agent capabilities and integrates very tightly with most Microsoft workloads for seamless restores. Unlike StorSimple, a restore does need to happen before data can be used. Data Protection Manager is best suited when live access to the data is not needed. It is a backup solution, not a local, real-time high-speed, high-resiliency storage solution like StorSimple. Data Protection Manager is better used for workloads with a higher RPO because some data loss is likely, depending on how the recovery points are configured. Data Protection Manager also gives you the ability to do tape archiving, whereas no such capability exists with StorSimple.

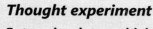

Thought experiment

Enterprise data archiving solution needed

In this thought experiment, apply what you've learned about this objective. You can find answers to these questions in the "Answers" section at the end of this chapter.

Your manager asks you to design a strategy to meet all of the needs of the organization. The following are system definitions and requirements.

Systems to backup and RPO/RTO associated with those workloads:

Systems and data	RPO	RTO	Performance requirements
File data from various servers, .docx, .xlxs, .pptx, and so on	24 hours	2 days	None
Daily market analysis, Excel files	1 hour	4 hours	High performance required
SharePoint data	4 hours	1 day	None
Exchange data	24 hours	2 days	None

With this in mind, answer the following questions:

1. What technology should you use to protect your daily market analysis Excel files? Why is this the best choice?

2. What technology should you use to protect other file data? Why?

3. What is the best technology to protect Exchange data? Why?

As you answer the why questions, consider not only why one technology is better, but also if the other technology could work and what are the limitations.

Objective summary

- Stand-alone Azure Backup is for backing up Windows Virtual Machines directly to Azure. It gives us a simple and efficient backup solution that is integrated directly into the backup that comes with Windows. It is best used for simple full-system backups. More specific, individual restores can be performed.

- Azure Backup with Data Protection Manager gives you much more capability including more specifically defined backup and restore of various Microsoft workloads such as SQL, SharePoint, Exchange, and Hyper-V. It can do everything that the stand-alone Backup can do, but it can do much more. It is a full backup and restore solution that can store data to hard drive, tape, and Azure. You can employ technologies like disk-2disk as well as disk2disk2tape, and even implement replication to multiple sites.

- StorSimple is more like a SAN solution that offers seemingly endless capacity by scaling-out to Azure for data that is not regularly accessed. You can use it to replicate and back up to Azure, but the real power of the system is in the high-performance and high-scalability multitier storage capability it provides. It is best used when low RPO or low RTO are required.

Objective review

Answer the following questions to test your knowledge of the information in this objective. You can find the answers to these questions and explanations of why each answer choice is correct or incorrect in the "Answers" section at the end of this chapter.

1. What type of backup and restore is possible with Azure Backup?
   A. Block-level backup with file-level restore
   B. File-level backup with file-level restore.
   C. System-level backup with system-level restore
   D. Block-level backup with block-level restore
   E. Block-level backup with System-level restore

2. How does Data Protection Manager differ from StorSimple? (Choose all that apply.)
   A. There are no differences other than the names.
   B. StorSimple offers instant restore capabilities, Data Protection Manager does not.
   C. Data Protection Manager Integrates with Azure Backup, StorSimple does not.
   D. Data Protection Manager provides for lower RPO and RTO capabilities than StorSimple.
   E. Data Protection Manager is part of System Center, StorSimple is not.
   F. StorSimple includes internal drives for storing data, Data Protection Manager does not.

3. Using Azure PowerShell, how would you display the schedule and retention information of an Azure Backup?
   A. *Get-ScheduledJob*
   B. *Get-ScheduledTask*
   C. *Get-AzureAutomationSchedule*
   D. *Get-OBPolicy*

Objective 6.5: Design Azure Automation and PowerShell workflows

Automating Azure is valuable for saving time and ensuring consistency in your deployment. Consistency reduces errors and increases efficiency. Windows PowerShell is an incredibly powerful tool that you can employ to implement this automation. In this Objective, we will look into Windows PowerShell and Windows PowerShell workflows to show what capabilities you have at your disposal as you design your Azure systems. There will likely be many questions on the exam related to Windows PowerShell.

> **This section covers the following topic:**
> - Create a Windows PowerShell script specific to Azure

Create a Windows PowerShell script specific to Azure

Windows PowerShell is an incredible tool. With it, you can do anything that is available in either the existing management portal or the new Preview Management Portal and more. It is easy to get started using Windows PowerShell with Azure.

Getting Started with Windows PowerShell

To begin, you need to download the Azure module for Windows PowerShell. You can download it directly from the management portal. To do this, in the upper-left corner of the management portal, click the arrow adjacent to Azure, and then click Downloads. You can also get the download directly by going to *http://azure.microsoft.com/en-us/downloads*. Scroll down to the Command-Line Tools section, and then, in the Windows PowerShell section, click Install. The installation is done through the Web Platform Installer.

When prompted, click Run and follow the installation instructions. After installation is complete, on your Start screen or Start menu locate Microsoft Azure PowerShell and start it.

You will then need to connect Azure PowerShell to your Azure subscription. There are two ways to do this. The first is the use the *Add-AzureAccount* cmdlet.

This method requires a user name and password to authenticate to Azure. The command will open a web browser sign-in screen for Azure. You enter your Microsoft account (formerly known as Windows Live ID) email address, and then click Continue. Next, type your password, and then click Sign In. Another way to connect to Azure from Windows PowerShell is through certificate authentication. This is not recommended if you are connecting from a shared computer. To use certificate authentication, run the following command:

```
Get-AzurePublishSettingsFile
```

Then, save the configuration file locally. Next, run the following command:

```
Import-AzurePublishSettingsFile -PublishSettingsFile "<SubscriptionName-SubDate-
credentials.publishsettings"
```

The full command looks similar like this:

```
Import-AzurePublishSettingsFile -PublishSettingsFile "Internal Consumption-3-19-
2015-credentials.publishsettings"
```

EXAM TIP

You can use either the *Add-AzureAccount* cmdlet or the *Get-AzurePublishSettingsFile* and *Import-AzurePublishSettingsFile* cmdlets to authenticate Windows PowerShell to Azure:

IMPORTANT **PUBLISH SETTINGS FILE AUTHENTICATION**

The *publishSettingsFile* has certificate credentials embedded in it. After adding it to Windows PowerShell, you should delete it from your computer to prevent others from gaining access to the file and gaining access to your Azure subscription.

You should also be familiar with the following cmdlets:

- *Get-AzureAccount*   List accounts of which Windows PowerShell is aware.
- *Remove-AzureAccount* <ID>   Remove an Azure account. The account is not removed from Azure, the credentials are simply removed from Windows PowerShell.
- *Get-Help* <Command> *-example*   Get help and example scripts to run a command.

After authenticating with Azure, you then need to set the subscription that you want to use. To do this, use *Get-AzureSubscription* to determine what subscriptions are available, and then use *Set-AzureSubscription* "Your Subscription Name" to set the default subscription.

Get-AzureSubscription will return something similar to the following:

```
SubscriptionId : 1942a221-7d86-4e10-9e4b-d5af26…
SubscriptionName : Internal Consumption
Environment : AzureCloud
SupportedModes : AzureServiceManagement
DefaultAccount : FFA287FE6305123BADED295286…
Accounts : {FFA287FE6305123BADED295286B5C25E…}
IsDefault : True
IsCurrent : True
```

You then use the *SubscriptionName* with the *Set-AzureSubscription* command, as follows:

```
Set-AzureSubscription "Internal Consumption"
```

Now, any subsequent commands you run will be run against this subscription. The *Set-AzureSubscription* command also has a switch (*-CurrentStorageAccount*) to set the default storage container. To test connectivity with your subscription, you could run a simple command such as *Get-AzureVM*. If you do not have any VMs, this command will return an empty set. If you are not successfully connected, Windows PowerShell will display an error.

We are now connected to Azure and have set up our default subscription.

Windows PowerShell basics

Let me point out a few generic Windows PowerShell tips that just might come in handy.

- You will be asked to read a script, identify what needs to be added to fill in multiple missing lines, and then drag the missing lines from a list of available script line options, dropping the proper line to where it belongs in the original script. To solve this type of problem, there are many standard Windows PowerShell syntax basics that you will need to understand, including the following:

```
$ : Variable
$_ : THIS token
| pipe : Catch output of the command and pass it to another
command. Pipes allow you to chain together cmdlets to create more
complex actions
` back tick    : Continue command on next line
 (on tilde key) : Escape Character - Next character is literal
# : Single Line / End of line comment
<#..#>: Multi-line Comment
$() : Evaluate sub-expression inside double-quoted string
eg: "Hello $($MyUser.First), how are you today?"
```

- Include other cmdlets (remember: parentheses indicate subexpression).

```
$storageAccessKey = (Get-AzureStorageKey -StorageAccountName
<storageaccountname>).Primary
```

- Combine commands using vaiables.

```
$uri = Get-AzureWinRMUri -ServiceName $cloudServiceName -Name $Name
$cred = Get-Credential
Enter-PSSession -ConnectionUri $uri -Credential $cred
```

- Dot properties and pipeline variables.

```
Get-Service | Where-Object {$_.status -eq "Running"}
```

- Built-in variables.

```
$true, $false, $PSVersionTable, $HOME
```

- Working with pipes and variables, we pipe the output of one command into the input of another and store results into variables that you can reuse. In the following case, we are creating an Azure VM Configuration that you can use later to create a VM.

```
$un = "myadminname"
$pwd = "mysecretpassword"
$image = "a699494373c04fc0bc8f2bb1389d6106__Windows-Server-2012-R2-
201411.01-en.us-127GB.vhd"
$newVM = New-AzureVMConfig -Name "Server2" -InstanceSize "Small"
-Image $image
| Add-AzureProvisioningConfig -Windows -AdminUserName $un -Password
$pwd | Set-AzureSubnet -SubnetNames "FirstSubnet"
Use the variable to deploy the virtual machine!
New-AzureVM -VMs $newVM -ServiceName "newcloudservice" -Location
"West US" -VNetName "myVNet"
```

Note that the *New-AzureVM* command does not have important parameters like username, password, or image, so those have to be set by using the *New-AzureVMConfig* command. You can learn more about the various commands from *https://msdn.microsoft.com/en-us/library/azure/jj554330.aspx*.

There are a few key areas of Windows PowerShell that you will likely see on the exam. They are connecting Windows PowerShell to Azure (which was just covered), getting and creating VMs, working with storage and storage containers, and working with websites. I will share what you are likely to see on the exam, but I strongly recommend that you play with these commands so that you really learn them well. The exam will not try to trick you by presenting erroneous commands, but it is easy to miss minor details and answer a question incorrectly.

Working with VMs

Let's look at the primary Windows PowerShell commands that you will need to understand, both for the exam and to begin using Windows PowerShell, to deploy and manage Azure Infrastructure as a Service (IaaS) VMs:

- *Get-AzureVM*   List Azure VM's.
- Create a new VM:
  - *New-AzureVMConfig*   Creates a new VM configuration object. You can then use this object to perform a new deployment as well as to add a new VM to an existing deployment.
  - *Add-AzureProvisioningConfig*   Adds the provisioning configuration to an Azure VM.
  - *Set-AzureSubnet*   Sets the subnet list for a VM configuration.

- *New-AzureVM* Adds a new VM to an existing Azure service, or creates a new VM and service in the current subscription if either the *-Location* or *-AffinityGroup* is specified.

  Example:

  ```
  New-AzureVMConfig -Name <VmName> -InstanceSize Small –ImageName
  <ImageNameVHDString> `
  | Add-AzureProvisioningConfig –Windows -Password <adminPassword> -AdminUsername
  <adminusername> `
  | Set-AzureSubnet 'AD-Production' `
  | New-AzureVM –ServiceName <MyServiceName> -VNetName <MyNetworkName>
  ```

- *Remove-AzureVM* Removes an Azure VM (Note that this command provides a *-DeleteVHD* switch to also remove the underlying drives when you remove the AzureVM).

- *Restart-AzureVM* Restarts an Azure VM.

- *Start-AzureVM* Requests the start of an Azure VM.

- *Stop-AzureVM* Requests a shutdown of a VM (includes deallocated status unless *-StayProvisioned* parameter is passed).

- *Update-AzureVM* Accepts update information for the specified VM and initiates the update. You can add or remove data drives, modify the cache mode of data or operating system disks, change the network endpoints, or change the size of the VM.

- You can use "VM Name" or VM.Object in all scripts; for example

  ```
  Restart-AzureVM [-Name] <String> [-ServiceName] <String> [<CommonParameters>]
  ```

  or:

  ```
  Restart-AzureVM -VM <PersistentVM> [-ServiceName] <String> [<CommonParameters>]
  ```

- *Add-AzureVhd* Uploads a VHD to Azure (as a fixed drive) and converts from dynamic to fixed.

- *Get-AzureDisk* [[-DriveName] <String>] [<CommonParameters>] Get a particular drive with which to work.

- *Add-AzureDisk* Adds a new drive to the Microsoft Azure drive repository in the current subscription. This drive is bootable if you specify the optional *-OS* parameter. If you don't specify it, the drive is a data drive. The required parameters are *DiskName* and *MediaLocation*.

- *Add-AzureDataDisk* Adds a new data drive to a VM object. Use the *-CreateNew* parameter to create a new data drive with a specified size and label, and then attach it. Use the *-Import* parameter to attach an existing drive from the image repository. Use the *-ImportFrom* parameter to attach an existing drive from a Blob in a storage account. Using this cmdlet, you can specify the host-cache mode of attached data drives.

Example:

```
Get-AzureVM -ServiceName 'ITCserviceDS01' -Name "SQL01"
  | Add-AzureDataDisk -CreateNew -DiskSizeInGB 128 -DiskLabel "SQLData" -LUN 0 `
  | Update-AzureVM
```

Notice in this example that all three of the lines are a single command. Each of the lines are feeding the others. You have to *Get-AzureVM* before you can do anything with it. When you get it, you can use *Add-AzureDisk* to add the Azure drive, and then you need to use *Update-AzureVM* to post any changes that you made. Also note that we are using the string representation of the VM name "SQL01".

Working with Storage

There is not much to be concerned with in the exam except the commands to create various storage accounts. For the exam, you will not need to remember the syntax of the commands, just the sequence. You should understand what each does just to make it easier to keep organized in your mind. Pay attention to the sequence!

- *New-AzureStorageAccount*   Create storage account; storage account name must be alpha all lower case
- *Get-AzureStorageKey*   Obtain the security key for the storage account
- *New-AzureStorageContext*   Create an Azure storage context using Azure Storage credentials
  - *<StorageContext>.BlobEndPoint*   URL of the Blob endpoint
- *Set-AzureStorageBlobContent*   Upload a file to the container and context
- *New-AzureStorageContainer*   Create a folder in Azure Storage

Example:

```
# Define Variables
$StoreName = "70534storagename"
$myLocation = "West US"
$SubName = "MSDN Subscription"
$ContainerName = "files"
$fqName = "C:\ToUpload.zip"
# set default subscription
Set-AzureSubscription -SubscriptionName $SubName
Write-Host "Creating Storage Account... $StoreName at $myLocation"
# Create Storage Account
New-AzureStorageAccount -Location $myLocation -StorageAccountName $StoreName `
    -Type "Standard_LRS"
# Get the primary key from the new storage account
$StorageAccountKey = Get-AzureStorageKey $StoreName | %{ $_.Primary }
# Get context for storage

$StoreContext = New-AzureStorageContext -StorageAccountName $StoreName `
    -StorageAccountKey $StorageAccountKey
# Display full path to newly created storage account
Write-Host $StoreContext.BlobEndPoint
```

```
# set default storage account
Set-AzureSubscription -SubscriptionName $SubName -CurrentStorageAccount $StoreName
# Create container/Folder on Azure
New-AzureStorageContainer $ContainerName -Permission Container `
    -Context $StoreContext
# Display full path to newly created storage container
Write-host ($StoreContext.BlobEndPoint.ToString() + $ContainerName.ToString())
# upload file from c:\ to …/files/ on Azure
Set-AzureStorageBlobContent -Container $ContainerName -File $fqName `
    -Context $StoreContext -Force
```

EXAM TIP

Following is the Azure PowerShell command to retrieve the primary storage account:

```
$StorageAccountKey = Get-AzureStorageKey $StoreName | %{ $_.Primary }
```

Working with Azure Websites

Dealing with Websites or Web Apps is very similar to working with other components within Azure PowerShell. The key element to understand on the exam for websites is the *-Slot* parameter. Following is a list of commands to manage websites via Azure PowerShell:

- *Get-AzureWebsite* [[-Name] <String>] [-Slot <String>] [<CommonParameters>]   List websites

- *Remove-AzureWebsite* [-Force] [[-Name] <String>] [-Slot <String>] [<CommonParameters>]   Delete a website

- *Start-AzureWebsite* [[-Name] <String>] [-Slot <String>] [<CommonParameters>]   Start a website that was previously stopped

- *Stop-AzureWebsite* [[-Name] <String>] [-Slot <String>] [<CommonParameters>]   Stop a website

- *Show-AzureWebsite*   Open in a browser

- *New-AzureWebsite*   Create a website

Windows PowerShell Workflows

Azure has automation built in via Windows PowerShell workflows. Workflows are often referred to as runbooks in many automation platforms. You can use the built-in workflows, as shown in Figure 6-11, or you can create your own. Windows PowerShell workflows are located in the management portal. You can find them in the left navigation bar, in the Automation section. Using runbooks, you can automate or orchestrate the creation, deployment, maintenance, and monitoring of services and resources in Azure.

EXAM TIP

You can find Windows PowerShell workflows in the management portal. Go to the main navigation, and then look in the Automation section.

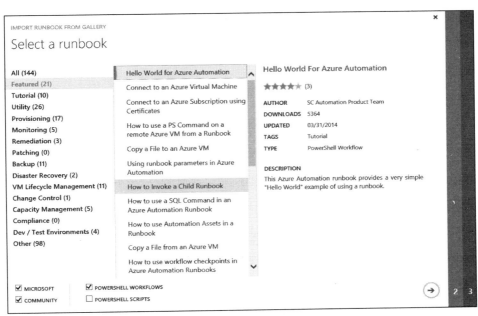

FIGURE 6-11 Categories of runbooks already available in Azure

Decomposing a workflow

The following sections of an Azure PowerShell Workflow New-AzureVMEndpoint script illustrate workflow concepts.

Use *Get-AutomationPSCredential* for the script to run with specific account permissions:

```
$Cred = Get-AutomationPSCredential -Name 'Azure AD Automation Account'
```

Connect to the Azure account the same way you would from Azure PowerShell:

```
$AzureAccount = Add-AzureAccount -Credential $Cred
```

The following example is for building and then running an Azure PowerShell script from a workflow using the InlineScript command. The *$Using:* variable is required within the InlineScript to reference variables and parameters that are external to the InlineScript.

```
$EndpointStatus = InlineScript {
$Status = Get-AzureVM -ServiceName $Using:ServiceName -Name $Using:VMName
|
Add-AzureEndpoint -Name $Using:AEName -Protocol $Using:AEProtocol
```

```
-PublicPort $Using:AEPublicPort -LocalPort $Using:AELocalPort | `
Update-AzureVM
Write-Output $Status}
```

Because we stored the result of the InlineScript into the *$EndpointStatus* variable, we can check the status, and then perform logging or write output. In the following script, we are displaying verbose - Success status information for the service, VM, Endpoint, Protocol, and Ports.

```
   if ($EndpointStatus.OperationStatus -eq "Succeeded") {
$SuccessMsg = "Service: {0} `nVM: {1} `nEndpoint: {2} `nProtocol: {3}
`nPublic Port: {4} `nLocal Port: {5} `nOperation: {6} `nOperation Id: {7}
`nOperation Status: {8} `n" `
 -f $ServiceName, $VMName, $AEName, $AEProtocol, $AEPublicPort,
$AELocalPort, $EndpointStatus.OperationDescription, $EndpointStatus.
OperationId, $EndpointStatus.OperationStatus
Write-Output $SuccessMsg
Write-Verbose $SuccessMsg }}
```

The full script will run from an Azure VM and does the following:

1. Get authentication credentials with *Get-AutomationPSCredential*.

2. Run *Add-AzureAccount*.

3. Invoke another script that is defined within this script. The invoked script will execute *Add-AzureEndPoint*.

4. Performs error checking and displays messages relative to the status.

Generally, parameters are going to be passed to workflows for the actions to be customized for particular services, machines, or items. For the exam, there will probably be only one or two questions on runbooks. It is likely that you will be shown a very simple workflow and asked to articulate the sequence in which the lines should be run in the script. The script that will be used in the workflow question will likely only have a few lines. It might have a comment line or a write-host line above it telling you what the line that is missing is supposed to be doing. If this is the case, you can just drag the correct line over to the script and drop it where it belongs.

Thought experiment
Automating Azure cloud VMs for training

In this thought experiment, apply what you've learned about this objective. You can find answers to these questions in the "Answers" section at the end of this chapter.

You are an administrator for Graphic Design Institute. You are asked to build a training lab that uses Azure as your infrastructure. You have 30 desks in your training room. Each student will connect to one or more VMs in Azure to do the training. You would like to automate the process of wiping or refreshing the training VMs after each class. You would also like the ability to have different VMs available for different classes. What would you need to do to implement this capability?

1. How would the users connect to the VMs assigned to their desks?

2. How would you create a very consistent training environment and how would you differentiate between different types of classes?

3. Are there things that you need to do to minimize the costs associated with this scenario? If yes, what?

Following are some things to consider when preparing an automation solution:

- Each desk points to a different set of VM's on Azure
- Building VMs
- Turning off VMs
- Turning on VMs
- Deleting VMs

Objective summary

- There are many Windows PowerShell commands and facts that you're likely to find on the exam. Here are some things that you should fully understand:
  - To download the Windows PowerShell Module, use Web Platform Installer.
  - To ascertain what accounts are connected to current Azure login, use the *Get-AzureAccount* cmdlet.

- To connect to Azure Account with a user name and password, use the *Add-AzureAccount* cmdlet.
- The sequence for getting started with Azure is as follows:
    A. Install the Azure PowerShell Module.
    B. Authenticate by using *Add-AzureAccount* or *Get-AzurePublishSettingsfile* (this also requires *Import-AzurePublishSettingsFile*).
    C. *Get-AzureSubscription* (so you know the exact name for below).
    D. *Set-AzureSubscription*. You can now work with Azure.

Objective review

Answer the following questions to test your knowledge of the information in this objective. You can find the answers to these questions and explanations of why each answer choice is correct or incorrect in the "Answers" section at the end of this chapter.

For questions 1–3, using the multiple choice options, fill in the missing lines of code in the following Windows PowerShell script. Select the letter of the line of code from the options that follow the script. Not all lines of code in the choices will be used. A line of code in the choices might be used more than once. On the exam, you will have questions like this where you must drag the line of code to the proper location.

Following are the multiple-choice options for questions 1–3:

A. *Set-AzureSubscription -SubscriptionName 'MSDN Subscription'*

B. *Set-AzureSubscription -SubscriptionName 'MSDN Subscription' -CurrentStorageAccount itcstore534*

C. *Add-AzureAccount*

D. *| Add-AzureProvisioningConfig -Windows -Password "My@Pass534!" -AdminUsername "sysadmin"* `

E. *Get-AzurePublishSettingsFile*

And here is the code to which you need to match the multiple-choice options:

```
# Setup Variables
$ITCLocation = 'East US 2'
$ITCSubName = 'Internal Consumption'
$ITCStoreName = 'itcstore534'
$ITCDC01Name = 'DCtest'
$ITCServiceName= 'ITC-70-534'
# Authenticate to Azure
```

1. What line of code should be inserted here?

```
# Set default Subscription
```

2. What line of code should be inserted here?

```
# Create New Storage Account
New-AzureStorageAccount -Location $ITCLocation -StorageAccountName $ITCStoreName
-Type 'Standard_LRS'
$ITCStorageAccountKey = Get-AzureStorageKey $ITCStoreName | %{ $_.Primary }
$ITCStoreContext = New-AzureStorageContext -StorageAccountName $ITCStoreName
-StorageAccountKey $ITCStorageAccountKey
# Set Default Storage
Set-AzureSubscription -SubscriptionName 'Internal Consumption'
-CurrentStorageAccount itcstore534
# Create new Azure Service
New-AzureService -Location $ITCLocation -ServiceName $ITCServiceName
#Create New Azure VM
New-AzureVMConfig -Name $ITCDC01Name -InstanceSize Small -ImageName
"a699494373c04fc0bc8f2bb1389d6106__Windows-Server-2012-R2-201412.01-en.us-127GB.
vhd" `
```

3. What line of code should be inserted here?

```
(

| Set-AzureSubnet 'AD-Production' `
| New-AzureVM –ServiceName $ITCServiceName -VNetName 'ITC-VNet'
```

4. Place in order the commands that you would need to execute to connect to Azure and get a list of VMs already built on Azure. You might not need all lines of code.

A. *Set-AzureSubscription -SubscriptionName 'MSDN Subscription'*

B. *Get-AzureWebsite*

C. *Get-AzureVM*

D. *Get-AzureAccount*

E. *Add-AzureAccount*

F. *Get-AzureSubscription*

Objective 6.6: Describe the use cases for Azure Automation configuration

The term "Infrastructure as Code" is how most refer to automation concepts for which software does the work to deploy or change infrastructure with constant management of compliance. There are several options for automating and carrying out desired configurations within Azure. Some of the tools that are embedded in Azure include Chef, Puppet, Windows PowerShell, and Desired State Configuration. Azure Automation boosts efficiency, reduces costs, increases agility, and boosts productivity—all this, and it is easy to implement, too. It is great for long running often-repeated tasks or tasks that are prone to errors. Some examples include backup SQL Azure on a schedule, patch VMs with no downtime, enabling regeneration of storage account keys, stage deployment of a service, or even deploy an application from Git.

This section covers the following topic:

- Understand when to use Azure Automation, Chef, Puppet, Windows PowerShell, or Desired State Configuration

---

Desired State Configuration

Desired State Configuration is the automated process of forcing a desired configuration onto a system. This is obtained by inspecting systems and automatically changing the configuration to match that of the desired state. This might be removing something that was added or adding something that was removed. It is used to make deployment easier and dependable as well as to enforce a particular configuration on a VM or series of VMs. As an example, if you have a bunch of web servers and for all of your web servers, you need to have PHP support turned on. You could set a desired configuration that forces the installation of Internet Information Services (IIS) and configuration of PHP. If someone later removes one of these capabilities, Desired State Configuration will reinstall and configure these components.

Some new terms are defined for a special syntax used for Windows PowerShell Desired State Configuration. *Configuration* is a keyword which is followed by a set of braces ({}) to delimit the block. Inside the configuration, you can define nodes, which is the computer name. The node has a braces ({}) block for action to be performed on that node. Keywords are used to define how the script engine should interpret the instructions. You use the term *Ensure* to make certain that the configuration is met; if it is not, make it so. *Absent* is a term that you use to make sure something is not present; if it is, remove it.

Practical applications of Desired State Configuration include the following:

- Install or remove windows roles and features
- Running Windows PowerShell scripts
- Managing registry settings
- Managing files and directories
- Starting, stopping, and managing processes and services
- Managing groups and user accounts
- Deploying new software
- Managing environment variables
- Discovering the actual configuration state on a given node
- Fixing a configuration that has drifted away from the desired state

The best use-case for Desired State Configuration is if you want to ensure that newly deployed servers configured a certain way. Another case is when you want to eliminate *configuration drift*; that is, guarantee the servers maintain their desired configuration at all times. The desired configuration not only monitors for misconfigurations of servers but corrects problems, eliminating configuration drift. Following is an example of a Desired State Configuration:

```
Example Configuration – IIS Installed
Configuration MyWebConfig
{
  # A Configuration block can have zero or more Node blocks
  Node "Server001"  # set to localhost for any server
  {
   # Next, specify one or more resource blocks
   # This example ensures the Web Server (IIS) role is installed
   WindowsFeature MyRoleExample
   {
     Ensure = "Present" # To uninstall the role, set Ensure to "Absent"
     Name = "Web-Server" #The name of the IIS feature
   }

   # File is a built-in resource you can use to manage files and directories
   # ensures files from source directory are present in the destination
   File MyFileExample
   {
     Ensure = "Present" # You can also set Ensure to "Absent"
     Type = "Directory" # Default is "File"
     Recurse = $true
     SourcePath = $WebsiteFilePath # This is a path that has web files
     DestinationPath = "C:\inetpub\wwwroot" # Make sure web files are present
DependsOn = "[WindowsFeature]MyRoleExample"
   # Ensures MyRoleExample completes before this block will runs
   }
  }
}
```

In the preceding example, I used two Desired State Configuration resources, *Windows-Feature* and the *File* resource. In this example, the *Name* of the *WindowsFeature* to ensure is *Web-Server*, which is IIS. For the *File*, the *SourcePath* and *DestinationPath* are defined. If the file is not present, it will be copied from the source to ensure that it is present. The reverse could also be established by using *Absent* instead of *Ensure*. As an example, if you want to make certain that default.aspx is removed, you could set that file and path to *Absent*. There are many other resources available, which you can find at *https://technet.microsoft.com/en-us/library/dn282125.aspx*. Desired State Configuration is a feature of Windows PowerShell so it is designed for configuring Windows Systems.

Windows PowerShell for automation

You can use Windows PowerShell by itself for automation. It is best used for automating repeated tasks that are identical. An example of this might be if you were setting up a training room and you want to deploy 15 VMs exactly the same way. You could have Windows PowerShell create these VMs, and they would be identical in every way. After the class is finished, you could then use Windows PowerShell to delete all of the VMs. You could also use Desired State Configuration, but the wrapper is a much more suitable solution for Desired State Configuration. To continue with our training class example, you would not necessarily want Desired State Configuration to reconfigure something that a user was doing in her lab. Any tasks that are very time consuming or prone to error are great examples of use-cases for Windows PowerShell automation.

Chef and Puppet

Chef is a third-party (non-Microsoft) product that you can use for systems management, automation, and producing analytics. A Chef client is installed on the VM that is being managed, and then that client checks in with the Chef server periodically to see if there are any updates that need to be applied. Chef is a well-known and popular platform built on Ruby, and it enjoys large adoption numbers and familiarity. Chef can manage Windows, Linux, and even Mac computers. To configure Chef to integrate with Azure, you can download a publishSettingsFile that you put on your Chef server so that it can authenticate with Azure to perform various tasks.

Chef *Cookbooks* are a group of scripts or instructions known as recipes that you can run to deploy systems or force compliance with a desired configuration on a system. A *knife* plugin is used to communicate with Azure, so resources on Azure can be fully managed by Chef (think of this as an agent).You also can create, modify, and delete resources with it.

Puppet is another option to automate and enforce consistency of systems. It is very similar to Chef. Azure has the ability to automatically add the Puppet Enterprise Agent as you deploy a new VM. When you deploy the VM, select the Puppet check box and type the name of your Puppet Master Server. You can also deploy a Puppet Enterprise Server using a template in the VM Gallery. Chef and Puppet both have a vast open-source catalog of modules that you can download and reuse.

If you have Linux infrastructure in Azure, Puppet and Chef can both manage and automate the infrastructure. A use-case for Chef is if you already have a Chef-managed infrastructure. A use-case for Puppet is if you are already using Puppet for systems management or deployment. You can very easily integrate your new Azure infrastructure and share all of the management scripts with your new cloud capabilities. Another use-case for either Chef or Puppet is if you have a broadly diverse infrastructure in many locations with many different operating systems that you want to bring under management. Chef and Puppet both have commands and examples available for Linux and Windows. And, each is a versatile and useful tool when need to prevent configuration drift of Linux-based systems.

Azure Automation

Azure Automation is a feature integrated in the Azure platform that uses Windows Power-Shell for its engine. It uses the term runbooks for the scripts that you can execute to auto-mate systems in Azure. Automation is designed for Azure systems; it does not integrate with on-premises systems unless they are accessible from the public cloud. Because PowerShell is the engine, you can perform almost any task on nearly any Windows-based computer as long as you can get to that computer and gain access from a Windows PowerShell workflow from the cloud. The best use-case for Automation is to automate systems running in Azure if you do not have any other automation system already adopted. Even though it has the brawn of Windows PowerShell behind it, Automation, does not have the graphical tools associated with higher-functioning runbook automation platforms such as System Center Orchestrator. After you create or import existing runbooks into Automation, you can schedule them against the server or servers at a particular time or times. It is designed to simplify tedious, long-running, or error-prone procedures and processes.

Thought experiment
Desired State Configuration in Azure

In this thought experiment, apply what you've learned about this objective. You can find answers to these questions in the "Answers" section at the end of this chapter.

On several occasions, various technology staff within your organization have made changes to systems that decreased performance and in some cases, even availability of systems. Your manager has asked you to determine if there is some way that you can easily prevent engineers from deploying improperly configured VMs or to mon-itor configuration changes of servers. All of the web servers should be deployed with Windows Server, IIS, PHP, and CGI turned on. There are other requirements, but this is likely the most difficult. If it is possible, she would also like to know if there is a way to automate the configuration so that if an out-of-scope change is made, it can be fixed automatically. All of the servers in your organization are run-ning Windows Server. Most of the servers are running in Azure. Azure is the primary front end and also stores the SQL data. There are a few on-premises servers that are maintained for less important systems or disaster recovery should Azure fail.

With this in mind, answer the following questions:

1. What are available options to ensure Desired State Configuration is met prior to deployment?

2. How can you automatically remediate changes if an engineer does incorrectly configure a server?

3. What is the easiest option to provide this capability given that there is no exist-ing Desired State Configuration systems in place now?

Objective summary

- Azure Automation is a method by which you can run Windows PowerShell commands to simplify and streamline long-running, error-prone or repetitive processes.

- A key tenet of Azure Automation is Desired State Configuration. This ensures that when a system is deployed, it conforms to the predefined state for this type of server. Additionally, desired state can be enforced post deployment, so if configuration changes are made, they are automatically set back to the desired state.

- There are several ways to perform deployment as well as post deployment enforcement of Desired State Configuration. You can do this by using Azure Automation, Windows PowerShell, Puppet, or Chef. Puppet and Chef are the most popular methods and can perform desired state compliance across Azure as well as on-premises machines. Each application has a large community following, so there are many scripts available online that you can use, either directly or as a base from which you can customize or modify. You can use Puppet and Chef on Linux as well as Windows computers.

- Azure automation and Windows PowerShell are the easiest to set up and configure. They do not require additional server or host integration to manage. Both Chef and Puppet require a central management server to administer Desired State Configuration.

Objective review

Answer the following questions to test your knowledge of the information in this objective. You can find the answers to these questions and explanations of why each answer choice is correct or incorrect in the "Answers" section at the end of this chapter.

1. What types of processes are best suited for Azure Automation? (Choose all that apply.)

    A. One-time configuration changes

    B. Error-prone tasks or configuration changes

    C. Changes that are often repeated

    D. One-time system deployments

    E. Linux-based VM configuration changes

2. What is Desired State Configuration designed to do? (Choose all that apply.)

    A. Create new instances of VMs to scale-out based on performance statistics

    B. Install or remove Windows roles and features

    C. Manage files and directories

    D. Start, stop, and manage processes and services

    E. Protect systems and data by providing Backup and Recovery Services

    F. Deploy new software

    G. Discover the actual configuration state on a given node

    H. Fix a configuration that has drifted away from the desired state

3. What are the key benefits of Chef and Puppet? (Choose all that apply.)

   A. Cross-platform configuration management (Linux and Windows).

   B. They are built on Windows PowerShell and integrate tightly with the Windows PowerShell engine.

   C. They are backed by strong user communities.

   D. They require no server infrastructure for management.

   E. They accelerate time-to-market by simplifying configuration management.

Answers

This section contains the solutions to the thought experiments and answers to the objective review questions in this chapter.

Objective 6.1: Thought experiment

1. System Center gives us all of the capabilities desired now and has very extensive cloud integration with which you can grow into the cloud with the same tools you use to manage on-premises systems.

2. System Center comes with Self-Service capabilities. You just need to set up and configure the self-service portal, configure quotas for users, and then show them how to access the portal.

3. System Center Configuration Manager and Windows System Update Service.

4. Migrating data that is not regularly used to Azure can free up existing SAN storage for more important and regularly accessed storage. You could also migrate your replica servers to Azure.

Objective 6.1: Review

1. **Correct answers:** A, B, C, D, E, and G

   A. **Correct:** Operations Manager is integrated by adding the Azure Management Pack.

   B. **Correct:** Configuration Manager has Cloud Distribution Points for direction integration with Azure.

   C. **Correct:** Virtual Machine Manager integrates with Azure through the creation of a Public Cloud connector.

   D. **Correct:** Orchestrator integrates with Azure through the Azure Connector.

   E. **Correct:** Data Protection Manager integrates directly with Azure to publish backup data to Azure by installing the Azure Online Backup agent on the Data Protection Manager server.

   F. **Incorrect:** Service Manager does not connect directly with Azure. All communications and integrations with Azure go through other components.

   G. **Correct:** App Controller integrates with Azure by configuring a Public Cloud Connector.

   H. **Incorrect:** Endpoint Protection does not integrate directly with Azure. The functionality is already available in Azure as a service.

2. **Correct answer:** E

    A.   **Incorrect**: Small businesses can benefit; however, this is not the best answer.

    B.   **Incorrect**: Medium-sized businesses can benefit; however, this is not the best answer.

    C.   **Incorrect**: Large businesses can benefit; however, this is not the best answer.

    D.   **Incorrect**: Extra-large or multisite businesses can benefit; however, this is not the best answer.

    E.   **Correct**: All of the above. All businesses can benefit from System Center and hybrid scenarios. They can benefit from many features such as Mapped Drive; extending storage to the cloud; monitoring, managing, automating and protecting servers, software, and patch distributions; and more.

3. **Correct answers:** B, D, and E

    A.   **Incorrect**: It is possible to turn on security for in-transit data as well as data at rest.

    B.   **Correct**: It is possible to secure data being stored on Azure. Each storage account has two keys if the storage container is private; the key is required to read or write data.

    C.   **Incorrect**: Most azure services require HTTPS or other ports for communication. If only 3389 were open, services would not be available.

    D.   **Correct**: It is possible to set up a VPN for encrypting data in transit to Azure.

    E.   **Correct**: You can use computer certificates for authentication to communicate with cloud services. Adding IPSec and computer authentication will provide additional security protection.

Objective 6.2: Thought experiment

1. Deep application insights with System Center Operations Manager and Azure Insights can tell you where the problems are. When you get the data, you can determine who needs to fix it.

2. Operations Manager can often see crashes long before they happen. An example of this is when a server's hard drive is at 75 percent capacity, you can be alerted to the issue so that it can be resolved long before the server is in jeopardy of crashing.

3. Yes, System Center is built for managing, monitoring, and protecting on-premises, cloud and hybrid infrastructure and services.

Objective 6.2: Review

1. **Correct answer:** D

   A. **Incorrect:** 0. While performing upgrades and updates, the servers in the update domain that is being updated can and usually do go down.

   B. **Incorrect:** 1 to 3. If you have 14 instances spread across 5 update domains, you would have 3 instances in each of 4 update domains (12) and the remaining 2 instances in the 5th update domain. The maximum number of instances that would go down is 3.

   C. **Incorrect:** 2. Two instances is the minimum number of servers that can go down, not the maximum.

   D. **Correct:** 3. If you have 14 instances spread across 5 update domains, you would have 3 instances in each of 4 update domains (12) and the remaining 2 instances in the fifth update domain. The maximum number of instances that would go down is 3.

2. **Correct answers:** B and D

   A. **Incorrect:** Windows PowerShell can read the application insight from other tools but it cannot create the data.

   B. **Correct:** You can use Operations Manager with APM to gain this insight

   C. **Incorrect:** Configuration Manger can only evaluate configuration information, not deep application performance.

   D. **Correct:** Application Insights gives deep application insight.

   E. **Incorrect:** Global Service Monitor can only monitor availability of a site; it cannot provide more detailed information such as the time it takes to retrieve a query.

3. **Correct answers:** B, C, and D

   A. **Incorrect:** Logging and monitoring must be enabled

   B. **Correct:** Verbose monitoring gives additional logging and statistical information capabilities.

   C. **Correct:** Application Logging (File, Table, Queue) all give additional information and are required to create logs.

   D. **Correct:** Azure Certificate Authentication is required for System Center Operations Manager to be able to read the logs off of Azure Storage.

Objective 6.3: Thought experiment

1. You should use Azure as the destination site because by doing so you eliminate any capital expenditures for hardware while providing a simple and fast migration platform, ensuring the least amount of downtime.

2. Migration Accelerator will be the primary tool to use for this migration. It can handle the physical and virtual servers regardless of operating system.

3. Performing replication and test migration to Azure without performing actual failover. As systems are fully tested, they can be switched to run in the recovery site, which is Azure.

Objective 6.3: Review

1. **Correct answers:** A ,B, C, and D

   A. **Correct:** RTO is the amount of time systems can be down in the event of a disaster before unacceptable business loss occurs.

   B. **Correct:** Scaling-up means to add more resources (CPU, Memory, and bandwidth) to an existing machine.

   C. **Correct:** RPO is the target window in time for which data loss can occur during a disaster.

   D. **Correct:** Scaling-out means to Add more machines with the same characteristics (CPU, Memory, and bandwidth) to take some of the load off of the existing VMs..

   E. **Incorrect:** Data Loss is data that has been collected by systems but cannot be recovered after a disaster. This could be in the form of lost data that was not saved or data that was saved but is corrupt and longer usable.

   F. **Incorrect:** A disaster is any event that causes system outages or data loss. It is generally a term that is used in only extreme cases such as natural disasters, but from a systems standpoint, any outage or data loss can be considered a disaster. This should also include accidental deletion of data.

2. **Correct answer:** B

   A. **Incorrect:** 99.90 is the SLA for Storage.

   B. **Correct:** 99.95 is the SLA for a highly available VM.

   C. **Incorrect:** VMs have an SLA as long as they are configured for high availability.

3. **Correct answer:** C

   A. **Incorrect:** Hyper-V cannot convert VMware or migrate to Azure.

   B. **Incorrect:** Azure Site Recovery does not natively migrate a VM. It orchestrates the migration through System Center. Also, as of this writing, ASR does not monitor VMware ESX hosts.

   C. **Correct:** Migration Accelerator is the tool created from the InMage Scout product acquisition.

   D. **Incorrect:** Microsoft does have a tool; it is the Migration Accelerator or InMage Scout.

Objective 6.4: Thought experiment

1. You should use StorSimple. It can give a significant performance boost for the live data because the data can be stored on SSD storage devices. Also, the very small RPO and RTO requirements make StorSimple a perfect solution because post disaster, the files can be used without having to wait for a restore of the data. It can be simply brought online. Data Protection Manager could provide the RPO by doing hourly backups, but the RTO of four hours would be difficult to achieve with Data Protection Manager. Also Data Protection Manager does not offer any performance advantages.

2. Data Protection Manager is the best choice. There is no need for enhanced performance. There is an RPO of 24 hours, which basically means a once per day backup would be sufficient to protect this data. The two-day RTO could easily be obtained by restoring the data from disk or tape when a restore is needed.

3. Data Protection Manager is the best choice. With the high 24-hour RPO and 2 days for RTO, this is plenty of time to retrieve data from disk or tape using Data Protection Manager when a restore is needed. Stand-alone Azure Backup cannot backup and restore Exchange data. Although the RPO/RTO could be achieved through scheduling and then backing up Exchange dumps, it would be an inefficient solution with many limitations.

Objective 6.4: Review

1. **Correct answers:** A

   A. **Correct:** Azure Backup uses a block-level backup but allows for a file-level restore.

   B. **Incorrect:** Azure Backup uses block-level Backup, not file level.

   C. **Incorrect:** Azure Backup can perform a system backup, but it still uses a block-level backup. It can do a system-level restore to an existing machine.

   D. **Incorrect:** Azure Backup cannot perform a block-level restore. It can only restore volumes, files, and folders. You cannot restore blocks.

   E. **Incorrect:** Azure Backup uses block-level backup, but it does not back up system state, so you cannot use it for a full system restore.

2. **Correct answers:** B, C, E, and F

   A. **Incorrect:** There are many differences; see the other answers for examples.

   B. **Correct:** StorSimple allows for instant restore capabilities; Data Protection Manager does not.

   C. **Correct:** Data Protection Manager integrates directly with Azure Backup; StorSimple does not. StorSimple is a stand-alone device.

   D. **Incorrect:** StorSimple provides much lower RPO and RTO capabilities than Data Protection Manager. StorSimple can do instant restores to reduce RTO.

E. **Correct:** Data Protection Manager is part of System Center, but StorSimple is not

F. **Correct:** StorSimple is a device that has internal drives; Data Protection Manager is software that is installed on a server.

3. **Correct answer:** D

A. **Incorrect:** The *Get-ScheduledJob* cmdlet gets scheduled jobs on the local computer. It has nothing to do with Online Backup, it retrieves Task Scheduler Jobs.

B. **Incorrect:** The *Get-ScheduledTask* cmdlet gets the task definition object of a scheduled task that is registered on a computer.

C. **Incorrect:** The *Get-AzureAutomationSchedule* cmdlet gets a Microsoft Azure Automation schedule.

D. **Correct:** The *Get-OBPolicy* cmdlet gets the current backup policy that is set for the server, including the details about scheduling backups, files included in the backup, and retention policy.

Objective 6.5: Thought experiment

You would need to use Windows PowerShell to do the following:

- Copy or create the right shortcuts on each desktop to their VMs. Using different public endpoint ports for each VM will make managing this very easy. For example, port 38901 for desk 1, 38902 for desk 2, 38903 for desk 3, and so on. Alternatively, you could use different cloud services for each workstation, using the same public port for all but a different public name.

- Write scripts for building the VMs in Azure for the upcoming class (different classes might require different scripts).

- Yes. Here's what you need to do:

  - Create and run a script for turning off and deallocating the VMs at night when they are not being used.

  - Create a script for deleting the VMs when the class is finished.

Objective 6.5: Review

1. **Correct answer:** C

A. **Incorrect:** You must use *add-account* before you can set subscription.

B. **Incorrect:** You must use *add-account* before you can set subscription. The storage container is not created yet so you cannot set the default storage.

C. **Correct:** *Add-AzureAccount.*

D. **Incorrect:** The pipe and add Azure provisioning has no context.

E. **Incorrect:** To authenticate with Azure using *Get-AzurePublishSettingsFile*, you must also import the file.

2. **Correct answer:** A

   A. **Correct:** The account is added, you can now set the subscription.

   B. **Incorrect:** The storage container is not created yet, so you cannot set the default storage.

   C. **Incorrect:** *Add-AzureAccount* was already run; you are trying to set the subscription in this line.

   D. **Incorect:** The pipe and add Azure provisioning has no context.

   E. **Incorrect**: You already authenticated, and to authenticate with Azure using *Get-AzurePublishSettingsFile*, you must also import the file.

3. **Correct answer**: D

   A. **Incorrect:** The account has been added already; adding it again would cause an error because this should be a continuation of the prior line

   B. **Incorrect:** This would cause an error because this should be a continuation of the prior line.

   C. **Incorrect:** This would cause an error because this should be a continuation of the prior line.

   D. **Correct:** The pipe and add Azure provisioning to set the user name and password goes here.

   E. **Incorrect:** This would cause an error because this should be a continuation of the prior line.

4. **Correct answers:** A, C, E, and F

   A. **Correct:** This is the third step.

   B. **Incorrect:** *Get-AzureWebsite* is not needed to meet the requirement.

   C. **Correct:** *Get-AzureVM* is the final step after authenticating and setting the subscripton.

   D. **Incorrect:** *Get-AzureAccount* is not required. It would not cause a problem, but it is not "required."

   E. **Correct:** *Add-AzureAccount* is the first required step which causes authentication.

   F. **Correct:** This is the second step. Before setting the Azure subscription, you must get it. You could also get this information from the management portal, but the Windows PowerShell command is the easier way.

Objective 6.6: Thought experiment

1. Create a template with the proper configuration already set and use that for deployment. Create a workflow or Windows PowerShell script that runs when the server is deployed that sets the configuration properly. Create Desired State Configuration scripts to force IIS, PHP, and CGI, and apply that script to all web servers. You could also deploy Puppet or Chef to perform the state configuration. You also could use

System Center and Orchestrator to check the configuration and fix it automatically if it changes.

2. Create Desired State Configuration scripts to force IIS, PHP, and CGI and apply that deploy script to all web servers. You also could deploy Puppet or Chef to perform the state configuration. You also could use System Center and Orchestrator to check the configuration and fix it automatically if it changes.

3. Microsoft Azure Desired State Configuration.

Objective 6.6: Review

1. **Correct answers**: B and C

    A. **Incorrect:** Configuration management can do one-time configuration changes, but this is not a best-suited scenario.

    B. **Correct:** Error-prone tasks or configuration changes.

    C. **Correct:** Changes that are often repeated.

    D. **Incorrect:** Writing scripts for one time system deployments is not a key use case.

    E. **Incorrect:** You can run Linux SSH commands by running putty-like commands through an external executable call, but they are not a best-suited scenario. XPlat-CLI is the Microsoft Cross Platform command-line client. It is not at all similar to Windows PowerShell. It can access Azure and perform many Azure actions, but the syntax and functionality is very different. Linux does not have direct Windows PowerShell support.

2. **Correct answers:** B, C, D, F, G, and H

    A. **Incorrect:** Desired State Configuration does not monitor based on performance, and scaling machines is beyond the scope of what Desired State Configuration is designed to do.

    B. **Correct:** WindowsFeature installs or removes Windows roles and features.

    C. **Correct:** File will allow managing files and directories.

    D. **Correct:** Starting, stopping, and managing processes and services.

    E. **Incorrect:** Desired State Configuration does not offer any data protection services, for Data Protection, you would need to use Azure Backup, DPM, or StorSimple.

    F. **Correct:** You could use Desired State Configuration to deploy new software. This is particularly helpful if you have many VMs that need the same application deployed and configured.

    G. **Correct:** To use Desired State Configuration to modify a configuration, it needs to discover the actual configuration state on a given node and then adjust it if needed.

    H. **Correct:** Fix a configuration that has drifted away from the desired state is the first and most important mission of Desired State Configuration.

3. **Correct answers:** A, C, and E

   A. **Correct:** Cross-platform configuration management (Linux and Windows).

   B. **Incorrect:** Chef and Puppet are not built on Windows PowerShell; they are built on Ruby or a Ruby-type language.

   C. **Correct:** Both are backed by strong user communities with scripts that can be easily downloaded and used.

   D. **Incorrect:** Both Chef and Puppet require an enterprise management server.

   E. **Correct:** Both Chef and Puppet accelerate time-to-market by simplifying configuration management and taking advantage of the work of the community

Index

A

D

About the authors

HAISHI BAI, senior technical evangelist at Microsoft, focuses on the Microsoft Azure compute platform, including IaaS, PaaS, networking, and scalable computing services

STEVE MAIER is an expert in Windows Store apps, mobile apps, and the cloud. He has been running a mobile phone community group for the past five years. He holds multiple certifications including Microsoft Specialist Architecting Microsoft Azure Solutions. You can reach Steve on his blog at *http://42base13.net* or on Twitter (@stevemaier3).

DAN STOLTS is a technology expert who is a master of systems management and security. You can reach him on his primary blog at *http://itproguru.com* or Twitter (@ITProGuru). He is proficient in many datacenter technologies (Windows Server, System Center, Virtualization, Cloud, and so on) and holds many certifications including MCT, MCITP, MCSE, and TS. Dan is currently specializing in system management, virtualization, and cloud technologies. He is and has been a very active member of the user group community. Dan is an enthusiastic advocate of technology and is passionate about helping others. To see more, go to *http://itproguru.com/about*.

Free ebooks

From technical overviews to drilldowns on special topics, get *free* ebooks from Microsoft Press at:

www.microsoftvirtualacademy.com/ebooks

Download your free ebooks in PDF, EPUB, and/or Mobi for Kindle formats.

Look for other great resources at Microsoft Virtual Academy, where you can learn new skills and help advance your career with free Microsoft training delivered by experts.

Now that you've read the book...

Tell us what you think!

Was it useful?
Did it teach you what you wanted to learn?
Was there room for improvement?

Let us know at http://aka.ms/tellpress

Your feedback goes directly to the staff at Microsoft Press,
and we read every one of your responses. Thanks in advance!

 Microsoft